GOD IS
A FRIEND
OF MINE

CLAIMING GOD'S PROMISES

An experience in Praise

Thanksgiving

Commitment

Recommitment

and

Journaling

by Dave Noland

xulon PRESS

God Is a Friend of Mine
by Dave Noland

Printed in the United States of America

ISBN 1-591607-01-9

Xulon Press
www.XulonPress.com

Xulon Press books are available in bookstores everywhere, and on the Web at www.XulonPress.com.

Acknowledgements

As with anyone who has tried to get a manuscript published, there are literally dozens of people I could, and should, thank. Over the years many have played an integral part in the growth of my Christian life. However, because I can't thank them all, I am going to keep the list very short.

First of all, I want to thank my Dad and Mom for providing me a model Christian home – a home that was filled with love and safety, yet an unlimited amount of freedom of expression in all ways. Although mom died a few years ago, I still have the privilege of having Dad alive and near, so that he and I can still meet regularly and enjoy the company of each other.

Then, I want to thank my seven children! Yes, seven! And what a wonderful family they have been to me. They have always been there with an unlimited amount of love and support, no matter what kind of an unusual path I might be following. I am so blessed to have them in my corner, as well as their spouses as – as of this date – 17 grandchildren, two step-grand-children and one step-great grandchild.

Then I want to thank my business contact, Peter, and my children Teri, Shellie, David and Troy, who gave me the encouragement as well as financial support to accomplish this self-publishing project.

Lastly, and an extremely important team player, I want to thank Julie Smith for her knowledge, her advice, and her contacts who made what was a circuitous route to self-publishing, an easy and straight road.

It was Julie who led me to Mary Lindsay, who typed the manuscript on to a disk. Thank you, Mary. And to Xulon Publishing and Karen Kochenburger at Xulon, who has been so cooperative with my questions and concerns.

And for all of you who should have been mentioned, and weren't, please know that I appreciate your thoughts, your prayer and your support.

Endorsements

"The discipline of spiritual formation does not come easy for most. David Noland presents in his *God Is a Friend of Mine: Claiming God's Promises* a tool that is a refreshing path for those who have yearned for a closer walk with God we have come to know in Jesus. Best of all, this tool lives up to the promises."

John A. Sundquist
Executive Director
American Baptist Churches International Ministries

"The material prepared by Dave Noland, *God Is a Friend of Mine,* is unique and very special. It is quite different to other devotional material available and has been meticulously prepared by a person who has put his whole heart and spirit into the preparation. I took personal delight in working through some of this material and was stimulated and challenged by the experience.

"There are Baptist people all over the world who would profit enormously from this particular material. For countless Baptists in remote parts of the world, the receipt of one book becomes a most precious possession. If the material that Dave Noland has prepared could be made available to Baptist pastors and seminary graduates in the developing world, it would make a big impact on the devotional lives and consequent ministries of many Christian workers.

"Without qualification, I heartily endorse *God Is a Friend of Mine* and hope and pray that it has a wide distribution because its effect will be immense."

Tony Cupit
Director of Study and Research
Baptist World Alliance

Although there are dozens of fine devotional books and aids, I am unaware of any that focus almost completely on just a couple of the great things that we can learn from God's Word, the Bible.

Those two things are how much God loves us and wants to be our friend, and how He has promised to forgive us when we return to Him with honesty and humility and confess our sins to Him.

With this devotional guide, a seeker of God's love and forgiveness does not have to sort through all of the many other great Bible stories, words of instruction, theological concepts, challenges, etc., that are found in God's Word.

Many verses in the Bible instruct the believing Christian in how to live. Another devotional book could be written just about the biblical instructions for the Christian.

This devotional book does not concentrate on what God wants you to do for Him, but rather on what He has promised to do for you. It is incredible to see all of the things that God wants to do for you when they are listed as they are in this devotional book.

Hopefully, no matter where you are in your walk with God—searching, questioning, fighting, or growing—these verses and prayers will be of help to you.

Personal Testimony

Although I make no claim whatsoever of being any kind of a theologian, over the years my own personal Bible study and reading have been of tremendous—and growing—importance and support in my life.

The Bible is replete with God's promises of love and care in all of the situations that we encounter in our everyday life—whether we are young people, workers at home, in the office or marketplace, professional people, hourly laborers, highly paid executives, etc.

Because of the incredible value of these promises to me personally over the years, I have had a desire to share my experience with God and my walk with God.

The verses, thoughts and prayers in this workbook constitute that attempt.

Let's start with a little resume of my background, my life, and my walk to date.

I was reared in a rural Midwestern community where there were two prominent separating identities of the neighborhood. One group consisted of those families who attended the little country Baptist church three times each week—Sunday morning, Sunday night, Wednesday night prayer meeting; and of course, "8 Great Days" of revival meetings every year or two, and the "R. R. Brown" tent meetings that were held every summer. The other group consisted of those families who spent almost every Sunday night and maybe another midweek night at one of the two local dance halls.

There was no animosity between the two groups. We lived in close but separate harmony. We simply lived different social lives. The two groups were fine acquaintances on the surface; but, when it came time to do things, whether is was socializing, running threshing crews, baling hay, partying, etc., there was little intermingling between the two groups.

I love my parents dearly, and respect them tremendously for the home, the love, the encouragement, and instilling in me the confidence that I could do anything I chose to do. But, there was no question that the religious teachings of that little Baptist group were certainly a religion of "DON'TS"! As a Christian you obviously don't dance, drink wine or liquor of any kind, smoke, go to movies, play cards—unless it was the permissible old standard of "Baptist Poker," otherwise known as Rook, shake dice, or do anything else like that that might "cause your brother to stumble!"

As you would expect, a basic tenet of that kind of conservatism was the "knowledge" that at your individual judgment day—whenever that occurred—you were going to be standing before God who would open this huge book in which He had kept track of your each and every sin! And, somehow you would be held accountable for each and every one of them.

I must admit that if you believe that, it does have a tendency to help keep you on the straight and narrow!

And, frankly, I was not at all unhappy with those ground rules. I wasn't one who rebelled. I liked my life. In fact, from a very young age I was comfortable not only with my life, but I was comfortable with my relationship with God. I loved and respected my parents. They gave me enormous freedom. Through a unique set of circumstances, my parents left the farm slightly before my 17th birthday, at which time they gave me the option of either moving with them to another state, or moving into the little town where I attended high school, and finishing my senior year. I choose to stay, and thus did not live with my parents since the end of my 16th year. That was pretty gutsy on their part!

However, in my years of growing as a Christian and a father, I went through a metamorphous—not a rebellion—simply a feeling of growing closer to God and understanding more of what I thought the Christian life could be.

There were three things that occurred about the same time that were the catalysts of this change.

One was my enormous love and pride in my children.

I remember walking behind my oldest son and one of his friends. We were doing something as simple as walking into a local shopping mall. As is typical of a couple of energetic young boys, they were running on ahead, laughing and talking. As I watched them the thought crossed my mind of how thankful I was to be blessed with such a great family and how much I loved each one of them. Somehow I was struck with the thought of what could this young son, who I loved so much, ever do to make me stop loving him. My conclusion was that the only thing that he could ever do to cause that kind of a change was to take me on personally—to reject me in every possible manner.

And, if I could feel that strongly, in my very human and weak love, how much more must God love me and accept me in His infinite love! Tears came to my eyes as I realized the extent of God's love for me.

In my own study, I ran across a writer who was discussing God's amazing forgiveness. The thoughts were along the lines that when we sin, and then ask God to forgive us of that sin, God not only forgives, He forgets! What a wonderful thought! He does not write each sin down in His big black book to throw it back in our faces when we see Him face to face. In fact, when we commit the same sin again, and return to our loving God again and confess again by saying, "God, I'm sorry. I did it again," God's response is, "Did what again my child. As far as the east is from the west, so far have I removed your transgressions from you. I have buried them in the depth of the sea." The Bible is very consistent on this issue. (Check the Bible references on page xiv following this introduction.)

What a wonderful promise and what a wonderful God! Who would want to rebel against a God like that?

Finally, about that same time, the Sunday School class I was attending was doing a study on Old Testament saints—and by coincidence, my own personal devotions were in the same place.

Now, this may sound like sacrilege, but from my opinion, they need to come up with another adjective for these men other than "saints." I am not sure that any of these Old Testament characters are the kind of men you would want to introduce to your virginal daughter!

Let's look at the three who are most prominently mentioned in the early part of the Jewish nation—the three who are most often considered as the founders of God's chosen people—Abraham, Isaac, and Jacob.

Abraham's faith is touted in the New Testament (Romans, chapter 4), but twice he lied about Sarah being his wife to save his own skin. (Genesis 12:11-20 & Genesis 20:1-14) According to the scriptures, Sarah was a very beautiful woman. As they traveled to the place God had sent them, they traveled through country where a local king took a fancy to Sarah and wanted her for a part of his harem. Abraham was afraid that if the king knew that Sarah was his wife, the king would kill Abraham to take Sarah for his own. Twice Sarah was put through the experience of being taken in the king's harem because of Abraham's lies.

If my arithmetic is correct, one of these times Sarah was somewhere south of 75 years old! I have always thought that being so beautiful at that age that a king wanted her in his harem would make a good challenge for any woman!

Much is made of Abraham's faith in offering Isaac as a sacrifice when God asked him to do so. (Genesis 22:1-18) No question, that would take a lot of faith on the part of Abraham to sacrifice a son he had waited so long to be born; but, did you ever think of the paradox of letting Sarah get taken into another man's harem—twice—to save his own skin and then being so willing to take the life of his only son? Based on his previous actions of lying about Sarah to save his life, I have often wondered if Abraham would have been so happy to oblige if the shoe had been on the other foot. What if he had been asked to be the sacrifice?

However, even with these thoughts, if we believe the Scriptures, we have no choice but to accept that Abraham was a man of faith.

Next, let's look at Isaac. He actually comes through without much of a blemish on his reputation. Some of it may be because there is so little written about him as compared to his father and family. Maybe that is a good lesson for all of us. We would probably all look better if our lives were not investigated too closely! Based on what is written, Isaac certainly looks like a real good guy compared to his father, Abraham, his wife Rebekah and his son, Jacob. Most of the scripture concerning Isaac relates to his life as it is intertwined with either his father, wife, or sons.

One statement that has always impressed me about Isaac occurs in the 67th verse of chapter 24 in Genesis. Here it is written that "he loved her very much and she was a special comfort to him." Wouldn't it be nice if every man and woman could say that about their spouse?

And, as we see in the later chapters, maybe Rebekah didn't deserve that kind of adulation!

However, even Isaac must have taken his survival training from his father, Abraham, because in the 26th chapter of Genesis, verses 6 through 8, Isaac also lied about Rebekah being his wife. According to the scriptures, when the men of the area asked about Rebekah, he—Isaac—said, "She is my sister," for he feared for his life if he told them she was his wife; he was afraid they would kill him to get to her for she was very attractive. Fortunately—or unfortunately—however you view the story, before Rebekah was taken from Isaac, his ruse was discovered.

So much for the special comfort she afforded him!

If you were God, would you have bet the future of your chosen nation on these men? Maybe so. They certainly were survivors in a hostile environment.

In spite of these things, according to Genesis 25:11, after Abraham's death, God poured out rich blessings upon Isaac.

Now let's look at Jacob, the father of the twelve tribes of Israel.

He connived with Rebekah to steal his older brother's birthright. They conspired to steal older brother Esau's blessing from old, blind Isaac. He was obviously so drunk on his wedding night that he didn't know which of two sisters he had married. He finagled the mating process in his father-in-law's flocks so that his animals were the strongest and his flocks grew the fastest. He tried to sneak out of his father-in-law's employment to avoid confronting him. And his twelve children were fathered with two wives and two servant girls! This all happens in Genesis 27 through 33.

This is some guy! A real survivor, but often at the expense of other people.

One of the great blessings that comes from the honesty of these Bible stories is that it confirms the fact that God can use anyone and everyone to fulfill his plans. And after studying these men and their sometimes dubious activities, I came to the conclusion that maybe I wasn't such a bad guy after all! If God could use these men to build his chosen race, he could certainly use me. And if he could love them, he could also love me!

That made me feel pretty good.

Soon after that, we had a minister who talked about praying God's Word back to him. I liked that idea.

Thus, much of the material in this devotional is based on taking God's Word at its face value and praying it back to him. Maybe some of the verses and prayers are taken out of context. Maybe some of the things that God said to—or promised—a particular Bible character were meant only for that character; however, if we love God, worship Him, and are trying to follow His leading, I think that the promises He made to others are also ours to claim.

It is also based on the assumption that what God wants more than any other thing is our honor, our praise, and our thanksgiving. That the real—and maybe the only—purpose of our lives is to honor Him, praise Him, and thank Him, in every circumstance in which we find ourselves.

Some of my theologian friends tell me that real communion with God consists of three things—praise and thanks, confession of sin and dependence on him, and petition for strength and wisdom for the day. I like that concept, and the pages that follow are petty consistently based on that structure.

You will notice that there are no divisions as to day, week, month, or year. There aren't 365 of them, so even if you were so consistent in your devotional time that you never missed a day, this devotional wouldn't come out even! There is no set pattern to use this devotional. If you have devotions only spasmodically, this guide is still timely. You won't get a guilt trip because you aren't keeping up with a set schedule. Maybe you only turn to God when you are in trouble. Maybe this guide will give you encouragement to make God a daily part of your life. Maybe this guide will become an addendum to whatever other devotions you are used to following.

In any event, there are roughly 400 verses from each the Old Testament and the New Testament contained in the following pages. Almost all of them are verses showing God's love for you, His care and concern for you, His promises to you; and maybe, above all, the consistency of his plan for our salvation from beginning to end. Hopefully you will grasp what a marvelous and loving God we have available to us if we will only accept His love and believe in His promises.

After each verse is a little prayer that may or may not fit how you feel about the verse and where you are in life on that particular day. There is a place where you can write a prayer of your own, but if you don't have another prayer on the tip of your tongue, maybe the prayer written for you will get you started talking to God. Then you can go on from there.

Depending on the length of the prayer you write, there is a place for you to do some journaling—a place to reflect where you are in life in several different areas—spiritually, emotionally, physically, financially, and generally. How you respond to the verses and what your prayer is for that day may often depend on where you are in life in one of more of these areas.

You will notice that a lot of the Old Testament verses come from the Psalms—many written by David. That is appropriate as the Bible tells us that David had a heart like God. I particularly like the King James Version when it comes to these verses. 1 Samuel 13; 14a states—and here Samuel is speaking of David—"The Lord has sought him a man after his own heart, and the Lord hath commanded him to be captain over his people." I Kings 11:4 states, "and his (Saul's) heart was not perfect with the Lord his God, as was the heart of David." Acts 13:22 reads, "He (God) raised up unto them David to be their king, to whom he also gave testimony and said I have found David the son of Jesse a man after mine own heart which shall fulfill my will."

So, if God thought that highly of David, it seems proper that a lot of the verses herein should be attributed to him.

There are a couple of different places in the back of the guide to make notes of any particular verse or prayer that may have struck a particularly meaningful chord in your life; and why you had that reaction.

You may also keep track of every verse and prayer that you read and where you were at that time of your life. My encouragement is for you to keep this guide as a permanent part of your life and relationship with God. That is one reason why your comments, prayers, and journaling are so important. Keep track of the times of special praise or special crises and revisit these items to see how God worked them out in your life. Maybe the outcome was not what you expected or wanted, but in the process you learned more about yourself and your relationship to God. Maybe it was a time of growing spiritually. Maybe it was a time to learn total dependence on Him. Maybe you cannot find any special purpose. It is just a special time in your life—either of joy or trial.

In your walk with God, be honest with Him. He knows your thoughts and innermost feelings anyway. So there is no purpose in trying to keep your true feelings from Him. If you hurt, tell Him so and why! If you are riding high, thank Him and acknowledge that he is the giver of all good things. And as you grow in your comfort with your relationship with God, try to buy into Paul's admonition to be thankful in all things. Ask for the wisdom to learn what God is trying to teach you.

Finally, how can I be so sure that God is my friend.

That's an easy one to answer. Let's just go back to the scriptures.

The Bible is very consistent about God being our friend if we do our part.

See all of the following verses that confirm God's desire to be your friend beginning on page xiii.

And remember, Christ said, "I came that you should have life and have it more abundantly," John 10:10. Learn to love God more, to rely on Him more, and to always thank Him for all He has done and is doing for you.

Remember, God loves you right now! Just the way you are! And He wants to be your friend too. So take Him up on His offer. Pray His promises back to Him. Claim them for yourself. Claim God as your friend, and Christ as your Savior, and live your life more abundantly!

God Is a Friend of Mine— Scriptures

John 15:13-15: And here is how to measure it—the greatest love is shown when a person lays down his life for his friends; and you are my friends if you obey me. I no longer call you slaves, for a master doesn't confide in his slaves; now you are my friends, proved by the fact that I have told you everything the Father told me.

Psalm 54:4: But God is my helper. He is a friend of mine.

Matthew 10:32: If anyone publicly acknowledges me as his friend, I will openly acknowledge him as my friend before my Father in heaven.

Psalm 25:14: Friendship with God is reserved for those who reverence him. With them alone he shares the secrets of his promises.

Luke 12:8: And I assure you of this: I, the Messiah, will publicly honor you in the presence of God's angels if you publicly acknowledge me here on earth as your Friend.

Romans 5:10-11: And since, when we were his enemies, we were brought back to God by the death of his Son, what blessings he must have for us now that we are his friends, and he is living within us! Now we rejoice in our wonderful new relationship with God—all because of what our Lord Jesus Christ has done in dying for our sins—making us friends of God.

I John 3:21-23: But, dearly loved friends, if your consciences are clear, we can come to the Lord with perfect assurance and trust, and get whatever we ask for because we are obeying him and doing the things that please him. And this is what God says we must do: believe on the name of his Son Jesus Christ and love one another.

Hebrews 9:24: For Christ has entered into heaven itself, to appear now before God as our Friend. It was not in the early place of worship that he did this, for that was merely a copy of the real temple in heaven.

Galatians 4:6: And because we are his sons, God has sent the spirit of his Son into our hearts: so now we can rightly speak of God as our dear Father. (This verse only works if you consider your father your friend!)

Colossians 1:20-21: It was through what his Son did that God cleared a path for everyone to come to him—all things in heaven and on earth—for Christ's death on the cross has made peace with God for all by his blood. This includes you who were once so far away from God. You were his enemies and hated him and were separated from him by your evil thoughts and actions, yet he has now brought you back as his friends.

I Corinthians 1:8-9: And he guarantees right up to the end that you will be counted free from all sin and guilt on the day when he returns. God will surely do this for you, for he always does just what he says, and he is the one who invited you into this wonderful friendship with his Son, even Christ our Lord.

God Forgives and Forgets— Scriptures

Psalm 25:6-7: Overlook my youthful sins, O Lord! Look at me instead through eyes of mercy and forgiveness, through eyes of everlasting love and kindness.

Psalm 32:1: What happiness for those who guilt has been forgiven! What joys when sins are covered over! What relief for those who have confessed their sins and God has cleared the record.

Psalm 51:1-2: O loving and kind God, have mercy. Have pity upon me and take away the awful stain of my transgressions. Oh, wash me, cleanse me from this guilt. Let me be pure again.

Psalm 65:3: Though sins fill our hearts, you forgive them all.

Psalm 103:10-12: He has not punished us as we deserve for our sins, for his mercy toward those who fear and honor him is as great as the heights of the heavens above the earth. He has removed our sins as far away from us as the east is from the west.

Isaiah 44:22: I've blotted out your sins; they are gone like morning mist at noon! Oh, return to me, for I have paid the price to set you free.

Isaiah 64:8-9: And yet, O Lord, you are our Father. We are the clay and you are the Potter. We are all formed by your hand. Oh, be not so angry with us, Lord, nor forever remember our sins. Oh, look and see that we are all your people.

Ezekiel 18:21-22: But if a wicked person turns away from all his sins and begins to obey my laws and do what is just and right, he shall surely live and not die. All his past sins will be forgotten, and he shall live because of his goodness.

John 16:8-11: And when he has come he will convince the world of its sin, and of the availability of God's goodness, and of deliverance from judgment. The world's sin is unbelief in me; there is righteousness available because I go to the Father and you shall see me no more; there is deliverance from judgment because the prince of this world has already been judged.

Acts 22:16: And now, why delay? Go and be baptized, and be cleansed from your sin, calling upon the name of the Lord.

Hebrews 10:10: Under this new plan we have been forgiven and made clean by Christ's dying for us once and for all.

Hebrews 10:14: For by this one offering he made forever perfect in the sight of God all those whom he is making holy.

Hebrews 10:17: And then he adds, I will never again remember their sins and lawless deeds.

Psalm 51:9: Don't keep looking at my sins—erase them from your sight.

Romans 4:6-8: King David spoke of this, describing the happiness of an undeserving sinner who is declared "not guilty" by God. "Blessed and to be envied," he said, "are those whose sins are forgiven and put out of sight. Yes, what joy there is for anyone whose sins are no longer counted against him by the Lord."

Psalm 130:3-5: Lord, if you keep in mind our sins then who can ever get an answer to his prayers? But you forgive! What an awesome thing this is! That is why I wait expectantly, trusting God to help, for he has promised.

Romans 8:30: And having chosen us, he called us to come to him; and when we came, he declared us "not guilty," filled us with Christ's goodness, gave us right standing with him, and promised us his glory.

Micah 7:18-19: Where is another God like you, who pardons the sins of the survivors among his people? You cannot stay angry with your people, for you love to be merciful. Once again you have compassion on us. You will tread our sins beneath your feet; you will throw them into the depths of the ocean!

I Corinthians 1:8-9: And he guarantees right up to the end that you will be counted free from all sin and guilt on the day when he returns. God will surely do this for you, for he always does just what he says, and he is the one who invited you into this wonderful friendship with his Son, even Christ our Lord.

Isaiah 43:25: I, yes, I alone am he who blots away your sins and will never think of them again.

Romans 3:23: Yes, all have sinned; all fall short of God's glorious ideal; yet now God declares us "not guilty" of offending him if we trust in Jesus Christ, who in his kindness freely takes away our sins.

Hebrews 8:12: And I will be merciful to them in their wrongdoings, and I will remember their sins no more.

I John 1:7: But if we are living in the light of God's presence, just as Christ does, then we have wonderful fellowship and joy with each other, and the blood of Jesus his Son cleanses us from every sin.

I John 1:9: But if we confess our sins to him, he can be depended on to forgive us and to cleanse us from every wrong. And it is perfect proper for God to do this for us because Christ died to wash away our sins.

II Corinthians 5:19: For God was in Christ, restoring the world to himself, no longer counting men's sins against them but blotting them out. This is the wonderful message he has given us to tell others.

Jeremiah 31:34: At that time it will no longer be necessary to admonish one another to know the Lord. For everyone, both great and small, shall really know me then, says the Lord, and I will forgive and forget their sins.

Colossians 2:13-15: You were dead in your sins, and your sinful desires were not yet cut away. Then he gave you a share in the very life of Christ, for he forgave all your sins, and blotted out the charges proved against you, the list of his commandments which you had not obeyed. He took this list of sins and destroyed it by nailing it to Christ's cross. In this way God took away Satan's power to accuse you of sin, and God openly displayed to the whole world Christ's triumph at the cross where you sins were all taken away.

I John 2:12: I am writing these things to all of you, my little children, because your sins have been forgiven in the name of Jesus our Savior.

Acts 13:38-39: Brothers! Listen! In this man Jesus, there is forgiveness for your sins! Everyone who trusts in him is freed from all guilt and declared righteous—something the Jewish law could never do.

Hebrews 1:3: God's Son shines out with God's glory, and all that God's Son is and does marks him as God. He regulates the universe by the mighty power of his command. He is the one who died to cleanse us and clear our record of all sin, and then he sat down in highest honor beside the great God of heaven.

Ephesians 1:4: Long ago, even before he made the world, God chose us to be his very own, through what Christ would do for us; he decided then to make us holy in his eyes, without a single fault—we who stand before him covered with his love.

Hebrews 10:18: Now, when sins have once been forever forgiven and forgotten, there is no need to offer more sacrifices to get rid of them.

Acts 26:17 & 18: And I will protect you from both your own people and the Gentiles. Yes, I am going to send you to the Gentiles to open their eyes to their true condition so that they may repent and live in the light of God instead of in Satan's darkness, so that they may receive forgiveness for their sins and God's inheritance along with all people everywhere whose sins are cleansed away, and who are set apart by faith in me.

Luke 24:47: —and that this message of salvation should be taken from Jerusalem to all the nations: There is forgiveness of sins for all who turn to me.

John 5:24: I say emphatically that anyone who listens to my message and believes in God who sent me has eternal life, and will never be damned for their sins, but has already passed out of death into life.

Acts 10:42 & 43: And he sent us to preach the Good News everywhere and to testify that Jesus is ordained of God to be the Judge of us all—living and dead. And all the prophets have written about him, saying that everyone who believes in him will have their sins forgiven in his name.

Isaiah 1:18: Come, let's talk this over! Says the Lord; no matter how deep the stain of your sins, I can take it out and make you as clean as freshly fallen snow. Even if you are stained as red as crimson, I can make you white as wool!

Romans 3:25 & 26: For God sent Christ Jesus to take the punishment for our sins and to end all God's anger against us. He used Christ's blood and our faith as the means of saving us from his wrath. In this way he was being entirely fair, even though he did not punish those who sinned in former times. For his was looking forward to the time when Christ would come and take away those sins. And now in these days also he can receive sinners in this same way, because Jesus took away their sins.

Romans 8:33: Who dares accuse us whom God has chosen for his own? Will God? No! He is the one who has forgiven us and given us right standing with himself.

Devotional Pages

Today's Date: _____

Old Testament verse for today: Genesis 1:26 thru 28

Then God said, "Let us make a man—someone like ourselves, to be the master of all life upon the earth and in the skies and in the seas." So God made man like his Maker. Like God did God make man; Man and maid did he make them. And God blessed them and told them, "Multiply and fill the earth and subdue it; you are masters of the fish and birds and all the animals."

One possible prayer for today:

God, that's a pretty awesome responsibility! First of all, to be made like you! Then to be master of all you have made and given to me to enjoy and to use. God, please grant me the wisdom and understanding to be a good steward of all you have given to me to enjoy. Thank you for your blessing, God. Let me do my best to return to you the praise and honor that is due you for all you have done for me. Thank you for giving me the help that I need, Lord.

New Testament verse for today: Romans 8:16 & 17a

For his Holy Spirit speaks to us deep in our hearts, and tells us that we really are God's children. And since we are his children, we will share his treasures—for all God gives to his Son Jesus is now ours too.

One possible prayer for today:

Thank you for reaffirming that I am one of your children, God. Thank you for letting me share in all your treasures. Thank you for giving me your greatest treasure—the gift of your Son, Jesus, through whose suffering I was given salvation. Thank you, Lord, for all your gifts to me, your child.

My prayer for today—including any journaling thoughts I may want to add. Where am I today spiritually, emotionally, physically, financially, generally?

Today's Date: _____

Old Testament verse for today: Genesis 8:22

As long as the earth remains, there will be springtime and harvest, cold and heat, winter and summer, day and night.

One possible prayer for today:

God, thank you for being a God of consistency and a God of permanence. Thank you for being an everlasting God. Thank you for being a God who can keep his promises. Thank you for giving me a place to live that is so wonderful and so full of variation. Thank you for being my personal God.

New Testament verse for today: II Peter 3:8

But don't forget this, dear friends, that a day or a thousand years from now is like tomorrow to the Lord.

One possible prayer for today:

God, thank you again for being a God of permanence. Thank you for being an everlasting God. Thank you for being a God who can keep his promises for a day, or for a year, or for thousands of years. Thank you for forgiving me when I get impatient to have things happen on my timetable instead of waiting for you to act. Thank you for being such a marvelous God.

My prayer for today—including any journaling thoughts I may want to add. Where am I today spiritually, emotionally, physically, financially, generally?

Today's Date: _____

Old Testament verse for today: Genesis 18:14a

Is anything too hard for God?

One possible prayer for today:

God, thank you for being a God who knows no limit to his power. Thank you for being a God for which nothing is too hard. Thank you for being an everlasting God. Thank you for always being there when I need you and call on you. Thank you for giving me the faith to know that there is nothing too hard for you.

New Testament verse for today: Ephesians 2:4 thru 6

But God is so rich in mercy; he loved us so much that even though we were spiritually dead and doomed by our sins, he gave us back our lives again when he raised Christ from the dead—only by his undeserved favor have we ever been saved—and lifted us up from the grave into glory along with Christ, where we sit with him in the heavenly realms—all because of what Christ Jesus did.

One possible prayer for today:

God, you certainly proved your power; you certainly proved that there was nothing too hard for you to do, when you sacrificed your one and only Son on the cross to wipe away my sins. And then, Lord, you raised him from the dead, again showing your unlimited power, and you did this out of love for me and all the other people like me, who are full of sin and rebellion against you. God, only you could show your power with that amount of love and the resulting plan of salvation. Thank you, God, for your unlimited power. Thank you that you are a God where nothing is too hard for you.

My prayer for today—including any journaling thoughts I may want to add. Where am I today spiritually, emotionally, physically, financially, generally?

Today's Date: _____

Old Testament verse for today: Exodus 15:2a

The Lord is my strength, my song, and my salvation. He is my God, and I will praise him.

One possible prayer for today:

God, thank you for being a God who is always worthy of my praise. Thank you for being a God of strength, and a God who is my strength. Thank you for being a God who is the author of my salvation. Thank you for being a God so wonderful that I can always sing of your blessings and know that they are always there for me. Thank you, God.

New Testament verse for today: II Corinthians 1:22

He has put his brand upon us—his mark of ownership—and has given us his Holy Spirit in our hearts as guarantee that we belong to him, and as the first installment of all that he is going to give us.

One possible prayer for today:

God, thank you for being my strength and my salvation. And, God, thank you for putting your brand upon me. Thank you for marking me as one who belongs to you. Thank you for giving me your wonderful, loving Holy Spirit to guide me and as a guarantee that I belong to you. Then I know that you can never forget me. Thank you for all the wonderful promises that you have given to me. Lord, let me do my best to return to you the worship and the praise that is due you for being such a wonderful God. And thank you for forgiving me when I fail to do my part. Thank you, God.

My prayer for today—including any journaling thoughts I may want to add. Where am I today spiritually, emotionally, physically, financially, generally?

Today's Date: _____

Old Testament verse for today: Exodus 15:26

If you will listen to the voice of the Lord your God, and obey it, and do what is right, then I will not make you suffer the diseases I sent on the Egyptians, for I am the Lord who heals you.

One possible prayer for today:

God, thank you for being a God who can heal. Thank you for being a God who heals me. Let me always listen to your voice, Lord. Let me obey your voice. Let me do what is right in your sight. Thank you for keeping me from suffering. Thank you for helping me. Thank you for being my God. Thank you.

New Testament verse for today: James 5:13

Is anyone among you suffering? He should keep on praying about it. And those who have reason to be thankful should continually be singing praises for the Lord.

One possible prayer for today:

Lord, thank you for hearing my prayers when I am hurting. Thank you for never getting tired of my pleading to you for your help. And, Lord, when I am not suffering, let me be as faithful in singing your praises about all the good things that you have done and are doing for me. Let me be always in prayer and communication with you, Lord. Thank you for being with me in both the good times and the bad times. Thank you for being my everlasting and ever faithful God.

My prayer for today—including any journaling thoughts I may want to add. Where am I today spiritually, emotionally, physically, financially, generally?

Today's Date: _____

Old Testament verse for today: Numbers 11:23

Then the Lord said to Moses, "When did I become weak? Now you shall see whether my word comes true or not."

One possible prayer for today:

God, thank you for being a God who never becomes weak. Thank you for being an everlasting God. Thank you for being a God whose words always come true. Thank you for being the one and only true God.

New Testament verse for today: Acts 17:24

He made the world and everything in it, and since he is Lord of heaven and earth, he doesn't live in man made temples; and human hands can't minister to his needs—for he has no needs.

One possible prayer for today:

God, thank you for being a God powerful enough to make heaven and earth, and all that is in the heavens and on the earth. Thank you for being the Lord of everything you have made. Thank you for being an all-powerful and all encompassing God. Thank you for being a God who does not need me to minister to your needs, and yet ardently desires me to love you and worship you because you loved me first. Thank you for being a God that even though all-powerful, still cares about me and cares about the things that concern me. Thank you for being all-powerful and yet all loving. Thank you for always being there for me.

My prayer for today—including any journaling thoughts I may want to add. Where am I today spiritually, emotionally, physically, financially, generally?

Today's Date: _____

Old Testament verse for today: Numbers 14:17, 18, & 19a

Oh, please, show the great power of your patience by forgiving our sins and showing us your steadfast love. Forgive us, even though you have said that you don't let sin go unpunished, and that you punish the father's guilt in the children to the third and fourth generation. Oh, I plead with you, pardon the sins of this people because of your magnificent, steadfast love.

One possible prayer for today:

God, thank you for showing me your steadfast love. Thank you for showing me your patience by forgiving my sins. Thank you for letting my sins go unpunished; because, if you punished me for all of the times I sin, I would be punished continually! Thank you for not punishing my family for my sins. Thank you for pardoning my sins because of your magnificent, steadfast love. Thank you, God.

New Testament verse for today: Hebrews 12:5

And have you forgotten the encouraging words God spoke to you, his child? He said, "My son, don't be angry when the Lord punishes you. Don't be discouraged when he has to show you where you are wrong. For when he punishes you, it proves that he loves you. When he whips you it proves you are really his child."

One possible prayer for today:

God, again I say thank you for not punishing me for all my sins. I know that you need to correct me. I know that I need your correction often. Lord, please be gentle with me in your punishment and in the times when you have to show me where I am wrong. Thank you for loving me. Thank you for making me your child. And, Lord, thank you for being gentle in your punishment and in your correction.

My prayer for today—including any journaling thoughts I may want to add. Where am I today spiritually, emotionally, physically, financially, generally?

Today's Date: _____

Old Testament verse for today: Deuteronomy 4:29

But you will also begin to search again for Jehovah your God, and you shall find him when you search for him with all your hearts and souls.

One possible prayer for today:

God, thank you for being a God who never moves away from me. I know that when I find myself feeling apart from you, it is because I have moved away from you, not that you have moved away from me. And, God, I know that when I again search for you, when I again move back to you, you will always be there waiting for me to come back to you. Thank you for always being there when I search for you with all my heart and soul.

New Testament verse for today: Acts 20:21

I have had one message for Jews and Gentiles alike—the necessity of turning from sin to God through faith in our Lord Jesus Christ.

One possible prayer for today:

God, I know that when I search for you with all my heart and soul, you will always be there to receive me into your kingdom. Lord, I know that you have prepared the way for my salvation through the gift of your Son, Jesus. I know that when I search for you, the path of my salvation goes through your Son, Jesus, who died and rose again so that my sins are all washed away, and thus, I can stand before you without the stain or blemish of sin because of what Jesus has done for me. Thank you for always being there when I diligently search for you. Thank you for making the path of salvation so simple that even I can understand it and avail myself of it. Thank you, God.

My prayer for today—including any journaling thoughts I may want to add. Where am I today spiritually, emotionally, physically, financially, generally?

Today's Date: _____

Old Testament verse for today: Deuteronomy 4:31

For the Lord your God is merciful—he will not abandon you nor destroy you nor forget the promises he made to your ancestors.

One possible prayer for today:

Thank you for being a merciful God to me. Thank you for never abandoning me when I abandon you. Thank you for not destroying me when I continue to sin against you. Thank you for never forgetting the promises you have made to me through your word. Thank you for being not only the one and only true God, but a loving, caring and forgiving God.

New Testament verse for today: Acts 14:15a thru 17

We have come to bring you the Good News that you are invited to turn from the worship of these foolish things and to pray instead to the living God who made heaven and earth and sea and everything in them. In bygone days he permitted the nations to go their own ways, but he never left himself without a witness; there were always his reminders—the kinds of things he did such as sending you rain and good crops and giving you food and gladness.

One possible prayer for today:

God, thank you for being such a merciful God that you are always reminding me of your love and concern. Thank you for being an everlasting God who will never abandon me or destroy me. Thank you for being an all-powerful God who made heaven and earth and sea and is in charge of everything that you made. Lord, you have given me—and the nations— a free will, and we often go our own ways, forgetting that you are the creator and author of all that we have. But, Lord, thank you for always being there with your gentle reminders. We take these things so much for granted, Lord, but let us always remember that the things that we take for granted are gifts from you. Thank you, God, for your many gifts.

My prayer for today—including any journaling thoughts I may want to add. Where am I today spiritually, emotionally, physically, financially, generally?

Today's Date: _____

Old Testament verse for today: Deuteronomy 4:39

This is your wonderful thought for the day: Jehovah is God both in heaven and down here upon the earth; and there is no God other than him.

One possible prayer for today:

God, that is a wonderful thought for any day! To think that you are the one and only true God of both heaven and earth, that there is no other God like you, and to know that you still love and care for me! That is, indeed, a wonderful thought. Thank you for being the God of both heaven and earth. Thank you for being a God like no other God. And, God, thank you for always loving me and caring for me. Thank you, God.

New Testament verse for today: I John 2:12

I am writing these things to all of you, my little children, because your sins have been forgiven in the name of Jesus our Savor.

One possible prayer for today:

God, thank you for being the God of heaven and earth. Thank you for being concerned about me while I am here on earth. Thank you for being so concerned about me that you sent your Son, Jesus, to die on the cross for my sins so that I might be blameless before you, and therefore know that I will spend eternity with you in heaven. Thank you for being such a wonderful, powerful, and yet caring and loving God. Thank you for being the God of both heaven and earth.

My prayer for today—including any journaling thoughts I may want to add. Where am I today spiritually, emotionally, physically, financially, generally?

Today's Date: _____

Old Testament verse for today: Deuteronomy 6:2

The purpose of these laws is to cause you, your sons, and your grandsons to reverence the Lord your God by obeying all of his instructions as long as you live; if you do, you will have long, prosperous years ahead of you.

One possible prayer for today:

Lord, you know that I try to obey your laws. I know that your laws are made for my benefit. But, Lord, you know that I don't always follow your laws. You know that I fall short of this ideal that you have given me to follow. But, Lord, I do reverence you. I worship you. I adore you. Thank you for forgiving me when I fail you.

New Testament verse for today: II Peter 3:9

He isn't really being slow about his promised return, even though it sometimes seems that way. But he is waiting, for the good reason that he is not willing that any should perish, and he is giving more time for sinners to repent.

One possible prayer for today:

God, thank you for your patience with me. Thank you for waiting for me to repent. Thank you for being unwilling that I should perish. Thank you for forgiving me when I fail you. Thank you for being patient with me when I fall short of your goals for me. And, thank you again, for saving me through the sacrifice of your Son, Jesus, who died for my sins. Lord, I believe in your Son, Jesus, as my Savior. Thank you, Lord.

My prayer for today—including any journaling thoughts I may want to add. Where am I today spiritually, emotionally, physically, financially, generally?

Today's Date: _____

Old Testament verse for today: Deuteronomy 6:4 & 5

O Israel, listen: Jehovah is our God, Jehovah alone. You must love him with all your heart, soul, and might.

One possible prayer for today:

God, thank you for being the one and only true God. You alone are God. Help me to love you more. Help me to love you with all my heart, soul, and might. Thank you for being such a mighty and awesome God, and yet a God who loves me and cares for me. Thank you for accepting my very frail and human love. Thank you, God.

New Testament verse for today: Revelation 4:11

O Lord, you are worthy to receive the glory and the honor and the power, for you have created all things. They were created and called into being by your act of will.

One possible prayer for today:

God, thank you for being the one and only true God. Thank you for being a God who is worthy to receive all the glory and honor and worship that I am capable of giving you. Thank you for being a God who is worthy to receive all the glory and honor and worship that the whole world is capable of giving you. Thank you for the wonderful creation that you have made available for me to enjoy. Thank you, God, for being such a wonderful, awesome, and yet caring and loving God.

My prayer for today—including any journaling thoughts I may want to add. Where am I today spiritually, emotionally, physically, financially, generally?

Today's Date: _____

Old Testament verse for today: Deuteronomy 6:25

For it always goes well with us when we obey all the laws of the Lord our God.

One possible prayer for today:

God, thank you loving me so much that when I do fail to keep all of your laws, you still forgive me because of the gift of your Son, Jesus, who died for me sins. Thank you for helping me in my life so that things do go well for me. Thank you for always being there for me. Thank you, God.

New Testament verse for today: Hebrews 3:14

For if we are faithful to the end, trusting God just as we did when we first became Christians, we will share in all that belongs to Christ.

One possible prayer for today:

God, I can be faithful in your eyes only if you continue to forgive me when I sin against you. I confess my sins to you, Lord, and thank you for forgiving me. Let me work at being more faithful to you. Let me work at keeping all of my promises to you. Thank you for giving me the promise that I will share in all that belongs to Christ if I am faithful in continuing to come before you, leaning on you for guidance and asking your forgiveness when I fail. Thank you for always being faithful to me, even when I am unfaithful to you and unworthy of your wonderful love. Thank you, God.

My prayer for today—including any journaling thoughts I may want to add. Where am I today spiritually, emotionally, physically, financially, generally?

Today's Date: _____

Old Testament verse for today: Deuteronomy 7:9

Understand, therefore, that the Lord your God is the faithful God who for a thousand generations keeps his promises and constantly loves those who love him and who obey his commandments.

One possible prayer for today:

God, what a wonderful God you are. Thank you for being a faithful God. Thank you for being an everlasting God, who can keep his promises for a thousand generations. Thank you for constantly loving me. Thank you for helping me to live as you want me to live; and, thank you for forgiving me when I fail to live as you want me to live. Thank you for being a God worthy of my love and my faith. Thank you, Lord.

New Testament verse for today: John 13:34 & 35

And so I am giving a new commandment to you now—love each other just as much as I love you. Your strong love for each other will prove to the world that you are my disciples.

One possible prayer for today:

God, thank you for sending your Son, Jesus, to give me a new commandment. You know how many times I have failed to live up to your original commandments. You know that even now, I fail many times to show love to others. I let me ego, my desires, my selfishness, all the things that please me get in the way of loving others. But, God, I know that you love me. I know that you sent your Son, Jesus, to provide a plan of salvation for me if I will only believe in him as my personal Savior. I do believe, Lord. Thank you for loving me so much, Lord. Thank you for forgiving me when I fail you. Help me to do a better job of loving you and showing my love for others.

My prayer for today—including any journaling thoughts I may want to add. Where am I today spiritually, emotionally, physically, financially, generally?

Today's Date: _____

Old Testament verse for today: Deuteronomy 7:11 thru 13a

Therefore obey all these commandments. I am giving you today. Because of your obedience, the Lord your God will keep his part of the contract which, in his tender love, he made with your fathers. And he will love you and bless you.

One possible prayer for today:

God, thank you so much for your tender love. Thank you for being a God who is trustworthy and who always keeps his promises. Thank you for loving me and blessing me. Lord, let me do a better joy of keeping my end of the bargain. Let me do a better job of living the way you want me to live. Thank you for being patience with me when I fail you, Lord. Thank you for forgiving me when I let you down. Thank you, Lord.

New Testament verse for today: II Corinthians 6:18

And I will be a father to you, and you will be my sons and daughters.

One possible prayer for today:

God, how wonderful it is to have you as my loving heavenly father. Thank you for calling me one of your children. Thank you for loving me and blessing me as you would one of your children whom you love and cherish. Thank you, God. Thank you.

My prayer for today—including any journaling thoughts I may want to add. Where am I today spiritually, emotionally, physically, financially, generally?

Today's Date: _____

Old Testament verse for today: Deuteronomy 8:1a

You must obey all the commandments I give you today. If you do, you will not only live, you will multiply.

One possible prayer for today:

God, you know that I try to live as you would have me live. You know that I love you and try to keep your commandments. But, God, you know that I fail often. I fail to keep your commandments. Yet God, you love me and continue to uphold me with your power and your strength if I will only come back to you, expressing my love for you and asking for your forgiveness one more time. Thank you for continuing to forgive me, Lord. Thank you for never getting tired of having me come back to you once I have failed you. Thank you for being such a great and loving God.

New Testament verse for today: Hebrews 10:24

In response to all he has done for us, let us outdo each other in being helpful and kind to each other and in doing good.

One possible prayer for today:

Lord, you know that I have a tendency to be a "taker." I am delighted to take all of the blessings you give me without thanking and praising you enough and without being a "giver" to others who either need my giving spirit, or who would just appreciate someone being kind and helpful to them. Lord, you have done so much for me. Thank you for all you have done for me. Help me to have a kinder and more helpful spirit to others in order to show your love working through me. Thank you for helping me, Lord.

My prayer for today—including any journaling thoughts I may want to add. Where am I today spiritually, emotionally, physically, financially, generally?

Today's Date: _____

Old Testament verse for today: Deuteronomy 8:3b
Real life comes from obeying every command of God.

One possible prayer for today:
God, help me to live more as you would have me to live. Help me to obey your commands and your instructions. Help me to turn to you for all of my needs and guidance. And, Lord, thank you for forgiving me—always—when I fail you in any way and return to you. Thank you for giving me the real life that only you can give.

New Testament verse for today: Titus 2:7b & 8
Let everything you do reflect your love of the truth and the fact that you are in dead earnest about it. Your conversation should be so sensible and logical that anyone who wants to argue will be ashamed of himself because there won't be anything to criticize in anything you say!

One possible prayer for today:
God, help me to have the consistency I need to live as you would want me to live. Help me to live so that everything I do reflects my love of the truth. Let my conversation be sensible and logical. Lord, I acknowledge that I can only do that if I rely completely on you and listen to your leading in my life. Let me always look to you for this guidance. Thank you, Lord, for helping me to live as you would have me live.

My prayer for today—including any journaling thoughts I may want to add. Where am I today spiritually, emotionally, physically, financially, generally?

Today's Date: _____

Old Testament verse for today: Deuteronomy 8:5

So you should realize that, as a man punishes his son, the Lord punishes you to help you.

One possible prayer for today:

God, it is really hard for me to thank you for the hard times that I face. I know that you either provide or permit hard times in my life for many reasons. If it is punishment, please be gentle with me. If it is for learning, please let me learn the lessons that you have in mind for me to learn. But, most of all, Lord, let my faith in you, my love for you, and my confidence in you as the Lord of my life, grow as I face these problems and work through them. Help me, Lord. Help me with solutions to these problems that will not only solve the problems, but bring honor to you as I work through to the solution. Thank you, Lord.

New Testament verse for today: Colossians 3:23 & 24

Work hard and cheerfully at all you do, just as though you were working for the Lord and not merely for your masters, remembering that it is the Lord Christ who is going to pay you, giving you your full portion of all he owns. He is the one you are really working for.

One possible prayer for today:

God, help me to keep in mind that you are in charge of everything in my life. Help me to remember that my main purpose in life is to honor you and your Son, Jesus. Lord, when things get tough for me, I have a hard time remembering that. I get so caught up in my own problems that I take my eye off the goal of pleasing you. I need your help right now, Lord. I need your help in solving my problems and I need your help in remembering to thank you for these problems—and really meaning it. I need your help to learn what you have in mind for me to learn. I need your help to work cheerfully through my problems. I need your help to remember that ultimately I am working for you. Help me, Lord. Thank you for helping me.

My prayer for today—including any journaling thoughts I may want to add. Where am I today spiritually, emotionally, physically, financially, generally?

Today's Date: _____

Old Testament verse for today: Deuteronomy 8:6

Obey the laws of the Lord your God. Walk in his ways and fear him.

One possible prayer for today:

God, thank you for loving me when I fail to obey your laws. Thank you for loving me when I fail to walk in your ways. Lord, I do try. I do fear you. And, God, I love you. Thank you for loving me so much that I know how to love you in return.

New Testament verse for today: I John 2:1 & 2

My little children, I am telling you this so that you will stay away from sin. But if you sin, there is someone to plead for you before the Father. His name is Jesus Christ, the one who is all that is good and who pleases God completely. He is the one who took God's wrath against our sins upon himself, and brought us into fellowship with God; and he is the forgiveness for our sins, and not only ours but all the world's.

One possible prayer for today:

God, thank you so much for sending Christ to plead for me before you. What a wonderful advocate! Thank you for sending Jesus to take away your wrath against me for me sins. Thank you for sending Jesus to bring me into direct fellowship with you. Thank you for sending Jesus to be the forgiveness for my sins. Thank you for making this marvelous plan of salvation just for me, and for everyone else just like I am; a sinner saved by the love of Jesus. Thank you, Lord.

My prayer for today—including any journaling thoughts I may want to add. Where am I today spiritually, emotionally, physically, financially, generally?

Today's Date: _____

Old Testament verse for today: Deuteronomy 8:13

You must walk blamelessly before the Lord your God.

One possible prayer for today:

God, you know that I am completely unable to walk blamelessly before you. You are perfect in every way and I have a sinful nature. So, Lord, I cannot be blameless before you without your continuing and continual forgiveness. Thank you for being a forgiving God. Thank you for being an everlasting God who always wipes away my sins when I return to you, so that with your forgiveness I may be blameless before you. Thank you, God, for your continuing and continual forgiveness.

New Testament verse for today: Ephesians 4:12 & 13

Why is it that he gives us these special abilities to do certain things best? It is that God's people will be equipped to do better work for him, building up the church, the body of Christ, to a position of strength and maturity; until finally we all believe alike about our salvation and about our Savior, God's Son, and all become full grown in the Lord—yes to the point of being filled full with Christ.

One Possible prayer for today:

God, thank you for giving me the ability that you have given me. Thank you for knowing that I was unable to walk blamelessly before you in my own strength. Thank you for helping me to be better equipped to live for you, living as Christ would have me to live and growing in my walk of faith with you. Thank you for giving me your Son, Jesus, through whom I receive my salvation by only believing in him—not by being blameless—a goal that I could not achieve. Thank you for letting me be filled with Christ. Thank you, God, for knowing me so well that you knew that I needed Christ to die for my sins so that I could walk blamelessly before you. Thank you, God.

My prayer for today—including any journaling thoughts I may want to add. Where am I today spiritually, emotionally, physically, financially, generally?

Today's Date: _____

Old Testament verse for today: Deuteronomy 8:18a
Always remember that it is the Lord your God who gives you power to become rich.

One possible prayer for today:
God, I acknowledge that you are the God of everything in the universe. I acknowledge that all things were made by you and are under your power. God, I thank you for the things that you have given me. I thank you for being so good to me. Lord, if you shower me with riches, let me do my part in giving back to you in a manner that is pleasing to you. Thank you, Lord, for being so good to me. Forgive me for the times I become unhappy because I don't have enough of what I want. Let me always acknowledge your Lordship in my life—both in times of plenty and in times of need. Thank you, Lord.

New Testament verse for today: John 15:4 & 5
Take care to live in me, and let me live in you. For a branch can't produce fruit when severed from the vine. Nor can you be fruitful apart from me. Yes, I am the vine; you are the branches. Whoever lives in me and I in him shall produce a large crop of fruit. For apart from me you can't do a thing.

One possible prayer for today:
Lord, let me always remember that you are the source of my strength and power. Let me remember that only what I do for you has any lasting effect. Let me remember that earthly riches may not be what you have in store for me. Let me produce the kind of fruit that you want me to produce. Let me be drawn ever closer to you and cling to you and your promises as a branch clings to the vine from which it grew. Let me grow in my knowledge and faith in you, Lord. Thank you for always being there for me.

My prayer for today—including any journaling thoughts I may want to add. Where am I today spiritually, emotionally, physically, financially, generally?

Today's Date: _____

Old Testament verse for today: Deuteronomy 10:12 thru 14

And now, ___, what does the Lord your God require of you except to listen carefully to all he says to you, and to obey for your own good the commandments I am giving you today, and to love him, and to worship him with all your hearts and souls? Earth and highest heaven belong to the Lord your God.

One possible prayer for today:

God, thank you for being the God of everything, whether it is here on earth or in the highest heaven. And yet, God, thank you for being concerned about me. Help me to listen as you speak to me. Help me to listen carefully. Let me do my best to obey the commandments you have given to me, knowing that such obedience is for my own good. But, Lord, most of all, help me to love you and worship you with all my heart and soul. Thank you for being such a great and glorious God so that worshipping you is so easy and natural. Thank you, God.

New Testament verse for today: Galatians 5:14

For the whole Law can be summed up in this one command: "Love others as you love yourself."

One possible prayer for today:

God, you knew that I could not obey your commandments. You knew that I would continuously fail. So, you made things so easy for me. "Just love others." Just follow the example of Christ, who you gave to me to die for my sins. What a wonderful, loving God are! Let me have more love for others Lord, so that I may show just a little bit more of the enormous love that you have given to me. And, God, thank you again for being patient with me when I don't show your love to me because I don't show love for others.

My prayer for today—including any journaling thoughts I may want to add. Where am I today spiritually, emotionally, physically, financially, generally?

Today's Date: _____

Old Testament verse for today: Deuteronomy 10:17a

Jehovah your God is God of gods and Lord of lords. He is the great and mighty God.

One possible prayer for today:

God, thank you for being the one and only true God. Thank you for being the God of gods and the Lord of lords. Thank you for your great power and might. And, God, thank you for being not only a great and mighty God, but a caring and loving God. Thank you for loving and caring for me—every day and all the time. Thank you, God.

New Testament verse for today: Colossians 1:15 thru 19

Christ is the exact likeness of the unseen God. He existed before God made anything at all, and, in fact, Christ himself is the Creator who made everything in heaven and earth, the things we can see and the things that we can't; the spirit world with its kings and kingdoms, its rulers and authorities; all were made by Christ for his own use and glory. He was before all else began and it is his power that holds everything together. He is the Head of the body made up of his people—that is, his church—which he began; and he is the leader of all those who arise from the dead, so that he is first in everything; for God wanted all of himself to be in his Son.

One possible prayer for today:

God, thank you for being the only true God. Thank you for being the God of gods and the Lord of lords. Thank you for your great power and might. Thank you for giving all that power and might to your Son, Jesus. Thank you for making Christ your exact likeness. Thank you for loving each one of us—and especially me—so much that you gave Christ the power to be such a magnificent Creator. Thank you for giving Christ the power to hold everything together. Thank you for having your marvelous plan of salvation through your Son, Jesus, so that I may have eternal life by simply believing in Christ as my Savior. God, I do believe. Thank you for wanting all of yourself to be in Christ so that from his life, we might know you better. Thank you, God.

My prayer for today—including any journaling thoughts I may want to add. Where am I today spiritually, emotionally, physically, financially, generally?

Today's Date: _____

Old Testament verse for today: Deuteronomy 10:20 & 21a

You must fear the Lord your God and worship him and cling to him and take oaths by his name alone. He is your praise and he is your God, the one who has done mighty miracles.

One possible prayer for today:

God, you know my heart. I cannot hide anything from you. So, you know that I fear you, as well as love you and worship you. You know that I cling to you as the only one who can help me through my times of trial. You know that you alone are the God who I praise. You know that you alone are the God who I worship. Thank you for being the one and only true God. Thank you for being my personal God. Thank you.

New Testament verse for today: Colossians 1:20 & 21

It was through what his Son did that God cleared a path for everything to come to him— all things in heaven and on earth—for Christ's death on the cross has made peace with God for all by his blood. This includes you who were once so far away from God. You were his enemies and hated him and were separated from him by your evil thoughts and actions, yet now he has brought you back as his friends.

One possible prayer for today:

God, what a wonderful loving and forgiving God you are! Thank you for giving me Christ who cleared a path for me to come to you. Thank you for giving me Christ, whose death on the cross has permitted me to have peace with you, because of Christ's shed blood for me. Thank you for letting me come to you, even though my sins were—and sometimes still are—many. Thank you for forgiving me of my evil thoughts and actions. Thank you for bringing me back as one of your friends. Thank you, God, for loving me so much.

My prayer for today—including any journaling thoughts I may want to add. Where am I today spiritually, emotionally, physically, financially, generally?

Today's Date: _____

Old Testament verse for today: Deuteronomy 11:1
You must love the Lord your God and obey every one of his commands.

One possible prayer for today:
Lord, you know that I am unable to always obey every one of your commands. You know that I fall short of your ideal for my life on a regular basis. You know my heart. You know that in my humanness I continue to sin against you. Thank you, Lord, for continuing to forgive me when I fail you. Thank you for always being there for me, even when I fall short of living for you. But, Lord, you know that I always love you. And, God, thank you for always loving me.

New Testament verse for today: I Thessalonians 5:11
So encourage each other to build each other up, just as you are already doing.

One possible prayer for today:
Lord, I know that you want me to show my love and encouragement to others as an indication of my love for you, and as an indication of how much you love me and encourage me. Help me to do a better job of caring for others. Help me to do a better job of encouraging others—not only in their faith in you—but in all areas of their life. Thank you for always being there to encourage me and to build me up. Thank you, God, for your everlasting love.

My prayer for today—including any journaling thoughts I may want to add. Where am I today spiritually, emotionally, physically, financially, generally?

Today's Date: _____

Old Testament verse for today: Deuteronomy 11:13 thru 15

And if you will carefully obey all of his commandments that I am going to give you today, and if you will love the Lord your God with all your hearts and souls, and will worship him, then he will continue to send both the early and the late rains that will produce wonderful crops of grain, grapes for your wine, and olive oil. He will give you lush pastureland for your cattle to graze in, and you yourselves shall have plenty to eat and be fully content.

One possible prayer for today:

God, you know that I am unable to keep all of your commandments. You know that I will fail you often in this area. But, God, you also know that I do love you with all my heart and soul. You know that I worship you and praise you for all that you have done for me. And, Lord, I claim your promise of taking care of me at all times. I claim your promise of giving me the things that I need in life. Lord, I claim your promise to give me more than my bare necessities, to give me some of the better things in life. And, Lord, most of all, I ask for your help in being completely satisfied with whatever you decide to give me. Thank you, Lord, for taking care of my needs.

New Testament verse for today: I Peter 1:15 & 16

But be holy now in everything you do, just as the Lord is holy, who invited you to be his child. He himself has said, "You must be holy, for I am holy."

One possible prayer for today:

God, you have set a very high standard for me to follow! You know that no matter how hard I try, I will fall short of always being holy. You know that there is no way that I can be as holy as you are holy. But, Lord, even as you know these things about me, you have still invited me to be your child. What a wonderful and incredible invitation! You have told me that you love me and that you will always love me. You have given me a challenge that I cannot obtain, and yet you will always be there to encourage me to work toward that goal. Thank you for being such a loving, encouraging, and—of great importance to me—a forgiving God. Thank you, God.

My prayer for today—including any journaling thoughts I may want to add. Where am I today spiritually, emotionally, physically, financially, generally?

Today's Date: _____

Old Testament verse for today: Deuteronomy 12:18b

Rejoice before the Lord your God in everything you do.

One possible prayer for today:

God, thank you for being such a loving and caring God. Thank you for wanting me to have a good life so that I might truly rejoice before you in everything that I do. Thank you for giving me the ability to experience those feelings that make rejoicing possible. Thank you for making me so that I may learn to love. Thank you for giving me sight and hearing and feelings so that I might rejoice in all the wonderful things that you have created for me. Thank you for giving me a plan of salvation so that I might rejoice in the knowledge that I have eternal life with you. Thank you, God.

New Testament verse for today: John 15:11

I have told you this so that you will be filled with my joy. Yes, your cup of joy will overflow!

One possible prayer for today:

God, thank you for all the wonderful promises that you have given me so that I can be filled with joy. Thank you for making me so that I can rejoice before you in all that I do. Thank you for letting my cup of joy overflow because of the bountiful blessings you have given to me. Thank you, Lord, for being so good to me; for loving me so much; and for caring about me all the time. Thank you, God.

My prayer for today—including any journaling thoughts I may want to add. Where am I today spiritually, emotionally, physically, financially, generally?

Today's Date: _____

Old Testament verse for today: Deuteronomy 30:10

He will rejoice if you but obey the commandments written in this book of the law, and if you turn to the Lord your God with all your hearts and souls.

One possible prayer for today:

God, you know my heart. You know that I have tried to keep all of your commandments. You know that I have tried to give you my heart and soul, and to live in a manner that would be pleasing to you. But, Lord, you know that I have often failed in that goal. You know that my very nature is sinful and that I continually fall short of the goals you have set down for me in your law. So, God, thank you for forgiving me for my sins. Thank you for understanding my sinful nature and letting me always come back to you for forgiveness.

New Testament verse for today: Galatians 6:4 & 5

Let everyone be sure that he is doing his very best, for then he will have the personal satisfaction of work well done, and won't need to compare himself with someone else. Each of us must bear some faults and burdens of his own. For none of us is perfect!

One possible prayer for today:

God, thank you for understanding that I am not perfect! Thank you for accepting my best as being good enough—as long as I turn to your Son, Jesus, to forgive me of my sins and make me perfect in your eyes. Lord, I do know that I must bear the burdens for my faults. I do know that I fail you often. But, Lord, I also know that anytime I return to you, you will once again forgive me and wipe my slate of sins clean so that I will again to be perfect in your sight. Thank you, Lord, for your patience with me.

My prayer for today—including any journaling thoughts I may want to add. Where am I today spiritually, emotionally, physically, financially, generally?

Today's Date: _____

Old Testament verse for today: Deuteronomy 31:6

Be strong! Be courageous! Do not be afraid! For the Lord your God will be with you. He will never fail you nor forsake you.

One possible prayer for today:

God, what a wonderful promise! Thank you for promising that you will never fail me nor forsake me. Thank you for always being there for me so that I can face any adversity knowing that you are there with me. Knowing that I can be strong and courageous and unafraid as I trust in your strength and not in my own. Thank you for always being with me, Lord. Thank you. Thank you.

New Testament verse for today: I Corinthians 12:7

Now God gives us many kinds of special abilities, but it is the same Holy Spirit who is the source of them all. There are different kinds of service to God, but it is the same Lord we are serving. There are many ways in which God works in our lives, but it is the same God who does the work in and through all of us who are his. The Holy Spirit displays God's power through each of us as a means of helping the entire church.

One possible prayer for today:

God, thank you for the abilities that you have given me. Thank you for sending your loving Holy Spirit to work in my life. Thank you for accepting what little service I can accomplish for you. Thank you for having your loving Holy Spirit empower me to do the things that I need to do. Thank you, Lord, for this promise so that I know that if I am one of yours, I can, indeed, be strong, courageous, and unafraid, knowing that you will always be with me, empowering me, and never failing or forsaking me. Thank you for always being there for me, Lord.

My prayer for today—including any journaling thoughts I may want to add. Where am I today spiritually, emotionally, physically, financially, generally?

Today's Date: _____

Old Testament verse for today: Deuteronomy 31:8 Today's date
Don't be afraid, for the Lord will go before you and will be with you: he will not fail nor forsake you.

One possible prayer for today:
God, thank you for that promise. Thank you for being there for me so that I have the confidence to charge ahead, as long as while I am charging ahead, I am leaning on you for strength and guidance. Thank you for promising to go before and for promising to always be with me. Thank you for the promise that you will never forsake me. Thank you, God, for being such a wonderful God to me.

New Testament verse for today: James 1:2 thru 4
Dear brothers, is your life full of difficulties and temptations? Then be happy, for when the way is rough, your patience has a chance to grow. So let it grow, and don't try to squirm out of your problems. For when your patience is finally in full bloom, then you will be ready for anything, strong in character, full and complete.

One possible prayer for today:
God, that is really hard for me to accept sometimes. When my life is full of difficulties and temptations, I want to complain about how tough I have it! I want sympathy from somebody. I may not feel happy at all. Then, Lord, I know that it is time to get down on my knees and humble myself before you and ask for your help; ask for another shot of faith in you. That is the time when I need to remember that you will always go before me and be with me. That is the time when I need to remember that you will never fail nor forsake me. Lord, when those times occur in my life, let my faith and confidence in you grow, so that my patience will grow; and, so that I will be strong in character, full and complete, and ready for anything. Lord, you know that I cannot accomplish that without your help. So, help me, Lord. Thank you for helping me.

My prayer for today—including any journaling thoughts I may want to add.
Where am I today spiritually, emotionally, physically, financially, generally?

Today's Date: _____

Old Testament verse for today: Deuteronomy 32:20a

Choose to love the Lord your God and to obey him and to cling to him, for he is your life and the length of your days.

One possible prayer for today:

God, I do choose to love you. I do choose to obey you. I do choose to cling to you. Thank you for accepting my love. Thank you for letting me cling to you in both good times and bad. Thank you for being the author and finisher of my life. Thank you for being so consistent that I know you will be there for me for the entire length of my days. Thank you, Lord.

New Testament verse for today: Revelation 21:3 & 4

I heard a loud shout from the throne saying, "Look, the home of God is now among men, and he will live with them and they will be his people; yes, God himself will be among them. He will wipe away all tears from their eyes, and there shall be no more death, nor sorrow, nor crying, nor pain. All of that has gone forever."

One possible prayer for today:

God, what wonderful promises you give me. Thank you for being there for me, not only for the length of my days, but also for eternity. Thank you for letting me cling to you in this life with the knowledge that you will be there for me for the ages to come. Thank you for the promise that someday your home will be where I am. Thank you for the promise that when that occurs, there will be no more tears. There will be no more death. There will be no more pain. Thank you, God, for being an eternal God.

My prayer for today—including any journaling thoughts I may want to add. Where am I today spiritually, emotionally, physically, financially, generally?

Today's Date: _____

Old Testament verse for today: Joshua 1:5

No one will be able to oppose you as long as you live, for I will be with you just as I was with Moses; I will never abandon you or fail to help you.

One possible prayer for today:

God, I know that you will never abandon me. I thank you and praise you for that. I know that you will be with me as long as I live. I thank you and praise you for that. I do know that I will be confronted with opposition during my life. I do know that I will encounter problems and disappointments. But, Lord, knowing that you are always there for me is a great encouragement to me in these times of trouble. Let my faith grow so that no matter what I am facing, I can turn to you with confidence and peace, knowing that you will walk with me through my trials, and help deliver me out of the other side. Thank you, God, for always being with me.

New Testament verse for today: Hebrews 4:14 & 15

But Jesus the Son of God is our great High Priest who has gone to heaven itself to help us; therefore let us never stop trusting him. This High Priest of ours understands our weaknesses, since he had the same temptations we do, though he never once gave way to them and sinned.

One possible prayer for today:

Thank you for sending your Son, Jesus, to be my great High Priest. Thank you for sending Jesus to earth so that he knows first hand the temptations that I have. Thank you for taking Jesus back to heaven with you to help me in my times of trouble and trial. Thank you for letting Jesus understand my weaknesses—which are plentiful! And even though Jesus was perfect and did not give into temptation, thank you, God, that you and Jesus understand that I do! I sin. But, God, you forgive me because of Jesus being the great High Priest. Thank you for giving me the faith to believe in Jesus as my great High Priest and Savior.

My prayer for today—including any journaling thoughts I may want to add. Where am I today spiritually, emotionally, physically, financially, generally?

Today's Date: _____

Old Testament verse for today: Joshua 1:7

You need only to be strong and courageous and to obey to the letter every law Moses gave you, for it you are careful to obey every one of them you will be successful in everything you do.

One possible prayer for today:

God, you know that I am totally incapable of obeying to the letter every one of the laws that you gave Moses. You know my heart. You know that no matter how hard I may try, I will fail in that attempt. So, Lord, thank you for giving me an alternative way to please you. Thank you for loving me even though I am not capable of keeping every law that you gave Moses. Lord, thank you for being with me even when I fail you and sin against you. And, thank you for giving me the courage and the strength to meet the challenges that I face daily in my life. Thank you for the success that you have given me. Thank you, Lord.

New Testament verse for today: Romans 5:11

Now we rejoice in our wonderful new relationship with God—all because of what our Lord Jesus Christ has done in dying for our sins—making us friends of God.

One possible prayer for today:

God, you are so wonderful to me. You knew that I could not keep every law of Moses. You knew what a failure I would be trying to meet that standard. So, you gave me a new standard—one that I could meet. You sent your Son, Jesus, to die on the cross to wipe my sins completely off the slate of my life. And all I have to do is believe in him! And, God, you know that I believe. Thank you for giving me the faith to believe. Thank you for that wonderful relationship that I can now have with you and your Son, Jesus—being one of your friends. Thank you, God, for being such a caring and loving God.

My prayer for today—including any journaling thoughts I may want to add. Where am I today spiritually, emotionally, physically, financially, generally?

Today's Date: _____

Old Testament verse for today: Joshua 1:9

Yes, be bold and strong! Banish fear and doubt! For remember, the Lord your God is with you wherever you go.

One possible prayer for today:

God, thank you for always being with me. Thank you for giving me the courage and the strength to be bold and strong. Thank you for giving me the courage and the strength to banish all fear and doubt from my mind. Thank you for being a God who is always there for me—to care for me, to love me, to protect me, to guide me, and most of all, Lord, to forgive me when I sin against you. Thank you, God.

New Testament verse for today: I John 1:24 & 25

So keep on believing what you have been taught from the beginning. If you do, you will always be in close fellowship with both God the Father and his Son. And he himself has promised us this: eternal life.

One possible prayer for today: .

What a wonderful God you are! You are a God who is with me today. A God who permits me and encourages me to be bold and strong. A God who encourages me to banish all fear and doubt from my mind today. And then, God, you have promised me eternal life with you and your Son, Jesus, if I will only believe that my salvation—ticket into eternal life—is simply based on my belief in your Son, Jesus. God, thank you for being with me here in this life, and for giving me such a simple plan of salvation for eternal life. Thank you, God.

My prayer for today—including any journaling thoughts I may want to add. Where am I today spiritually, emotionally, physically, financially, generally?

Today's Date: _____

Old Testament verse for today: Joshua 2:11b

For your God is the supreme God of heaven, not just an ordinary god.

One possible prayer for today:

God, thank you for being the supreme God of heaven. Thank you for not being just an ordinary god. Thank you for being a God who rules over all. And, God, even with all your power and might, thank you for being a God who loves me and care about me. Thank you, God.

New Testament verse for today: Revelation 15:4

Who shall not fear, O Lord, and glorify your Name? For you alone are holy. All nations will come and worship before you, for your righteous deeds have been disclosed.

One possible prayer for today:

God, thank you for being the supreme God of heaven. Thank you for alone being the God who is holy. Thank you for your wonderful plan of salvation through the blood of your Son, Jesus, which you have disclosed to me. Thank you for being a God who is so mighty that your name is worthy of being glorified. And, God, thank you for loving and caring for me.

My prayer for today—including any journaling thoughts I may want to add. Where am I today spiritually, emotionally, physically, financially, generally?

Today's Date: _____

Old Testament verse for today: Joshua 4:24

He did this so that all the nations of the earth will realize that Jehovah is the mighty God, and so that all of you will worship him forever.

One possible prayer for today:

God, thank you for being such a mighty God. Thank you for being a God who is worthy of everlasting worship. Thank you for showing your power and might so that I am constantly reminded to worship and glorify your name. Thank you for being the ruler of all nations in the whole earth. Thank you for being an eternal God who loves me eternally. Thank you, God.

New Testament verse for today: Luke 1:32 & 33

He shall be very great and shall be called the Son of God. And the Lord God shall give him the throne of his ancestor David. And he shall reign over Israel forever; his Kingdom shall never end.

One possible prayer for today:

God, thank you for making Jesus, your Son, a ruler whose Kingdom will never end. Thank you for making a plan of salvation that all nations can embrace if they will only believe in your Son, Jesus. Thank you for not only being a great and glorious God, and an everlasting God; but a loving and caring God who cares for all those who love him and glorify his name. Thank you for letting me accept your plan of salvation so that I can look forward to spending eternity with you and your Son, Jesus. Thank you, God, for your power, your might, and also your love and your care.

My prayer for today—including any journaling thoughts I may want to add. Where am I today spiritually, emotionally, physically, financially, generally?

Today's Date: _____

Old Testament verse for today: Joshua 10:25

Don't ever be afraid of discouraged, Joshua said to his men. Be strong and courageous, for the Lord is going to do this to all your enemies.

One possible prayer for today:

God, thank you for being with me to defeat my enemies, just as you were with Joshua to defeat his. I know, Lord, that for that to happen, I must have the faith, the discipline, and the trust in you that Joshua had. Give me the faith and the strength that I need, Lord, to never let my trust and confidence in you wane. Let me always be strong and courageous in my belief in you. Then I can have the confidence that I never need to be afraid or discouraged, because you are with me at all times. Thank you, Lord, for that confidence.

New Testament verse for today: I Corinthians 15:58

So, my dear brothers, since future victory is sure, be strong and steady, always abounding in the Lord's work, for you know that nothing you do for the Lord is ever wasted as it would be if there were no resurrection.

One possible prayer for today:

God, thank you for the assurance of the final victory—an eternity with you! Thank you for giving me the strength to be strong and steady in my belief in you and my work for you. Thank you for helping me never to be discouraged in my attempt to live as you would want me to live. Thank you for the promise of Christ's resurrection, giving me the knowledge that nothing that I do for you is ever wasted. Thank you for being an everlasting God. Thank you for being a God who everlastingly loves, cares and forgives me. Thank you, God.

My prayer for today—including any journaling thoughts I may want to add. Where am I today spiritually, emotionally, physically, financially, generally?

Today's Date: _____

Old Testament verse for today: Joshua 24:15

As for me and my family, we will serve the Lord.

One possible prayer for today:

God, thank you for making yourself known to me. Thank you for permitting me to be one of your children. Thank you for letting me serve you to the best of my ability. Thank you, Lord, for being a God worthy of my service and my praise.

New Testament verse for today: I John 3:10 & 11

So now we can tell who is a child of God and who belongs to Satan. Whoever is living a life of sin and doesn't love his brother shows that he is not in God's family; for the message to us from the beginning has been that we should love one another.

One possible prayer for today:

God, again I thank you for making yourself known to me. Again, I thank you for letting me be one of your children. But, Lord, I need your help to live as you want me to live. I need your help to not only love you, but to love others more. I need your help to resist temptation, which leads to sinning against you. God, thank you for helping me in these areas; and, God, thank you for forgiving me when I fail you in any way. Thank you, God.

My prayer for today—including any journaling thoughts I may want to add. Where am I today spiritually, emotionally, physically, financially, generally?

Today's Date: _____

Old Testament verse for today: I Samuel 12:24

Trust the Lord and sincerely worship him; think of all the tremendous things he has done for you.

One possible prayer for today:

Lord, thank you for all the tremendous things that you have done for me. Thank you for being such a wonderful and consistent God that I can trust you completely. Thank you for being a God who is worthy of my sincere worship. God, thank you for accepting my complete trust and my sincere worship, even though my trust and my worship are limited by my human frailty. Thank you for loving me just as I am. Thank you, God.

New Testament verse for today: Romans 12:2

Don't copy the behavior and customs of the world, but be a new and different person with a fresh newness in all you do and think. Then you will learn from your own experience how his ways will really satisfy you.

One possible prayer for today:

God, help me to be strong enough not to copy the behavior and custom of the world. Give me the strength and the resolve to trust you more completely and worship you more sincerely. Help me to be a person who exudes a fresh newness in all that I do and think. Let me learn more about you. Let me always remember all the tremendous things that you have done for me. Let me be satisfied by you alone. Let my confidence and trust in you be so strong that I never question the plans you have for my life. Thank you, Lord, for giving me the faith that I need to trust you more, to worship you more fully, and to be the kind of new and different person that you would have me to be. And, Lord, thank you for never giving up on me when I fail to be that new and different person. Thank you for your ever-lasting love and your continuing forgiveness. Thank you, God.

My prayer for today—including any journaling thoughts I may want to add. Where am I today spiritually, emotionally, physically, financially, generally?

Today's Date: _____

Old Testament verse for today: I Samuel 15:22

Has the Lord as much pleasure in your burnt offerings and sacrifices as in your obedience? Obedience is far better than sacrifice. He is much more interested in your listening to him than in your offering the fat ram to him.

One possible prayer for today:

Lord, let me do a better job of listening to you. Let me do a much better job of obeying you. I know that above all you want me to honor and praise you with my life—my words and my actions. Lord, thank you for giving me the strength to love you and obey you more fully. And, Lord, thank you for forgiving me when I fail you. Thank you, Lord.

New Testament verse for today: Romans 3:20

Now do you see it? No one can ever be made right in God's sight by doing what the law commands. For the more we know of God's laws, the clearer it becomes that we aren't obeying them; his laws serve only to make us see that we are sinners.

One possible prayer for today:

God, I know that I don't have the ability or the discipline to always obey you and your laws. I know that I cannot ever be righteous in your eyes by attempting to obey your laws. It's true. The more I know of how your laws want me to live, the more apparent it becomes that I am missing the mark. So, Lord, thank you for providing a way that does work for me. Thank you for sending your Son, Jesus, to die on the cross for my sins. Thank you for sending Jesus to make me righteous in your eyes. Thank you for loving me so much that you came up with a plan that works for me. Thank you, Lord.

My prayer for today—including any journaling thoughts I may want to add. Where am I today spiritually, emotionally, physically, financially, generally?

Today's Date: _____

Old Testament verse for today: I Samuel 16:7

But the Lord said to Samuel, "Don't judge by a man's face or height, for this is not the one. I don't make decisions the way you do! Men judge by outward appearance, but I look at a man's thoughts and intentions."

One possible prayer for today:

God, let me remember this statement of yours to Samuel. I get all caught up in impressing people with how I look, when I should be trying to please you with my thoughts and my intentions. Thank you for forgiving me, Lord, for getting my priorities all confused. Let me concentrate more on the things that please you, and less on the things that please me, or the things that I may do attempting to impress others. Thank you for your continued patience with me, Lord, as me ego keeps getting in the way of what I should be doing.

New Testament verse for today: Romans 13:9b & 10

All ten (commandments) are wrapped up in this one, to love your neighbor as you love yourself. Love does no wrong to anyone. That's why it fully satisfied all of God's requirements. It is the only law you need.

One possible prayer for today:

God, if I could just remember this verse, I wouldn't try to impress anyone. I would treat others as I want to be treated. It is pretty tough for me to go around loving some of my neighbors, fellow workers, etc.; and the only way that I can even attempt that kind of an attitude is to turn fully to you for your help! Let me work harder at trying to satisfy your requirement for my life by following this challenge! Thank you, Lord, for helping me in this area of my thinking and my intent.

My prayer for today—including any journaling thoughts I may want to add. Where am I today spiritually, emotionally, physically, financially, generally?

Today's Date: _____

Old Testament verse for today: II Samuel 7:21 & 22

You are doing all these things just because you promised to and because you want to! How great you are, Lord God! We have never heard of any other god like you. And there is no other god.

One possible prayer for today:

God, thank you for being the one and only true God. Thank you for all the promises that you have given to me. Thank you for being a God who keeps all of your promises. Thank you for being a God like no other. Lord, thank you for choosing me to be one of your children. Thank you, God.

New Testament verse for today: II Thessalonians 3:3

But the Lord is faithful; he will make you strong and guard you from satanic attacks of every kind.

One possible prayer for today:

God, thank you for all the wonderful promises you have given me just because you want to. Thank you for promising me that you will guard me from satanic attacks of all kinds. Thank you for keeping me strong and safe. Thank you for being a faithful God. Thank you for being a God like no other God. Thank you for being a God who cares about me.

My prayer for today—including any journaling thoughts I may want to add. Where am I today spiritually, emotionally, physically, financially, generally?

Today's Date: _____

Old Testament verse for today: II Samuel 7:28 & 29a

For you are indeed God, and your words are truth; and you have promised me these good things—so do as you have promised! Bless me and my family forever!

One possible prayer for today:

Thank you for being a God whose words are truth. Thank you for being a God who keeps his promises. Thank you for being God who I can trust. Thank you for being a God who has chosen to bless me and my family with salvation. Thank you for that promise, Lord.

New Testament verse for today: I Timothy 2:4 thru 6

For he longs for all to be saved and to understand this truth: That God is on one side and all the people on the other side, and Christ Jesus, himself man, is between them to bring them together, by giving his life for all mankind.

One possible prayer for today:

God, thank you for your words being truth. Thank you for wanting all these good things for me. Thank you for longing for my salvation. Thank you for sending your Son, Jesus, to bridge the gap that existed between you and me. Thank you for letting me come to you through Jesus so that I may experience your salvation. Thank you, Lord, for promising me all these good things, and then letting me experience them because of your love for me. Thank you, Lord.

My prayer for today—including any journaling thoughts I may want to add. Where am I today spiritually, emotionally, physically, financially, generally?

Today's Date: _____

Old Testament verse for today: I Kings 3:14

And I will give you a long life if you follow me and obey my laws as your father David did.

One possible prayer for today:

Lord, thank you for your promises of blessings if I follow the path that you have set for me. Thank you for the promise of a long life. Thank you for all the other promises that you have made to me through your wonderful book of promises, the Bible. Give me the strength and the faith to follow your instructions for me. Give me a mind more like yours as you gave your servant, David. Thank you for your promises, Lord.

New Testament verse for today: James 1:22 thru 25

And remember, it is a message to obey, not just to listen to. So don't fool yourselves. For if a person just listens and doesn't obey, he is like a man looking at his face in a mirror; as soon as he walks away, he can't see himself anymore or remember what he looks like. But if anyone keeps looking steadily into God's law for free men, he will not only remember it but he will do what it says, and God will greatly bless him in everything he does.

One possible prayer for today:

God, thank you for giving me your law for free men. Thank you for giving me the faith and the strength to accept your law for free men that entails belief in your Son, Jesus, as my Savior. Lord, don't let me fool myself. Let me keep looking to you for guidance in my life so that I will always be inspired to do the best that I can in living as you want me to live. And, God, I claim this promise that if I do what you want me to do, you will bless me greatly in everything that I do. Lord, you know that I will fail you often in trying to live as you want me to live. But, Lord, I know that you will never fail me. Thank you, Lord, for being an unfailing God to me.

My prayer for today—including any journaling thoughts I may want to add. Where am I today spiritually, emotionally, physically, financially, generally?

Today's Date: _____

Old Testament verse for today: I Kings 8:23

O Lord God of Israel, there is no god like you in heaven or earth, for you are loving and kind and you keep your promises to your people if they do their best to do your will.

One possible prayer for today:

God, thank you for being the one and only true God. Thank you that there is no other god like you in either heaven or earth. Thank you for being so loving and kind. Thank you for keeping your promises to me if I do my best to do your will. Lord, it is great that Solomon, in this prayer, did not say that this applied only to me if I always do your will; because I know that I don't always do that. But, God, Solomon said this applies to me if I do my best to do your will. Lord, give me the strength and the discipline to always try my best to do your will; and, then, Lord, I claim all of your promises of goodness for me. Thank you, Lord.

New Testament verse for today: II Timothy 3:16

The whole Bible was given to us by inspiration from God and is useful to teach us what is true and to make us realize what is wrong with our lives; it straightens us out and helps us to do what is right. It is God's way of making us well prepared at every point, fully equipped to do good to everyone.

One possible prayer for today:

God, thank you for giving me your words—to give me inspiration; to teach me; to help me realize what is wrong with my life; to straighten me out; to prepare and equip me. Thank you for being so loving and kind and for keeping your promises. Help me to look to you and your word—the Bible—more often so that I do a better job of following your instructions. Thank you for forgiving me when I fall short of your goals for me. Thank you for straightening me out gently when I fail! Thank you for equipping me to meet the rigors of life in a way that would be pleasing to you. Thank you, God.

My prayer for today—including any journaling thoughts I may want to add. Where am I today spiritually, emotionally, physically, financially, generally?

Today's Date: _____

Old Testament verse for today: I Kings 8:30 Today's date
Listen to every plea of the people ___; yes, hear in heaven where you live, and when you hear, forgive.

One possible prayer for today:
God, thank you for always hearing and listening to my prayers. Thank you for responding to my pleas. Thank you for not only hearing; but, answering my prayers when I ask for forgiveness. Thank you for being such a marvelous God, who can span the distance from heaven to reach me to hear and forgive. Thank you, Lord.

New Testament verse for today: II Corinthians 3:5b
Our only power and success comes from God.

One possible prayer for today:
God, how wonderful it is to rely totally on you and your lovingkindness. Let me always give you thanks for what you have done for me. Let me always acknowledge that all my power and success is a gift from you; and, gifts that you give generously and compassionately. Don't let me ever even give a thought to believing that I can go through life without you as my God and my help. Let me start every day with worship of you and acknowledgment that I want you to be the Lord of my life that day. Thank you for the success that you have given me and for the power and success that you have in store for me. Thank you, Lord.

My prayer for today—including any journaling thoughts I may want to add. Where am I today spiritually, emotionally, physically, financially, generally?

Today's Date: _____

Old Testament verse for today: I Kings 8:37b, 38 & 39

Whatever the problem is—when the people realize their sin and pray, hear them from heaven and forgive and answer all who have made an honest confession; for you know each heart.

One possible prayer for today:

God, I know that you know my heart. I cannot keep anything from you. You know the problems that I have and you know how many of them I have created because of my own greed, lust, dishonesty, selfishness, pride, etc. Thank you for being there for me when I finally wake up and realize my sin. Thank you for hearing me when I pray to you. Thank you for answering me when I make an honest confession of my sin. Thank you for knowing my heart and still forgiving me when I return to you. Thank you, God.

New Testament verse for today: James 4:10

Then when you realize your worthlessness before the Lord, he will lift you up, encourage and help you.

One possible prayer for today:

God, when I compare my life with the ideal that you have given me to follow—your Son, Jesus, there is no question that I am a huge failure. And yet, Lord, you love me. You care for me. You are always there to lift me up, and to encourage and help me. Thank you, Lord, for not considering me worthless in your eyes. What a wonderful, loving, caring, and forgiving Lord you are.

My prayer for today—including any journaling thoughts I may want to add. Where am I today spiritually, emotionally, physically, financially, generally?

Today's Date: _____

Old Testament verse for today: I Kings 8:57 thru 61

May the Lord our God be with us as he was with our fathers; may he never forsake us. May he give us the desire to do his will in everything, and to obey all the commandments and instructions he has given our ancestors. And may these words of my prayer be constantly before him day and night, so that he helps me and all of Israel in accordance with our daily needs. May people all over the earth know that the Lord is God, and that there is no other god at all. O my people, may you live good and perfect lives before the Lord our God; may you always obey his laws and commandments, just as you are doing today.

One possible prayer for today:

God, what a wonderful prayer this is that Solomon prayed. I know that you will do your part of never forsaking me and giving me the desire to always do your will; but, God, you know that I can't keep my end of the bargain! You know that I can't always obey all of your commandments and instructions. You know that I can't live a good and perfect life. So, Lord, thank you for always loving me just as I am. Thank you for giving me another alternative. Thank you, God.

New Testament verse for today: John 3:3

Jesus replied, "With all the earnestness I possess I tell you this: Unless you are born again, you can never get into the Kingdom of God."

One possible prayer for today:

God, thank you for giving me a solution that I can achieve. All I have to do to inherit your Kingdom is to just believe! What a wonderful alternative for me. That is something that I can do! I do believe, God. Thank you for knowing that I needed this alternative to living a good and perfect life and always obeying your commandments and instructions. I failed at that, Lord. Thank you for giving me a fail-safe alternative! Thank you, God.

My prayer for today—including any journaling thoughts I may want to add. Where am I today spiritually, emotionally, physically, financially, generally?

Today's Date: _____

Old Testament verse for today: II Kings 17:38 Today's date

For God had said, "You must never forget the covenant I made with you; never worship other gods. You must worship only the Lord; he will save you from all your enemies."

One possible prayer for today:

God, you know that I worship only you. You know my heart. You know that I believe that you are the one and only true God. Lord, let my life reflect this belief: and, Lord, I claim the promise of this verse that you will save me from all my enemies. Thank you, Lord, for saving me from my enemies.

New Testament verse for today: Hebrews 2:18

For since he himself has now been through suffering and temptation, he knows what it is like when we suffer and are tempted, and he is wonderfully able to help us.

One possible prayer for today:

God, thank you for understanding my pain. Thank you for understanding my suffering. Thank you for understanding my temptations. Thank you for always being there for me when I am in pain; when I am suffering; when I am tempted. And, God, thank you for always being there to save me from these enemies that take away the peace that only you can give. Thank you for being such a caring and consistent God.

My prayer for today—including any journaling thoughts I may want to add. Where am I today spiritually, emotionally, physically, financially, generally?

Today's Date: _____

Old Testament verse for today: II Kings 19:15 & 16a
O Lord God of Israel, sitting on your throne high above the angels, you alone are the God of all the kingdoms of the earth. You created the heavens and the earth. Bend low, O Lord, and listen. (This was King Hezekiah's prayer when the Assyrians were threatening Israel. God responded by killing 185,000 Assyrian troops! Verse 35)

One possible prayer for today:
Lord, God thank you for being the God of all the kingdoms of the world; but, most of all, thank you for being my god! Thank you for creating this beautiful world for me to enjoy. And, God, thank you for bending down to hear my prayers when I need help. Thank you for being as powerful now as you were in King Hezekiah's day, and thank you for being as concerned about my problems now as you were about King Hezekiah's problem. Thank you, God, for hearing me today.

New Testament verse for today: John 8:31 & 32
Jesus—"You are truly my disciples if you live as I tell you to, and you will know the truth, and the truth will set you free."

One possible prayer for today:
God, thank you for sending Christ as my personal Savior. Thank you for choosing me to be a believer of Christ. Lord, I know that I am not capable of always living as Christ told me to; but, Lord, your love and Christ's love is everlasting and that love erases my sins from your sight if I will only confess them to you. So, just now, I confess my sins and thank you for forgiving me of those sins.

My prayer for today—including any journaling thoughts I may want to add. Where am I today spiritually, emotionally, physically, financially, generally?

Today's Date: _____

Old Testament verse for today: I Chronicles 4:10

He (Jabez) was the one who prayed to the God of Israel, "Oh that you would wonderfully bless me and help me in my work; please be with me in all that I do, and keep me from all evil and disaster!" And God granted him his request.

One possible prayer for today:

God, what a wonderful prayer and how wonderful to know that you answered this prayer. Lord, I too pray this prayer. I too ask that you would wonderfully bless me and help me in my work. I too pray that you will be with me—and my family—and keep all of us from all evil and disaster. And, God, I too ask that you will hear my prayer and grant my request. Thank you, God, for hearing me and granting my request.

New Testament verse for today: I Timothy 4:16

Keep a close watch on all you do and think. Stay true to what is right and God will bless you and use you to help others.

One possible prayer for today:

God, help me to have the strength, the faith, the discipline, to live as you would have me to live. Help me to always be mindful of what I do and what I think. Help me to stay true to the things that you would have me do. And, God, thank you for blessing me. Use me as it fits into your plans, Lord; but, if I may be selfish, please use me gently until my faith grows so that you may use me mightily. Thank you, Lord, for working with me as I grow in my faith and trust in you.

My prayer for today—including any journaling thoughts I may want to add. Where am I today spiritually, emotionally, physically, financially, generally?

Today's Date: _____

Old Testament verse for today: I Chronicles 16:34

Oh, give thanks to the Lord, for he is good; His love and his kindness go on forever.

One possible prayer for today:

How wonderful to know that your love and kindness go on forever for me, Lord. Thank you for that promise. Thank you for being so good to me. Thank you, Lord.

New Testament verse for today: Romans 4:6 thru 8

King David spoke of this, describing the happiness of an undeserving sinner who is declared "not guilty" by God. "Blessed and to be envied," he said, "are those whose sins are forgiven and put out of sight. Yes, what joy there is for anyone whose sins are no longer counted against him by the Lord."

One possible prayer for today:

God, I agree with David. What joy and peace there is in my life knowing that even though I am an undeserving sinner, you have chosen to save me. You have chosen to forgive me through the gift of your Son, Jesus. Thank you for putting my sins out of your sight. Thank you for no longer counting them against me. Thank you for giving me the happiness that comes from that knowledge. Thank you, God.

My prayer for today—including any journaling thoughts I may want to add. Where am I today spiritually, emotionally, physically, financially, generally?

Today's Date: _____

Old Testament verse for today: I Chronicles 17:19 & 20

O Lord, you have given me these wonderful promises just because you want to be kind to me, because of your own great heart. O Lord, there is no one like you—there is no other God. In fact, we have never even heard of another god like you.

One possible prayer for today:

God, thank you for being so good to me. Just as you gave wonderful promises to your servant, David, you have given me wonderful promise for my own life. Thank you for being so kind to me. Thank you for wanting to be so kind to me. Thank you for being the one and only true God. Thank you that there are no others gods like you. And, Lord, thank you for being my personal God.

New Testament verse for today: James 5:16b

The earnest prayer of a righteous man has great power and wonderful results.

One possible prayer for today:

Thank you, God, for being such a great and powerful God, and yet a God who is concerned about me and the things that concern me. In addition, God, you are a God who listens to my prayers. Thank you for listening to my prayers, Lord. Let my life be righteous in your eyes, Lord, because in your love, you forgive me when I fail you. Thank you for listening to my prayers and pleading, Lord, so that, because you have made me righteous in your eyes, my prayers have great power and achieve wonderful results. Thank you, Lord.

My prayer for today—including any journaling thoughts I may want to add. Where am I today spiritually, emotionally, physically, financially, generally?

Today's Date: _____

Old Testament verse for today: I Chronicles 28:6b, 9, & 10a & c

I am instructing you to search out every commandment of the Lord so that you may continue to rule this good land and leave it to your children to rule forever. Solomon, my son, get to know the God of your fathers. Worship and serve him with a clean heart and a willing mind, for the Lord sees every heart and understands and knows every thought. If you seek him, you will find him, but, if you forsake him, he will permanently throw you aside. So be very careful—. Be strong and do as he commands.

One possible prayer for today:

God, thank you for instructing me as you want me to live and as you want me to act. Thank you for letting me get to know you. Thank you for being a friend of mine. Help me to worship you with a clean heart and a willing mind. Thank you for seeing my heart and knowing my every thought. And, God, thank you for forgiving me when you see things in my heart and in my thought that are not pleasing to you. Thank you for letting me find you and come back to you when I seek you. Thank you for always being there for me. Thank you, God.

New Testament verse for today: Matthew 12:6-9

God has given each of us the ability to do certain things well. So, if God has given you the ability to prophesy, then prophesy whenever you can—as often as your faith is strong enough to receive a message from God. If your gift is that of serving others, serve them well. If you are a teacher, do a good job of teaching. If you are a preacher, see to it that your sermons are strong and helpful. If God has given you money, be generous in helping others with it. If God has given you administrative ability and put you in charge of the work of others, take the responsibility seriously. Those who offer comfort to the sorrowing should do so with Christian cheer. Don't just pretend that you love others: really love them.

One possible prayer for today:

God, you know my every thought. You know my heart. You know the ability that you have given me. You know what you expect of me in the use of that ability. Give me the love and faith to use that gift to the best of my ability and for your service. Thank you for making me the way that I am. Thank you for using me. Let me always be receptive to your leading in my life to use the ability that you have given me as you want.

My prayer for today—including any journaling thoughts I may want to add. Where am I today spiritually, emotionally, physically, financially, generally?

Today's Date: _____

Old Testament verse for today: I Chronicles 28:20

Be strong and courageous and get to work. Don't be frightened by the size of the task, for the Lord my God is with you: he will not forsake you. He will see to it that everything is finished correctly.

One possible prayer for today:

God, even though this was David's instruction to Solomon, I know that it applies to me if I am living within your will. I know that I can charge ahead with confidence if you are with me—and you will be with me if I look to you for guidance and help—and then follow your direction. Then I know that I can move ahead strongly and courageously and don't have to be afraid of the size of the task that I am contemplating. I know that you will be with me and will not forsake me. And I know that you will see to it that everything is finished correctly. Thank you for being with me today, Lord, as I dig into the tasks before me today. Thank you for seeing that everything will be finished correctly. Thank you, God.

New Testament verse for today: Romans 11:36

For everything comes from God alone. Everything lives by his power, and everything is for his glory. To him be glory forevermore.

One possible prayer for today:

God, thank you for being in charge of everything. Thank you for giving me all that you have given me. Thank you for your power, the same power that permits me to charge ahead full steam knowing that if you are in charge, it will be O.K. and everything will turn out all right. Let me live in such a way that I give you all the glory and adoration that I can. I know, Lord, that you deserve much more glory than I am capable of giving you; but, Lord, thank you for all that you have given me. Thank you for giving me the life that I have.

My prayer for today—including any journaling thoughts I may want to add. Where am I today spiritually, emotionally, physically, financially, generally?

Today's Date: _____

Old Testament verse for today: II Chronicles 6:14

O Lord God of Israel, there is no God like you in all of heaven and earth. You are the God who keeps his kind promises to all those who obey you, and who are anxious to do your will.

One possible prayer for today:

God, thank you for being such a consistent God. Thank you for being a one of a kind God. Thank you for being a God like no other God in heaven or earth. Thank you for all the kind promises you have given me. Thank you for always keeping your promises. Lord, let me do my part. Let me do my best to obey you. Let me always be anxious to do your will. Thank you for your

forgiveness, God, when I fail you. And, God, thank you for never failing me.

New Testament verse for today: James 1:5 thru 8

If you want to know what God wants you to do, ask him, and he will gladly tell you, for he is always ready to give a bountiful supply of wisdom to all who ask him; he will not resent it. But when you ask him, be sure that you really expect him to tell you, for a doubtful mind will be as unsettled as a wave of the sea that is driven and tossed by the wind; and every decision you then make will be uncertain, as you turn first this way, and then that. If you don't ask with faith, don't expect the Lord to give you a solid answer.

One possible prayer for today:

God, thank you again for being such a consistent God. Thank you for being a God who listens to my prayers and who gives me answers. Lord, give me the faith that I need to ask you for help without having a doubtful mind. Let me always ask for your help and advice with faith. Give me a little more of your consistency and steadfastness. Give me the faith to ask and expect a solid answer. Thank you, Lord, for helping me rely more completely and confidently on you.

My prayer for today—including any journaling thoughts I may want to add. Where am I today spiritually, emotionally, physically, financially, generally?

Today's Date: _____

Old Testament verse for today: II Chronicles 6:21b

Yes, hear from heaven, and when you hear, forgive.

One possible prayer for today:

God, thank you for always hearing from heaven. Thank you for always hearing and forgiving. Thank you for never giving up on me. Thank you for helping me to have more strength and personal discipline to live as you would have me live. Thank you, Lord.

New Testament verse for today: I Timothy 2:8

So I want men everywhere to pray with holy hands lifted up to God, free from sin and anger and resentment.

One possible prayer for today:

God, I know that you are always there and that I may always pray to you, and I try hard to be in constant communication with you; but, Lord, you know that I am not free from sin—except that you continue to forgive me. Lord, remove from me any anger and resentment. Forgive me for any anger and resentment that I have been feeling. Lord, I do just now, lift up my hands and pray and praise and thank you, my Holy God and the author of my salvation. Thank you, Lord.

My prayer for today—including any journaling thoughts I may want to add. Where am I today spiritually, emotionally, physically, financially, generally?

Today's Date: _____

Old Testament verse for today: II Chronicles 7:14

Then if my people will humble themselves and pray, and search for me, and turn from their wicked ways, I will hear them from heaven and forgive their sins and heal their land.

One possible prayer for today:

God, thank you for always letting me come back to you after I have sinned. Let me humble myself before you and ask for your forgiveness. Let me search for you and turn to you, rejecting the sinful things I have been doing. Then, Lord, thank you for hearing me from your place in heaven. Thank you for forgiving my sins. Thank you for healing me and my land. Let me do my part to be a light for you and your salvation in the place where I live.

New Testament verse for today: I Peter 3:4

Be beautiful inside, in your hearts, with the lasting charm of a gentle and quiet spirit which is so precious to God.

One possible prayer for today:

God, this is an area where I need a lot of help! My spirit is sometimes not so gentle and quiet! My heart and my ego get caught up in the challenges of my everyday life. But, Lord, I know that you do find a gentle and quiet spirit precious. I know that you love me just the way that I am; but, I also know that I could be more pleasing to you if I did a better job of following these directions for my life. So, help me, Lord. Give me the strength and courage I need to have a spirit more in tune with you. And, Lord, thank you for continuing to forgive me when I continue to fail you. Thank you, Lord, for your patience with me.

My prayer for today—including any journaling thoughts I may want to add. Where am I today spiritually, emotionally, physically, financially, generally?

Today's Date: _____

Old Testament verse for today: II Chronicles 14:11

"O Lord," he (King Asa) cried out to God, "no one else can help us! Here we are, power-less against this mighty army. Oh, help us, Lord our God! For we`trust in you alone to rescue us, and in your name we attack this vast horde. Don't let mere men defeat you!"

One possible prayer for today:

Lord, I may not be in a situation where I am being attacked by an army of 1,000,000 troops like King Asa was; but, there are many days when I feel besieged and overwhelmed by all my problems. And like King Asa, Lord, I have no place to turn but to you. No one else can help me! I am powerless to solve my problems without your help and your guidance. So, help me, Lord! Help me right now! I trust in you alone to give me the guidance, the direction, and the strength that I need right now! Don't let me be defeated, Lord. Please come quickly to my aid. Thank you, Lord, for hearing and heeding my prayer.

New Testament verse for today: II Corinthians 1:7

But in our trouble God had comforted us—and in this too, to help you: to show you from our personal experience how God will tenderly comfort you when you undergo these same sufferings. He will give you the strength to endure.

One possible prayer for today:

God, what a wonderful promise. Thank you for the promise that you will give me the strength to endure. Lord, you have not promised to make my life easy. You have not promised that I won't have problems. But you have promised that you will always be there for me. You have promised that I can always lean on you. You have promised that you will tenderly comfort me and give me the strength to endure. Thank you for that promise, Lord. Thank you for giving me the faith to confront my problems knowing that you are there to help me.

My prayer for today—including any journaling thoughts I may want to add. Where am I today spiritually, emotionally, physically, financially, generally?

Today's Date: _____

Old Testament verse for today: II Chronicles 16:9a

For the eyes of the Lord search back and forth across the whole earth, looking for people whose hearts are perfect toward him, so that he can show his great power in helping them.

One possible prayer for today:

God, I know that I fall short of meeting that requirement that my heart is always perfect toward you; but, Lord, you know that I try. You know that I always come back and ask for your forgiveness; and you have promised that you will always forgive me; so, at that point, my heart is perfect toward you, because you have made it perfect. So, Lord, show your great power in helping me. Continue to help me, Lord. Let me plug into your great power. Then I know that I can do anything that is in line with your will for my life. Thank you, Lord, for making that great power available to me.

New Testament verse for today: Romans 3:21 thru 24

But now God has shown us a different way to heaven—not by "being good enough" and trying to keep his laws, but by a new way (though not new, really, for the Scriptures told about it long ago). Now God says he will accept us and acquit us—declare us "not guilty"—if we trust Jesus Christ to take away our sins. And we all can be saved in this same way, by coming to Christ, no matter who we are or what we have been like. Yes, all have sinned; all fall short of God's glorious ideal; yet now God declares us "not guilty" of offending him if we trust in Jesus Christ, who in his kindness freely takes away our sins.

One possible prayer for today:

God, how wonderful you are and how wonderful your plan for salvation is for me. I am not able to keep my heart perfect toward you, so you have given me a new plan. A plan that I can keep. All I have to do is trust in Jesus Christ. I can do that, Lord! Thank you for giving me this different plan to get to heaven. Thank you for giving me this new way. Thank you for declaring me "not guilty" if I only trust in Jesus Christ. Thank you for declaring me "not guilty" no matter what I have done if I only trust in Jesus Christ. Thank you for sending your Son, the Christ to freely take away all my sins.

My prayer for today—including any journaling thoughts I may want to add. Where am I today spiritually, emotionally, physically, financially, generally?

Today's Date: _____

Old Testament verse for today: II Chronicles 19:9

In a time like this—whenever we are faced with any calamity such as war, disease, or famine—we can stand here before you—and cry out to you to save us; and that you will hear us and rescue us.

One possible prayer for today:

Lord, thank you for always being there for me. Thank you for letting me come to you whenever I have any problems. Thank you for letting me cry out to you to save me. Thank you for hearing me. Thank you for rescuing me when I call out to you. Thank you, Lord.

New Testament verse for today: II Timothy 2:19a

But God's truth stands firm like a great rock, nothing can shake it. It is a foundation stone with these words written on it: "the Lord knows those who are really his."

One possible prayer for today:

God, thank you for being such a wonderful God whose truth stands firm like a great rock. Thank you for being a God that nothing can shake. Thank you for being a foundation stone for me that I can count on always being there. Thank you for knowing me—knowing that I am really yours. Thank you for letting me stand before you and cry out to you. Thank you for hearing me and saving me when I call to you. Thank you, Lord.

My prayer for today—including any journaling thoughts I may want to add. Where am I today spiritually, emotionally, physically, financially, generally?

Today's Date: _____

Old Testament verse for today: II Chronicles 20:6

O Lord God of our fathers—the only God in all the heavens, the Ruler of all the kingdoms of the earth—you are so powerful, so mighty. Who can stand against you?

One possible prayer for today:

God, thank you for being such a great God. Thank you for your power and your might. And with all that power and might, it is overwhelming to think that you care about me as an individual. You rule the heavens and all the kingdoms of the earth, and yet, you hear my prayers when I call to you. You are so powerful and mighty, and yet, you are always there for me when I call. Lord, no one can stand against you. Thank you for standing there for me to lean on when I need you. Thank you for letting me plug into your power and might when I am in trouble. Thank you, Lord.

New Testament verse for today: Romans 8:26 thru 28

And in the same way—by our faith—the Holy Spirit helps us with our daily problems and in our praying. For we don't even know what we should pray for, nor how to pray as we should; but the Holy Spirit prays for us with such feeling that it cannot be expressed in words. And the Father who knows all hearts knows, of course, what the Spirit is saying as he pleads for us in harmony with God's own will. And we know that all that happens to us is working for our good if we love God and are fitting into his plans.

One possible prayer for today:

God, there are many times when, in my troubles and confusion, I don't feel like praying. I don't know how to pray or for what to pray. So, this promise that—if I have faith—your loving Holy Spirit will help me with my problems and help me with my prayers is a great promise. Thank you, Lord. Thank you for giving us your loving Holy Spirit who communicates with you for me in such a manner that you know what I need and the things for which I should be praying. Thank you for having the Spirit plead for me in harmony with your will for me. And, Lord, let me have peace knowing that whatever happens is what you have planned for me. And the seed that makes it all happen is my faith. Give me the faith that I need, Lord, both in the good times and in the bad times. Thank you, Lord, for granting me the faith that I need.

My prayer for today—including any journaling thoughts I may want to add. Where am I today spiritually, emotionally, physically, financially, generally?

Today's Date: _____

Old Testament verse for today: II Chronicles 20:17b
Don't be afraid or discouraged! Go out there tomorrow, for the Lord is with you!

One possible prayer for today:
God, what a wonderful verse this is for me to remember when I get discouraged or afraid of what tomorrow will bring. How wonderful it is to know that you are always with me. Thank you for that promise. With that promise, Lord, I know that I can go out into my world tomorrow and face whatever challenges are there for me—knowing that you are with me. You will protect me. You will give me the strength that I need to not only face the challenges, but to succeed in my assigned tasks. Thank you for being such a wonderful, supportive God.

New Testament verse for today: Romans 8:15
And so we should not be like cringing, fearful slaves, but we should behave like God's very own children, adopted into the bosom of his family, and calling to him, "Father, Father."

One possible prayer for today:
God, no wonder I don't have to be afraid or discouraged. No wonder I can go out and face the problems in my world. You have adopted me into the bosom of your very own family! What a wonderful promise, Lord. What a wonderful God you are to me! Thank you for letting me call you "Father" and letting me be a part of your very own family. Thank you for giving me the strength and the protection and the guidance that I need to face tomorrow. Thank you, God.

My prayer for today—including any journaling thoughts I may want to add. Where am I today spiritually, emotionally, physically, financially, generally?

Today's Date: _____

Old Testament verse for today: II Chronicles 20:20b

Believe in the Lord your God, and you shall have success.

One possible prayer for today:

God, I acknowledge that you are an all powerful God. I acknowledge that the moon, the stars, the heavens, and the earth move at your discretion and your will. I acknowledge that if I put my trust completely in you that you will give me the success that you want me to have. You will give me the money, the power, the fame and the life style that you want me to have. Lord, let me have the faith to put my trust completely in you. And, Lord, let me have the faith to accept that whatever occurs in my life, that if you are in charge, then that is what you want for me; and, my obligation to you is to thank you for that and respond in a manner that is pleasing to you. Give me that faith, Lord. And if it be your will, give me success.

New Testament very for today: Matthew 5:48

But you are to be perfect, even as your Father in heaven is perfect.

One possible prayer for today:

God, what a challenge! How can I be perfect? I am human, with all the imperfections that go with my humanity! The only way that I can ever be perfect is because you have made me perfect in your eyes by forgiving me of all my sins through the blood of your Son, Jesus. God, what a wonderful plan you have for me to give me perfection in your eyes. Thank you, Lord. Thank you for forgiving me. And, God, thank you for continuing to forgive me when I continue to show my humanity by continuing to fail. Thank you, Lord, for your consistency even when I am inconsistent. Lord, being made perfect in your eyes is probably the greatest success that I could ever have. Thank you, Lord.

My prayer for today—including any journaling thoughts I may want to add. Where am I today spiritually, emotionally, physically, financially, generally?

Today's Date: _____

Old Testament verse for today: I Chronicles 29:10b thru 13

O Lord God of our father Israel, praise your name for ever and ever! Yours is the mighty power and glory and victory and majesty. Everything in the heavens and earth is yours, O Lord, and this is your kingdom. We adore you as being in control of everything. Riches and honor come from you alone, and you are the Ruler of all mankind; your hand controls power and might, and it is at your discretion that men are made great and given strength. O our god, we thank you and praise your glorious name.

One possible prayer for today:

God, let me always praise your name in all that I do. Thank you for being mighty, powerful, glorious, victorious, and majestic. Thank you for being the God of all the heavens and the earth; and yet so loving that you permit me to enjoy all of your wonderful blessings. Thank you for being in control of everything. Thank you for giving me the riches and honor that you have chosen to give me. Give me the strength that you want me to have, Lord; and, let me always thank and praise your glorious name.

New Testament verse for today: I Peter 5:10 & 11

After you have suffered a little while, our God, who is full of kindness through Christ, will give you his eternal glory. He personally will come and pick you up, and set your firmly in place, and make you stronger than ever. To him be all power over all things, forever and ever. Amen.

One possible prayer for today:

God, thank you for being all powerful. Thank you for seeing me through my suffering. Please make it as short as possible! Please come and pick me up and make me stronger than ever. Thank you for having power over all things. Thank you for giving me your eternal glory. Thank you, God.

My prayer for today—including any journaling thoughts I may want to add. Where am I today spiritually, emotionally, physically, financially, generally?

Today's Date: _____

Old Testament verse for today: II Chronicles 30:9b

For the Lord your God is full of kindness and mercy and will not continue to turn away his face from you if you return to him.

One possible prayer for today:

God, thank you for being full of kindness and mercy to me. Thank you for always letting me return to you, no matter how badly I have sinned. Thank you for taking me back into your loving arms when I return to you. Thank you for not continuing to turn your face from me when I return to you. Thank you for being such a kind, merciful, and gracious God. Thank you.

New Testament verse for today: Romans 3:29 thru 31

And does God save only the Jews in this way? No, the Gentiles, too, may come to him in this same manner. God treats us all the same; all, whether Jews or Gentiles, are acquitted if they have faith. Well then, if we are saved by faith, does this mean that we no longer need to obey God's laws? Just the opposite! In fact, only when we trust Jesus can we truly obey him.

One possible prayer for today:

God, thank you for being such a loving God to all of your people. Thank you for treating us all the same, no matter what our color, background, family history, or whatever. Thank you for letting us come to you by faith through your Son, Jesus. Thank you for turning your face back to me when I come to you. Lord, I know that I break your laws. I know that I cannot stand up to your rigid set of rules. I know that you then made a better plan for me by sending your Son, Jesus, to die on the cross for my sins. Thank you for letting me come back to you in faith. Thank you, God.

My prayer for today—including any journaling thoughts I may want to add. Where am I today spiritually, emotionally, physically, financially, generally?

Today's Date: _____

Old Testament verse for today: Nehemiah 1:5

"O Lord God," I cried out; "O great and awesome God who keeps his promises and is so loving and kind to those who love and obey him! Hear my prayer!"

One possible prayer for today:

God, I too cry out to you. I acknowledge that you are a great and awesome God. I know that you always keep your promises. I know that you are loving and kind to those who love and obey you. I know that you hear my prayer. God, help me today. Listen to my pleas. I need your help. I need your guidance. I need your direction. I don't know which way to turn. Oh great and awesome God, I need to feel your loving arms holding me and protecting me in this time of trouble. I know that you are always there, God. Please let me feel you being there for me—right now. Thank you, Lord, for answering my prayer.

New Testament verse for today: Romans 15:13

So I pray for you—that God who gives you hope will keep you happy and full of peace as you believe in him. I pray that God will help you overflow with hope in him through the Holy Spirit's power within you.

One possible prayer for today:

God, I claim your Holy Spirit's power within me to help me today. I claim the hope that only your loving Holy Spirit can give me when I am desperate. I claim the peace that comes only from trusting you completely when I don't know where else to turn. I claim the happiness that you will return to me as I trust in you to help me. I thank you for the gift of hope to believe that you will give me the strength to meet today's challenges and once again be able to be genuinely happy. Thank you for hearing my pleas, Lord. Thank you for restoring me to happiness and peace. Thank you for the gift of your loving Holy Spirit to help me in this time of challenge. Thank you, God.

My prayer for today—including any journaling thoughts I may want to add. Where am I today spiritually, emotionally, physically, financially, generally?

Today's Date: _____

Old Testament verse for today: Nehemiah 1:11a
O Lord, please hear my prayer! Heed the prayers of those of us who delight to honor you. Please help me now.

One possible prayer for today:
Lord, thank you for always hearing my prayers. Thank you for heeding my prayers. But, Lord, let me do my part by always delighting to honor you. Help me now as I go to meet the challenges of this hour. Help me to look to you for guidance. Give me success in my goals for this day. Thank you, God.

New Testament verse for today: Ephesians 5:20
Always give thanks for everything to our God and Father in the name of our Lord Jesus Christ.

One possible prayer for today:
Lord, let me remember to always be thankful to you. Let me remember that you are always hearing and heeding my prayers. Let me delight in honoring you by giving you thanks at all times and in all things in the name of your Son, Jesus. Thank you, God, for being my personal God.

My prayer for today—including any journaling thoughts I may want to add. Where am I today spiritually, emotionally, physically, financially, generally?

Today's Date: _____

Old Testament verse for today: Nehemiah 9:5a

Then the Levite leaders called out to the people, "Stand up and praise the Lord your God, for he lives from everlasting to everlasting. Praise his glorious name! It is far greater than we can think or say."

One possible prayer for today:

God, let me always take a stand for you and always remember to praise you for all the good things that you do for me and for all the good things that you have given me to enjoy. Lord, even on the bad days, let me remember to praise you because my bad days are still the lessons that you want me to learn. Thank you for being the everlasting God. Thank you for being far greater than I can imagine. Let me always praise your glorious name. Thank you, God, for being my own personal glorious God.

New Testament verse for today: Luke 8:50

Bu when Jesus heard what had happened, he said to the father, "Don't be afraid! Just trust me, and she'll be all right."

One possible prayer for today:

Lord, when things don't go as I want them to go, let me trust you completely. Give me the faith so that I am not afraid of my problems. And, Lord, as Christ said to this man, I claim the promise that you will also make my problems be resolved "all right!" You are a great and glorious God who is everlastingly in charge of all things, so let me stand up and praise you in all my circumstances. Give me the faith that I need to praise you at all times, Lord. Thank you for giving me this faith. Let me comfortably and completely acknowledge your Lordship in my life.

My prayer for today—including any journaling thoughts I may want to add. Where am I today spiritually, emotionally, physically, financially, generally?

Today's Date: _____

Old Testament verse for today: Nehemiah 9:6

Then Ezra prayed, "You alone are God. You have made the skies and the heavens, the earth and the seas, and everything in them. You preserve it all; and all the angels in heaven worship you."

One possible prayer for today:

God, how wonderful you are! Thank you for being the one and only true God. Thank you for making the skies, the heavens, the earth, the seas, and everything in them, and making them for me to enjoy. Thank you for preserving it all in this troubled world in which we all live. Thank you for being the one point of stability on which I can count. Along with the angels, Lord, let me never quit worshipping you. Thank you, God.

New Testament verse for today: John 9:25

"I don't know whether he is good or bad," the man replied, "but I know this: I was blind and now I see!"

One possible prayer for today:

God, thank you for opening my eyes to see the glorious world that you have made and preserved. Like this blind man, let me acknowledge that it is your power that permits me to see and to enjoy all the wonderful things that you have provided for me. Let me never be blind to the fact that all things are made by you and are made for me to enjoy. Thank you, God, for the many blessings that you have provided for me so that I may live life more abundantly. Thank you, God.

My prayer for today—including any journaling thoughts I may want to add. Where am I today spiritually, emotionally, physically, financially, generally?

Today's Date: _____

Old Testament verse for today: Nehemiah 9:28b

Yet whenever your people returned to you and cried to you for help, once more you listened from heaven, and in your wonderful mercy delivered them!

One possible prayer for today:

Lord, what a wonderful God you are! So merciful in every way! When I return to you after sinning, you forgive—and you forget my sins! When I return to you and cry to you for help, you always listen from heaven, and in your wonderful mercy, you welcome me back into your loving arms. You are always there for me to deliver me from the problems of my life. Thank you, Lord, for hearing from heaven and delivering me.

New Testament verse for today: Luke 1:50

His mercy goes on from generation to generation, to all who reverence him.

One possible prayer for today:

Thank you again, for being such a merciful God to me. Lord, I do reverence you. I do worship you. I do adore you. I do thank you for all you have done to me. Thank you for your continuing mercy.

My prayer for today—including any journaling thoughts I may want to add. Where am I today spiritually, emotionally, physically, financially, generally?

Today's Date: _____

Old Testament verse for today: Nehemiah 9:31b

What a gracious and merciful God you are!

One possible prayer for today:

God, thank you for being so gracious and merciful to me. Thank you for never giving up on me. Thank you for giving me the faith that I need to worship you in all things and at all times. Thank you for your graciousness and your mercy. Thank you, God.

New Testament verse for today: II Timothy 2:13

Even when we are too weak to have any faith left, he remains faithful to us and will help us, for he cannot disown us who are part of himself, and he will always carry out his promises to us.

One possible prayer for today:

God, how wonderful you are! Thank you for being there for me even when I am too weak to have any faith left. Thank you for your great faithfulness. Thank you for still being there to help me, even when I don't have the strength or the courage to worship and honor you the way that I should. Thank you for making me a part of yourself so that you can never disown me. Thank you for always keeping your promises to me even when I am too weak to keep my promises to you. Thank you. Thank you. Thank you for being such a wonderful and faithful God to me.

My prayer for today—including any journaling thoughts I may want to add. Where am I today spiritually, emotionally, physically, financially, generally?

Today's Date: _____

Old Testament verse for today: Nehemiah 9:32a

And now, O great and awesome God, you who keep your promises of love and kindness.

One possible prayer for today:

God, thank you for being so great and awesome. Thank you for always keeping your promises of love and kindness. Thank you for always loving me, even when I am not lovable. Thank you for being kind to me, even when I do not deserve kindness. But, Lord, when I fall away from you; when I fail you, thank you for never failing me. Thank you for your commitment of love and kindness to me.

New Testament verse for today: I John 5:11 thru 13

And what is it that God has said? That he has given us eternal life, and that this life is in his Son. So whoever has God's Son has life; whoever does not have the Son, does not have life. I have written this to you who believe in the Son of God so that you may know that you have eternal life.

One possible prayer for today:

God, thank you for being a God who always keeps your promises. Thank you for the promise of eternal life if I will only believe in your Son, Jesus, I do believe. Thank you for giving me your Son so that I might have eternal life. Thank you for that promise and that confirmation. Thank you for keeping that promise to me.

My prayer for today—including any journaling thoughts I may want to add. Where am I today spiritually, emotionally, physically, financially, generally?

Today's Date: _____

Old Testament verse for today: Job 17:8-b & 9

Yet, finally, the innocent shall come out on top, above the godless; the righteous shall move onward and forward; those with pure hearts shall become stronger and stronger.

One possible prayer for today:

God, I know that my problems cannot in any way compare with the problems that Job confronted. I don't know why you let Satan be so hard on him. Frankly, sometimes, I don't even know why you permit me to have all the troubles that I am experiencing! And, sometimes, I don't know that I am going to come out on top! But, today, I claim the promise that is contained in Job's statement. You ended up blessing Job more at the end of his life than at the beginning, so I am assuming that you agree with this statement by Job, and that I can count on it for my life! Lord, I need to become stronger and stronger in all ways—spiritually, physically, financially. I am counting on you to help me do that. Thank you for helping me. Forgive me for the times that my faith in you and my faith in your promises gets too weak.

New Testament verse for today: Matthew 6:6 thru 9

"Happy are those who long to be just and good, for they shall be completely satisfied. Happy are the kind and merciful, for they shall be shown mercy. Happy are those whose hearts are pure, for they shall see God. Happy are those who strive for peace—they shall be called the sons of God."

One possible prayer for today:

God, sometimes these words of Christ seem really hollow to me! I am not completely satisfied! Right now, no one seems to be showing me mercy! Maybe I am not trying hard enough to be just and good, kind and merciful, striving for peace with a pure heart! Forgive me for my shortcomings, Lord. I really need your help! I need your encouragement! I need a little break in my problems! Forgive my lack of faith, Lord. Please give me a shot of encouragement so that I can get started on the road back to faith and satisfaction in you and your love. Thank you, Lord, for listening to me and putting up with me when I feel like this.

My prayer for today—including any journaling thoughts I may want to add. Where am I today spiritually, emotionally, physically, financially, generally?

Today's Date: _____

Old Testament verse for today: Job 19:25 thru 27

But as for me, I know that my Redeemer lives, and that he will stand upon the earth at last. And I know that after this body has decayed, this body shall see God! Then he will be on my side! Yes, I shall see him, not as a stranger, but as a friend! What a glorious hope!

One possible prayer for today:

God, please give me the faith that Job had. What a wonderful testimony Job has given for me to read. Thank you for being Job's redeemer and thank you for being my redeemer. Thank you for the confidence that after I die I will see you face to face—as a friend! God, that is a glorious hope. Thank you for that hope. Thank you for the faith that you have given me and that you will continue to give me. Thank you for being on my side even now. Thank you, God.

New Testament verse for today: Mark 13:26 & 27

"Then all mankind will see me, the Messiah, coming in the clouds with great power and glory. And I will send out the angels to gather together my chosen ones from all over the world—from the farthest bounds of earth and heaven."

One possible prayer for today:

God, thank you for sending your Son, Jesus, to fulfill your promise that I should someday see you face to face. Thank you for having such a marvelous plan so that I can have the confidence that my Redeemer will once more stand upon the earth and gather me to him. Thank you for choosing me. Thank you for the excitement of knowing that this is in store for me as one of your believers. Thank you, God, for these wonderful promises.

My prayer for today—including any journaling thoughts I may want to add. Where am I today spiritually, emotionally, physically, financially, generally?

Today's Date: _____

Old Testament verse for today: Job 22:23 thru 28

If you return to God and put right all the wrong in your home, then you will be restored. If you give up your lust for money, and throw your gold away, then the Almighty himself shall be your treasure; he will be your precious silver! Then you will delight yourself in the Lord, and look up to God. You will pray to him, and he will hear you, and you will fulfill all your promises to him. Whatever you wish will happen! And the light of heaven will shine upon the road ahead of you.

One possible prayer for today:

God, I do want to put you first in my life. I do want to correct any wrongs that are in my home. I do ask for your forgiveness for any of these wrongs and thank you for forgiving me all my sins when I bring them to you and repent of them. Thank you for restoring me into the fullness of your kingdom. Lord, help me to lust after a better relationship with you rather than the materialistic things that the world has to offer. Let me look to you to be my treasure. Let me delight myself in you and look up to you at all times. Thank you for hearing me when I pray to you. Help me to fulfill all my promises to you. And, Lord, then I know that you will indeed make my every wish come true, because my wishes will be in line with your will for my life. And, Lord, thank you for making the light of heaven shine upon the road ahead of me as I trust in you. Thank you, God.

New Testament verse for today: I Corinthians 9:24 & 25

In a race, everyone runs but only one person gets first prize. So run your race to win. To win the contest you must deny yourselves many things that would keep you from doing your best. An athlete goes to all this trouble just to win a blue ribbon or a silver cup, but we do it for a heavenly reward that never disappears.

One possible prayer for today:

Lord, let me keep my eyes on you and your goals for me as I run my race in this life. Let me run to live for you. Let me give up those things that would interfere with my ability to keep my eyes on your goals for me. Help me to fulfill my promises to you. Let me delight myself in you and look up to you so that my reward is a reward that never disappears—eternal life with you. Thank you for helping me accomplish this goal, God.

My prayer for today—including any journaling thoughts I may want to add. Where am I today spiritually, emotionally, physically, financially, generally?

Today's Date: _____

Old Testament verse for today: Job 23:10

But he knows every detail of what is happening to me; and when he has examined me, he will pronounce me completely innocent—as pure as solid gold!

One possible prayer for today:

God, thank you for knowing every detail of my life. Thank you for being concerned about every detail of my life that is of concern to me. Thank you for knowing my heart, and in knowing all my human frailties, still loving me. Thank you for always being there to forgive me when I return in honest humility and ask for your forgiveness. Thank you for pronouncing me completely innocent once you have forgiven me. Thank you for being such a loving, caring, and forgiving Lord. Thank you, God.

New Testament verse for today: Hebrews 9:27 & 28

And just as it is destined that men die only once, and after that comes judgment, so also Christ died only once as an offering for the sins of many people; and he will come again, but not to deal with our sins. This time he will come bringing salvation to all who are eagerly and patiently waiting for him.

One possible prayer for today:

God, thank you for sending Christ to die once and for all for all of my sins. Thank you for your promise that when I stand before you in judgment, if I have been eagerly and patiently waiting for the return of Christ, he will be there with me—not to deal with my sins—those he has washed away with his blood on the cross—but to complete my salvation. This is when you and Christ will examine me and find me completely innocent—as pure as solid gold—because of your marvelous plan of salvation and because of what Christ has done for me on the cross. Thank you for giving me that assurance, Lord. Thank you for the gift of my salvation through the sacrifice of your Son. Thank you, God.

My prayer for today—including any journaling thoughts I may want to add. Where am I today spiritually, emotionally, physically, financially, generally?

Today's Date: _____

Old Testament verse for today: Job 28:27 & 28

He knows where wisdom is and declares it to all who will listen. He established it and examined it thoroughly. And this is what he says to all mankind: 'Look, to fear the Lord is true wisdom; to forsake evil is real understanding.'

One possible prayer for today:

Lord, please give me the wisdom that comes from you. Give me the wisdom that is pure and holy. Give me the wisdom that you have examined thoroughly and established. Let me have the proper fear of you, Lord. Let me forsake evil. But, Lord, you know that even though I have a fear of your awesome power, I love you and I consider you a great friend, one to whom I can come and pray and talk and get comfort. Thank you for being such a powerful, and yet such a loving and caring God. Thank you, Lord.

New Testament verse for today: Ephesians 3:17 thru 19

And I pray that Christ will be more and more at home in your hearts, living within you as you trust in him. May your roots go down deep into the soil of God's marvelous love; and may you be able to feel and understand, as all God's children should, how long, how wide, how deep, and how high his love really is; and to experience this love for yourselves, though it is so great that you will never see the end of it or fully know or understand it. And so at last you will be filled up with God himself.

One possible prayer for today:

God, how marvelous you are. How I praise you. How I thank you for all that love. Lord, let me live my life so that Christ is truly more and more at home in my heart. Give me the wisdom and faith to trust him more and more all the time. Let my roots go down deep into the soil of your marvelous love. Let me understand more and more about the depth, the width, the length, the heights of your love. Let me be filled with your loving Holy Spirit, God. Thank you for all that unlimited love for me.

My prayer for today—including any journaling thoughts I may want to add. Where am I today spiritually, emotionally, physically, financially, generally?

Today's Date: _____

Old Testament verse for today: Job 41:11

God speaking: I owe no one anything. Everything under heaven is mine.

One possible prayer for today:

God, thank you for being such an awesome God that you owe no one anything, and yet you are so loving and kind to me. Thank you for giving so generously to me even though everything under heaven is yours. Thank you for caring for the things that are of concern to me. Thank you for being so wonderful, so powerful, and yet so loving and caring. Thank you, God.

New Testament verse for today: II Corinthians 9:9 & 10

It is as the Scriptures say: The godly man gives generously to the poor. His good deeds will be an honor to him forever. For God, who gives seed to the farmer to plant, and later on, good crops to harvest and eat, will give you more and more seed to plant and will make it grow so that you can give away more and more fruit from your harvest.

One possible prayer for today:

Lord, when you own everything under heaven and owe no one anything and yet are so loving and generous, why shouldn't I be more loving and generous to those who have less than I do? Let me be generous with what you have given me. Let me follow your lead in giving to others. And, Lord, I do claim your promise that if I do my part in giving generously, you will continue to bless me and make it possible for me to give more and more. Let me do my part, Lord; because, I know that you will do your part. Thank you, God, for being a God upon whom I can always count to do your part.

My prayer for today—including any journaling thoughts I may want to add. Where am I today spiritually, emotionally, physically, financially, generally?

Today's Date: _____

Old Testament verse for today: Psalm 1:1 & 2

Oh, the joys of those who do not follow evil men's advice, who do not hang around with sinners, scoffing at the things of God: But they delight in doing everything God wants them to, and day and night are always meditating on his laws and thinking about ways to follow him more closely.

One possible prayer for today:

God, thank you for the joy you give me if I only trust in you. Give me the good judgment to use my time and to pick my friends wisely. Let me delight in following what you would have me to do with my life more closely. Thank you for helping me to shun bad advice. Thank you for leading me, Lord.

New Testament verse for today: Galatians 3:24 thru 29

Until Christ came we were guarded by the law, kept in protective custody, so to speak, until we could believe in the coming Savior. Let me put it another way. The Jewish laws were our teacher and guide until Christ came to give us right standing with God through faith. But now that Christ has come, we don't need those laws any longer to guard us or lead us to him. For now we are all children of God through faith in Jesus Christ, and we who have been baptized into union with Christ are enveloped by him. We are no longer Jews or Greeks or slaves or free men or even merely men or women, but we are all the same—we are Christians; we are one in Christ Jesus. And now that we are all Christ's we are all true descendants of Abraham, and all of God's promises to him belong to us.

One possible prayer for today:

God, thank you for giving me Christ so that I am able to be acceptable to you as I am. You know that I am not capable of keeping all of your laws, no matter how much I may meditate on them. So, Lord, thank you for giving me a new plan that does work for me. All I have to do is believe on your Son, Jesus, to be in right standing with you. All I now need is faith. Thank you for permitting me to be one of your children, Lord. Thank you for letting Christ envelope me. Thank you for letting me be the recipient of all of your promises. Thank you, Lord.

My prayer for today—including any journaling thoughts I may want to add. Where am I today spiritually, emotionally, physically, financially, generally?

Today's Date: _____

Old Testament verse for today: Psalm 1:6

For the Lord watches over all the plans and paths of godly men (and women), but the paths of the godless lead to doom.

One possible prayer for today:

Thank you, Lord, for watching over my plans and paths for today. I know that I will stumble and I know that I will fail you; but, I also know that if I do not turn away from you, you will continue to watch over me every minute of the day. Forgive me for the times I fail you; and, thank you for never failing me. Don't let me even consider going the way of the godless. I don't want to lose your love and your watching over me.

New Testament verse for today: Matthew 3:16 & 17

After His (Christ's) baptism, as soon as Jesus came up out of the water, the heavens were opened to Him and He saw the Spirit of God coming down in the form of a dove. And a voice from heaven said, "This is my beloved Son, and I am wonderfully pleased with Him."

One possible prayer for today:

Thank you for giving me your Son, and thank you that Christ lived His life in a manner pleasing to you and carrying out all of Your plans. God, I know that I cannot live my life so that I am always pleasing to you; but, I also know that because Christ lived His life to please you and carry out all your plans, that you will always forgive me my failings, if I only confess them to you and ask for your forgiveness. And, once that occurs, them I am once more perfect in your sight, just as Christ was perfect in your sight, and only because of what Christ has done for me. Thank you, God, for forgiving me my shortcomings this day, and I confess them to you

My prayer for today—including any journaling thoughts I may want to add. Where am I today spiritually, emotionally, physically, financially, generally?

Today's Date: _____

Old Testament verse for today: Psalm 2:11 & 12b

Serve the Lord with reverent fear; rejoice with trembling. But, oh, the joys of those who put their trust in Him!

One possible prayer for today:

God, I am having a great day! Thank you! I needed a day like this. And today I can claim the Psalmist's promise that if I put my trust in you, I will experience joy! How great you are, oh Lord! And greatly to be praised! Today, I am truly rejoicing with trembling at your great power and your unlimited love. Thank you. Thank you. Thank you.

New Testament verse for today: Matthew 6:19b

"Those who teach God's laws and obey them shall be great in the Kingdom of Heaven."

One possible prayer for today:

Let me live my life in such a manner, God, that I am really striving to obey your laws; and maybe, by so doing, I will also be teaching them by example. I know that I can do better; but, God, you know that I have been trying. Thank you for forgiving me when I fail to reach the goal that you have set for me. Thank you for being so patient and kind to me. Please give me wisdom to more fully understand what you have for me and want from me on a daily basis. And, God, thank you for loving me even when I do fail. Thank you for always giving me another chance.

My prayer for today—including any journaling thoughts I may want to add. Where am I today spiritually, emotionally, physically, financially, generally?

Today's Date: _____

Old Testament verse for today: Psalm 3:3

But Lord, you are my shield, my glory, my only hope. You alone can lift my head, now bowed in shame.

One possible prayer for today:

Lord, when I have goofed real bad; when I have either let you down or have let down others who are counting on me, I am so ashamed. My head is indeed bowed in shame. When that happens, you are the only place I know to turn until you forgive me and give me to strength to go out and meet the world, acknowledge my errors and my shame, and get on with my life. Thank you, Lord, for never turning your back on me when I come back to you with honest humility and ask for your forgiveness. Thank you for giving me the strength to go back to those whom I have harmed or failed and ask their forgiveness. Thank you for guiding me through the rough times, Lord. Thank you.

New Testament verse for today: I Timothy 1:19

Cling tightly to your faith in Christ and always keep your conscience clear, doing what you know is right. For some people have disobeyed their consciences and deliberately done what they knew was wrong. It isn't surprising that soon they lost their faith in Christ after defying God like that.

One possible prayer for today:

God, I know that I sin. I know that I defy you and do what my conscience tells me is wrong. I know that I have deliberately disobeyed both my conscience and you. Forgive me, God. Thank you for forgiving me. I don't in any manner want to lose my faith in your Son, Jesus. I don't want to defy you. Yet I sin. And, Lord, you are always there to forgive me when I return to you in honest humility. Thank you, God, for never giving up on me.

My prayer for today—including any journaling thoughts I may want to add. Where am I today spiritually, emotionally, physically, financially, generally?

Today's Date: _____

Old Testament verse for today: Psalm 3:4 & 5

I cried out to the Lord, and he heard me from his Temple in Jerusalem. Then I lay down and slept in peace and woke up safely, for the Lord was watching over me.

One possible prayer for today:

Lord, thank you for hearing me when I pray. Thank you for hearing me from your place on high. Thank you for giving me a peace that can only come from you. Thank you for being there when I need you. Thank you for always watching over me.

New Testament verse for today: II Timothy 4:8

In heaven a crown is waiting for me which the Lord, the righteous Judge, will give me on that great day of his return. And not just to me, but to all those whose lives show that they are eagerly looking forward to his coming back again.

One possible prayer for today:

Lord, thank you for being concerned about me. Thank you for caring for me. Thank you for hearing me when I call out to you. Lord, you know my heart. You know that I love you. You know that even as I go through this life, whether I am riding on top of the world or whether I am struggling, that I am counting on you being there for me—now and for eternity. And you know that I am looking forward to spending that eternity with you. Thank you for preparing a crown in heaven for me. Thank you for the gift of my salvation through the death and resurrection of your Son, Jesus. Thank you for giving me the faith to eagerly look forward to your coming back for me. Thank you, God.

My prayer for today—including any journaling thoughts I may want to add. Where am I today spiritually, emotionally, physically, financially, generally?

Today's Date: _____

Old Testament verse for today: Psalm 3:8

For salvation comes from God. What joy he gives to all his people.

One possible prayer for today:

God, thank you for my salvation. Thank you for the joy you give me as I trust in you for not only my salvation; but, for guiding my life as I go through my daily challenges. Thank you for my salvation, Lord. Thank you for the joy that you give me.

New Testament verse for today: Colossians 3:12 & 13

Since you have been chosen by God who has given you this new kind of life, and because of his deep love and concern for you, you should practice tenderhearted mercy and kindness to others. Don't worry about making a good impression on them but be ready to suffer quietly and patiently. Be gentle and ready to forgive; never hold grudges. Remember, the Lord forgave you, so you must forgive others.

One possible prayer for today:

Lord, thank you for choosing me. Thank you for giving me your salvation, which has resulted in this new kind of life; a life of freedom from guilt; a life of feeling your deep love and concern for me. Lord, I know that many times I am not very good at passing on that feeling of love and concern for others. I need your help in that area, Lord. Let me do a better job of practicing mercy and kindness to others. Let me be as ready to forgive those who I feel have wronged me as you are always ready to forgive me. Let me free myself from the grudges I hold, Lord. Thank you again for forgiving me, Lord. Again, I pray for your help and guidance to me in forgiving others. Thank you for helping me in this area of my life, Lord.

My prayer for today—including any journaling thoughts I may want to add. Where am I today spiritually, emotionally, physically, financially, generally?

Today's Date: _____

Old Testament verse for today: Psalm 4:1

O God, you have declared me perfect in your eyes; you have always cared for me in my distress; now hear me as I call again. Have mercy on me. Hear my prayer.

One possible prayer for today:

God, I can be perfect only because you have made me perfect in your eyes by washing away my sins from your sight to remember them no more. Because of that, I know how much you care for me. I know that when I am distressed, you are distressed for me. So, Lord, hear me as I plead for an answer to my problems. Hear me as I call again. Continue to have mercy on me. Thank you for hearing my prayer, O Lord. Thank you for listening to me. Thank you for giving me an answer that will be clear as to which way you want me to turn. Help me, Lord. Thank you, Lord.

New Testament verse for today: Ephesians 3:12

Now we can come fearlessly right into God's presence, assured of his glad welcome when we come with Christ and trust in him.

One possible prayer for today:

God, thank you for that promise. And, God, I am! I am coming fearlessly to you and asking you—begging you—pleading with you—to help me now. God, I know that you love me. God, I know that you care for the things that are important to me. God, this is a very important issue with me. I really need your help and your guidance. So, I am coming back to you again and again—fearlessly pleading and begging for your help and your guidance. Thank you for hearing and answering my prayer, God.

My prayer for today—including any journaling thoughts I may want to add. Where am I today spiritually, emotionally, physically, financially, generally?

Today's Date: _____

Old Testament verse for today: Psalm 4:3

Mark this well. The Lord has set apart the redeemed for himself. Therefore he will listen to me and answer when I call to him.

One possible prayer for today:

Lord, I claim this promise that the Psalmist has written. I love you and I have given my life to you. I have asked your Son to be my personal Savior. Today, Lord, I am suffering. I have a problem that I cannot solve and I don't even know how I want it solved! So, Lord, I am one of your redeemed. I am calling to you. I am asking for wisdom in solving this problem. I am asking for clear guidance at this moment in my life. Lord, thank you for listening to me. Thank you for hearing me. Thank you for answering me as I call to you. Thank you, Lord.

New Testament verse for today: Colossians 4:2

Don't be weary in prayer; keep at it; watch for God's answers and remember to be thankful when they come.

One possible prayer for today:

God, I do keep on praying. I keep on praising you for all the good things that you have given me and for all the good things that have happened and are happenings in my life. Yet, Lord, today, I am back pleading for your help. I am not getting weary of asking for your help and your guidance. Hopefully, you aren't getting weary of my continual pleadings for your answers. God, I am waiting and watching for your answers. And, God, I am thanking you in advance for the answers you are going to give me. Thank you, God.

My prayer for today—including any journaling thoughts I may want to add. Where am I today spiritually, emotionally, physically, financially, generally?

Today's Date: _____

Old Testament verse for today: Psalm 4:4

Stand before the Lord in awe, and do not sin against him. Lie quietly upon your bed in silent meditation. Put your trust in the Lord, and offer him pleasing sacrifices.

One possible prayer for today:

Lord, I do stand before you in awe. But even in my awe, my human weaknesses continue to come through strong and clear. I continue to sin against you. I'm sorry. I try to do better; but, I continue to fail you. God, thank you for never failing me. I do meditate on what a great God you are and how good you are to me. I do put my trust in you and in you alone. Lord, the only pleasing sacrifice I can make to you is the offering of my life to you, loving you, trusting you, trying to please you more and sin less. Thank you for helping me in this area of my life, Lord.

New Testament verse for today: Hebrews 1:3

God's Son shines out with God's glory, and all that God's Son is and does marks him as God. He regulates the universe by the mighty power of his command. He is the one who died to cleanse us and to clear our record of all sin, and then sat down in highest honor beside the great God of heaven.

One possible prayer for today:

God, thank you for the gift of your Son, Jesus. Thank you for letting Jesus shine out with all of your glory. Thank you for the power you have given him. And, God, thank you so much for your plan of having Christ die to not only cleanse me from my sins, but to clear the record of all my sin! What a wonderful God you are. What a wonderful Savior I have in Jesus. What a wonderful plan of salvation you made for me. Thank you for giving me the faith to believe in your Son, Jesus. Thank you for always being there to forgive me through your Son's sacrifice when I continue to sin. Thank you, God.

My prayer for today—including any journaling thoughts I may want to add. Where am I today spiritually, emotionally, physically, financially, generally?

Today's Date: _____

Old Testament verse for today: Psalm 4:6 & 8

Many say that God will never help us. Prove them wrong, O Lord, by letting the light of your face shine down upon us. I will lie down in peace and sleep, for though I am alone, O Lord, you will keep me safe.

One possible prayer for today:

God, I know that you area always there to help me. I count on that. In my own life you have proved those who doubt you wrong many times. Thank you for what you have done for me, Lord. Thank you for letting the light of your face shine down upon me. Thank you for giving me the peace that can only come from you. Thank you for letting me rest in you. Thank you for keeping me safe.

New Testament verse for today: John 16:33

I have told you all this so that you will have peace of heart and mind. Here on earth you will have many trials and sorrows; but cheer up, for I have overcome the world.

One possible prayer for today:

God, thank you for the peace that only you can give. Thank you for giving me peace of heart and mind. Thank you for letting the light of your face shine down upon me. Thank you for keeping me safe amid my trials and sorrows. Thank you for giving me the confidence that I can look forward to better things. Thank you for sending your Son, Jesus to overcome the world so that I can look forward to spending my eternity with you and your Son, Jesus. Thank you, God.

My prayer for today—including any journaling thoughts I may want to add. Where am I today spiritually, emotionally, physically, financially, generally?

Today's Date: _____

Old Testament verse for today: Psalm 5:1 thru 3

O Lord, hear me praying; listen to my plea, O God my King, for I will never pray to anyone but you. Each morning I will look to you in heaven and lay my requests before you, praying earnestly.

One possible prayer for today:

God, thank you for always hearing my prayers and listening to me. Thank you for never turning your back on my pleas. Thank you for being the one and only true God. It would do me no good to pray to any other entity, so I pray only to you and have praise only for you. Thank you for letting me start my every day with you, laying my requests at your feet, praying earnestly, and knowing that you hear me. Lord, I know that you don't always give me the answer that, in my selfishness, I want; so, Lord, give me the faith and the peace to accept the answers that you give me. Thank you for that faith and peace, Lord.

New Testament verse for today: Romans 4:16a

So God's blessings are given to us by faith, as a free gift.

One possible prayer for today:

God, thank you for all the blessings you give to me and have given to me. Thank you for the free gift of my salvation and the free gift of listening to my prayers and my pleas. Thank you for the gift of faith so that I may take full benefit of all your free blessings. Thank you, Lord, for your kindness to me.

My prayer for today—including any journaling thoughts I may want to add. Where am I today spiritually, emotionally, physically, financially, generally?

Today's Date: _____

Old Testament verse for today: Psalm 5:7

But as for me, I will come into your Temple protected by your mercy and your love: I will worship you with deepest awe.

One possible prayer for today:

Lord, you know my heart. You know that I do hold you in awe. I am in awe of your mighty power. I am in awe of your unlimited love for me. I am in awe of your tremendous imagination exemplified by the beautiful world surrounding me. And, Lord, I continue to be in awe that you can care for me at all times. Thank you for protecting me with your mercy and love. Thank you for accepting my worship. Thank you, Lord.

New Testament verse for today: I John 3:2

Yes, dear friends, we are already God's children, right now, and we can't even imagine what it is going to be like later on. But we do know this, that when he comes we will be like him, as a result of seeing him as he really is.

One possible prayer for today:

God, I am in awe to think that you already consider me one of your children! And, yes, I can't even imagine what it is going to be like to actually be in your presence; to see you as you really are. I am in awe of your love and concern for me; for your promise to come back and get me because of your marvelous plan of salvation through your Son, Jesus. God, thank you for making me one of your children. Thank you for your plan of salvation for me. Thank you for your promise that one day I will see you face to face. Thank you for giving me the faith to believe. Thank you, God.

My prayer for today—including any journaling thoughts I may want to add. Where am I today spiritually, emotionally, physically, financially, generally?

Today's Date: _____

Old Testament verse for today: Psalm 5:8

Lord, lead me as you promised me you would; otherwise my enemies will conquer me. Tell me clearly what to do, which way to turn.

One possible prayer for today:

Lord, that is exactly where I am today! I don't know which way to turn. I have a problem for which I have no solution. In fact, I don't even know what I think the solution should be! So, Lord, I pray. Tell me clearly what to do. Tell me clearly which way to turn. Lead me as you promised you would. Lord, I need your direction, I am counting on you telling me clearly which way to turn. Don't let this problem conquer me, Lord. I am turning it over to you. Thank you for solving it with me and for me. Thank you, God.

New Testament verse for today: Ephesians 1:19 & 20

I pray that you will began to understand how incredibly great his power is to help those who believe in him. It is the same mighty power that raised Christ from the dead and seated him in the place of honor at God's right hand in heaven.

One possible prayer for today:

God, thank you for your mighty power. Lord, I know that my problems are so small compared to your mighty power. I also know that you care about everything that it important to me. So, Lord, I call on your mighty power to help me with my problem today. It may not look like a big problem to you; but, it looks big to me! I am sure that I can never understand how incredibly great your power really is; but, Lord, I know that it is there for me and that I can call on it to help me. So, Lord, I am calling on that power now. Thank you for using your power to raise Christ from the dead so that I might have salvation. Thank you for seating Christ at your right hand. Thank you for having Christ intercede for me with you to help me today. Thank you, God.

My prayer for today—including any journaling thoughts I may want to add. Where am I today spiritually, emotionally, physically, financially, generally?

Today's Date: _____

Old Testament verse for today: Psalm 5:11 & 12

But make everyone rejoice who puts his trust in you. Keep them shouting for joy because you are defending them. Fill all who love you with happiness. For you bless the godly man, O Lord; you protect him with your shield of love.

One possible prayer for today:

God, thank you for protecting me with your shield of love. Thank you for blessing me. Thank you for filling me with happiness. Thank you for defending me so that I may truly shout with joy because of it. Thank you for letting me rejoice. Thank you for giving me the faith to trust in you. Thank you, God.

New Testament verse for today: Acts 4:12

There is salvation in no one else! Under all heaven there is no other name for men to call upon to save them.

One possible prayer for today:

Thank you for being so loving, so protecting, and so generous, that you provided for my salvation through the death and resurrection of your Son, Jesus. Lord, I know, and I acknowledge that there is no other way. There is no other name upon whom to call to be saved. Thank you for your great plan of salvation for me. Thank you for that wonderful blessing.

My prayer for today—including any journaling thoughts I may want to add. Where am I today spiritually, emotionally, physically, financially, generally?

Today's Date: _____

Old Testament verse for today: Psalm 7:1

I am depending on you, O Lord my God, to save me from my persecutors.

One possible prayer for today:

God, thank you for being a God upon whom I can always depend. Thank you for being a God who can protect me from my persecutors. Thank you for being a God who cares about me and cares about the things that are important to me. Thank you for being such an awesome God, and yet such a loving God. Thank you, God.

New Testament verse for today: John 9:31

Well, God doesn't listen to evil men, but he has open ears to those who worship him and do his will.

One possible prayer for today:

God, thank you for listening to me. Thank you for forgiving me so that you do not consider me evil in your eyes. Thank you for permitting me to worship you and to return to you to be forgiven when I humbly return to you, even after I have failed you again and again. Thank you for knowing my heart and accepting that even though I continue to sin, it is my plan to always do your will. Thank you for always having an open ear to my praises and my pleas to you. Thank you for being such a caring and loving God.

My prayer for today—including any journaling thoughts I may want to add. Where am I today spiritually, emotionally, physically, financially, generally?

Today's Date: _____

Old Testament verse for today: Psalm 7:9b

Bless all who truly worship God; for you, the righteous God, look deep within the hearts of men and examine all their motives and their thoughts.

One possible prayer for today:

God, examine my thoughts and my motives; and, Lord, thank you for forgiving me when my thoughts and my motives are not what you would have them to be. God, I do try to worship you in a manner that is pleasing to you. Thank you for being a God truly worthy of my worship. Thank you for being a righteous God. Thank you for being gentle with me when I fail you in my thoughts and motives. Thank you, God.

New Testament verse for today: Hebrews 10:35 & 36

Do not let this happy trust in the Lord die away, no matter what happens. Remember your reward! You need to patiently keep on doing God's will if you want him to do for you all that he has promised.

One possible prayer for today:

God, don't ever let my happiness in you die. No matter what happens, please continue to give me the gift of faith to trust you completely. Let me always praise you, knowing that you have prepared a place for me with you for eternity. Help me to have the strength to keep on doing your will in every circumstance. And, God, thank you for being a God so loving and so consistent that I can always count on you to do for me all the things that you have promised. Thank you, God.

My prayer for today—including any journaling thoughts I may want to add. Where am I today spiritually, emotionally, physically, financially, generally?

Today's Date: _____

Old Testament verse for today: Psalm 7:10

God is my shield; he will defend me. He saves those whose hearts and lives are true and right.

One possible prayer for today:

God, thank you for being my shield. Thank you for defending me. Thank you for saving me. Lord, I try to live so that my heart and life are true and right; but, Lord, I continue to fail. So, the only way that my heart and life can be true and right is if you continue to forgive me—if you continue to forgive my sins and forget about them. Thank you for doing that for me. Thank you for making my heart and life true and right so that I can count on your shielding me and defending me. Thank you, Lord.

New Testament verse for today: Ephesians 1:4

Long ago, even before he made the world, God chose us to be his very own, through what Christ would do for us; he decided then to make us holy in his eyes, without a single fault—we who stand before him covered with his love.

One possible prayer for today:

Wow! What a wonderful promise, Lord. To think that you chose me to be your very own and sent Jesus to pay the price for my sins. Thank you for making me holy in your eyes—something that I would be totally unable to accomplish on my own. Thank you for looking at me without seeing any of my faults! Thank you for covering me with your love. What a wonderful, loving, generous God you are to me. Thank you for your wonderful plans for my life and my salvation. Thank you for always being my shield and my defender.

My prayer for today—including any journaling thoughts I may want to add. Where am I today spiritually, emotionally, physically, financially, generally?

Today's Date: _____

Old Testament verse for today: Psalm 7:17

Oh, how grateful and thankful I am to the Lord because he is so good. I will sing praise to the name of the Lord who is above all lords.

One possible prayer for today:

God, I am grateful and thankful to you for all things. You are so good to me—much better than I deserve! Thank you for being above all other lords. Thank you for being a God who listens when I sing your praises and responds when I call. Thank you, Lord.

New Testament verse for today: Acts 10:34 & 35

Then Peter replied, "I see very clearly that the Jews are not God's only favorites! In every nation he has those who worship him and do good deeds and are acceptable to him."

One possible prayer for today:

Thank you, God, for extending your plan of salvation to all people—including me! Thank you for permitting me to be one of your favorites! Let me try to be more worthy to warrant this claim. I know that I can be worthy in your eyes only with faith. Please give me the faith that I need. Let me worship you in my everyday life and with my everyday actions. Thank you for permitting me to be acceptable to you.

My prayer for today—including any journaling thoughts I may want to add. Where am I today spiritually, emotionally, physically, financially, generally?

Today's Date: _____

Old Testament verse for today: Psalm 8:1 & 3 thru 6

O Lord our God, the majesty and glory of your name fills all the earth and overflows the heavens. When I look up into the night skies and see the work of your fingers—the moon and the stars that you have made—I cannot understand how you can bother with mere puny man, to pay any attention to him! And yet you have made him only a little lower than the angels, and placed a crown of glory and honor on his head. You have put him in charge of everything you made; everything is put under his authority.

One possible prayer for today:

God, how wonderful you are to me. Thank you for being so majestic and glorious. Thank you for letting that majesty and glory not only overflow the heavens, but fill the earth. Thank you for being the creator of all things—heavens, the moon, the stars, and everything else you have made. And, God, even with all your majesty and glory, you still care about little me! Thank you for caring about me. Thank you for placing your crown of glory and honor on my head. Lord, let me be a good manager of all the things that you have put under my authority. Let me be a good steward of all that you have given me. Thank you for your many blessings, Lord.

New Testament verse for today: Romans 8:35 & 36a

Who then can ever keep Christ's love from us? When we have trouble or calamity, when we are hunted down or destroyed, is it because he doesn't love us anymore? And if we are hungry, or penniless, or in danger, or threatened with death, has God deserted us? No!

One possible prayer for today:

Lord, thank you for making me only a little lower than the angels. Thank you for placing your crown of glory and honor on my head. Lord, knowing that you care so much for me, I can have confidence that you will always love me. You will never forsake me. Thank you for giving me Christ's love to uphold me whatever is happening in my life. Lord, I know that I will have troubles. I know that there will be bad times. But, Lord, thank you for the promise that you and your Son Jesus will never forsake me. Thank you for that assurance, God.

My prayer for today—including any journaling thoughts I may want to add. Where am I today spiritually, emotionally, physically, financially, generally?

Today's Date: _____

Old Testament verse for today: Psalm 8:9

O Jehovah, our Lord, the majesty and glory of your name fills the earth.

One possible prayer for today:

God, how true! You have created such a wonderful world for us to enjoy. Everywhere I look I can see the grandeur of your creation and the imagination you had in that creation. I can see trees and flowers that are beautiful to behold. I went to the zoo the other day and saw animals that even in my wildest imagination I could never have conceived. And, Lord, these things mentioned don't even scratch the surface of what you have created. In every area, your majesty and glory fill the earth. Thank you, Lord, for making this such a wonderful place for me to enjoy.

New Testament verse for today: Ephesians 1:6 & 7

Now all praise to God for his wonderful kindness to us and his favor that he has poured out upon us, because we belong to his dearly loved Son. So overflowing is his kindness towards us that he took away all our sins through the blood of his Son, by whom we are saved; and he has showered down upon us the richness of his grace—for how well he understands us and knows what is best for us at all times.

One possible prayer for today:

God, your majesty, your glory, your love, your kindness, and your favor continue to pour down upon me at all times. Thank you, God. Thank you for your overflowing kindness. Thank you for taking away all my sins through the blood of your Son, Jesus. Thank you for making that plan of salvation available to me. Thank you for understanding me and knowing what is best for me at all times. Lord, when things don't go the way I would like them to go, let me remember that you always know what is best for me. Let me be thankful and joyful at all times as I rely on your direction for my life.

My prayer for today—including any journaling thoughts I may want to add. Where am I today spiritually, emotionally, physically, financially, generally?

Today's Date: _____

Old Testament verse for today: Psalm 9:1

Oh Lord, I will praise you with all my heart, and tell everyone about the marvelous things you do. I will be glad, yes, filled with joy because of you. I will sing your praises, O Lord God above all gods.

One possible prayer for today:

What a wonderful God you are! Thank you for being a wonderful God and a God worthy of all my praise and adoration. Thank you for the wonderful things you do for me. Thank you for filling me with joy. Thank you for being a God above all other gods.

New Testament verse for today: I John 4:17

And as we live with Christ, our love grows more perfect and complete: so we will not be ashamed and embarrassed at the day of judgment, but can face him with confidence and joy, because he loves us and we love him too.

One possible prayer for today:

God, thank you for your love for me—love that was so great that you gave your only Son, Jesus, to die on the cross for my sins. What a wonderful, loving God you are. How can I help but sing your praises? How can I help but adore you? How can I help being filled with joy? God, you are worthy of my praise and adoration. Thank you for being the one and only true God. Thank you for caring about me. Thank you, Lord.

My prayer for today—including any journaling thoughts I may want to add. Where am I today spiritually, emotionally, physically, financially, generally?

Today's Date: _____

Old Testament verse for today: Psalm 9:7 & 8

But the Lord lives on forever; he sits upon his throne to judge justly the nations of the world. All who are oppressed may come to him. He is a refuge for them in their time of troubles.

One possible prayer for today:

God, thank you for being my refuge when I am oppressed. Thank you for being an everlasting God who sits upon your throne forever. Thank you for always being there when I need you. Thank you for being such a loving and caring God.

New Testament prayer for today: I Peter 4:12 & 13

Dear friends, don't be bewildered or surprised when you go through the fiery trials ahead, for this is no strange, unusual thing that is going to happen to you. Instead, be really glad—because these trials will make you partners with Christ in his suffering, and afterwards you will have the wonderful joy of sharing his glory in that coming day when it will be displayed.

One possible prayer for today:

God, I really need help in this area! I have a real hard time being glad when I go through bad times. And, if I am honest with myself, I know that most of these bad times are my own fault! I know that I have taken things into my own hands, made my own decisions without relying on you, and really made a mess of things. Lord, I know that if I keep my faith through these bad times that I will grow stronger as a person and stronger in my relationship with Christ. So, help me right now, Lord. Give me a shot of faith! Help me to trust you more during this time. And, Lord, when I fail you during these difficult times, thank you for forgiving me when I come back to you and humbly confess my failures and my sins to you. Thank you for never giving up on me, Lord, even when I go through periods when I may have given up on having the faith that I needed to have in you.

My prayer for today—including any journaling thoughts I may want to add. Where am I today spiritually, emotionally, physically, financially, generally?

Today's Date: _____

Old Testament verse for today: Psalm 9:12b
He does not ignore the prayers of men in trouble when they call to him for help.

One possible prayer for today:
God, thank you for that promise that you will not ignore my prayer when I am in trouble and call to you for help. Thank you for always being there and always listening to my pleas. Lord, I get in trouble a lot; and, most of the time it is because I am not following the guidelines that you have asked me to follow. But, you are always there to forgive and to help when I call. Thank you, God, for being such a consistent God.

New Testament verse for today: I Thessalonians 5:16 thru 18
Always be joyful. Always keep on praying. No matter what happens, always be thankful, for this is God's will for you who belong to Christ Jesus.

One possible prayer for today:
Lord, that is great advice for me; but, sometimes real hard to do! But, Lord, I know that if you give me enough faith in you, I can do that! Let me accept that no matter what is happening in my life, if I am trusting in you, then these events are your will for my life at that time. But, Lord, you have also told me to keep on praying all the time. You have told me to be joyful and thankful, no matter what. So, Lord, I try. I really do. Sometimes I fall short of the goal of being joyful and thankful; but, even in those times, I keep on pleading with you to help me so that I can be genuinely joyful and thankful again. Thank you for helping me through the tough times, Lord. Thank you for never giving up on me, even when I fail you in this area of my life.

My prayer for today—including any journaling thoughts I may want to add. Where am I today spiritually, emotionally, physically, financially, generally?

Today's Date: _____

Old Testament verse for today: Psalm 10:17

Lord, you know the hopes of humble people. Surely you will hear their cries and comfort their hearts by helping them.

One possible prayer for today:

Lord, you know my heart. You know my thoughts. You know my hopes and fears. You know everything about me, and still you choose to love me. You choose to care for me in all situations. Thank you for always being there to hear my cries. Thank you for always being there to comfort my heart. Thank you for always being there to help me when I call on you. Thank you for being concerned about me. Thank you for always loving and caring for me. Thank you, Lord.

New Testament verse for today: Colossians 3:2

Let heaven fill your thoughts; don't spend your time worrying about things down here.

One possible prayer for today:

God, that sounds real good in principle, but, I have some real problems down here that I need to solve and I need your help and guidance in solving them. I know that you hear my cries. I know that you know my hopes and fears. And, Lord, I know that you can give me the guidance and the common sense that I need to solve my problems. So, thank you for hearing my cries. Thank you for giving me the wisdom and guidance that I need right now. Thank you for being there to comfort me. Thank you, Lord.

My prayer for today—including any journaling thoughts I may want to add. Where am I today spiritually, emotionally, physically, financially, generally?

Today's Date: _____

Old Testament verse for today: Psalm 11:4

But the Lord is still in his holy temple; he still rules from heaven. He closely watches everything that happens here on earth.

One possible prayer for today:

Lord, I really need the comfort of knowing that this is true. Our world seems to be in such a mess! Our leaders seem to have no regard for honesty or morality. So, thank you for being the stability I need in this unstable world. Thank you for continuing to be in your holy temple. Thank you for still ruling from heaven. Thank you for closely watching what happens here on earth. Thank you for closely watching me and continuing to help me, to protect me, and to forgive me when I fail you. Thank you for being constant and consistent even when I am not, and the world in which I live is not. Thank you, Lord.

New Testament verse for today: I Corinthians 5:8

So let us feast upon him and grow strong in the Christian life, leaving entirely behind us the cancerous old life with its hatreds and wickedness. Let us feast instead upon the pure bread of honor and sincerity and truth.

One possible prayer for today:

Lord, that is obviously the answer. Let me learn more about you and your Son, Jesus. Let me grow strong in my Christian faith. Let me leave behind the cancerous life of the world with its hatreds and wickedness. Let me live my life with honesty, purity, sincerity, and truth. And, Lord, I know that I cannot accomplish that without your help. So, help me, Lord. Help me to grow strong and be a witness to your love and to the stability that that love can bring to my life and the lives of those around me. Maybe by changing myself, I can be a witness to help to change others. Thank you for helping me, Lord.

My prayer for today—including any journaling thoughts I may want to add. Where am I today spiritually, emotionally, physically, financially, generally?

Today's Date: _____

Old Testament verse for today: Psalm 11:7

For God is good, and he loves goodness; the godly shall see his face.

One possible prayer for today:

God, thank you for being such a good and kind God. Thank you for loving goodness. Thank you for loving me even when I fail to live up to your standard of goodness. Thank you for letting me see your face if I will only trust in your Son, Jesus, to be my Savior. Thank you for letting me be godly, not because of anything that I have done; but, because in your love for me you provided a plan that makes it possible for me to be godly in your sight. Thank you, Lord, for your wonderful love.

New Testament verse for today: Ephesians 5:15 thru 17

So be careful how you act; these are difficult days. Don't be fools; be wise: make the most of every opportunity you have for doing good. Don't act thoughtlessly, but try to find out and do whatever the Lord wants you to.

One possible prayer for today:

God, I always need your help to act wisely. I always need your help to remember to make the most of every opportunity to do good. I always need your help to act thoughtfully. Lord, help me to listen to your leading in my life so that I may find out what you would have me to do. Thank you, Lord, for being patient with me as I try to learn to live more closely to how you would have me live.

My prayer for today—including any journaling thoughts I may want to add. Where am I today spiritually, emotionally, physically, financially, generally?

Today's Date: _____

Old Testament verse for today: Psalm 12:6 & 7

The Lord's promise is sure. He speaks no careless word; all he says is purest truth, like silver seven times refined. O Lord, we know that you will forever preserve your own from the reach of evil men.

One possible prayer for today:

God, thank you for being a God so consistent in all your ways that I can always count on you. I can always count on your promises. I can always count on your words being true. Thank you for your promises to me. Thank you for preserving me from evil. Thank you for caring for me at all times. Thank you, God.

New Testament verse for today: I John 2:28 & 29

And now, my little children, stay in happy fellowship with the Lord so that when he comes you will be sure that all is well, and will not have to be ashamed and shrink back from meeting him. Since we know that God is always good and does only right, we may rightly assume that all those who do right are his children.

One possible prayer for today:

God, thank you for being a God who only does good and only does right. Thank you for being a consistent God whose words are always true and never careless. Thank you for giving me the strength and the faith to do my best to always stay in fellowship with you. Thank you for helping me to live my life so that you are not ashamed of me and that I am not ashamed to come into your presence. But, Lord, you know that no matter how hard I try, I will always fail you. I will always let sin creep into my life. You know that I will not always do right. So, Lord, thank you for always being there to forgive me when I return to you. Thank you for forgiving me, Lord. Thank you for erasing my sins from my record to that I may appear blameless before you. Thank you, Lord.

My prayer for today—including any journaling thoughts I may want to add. Where am I today spiritually, emotionally, physically, financially, generally?

Today's Date: _____

Old Testament verse for today: Psalm 13:5 & 6

But I will always trust in you and in your mercy and shall rejoice in your salvation. I will sing to the Lord because he has blessed me so richly.

One possible prayer for today:

God, thank you for being so trustworthy. Thank you for being merciful. Thank you for giving me salvation. Let me always praise you for what you are doing in my life. Thank you for the good times, Lord. Thank you for blessing me so richly. And, Lord, when I am having problems, don't let me forget to thank you for the problems, because I know that if I am trusting you, the problems are also a part of your plan for my life. Thank you for my life, Lord. Thank you again for being so merciful to me.

New Testament verse for today: II Corinthians 5:19

For God was in Christ, restoring the world to himself, no longer counting men's sins against them but blotting them out. This is the wonderful message he has given us to tell others.

One possible prayer for today:

God, thank you for being trustworthy to blot out my sins. Thank you for giving me Jesus through whom I may have eternal life. Thank you for being so merciful that you are no longer counting my sins—which are many—against me. Lord, let me live my life so that I may be a personal witness to this wonderful message. Thank you, Lord.

My prayer for today—including any journaling thoughts I may want to add. Where am I today spiritually, emotionally, physically, financially, generally?

Today's Date: _____

Old Testament verse for today: Psalm 14:2

The Lord looks down from heaven on all mankind to see if there are any who are wise, who want to please God.

One possible prayer for today:

God, you know my heart. When you look down from heaven, you see me. You know me. You know my thoughts and my actions. You know that I do want to please you, even though I often fail you with my sins. Lord, give me the wisdom that I need to do a better job of pleasing you. And, God, thank you for continuing to forgive me when I fail you. Thank you for forgiving my sins when I humbly return to you and confess these sins. Thank you for watching me from heaven. Thank you for caring for me. Thank you for giving me additional wisdom. Thank you for forgiving me. Thank you, God.

New Testament verse for today: Acts 3:19

Now change your mind and attitude to God and turn to him so that he can cleanse away your sins and send you wonderful times of refreshment from the presence of the Lord.

One possible prayer for today:

God, thank you for letting me turn to you. Thank you for giving me the offer of letting me turn from my sinful ways and turn to you. Thank you for giving me the choice of changing my mind and attitude and turning to you. Thank you for cleansing me from my sins. And, Lord, thank you for giving me the wonderful times of refreshment that can only come from being in your presence. Thank you, God, for this wonderful promise.

My prayer for today—including any journaling thoughts I may want to add. Where am I today spiritually, emotionally, physically, financially, generally?

Today's Date: _____

Old Testament verse for today: Psalm 15:1 & 2

Lord, who may go and find refuge and shelter in your tabernacle up on your holy hill? Anyone who leads a blameless life and is truly sincere.

One possible prayer for today:

Lord, you know that my life is not blameless; but, you also know my heart. You know that I sincerely try to worship you and adore you and please you. You know how often I fail you; and, yet you continue to forgive me when I humbly return to you and ask for your forgiveness. And, Lord, you are always there to give me refuge and shelter when I return to you. Thank you for forgiving me and making me blameless in your eyes because of your forgiveness. Thank you for loving me and caring for me, Lord.

New Testament verse for today: John 14:21

The one who obeys me is the only who loves me; and because he loves me, my Father will love him; and I will too, and I will reveal myself to him.

One possible prayer for today:

God, you know that I love you. You know that I try to obey you at all times. And, Lord, thank you for loving me. Thank you for revealing your Son, Jesus, to me. Thank you for having Jesus love me and give me salvation through the marvelous plan of salvation that you authored for me. Thank you for forgiving me so that I may appear blameless before you. Thank you for refuge and shelter here on earth and for eternal refuse and shelter with you and your Son, Jesus, in eternity.

My prayer for today—including any journaling thoughts I may want to add. Where am I today spiritually, emotionally, physically, financially, generally?

Today's Date: _____

Old Testament verse for today: Psalm 16:1

Save me, O God, because I have come to you for refuge. I said to him, "You are my Lord; I have no other help but yours."

One possible prayer for today:

God, how true that is! When the chips are down, I really don't have any other place to turn! You are the only refuge on whom I can count when all else fails. You are the Lord of my life, and I have no choice but to trust you completely. I have no other help but yours, Lord. Please come to my aid   quickly! Please be my refuge right now when I need your loving and protecting arms around me. Thank you, Lord, for being my refuge when I need it.

New Testament verse for today: I Corinthians 1:30

For it is from God alone that you have your life through Christ Jesus. He showed us God's plan of salvation; he was the one who made us acceptable to God: he made us pure and holy and gave himself to purchase our salvation.

One possible prayer for today:

God, thank you for giving me Jesus who made me acceptable to you. Thank you for the life you have given me through your Son, Jesus. Thank you for permitting me to come directly to you and plead for your help and your refuge. Thank you for giving me salvation, if I only believe in your Son, Jesus. Thank you for permitting Jesus to make me pure and holy in your eyes. Thank you for hearing my prayer when I need you so much. Even though you have given me salvation, I still have problems today and I look to you for help at all times—for eternity and for today. Thank you for being the Lord of today as well as tomorrow. Thank you for giving me the help I need today.

My prayer for today—including any journaling thoughts I may want to add. Where am I today spiritually, emotionally, physically, financially, generally?

Today's Date: _____

Old Testament verse for today: Psalm 16:8, 9, & 11

I am always thinking of the Lord: and because he is so near, I never need to stumble or to fall. Heart, body, and soul are filled with joy. You have let me experience the joys of life and the exquisite pleasures of your eternal presence.

One possible prayer for today:

God, I am always thinking of you and praising you for being so good to me. And, Lord, I know that you are near. I know that I never need to stumble or to fall in your eyes; but, Lord, today I am suffering. My heart, body, and soul are not filled with joy. I am hurting. Yet, I know that you are as near as always. You are always there for me. I can call on you and I can lean on you for help. I can ask for guidance and support in this difficult time. And, Lord, I know you will hear me. I thank you for hearing me and helping me. I thank you that once again, I, like the Psalmist can say that my heart, body, and soul are filled with joy; and, that I can once again experience the joys of life. Lord, even when I am not experiencing the joys of life, I know that I can revel in the exquisite pleasures of your eternal presence and know that I can count on you to help me and once again rescue me. Thank you, God.

New Testament verse for today: Colossians 3:15

Let the peace of heart which comes from Christ be always present in your hearts and lives, for this is your responsibility and privilege as members of his body. And always be thankful.

One possible prayer for today:

Lord, thank you for that peace of heart which comes from Christ and can be present in my heart and my life, even during these troubled times. Thank you for giving me this privilege—and responsibility. Thank you for giving me the faith to really believe that and accept it fully. Thank you for the promise of restored joy and pleasure. And, Lord, don't let my faith waver during this time. I need that faith and the promises you give me even more when I am hurting. So, let me cling to your promises for me, accepting your will for my life and thanking you for what you are doing in my life, even at this time; because, I know that whatever is occurring is your will for me at this moment. So, thank you, Lord. Thank you for giving me the strength and the guidance to get through this period in my life—and for giving me peace of heart in this troubled time.

My prayer for today—including any journaling thoughts I may want to add. Where am I today spiritually, emotionally, physically, financially, generally?

Today's Date: _____

Old Testament verse for today: Psalm 18:1

Lord, how I love you! For you have done such tremendous things for me.

One possible prayer for today:

Lord, I do love you. I love you because you first loved me; and, you have done, and continue to do, such great things for me. Thank you for all you have done for me, Lord. Thank you for loving me. Thank you for putting up with all of my human frailty and my inability to always be consistent in my living for you. Thank you for your everlasting love.

New Testament verse for today: Acts 15:11

Don't you believe that all are saved the same way, by the free gift of the Lord Jesus?

One possible prayer for today:

God, how could you have possibly shown your love more dramatically than you have done by giving your only Son as a sacrifice so that I could be saved through that act? Thank you for that wonderful plan, Lord; and, thank you for your free gift of your Son, Jesus. I do believe, Lord; and, I thank you for my salvation because of your plan and giving me the faith to believe. Thank you, Lord.

My prayer for today—including any journaling thoughts I may want to add. Where am I today spiritually, emotionally, physically, financially, generally?

Today's Date: _____

Old Testament verse for today: Psalm 18:2 & 3

The Lord is my fort where I can enter and be safe; no one can follow me in and slay me. He is a rugged mountain where I hide; he is my Savior, a rock where none can reach me, and a tower of safety. He is my shield. He is like the strong horn of a mighty fighting bull. All I need to do is cry to him—oh, praise the Lord—and I am saved from all my enemies.

One possible prayer for today:

God, how wonderful it is to know that you are my fort where I can enter and be safe. Thank you for being my hiding place; my Savior; my rock where none can reach me; my tower of safety. Thank you for being my shield. Thank you for being like a strong horn of a mighty bull that will protect me. Thank you for hearing me when I cry to you. Lord, let me always praise you. And, Lord, thank you for hearing me and saving me from my enemies when I call to you.

New Testament verse for today: I Peter 1:3 thru 5

All honor to God, the God and Father of our Lord Jesus Christ: for it is his boundless mercy that has given us the privilege of being born again, so that we are now members of God's own family. Now we live in the hope of eternal life because Christ rose again from the dead. And God has reserved for his children the priceless gift of eternal life; it is kept in heaven for you, pure and undefiled, beyond the reach of change and decay. And God, in his mighty power, will make sure that you get there safely to receive it, because you are trusting him. It will be yours in that coming last day for all to see.

One possible prayer for today:

God, I do honor you. Thank you for being the God and Father of Jesus. Thank you for your boundless mercy to me so that I might have eternal life if I only believe in Jesus as my personal Savior. Thank you for raising Jesus from the dead for me. Thank you for reserving the priceless gift of eternal life for me. Thank you for being an unchanging and forever loving God. Thank you for guaranteeing that you will make sure that I get there safely to receive this wonderful gift. Thank you for guarding me in this life and always being there to hear my prayers. Thank you, God.

My prayer for today—including any journaling thoughts I may want to add. Where am I today spiritually, emotionally, physically, financially, generally?

Today's Date: _____

Old Testament verse for today: Psalm 18:6

In my distress I screamed to the Lord for his help. And he heard me from heaven; my cry reached his ears.

One possible prayer for today:

Lord, thank you for always hearing me in heaven when I scream to you for your help. Thank you for caring about me when I am in distress. Thank you for listening to my cries for help. Lord, thank you for being an everlasting caring and hearing God.

New Testament verse for today: Galatians 3:14b

All of us as Christians can have the promised Holy Spirit through this faith.

One possible prayer for today:

God, thank you for giving me the faith to cry to you when I need your help. Thank you for listening to me when I cry to you. Thank you for letting my cries reach your ears. Thank you for giving me your wonderful Holy Spirit to guide me through the deep waters of my life. Thank you for that promise and thank you for giving me the faith to believe that promise.

My prayer for today—including any journaling thoughts I may want to add. Where am I today spiritually, emotionally, physically, financially, generally?

Today's Date: _____

Old Testament verse for today: Psalm 18:25 thru 28

Lord, how merciful you are to those who are merciful. And you do not punish those who run from evil. You give blessings to the pure but pain to those whom leave you paths. You deliver the humble but condemn the proud and haughty ones. You have turned on my light! The Lord my God has made my darkness turn to light.

One possible prayer for today:

God, thank you for being merciful to me, even when I don't deserve it. Thank you for helping me to run from evil. Thank you for giving me blessings that I don't deserve, just because you love me. Thank you for bringing me out of the darkness of sin into the light of your salvation. Thank you for your everlasting love to me.

New Testament verse for today: Colossians 2:2 & 3

This is what I have asked of God for you: that you will be encouraged and knit together by strong ties of love, and that you will have the rich experience of knowing Christ with real certainty and clear understanding. For God's secret plan, now at last made known, is Christ himself. In him lie hidden all the mighty, untapped treasures of wisdom and knowledge.

One possible prayer for today:

God, thank you for giving me the rich experience of knowing Christ as my personal Savior. Thank you for making Christ real to me. Thank you for opening my eyes so that I may have a clear understanding of what Christ has done for me and that by believing in him, I may experience salvation. Thank you for making this plan of salvation so simple and so easy to understand. Thank you for making Christ the treasure trove of wisdom and knowledge. Thank you for letting me tap into that wisdom and knowledge though my belief in Christ. Thank you, God, for being so good to me.

My prayer for today—including any journaling thoughts I may want to add. Where am I today spiritually, emotionally, physically, financially, generally?

Today's Date: _____

Old Testament verse for today: Psalm 18:30 thru 32

What a God he is! How perfect in every way! All his promises prove true. He is a shield for everyone who hides behind him. For who is God except our Lord? Who but he is as a rock? He fills me with strength and protects me wherever I go.

One possible prayer for today:

I agree, Lord. What a God you are! Thank you for being perfect in every way. Thank you for your promises and thank you that they always prove true. Thank you for shielding me when I hide behind you. Thank you for being the one and only God. Thank you for being my rock. Thank you for protecting me wherever I go, and thank you for the strength that you give me to do the work you have sent me to do. Thank you, Lord. Thank you.

New Testament verse for today: Acts 7:49

"The heaven is my throne" says the Lord through his prophets, "and the earth is my foot-stool".

One possible prayer for today:

God, not only are you perfect, you are majestic! I really cannot comprehend a God who makes the heaven his throne and the earth his footstool; but, when I look at around at the incredible imagination and beauty you have created, Lord, I know that you are in charge of all things—above and below. How wonderful to have a God like you. Add to that, Lord, the fact that you love me and care about me and are concerned about the things that concern me. What a wonderful, majestic, and yet personal God you are. Thank you for being my personal God.

My prayer for today—including any journaling thoughts I may want to add. Where am I today spiritually, emotionally, physically, financially, generally?

Today's Date: _____

Old Testament verse for today: Psalm 18:35 & 36

You have given me your salvation as my shield. Your right hand, O Lord, supports me; your gentleness has made me great. You have made wide steps beneath my feet so that I need never slip.

On possible prayer for today:

Lord, thank you for my salvation. Thank you for being such a great and loving God. Thank you for supporting me with your strong right hand. Thank you for your gentleness with me even when I continue to fail you in my human weakness. Thank you for making wide steps beneath my feet so that I need never slip. Thank you for being such a caring and loving God to me.

New Testament verse for today: James 1:12 & 13

Happy is the man who doesn't give in and do wrong when he is tempted, for afterwards he will get as his reward the crown of life that God has promised to those who love him. And remember, when someone wants to do wrong it is never God who is tempting him, for God never wants to do wrong and never tempts anyone else to do it.

One possible prayer for today:

God, thank you for helping me resist temptation. Thank you for my salvation. Thank you for making wide steps beneath my feet so that I need never slip into temptation and sin. But you know that because of my human weakness, I do slip and, I do fail you. Thank you for forgiving me when I return to you and repent—no matter what the scope of my sin. Thank you for the promise of your crown of life as my reward for loving you and following you. Thank you for being such a loving and caring God.

My prayer for today—including any journaling thoughts I may want to add. Where am I today spiritually, emotionally, physically, financially, generally?

Today's Date: _____

Old Testament verse for today: Psalm 18:46, 48 & 50b

God is alive! Praise him who is the great rock of protection. He rescues me from my enemies; he holds me safely out of their reach and saves me from these powerful opponents. You have been loving and kind to me and will be to my descendants.

One possible prayer for today:

God, thank you for being the living God! Thank you for being my rock of protection. Thank you for being my rescuer and holding me safely out of the reach of those who are trying to harm me. Thank you for being loving and kind, and thank you for being there for my children and their children. Thank you for being forever!

New Testament verse for today: Matthew 9:13b

It isn't your sacrifices and your gifts I want. I want you to be merciful.

One possible prayer for today:

God, I know that I need to work on being less judgmental of others and to show more mercy to those who need help. Who am I to judge others when I have so many failings of my own? I expect you to help me, and then I don't always treat others as I want you to treat me. So, help me to learn to be more concerned. Help me to try harder to emulate the life that you lived in concern for others. Thank you for forgiving me when I fail, and thank you for never giving up on me.

My prayer for today—including any journaling thoughts I may want to add. Where am I today spiritually, emotionally, physically, financially, generally?

Today's Date: _____

Old Testament verse for today: Psalm 19:1 thru 5

The heavens are telling the glory of God: they are a marvelous display of his craftsmanship. Day and night they keep on telling about God. Without a sound or word, silent in the skies, the message reaches out to all the world. The sun lives in the heavens where God placed it and moves out across the skies as radiant as a bridegroom going to his wedding, or as joyous as an athlete looking forward to a race.

One possible prayer for today:

What a glorious God you are! You have given me such a wonderful and beautiful world to enjoy. All of your creation is here for me to enjoy. Thank you for making your world so wonderful for me. Lord, forgive me for all the times I take your many gifts to me for granted. Each day, let me take a moment and give thanks to you for your wonderful natural gifts that you have given me to enjoy.

New Testament verse for today: I Timothy 1:7

Glory and honor to God forever and ever. He is the King of the ages, the unseen one who never dies; he alone is God, and full of wisdom. Amen.

One possible prayer for today:

God, you do deserve my honoring you forever. Thank you for being the King of the ages. And even though I cannot see you, I can see your wonderful creation. I can see what a marvelous God you are because of the marvelous things you have created for me to enjoy. God, thank you for your wisdom and your imagination. And God, with all your power, your might, your wisdom, and your imagination, thank you for being a God who cares about me and loves me. Thank you, God.

My prayer for today—including any journaling thoughts I may want to add. Where am I today spiritually, emotionally, physically, financially, generally?

Today's Date: _____

Old Testament verse for today: Psalm 19:7 thru 13

God's laws are perfect. They protect us, make us wise, and give us joy and light. God's laws are pure, eternal, just. They are more desirable than gold. They are sweeter than honey dripping from a honeycomb. For they warn us away from harm and give success to those who obey them. But how can I know what sins are lurking in my heart? Cleanse me from these hidden faults. And keep me from deliberate wrongs; help me to stop doing them. Only then can I be free of guilt and innocent of some great crime.

One possible prayer for today:

God, you know that I am unable to keep your laws, even though your laws are perfect. Even though, if I could follow them, they would make me wise and give me joy and light. If I could consistently obey them, they would warn me away from harm and give me success. But, Lord, you know that I continue to fail to keep your laws all the time. You know that there is always sin lurking in my heart. Help me to stay away from deliberate wrongs. And, Lord, thank you for cleansing me from my hidden faults. Thank you for freeing me of the guilt that I deserve because I continue to let you down. Thank you for loving me and always taking me back into your care when I confess my sins and return to you.

New Testament verse for today: Galatians 3:12 & 13a

How different from this way of faith is the way of law which says that a man is saved by obeying every law of God, without one slip. But Christ has bought us out of the doom of that impossible system by taking the curse for our wrongdoing upon himself.

One possible prayer for today:

God, thank you for giving me another method of salvation; one that I can understand and one that makes it possible for me to be acceptable to you. You knew that I could not keep every one of your laws all of the time. You knew that there was sin lurking in my heart and that I was filled with hidden faults and continued to deliberately go my own way. So, Lord, you loved me so much that you sent your Son, Jesus, to buy me out of the doom of failing to obey each and every one of your laws. Thank you for sending Christ to take the curse of my sins upon himself so that I might be acceptable to you. Thank you, Lord, for loving me so much.

My prayer for today—including any journaling thoughts I may want to add. Where am I today spiritually, emotionally, physically, financially, generally?

Today's Date: _____

Old Testament verse for today: Psalm 19:14

May my spoken words and unspoken thoughts be pleasing even to you, O Lord my Rock and my Redeemer.

One possible prayer for today:

God, I know that I often fail you in both my spoken words and unspoken thoughts. Thank you for always forgiving me when I return to you and confess my failings to you. Help me to do a better job of controlling my words and my thoughts. Help me to be more concerned about my words and my thoughts being pleasing to you. Thank you for always being there as my Rock and my Redeemer. Thank you, Lord.

New Testament verse for today: Colossians 4:6

Make the most of your chances to tell others the Good News. Be wise in all your contacts with them. Let your conversation be gracious as well as sensible, for then you will have the right answer for everyone.

One possible prayer for today:

God, help me to have both my spoken words and unspoken thoughts be acceptable to you. Lord, you have done so much for me. Thank you for doing so much for me. The least that I can do for you is to tell others about how good you are. Help me to make the most of my chances to do that. Help me to be gracious and sensible in my conversations with others. Help me to have the right answers in telling others about you and how wonderful you are. Thank you for giving me the wisdom that you have given me. Help me to do a better joy of using that wisdom for your honor and glory.

My prayer for today—including any journaling thoughts I may want to add. Where am I today spiritually, emotionally, physically, financially, generally?

Today's Date: _____

Old Testament verse for today: Psalm 20:4

May he grant you your heart's desire and fulfill all your plans.

One possible prayer for today:

God, that is a little scary for me; because, I know that sometimes my heart's desires may not be desires that would please you. Sometimes my plans are not those that would bring honor and glory to your name. So help me, Lord. Help me to have desires and plans that are in line with your will for my life. Give me the wisdom and the discipline to look to you for guidance before I make my plans and before I get my heart set on desire. Thank you for helping me, Lord. And, thank you for being patient with me when my heart's desires and my plans stray from the path that you have set for me.

New Testament verse for today: Titus 3:4 thru 7

But when the time came for the kindness and love of God our Savior to appear, then he saved us—not because we were good enough to be saved, but because of his kindness and pity—by washing away our sins and giving us the new joy of the indwelling Holy Spirit whom he poured out upon us with wonderful fullness—and all because of what Jesus Christ our Savior did so that he could declare us good in God's eyes—all because of his great kindness; and now we can share in the wealth of the eternal life he gives us, and we are eagerly looking forward to receiving it.

One possible prayer for today:

God, thank you for your kindness and your pity to me. Thank you for washing away my sins, even though I was undeserving of such an act. Thank you for your limitless love to me even when my heart's desires and my plans are not in line with your will for my life. Thank you for caring for me so much that you gave me the indwelling of your Holy Spirit with all of his wonderful fullness. Thank you for giving me Jesus, who made all of this possible for me. Thank you for letting me share in the wealth of the eternal life that Christ gives to me. Thank you, God, for your love and your faithfulness to me—even though I am undeserving of it.

My prayer for today—including any journaling thoughts I may want to add. Where am I today spiritually, emotionally, physically, financially, generally?

Today's Date: _____

Old Testament verse for today: Psalm 23

Because the Lord is my shepherd, I have everything I need! He lets me rest in the meadow grass and leads me beside the quiet streams. He restores my failing health. He helps me do what honors him most. Even when walking through the dark valley of death I will not be afraid, for you are close beside me, guarding, guiding all the way. You provide delicious food for me in the presence of my enemies. You have welcomed me as your guest; blessings overflow! Your goodness and unfailing kindness shall be with me all of my life, and afterwards I will live with you forever in your home.

One possible prayer for today:

God, what wonderful thoughts these are! Thank you for being my shepherd. Thank you for giving me the things that you think that I need. Thank you for restoring my health when it fails. And, Lord, I need to remember that you help me do those things which honor you the most. Thank you for guarding me and guiding me every step along my way of life. Thank you for giving me my physical needs. Thank you for making me your guest and letting your blessings, your goodness, and your unfailing kindness overflow all of my life. And, Lord, thank you for your promise that I will spend eternity with you in your home. Thank you, Lord.

New Testament verse for today: I Peter 5: 6 & 7

If you will humble yourselves under the mighty hand of God, in his good time he will lift you up. Let him have all your worries and cares, for he is always thinking about you and watching everything that concerns you.

One possible prayer for today:

God, thank you for caring about the things that concern me. I do humble myself before you and ask for your continued love and care. Thank you for lifting me up when it fits your purposes for my life. Lord, thank you for shouldering all my worries and cares. Thank you for letting me give them to you. Thank you for always thinking about me and watching over me. Thank you, God.

My prayer for today—including any journaling thoughts I may want to add. Where am I today spiritually, emotionally, physically, financially, generally?

Today's Date: _____

Old Testament verse for today: Psalm 24:8

Our help is from the Lord who made heaven and earth.

One possible prayer for today:

What an awesome God you are! All things that have been made have been made by you, God. And to think that with all your glory, power, and might, that you still care about me and are willing to help me. I honor you and give you glory, oh God; and, ask that you will help me this day. Give me wisdom to conduct my affairs in all areas. Give me efficiency and effectiveness in all that I do. And, Lord, let me always remember to give you thanks for all your help.

New Testament verse for today: Matthew 5:44 & 45

But I say: Love your enemies! Pray for those who persecute you! In that way you will be acting as true sons of your Father in heaven.

One possible prayer for today:

God, that is really tough for me to do! I don't want to pray for my enemies and those who persecute me! I want to get even! What I would really like to pray, is that you take them down a notch, and help me get even! But, Lord, I know that that is not what Christ taught. I know that I cannot fulfill that challenge without your help. And, first of all, I need a real change of heart. Only you can change my heart, Lord. So, help me. Help me to have the right attitude and help me be more receptive to listening to your leading in my life. Lord, I probably can't make this change all at once; but, with your help, I can make one small step in that direction today. Thank you for helping me.

My prayer for today—including any journaling thoughts I may want to add. Where am I today spiritually, emotionally, physically, financially, generally?

Today's Date: _____

Old Testament verse for today: Psalm 25:1 thru 3a

To you, O Lord, I pray. Don't fail me, Lord, for I am trusting you. Don't let my enemies succeed. Don't give them victory over me. None who have faith in God will ever be disgraced for trusting him.

One possible prayer for today:

God, I do pray to you and plead with you; for I have no place else to turn! I am trusting you—and you alone! Don't let my enemies have victory over me. Don't let them win! Lord, give me greater faith in your power and greater confidence in your plans for my life today. Let my faith and my trust increase; and, God, I claim the Psalmist's promise that I will never be disgraced for trusting you.

New Testament verse for today: Matthew 6:15 & 16

"Don't hide your light! Let it shine for all; let your good deeds glow for all to see, so that they will praise your heavenly Father."

One possible prayer for today:

God, give me the power to actually do some good deeds for your honor today! But, Lord, let me remember that it is your power that I am using. I know that I cannot do your work properly without plugging into your power. And, Lord, even if I do have some success today, and it is noticed, don't let me get into an ego trip over any success that I have. Let anything I do today be done in such a manner that it will bring praise to you. Thank you, Lord, for letting me have some wins today that will bring glory and honor to you.

My prayer for today—including any journaling thoughts I may want to add. Where am I today spiritually, emotionally, physically, financially, generally?

Today's Date: _____

Old Testament verse for today: Psalm 25:4 thru 7

Show me the path where I should go, O Lord; point out the right road for me to walk. Lead me; teach me; for you are the God who gives me salvation. I have no hope except in you. Overlook my youthful sins, O Lord! Look at me instead through eyes of mercy and forgiveness, through eyes of everlasting love and kindness.

One possible prayer for today:

God, do show me the path where I should go. Always point out the right road for me; but, Lord, especially do that for me today, I pray. Do lead me and teach me. Thank you for being the God who gives me salvation. Lord, I do not have any hope except in you, and thank you for that hope. And, God, thank you for forgiving my sins—not only of my youth; but, of every age; because I continue to sin! And, God, thank you for looking at me through your eyes of mercy, forgiveness, everlasting love, and kindness. Lord, what a great God you are. Thank you for being such a great God to me.

New Testament verse for today: I Corinthians 1:8 & 9

And he (God) guarantees right up to the end that you will be counted free from all sin and guilt on the day when he returns. God will surely do this for you, for he always does just what he says, and he is the one who invited you in to this wonderful friendship with his Son, even Christ our Lord.

One possible prayer for today:

God, thank you for that guarantee! Thank you for counting me free from all my sin and guilt if I will only accept your invitation into this wonderful friendship with Christ. God, thank you for being a God upon whom we can count to do what you say. Thank you for that wonderful invitation. Thank you for doing this for me.

My prayer for today—including any journaling thoughts I may want to add. Where am I today spiritually, emotionally, physically, financially, generally?

Today's Date: _____

Old Testament verse for today: Psalm 25:8 thru 11

The Lord is good and glad to teach the proper path to all those who go astray; he will teach the ways that are right and best to those who humbly turn to him. And when we obey him, every path he guides us on is fragrant with his lovingkindness and his truth. But, Lord, my sins! How many they are. Oh, pardon them for the honor of your name.

One possible prayer for today:

God, thank you for being such a good God. Thank you for being glad to teach me the proper path. Thank you for teaching me the ways that are right and best for me. Thank you for guiding my paths and making them fragrant with your lovingkindness and truth. And, Lord, when I sin, which is often, thank you for pardoning me for the honor of your name anytime I humbly turn to you. Thank you, Lord, for your guidance, for your teaching, for your lovingkindness, and for your eternal pardon.

New Testament verse for today: Hebrews 10:18 thru 20

Now, when sins have once been forever forgiven and forgotten, there is no need to offer more sacrifices to get rid of them. And so, dear brothers, now we may walk right into the very Holy of Holies where God is, because of the blood of Jesus. This is the fresh, new, life-giving way which Christ has opened up for us by tearing the curtain—his human body—to let us into the holy presence of God.

One possible prayer for today:

God, what a wonderful God you are! To think that because of Christ's sacrifice, by sins are not only forgiven; but, they are forever forgotten! That is a concept almost too incredible for me to understand! Thank you for letting me come directly to you with my praises and my prayers. Thank you for providing this fresh, new, life-giving way for me to come into your presence. Thank you for being not just a holy God, but, a God full of lovingkindness. Thank you, God.

My prayer for today—including any journaling thoughts I may want to add. Where am I today spiritually, emotionally, physically, financially, generally?

Today's Date: _____

Old Testament verse for today: Psalm 25:12 & 13

Where is the man who fears the Lord? God will teach him how to choose the best. He shall live within God's circle of blessing, and his children shall inherit the earth.

One possible prayer for today:

God, you know that I honor and worship you. You know that I fear your awesome power. God, thank you for your promise that you will always be there with me to help me choose the best way, if I will only turn to you for your help. Lord, thank you for letting me live within your circle of blessing. Thank you for letting your blessing flow to my children. Thank you for being such a loving, caring, patient God.

New Testament verse for today: James 4:5 & 6

Or what do you think the Scripture means when it says that the Holy Spirit, whom God has placed within us, watches over us with tender jealousy? But he gives us more and more strength to stand against all such evil longings. As the Scripture says, God gives strength to the humble, but sets himself against the proud and haughty.

One possible prayer for today:

God, thank you for your loving Holy Spirit. Thank you for giving me your loving Holy Spirit. Thank you for having your loving Holy Spirit watch over me with tender jealousy. Thank you for the strength to stand against the evil desires that are a part of my human nature. Lord, don't let me ever be proud and haughty enough to believe that I can make it in this life without your love and the love of your Holy Spirit. Thank you for being there for me to help me choose the best way for me life. Thank you for keeping me in your wonderful circle of blessing.

My prayer for today—including any journaling thoughts I may want to add. Where am I today spiritually, emotionally, physically, financially, generally?

Today's Date: _____

Old Testament verse for today: Psalm 25:14

Friendship with God is reserved for those who reverence him. With them alone he shares the secrets of his promises.

One possible prayer for today:

God, thank you for reserving a place for me among those you call your friends. God, you know that I do reverence you. You know my heart. You know that I often fail to live up to your expectations for me. Thank you for forgiving me when I fail you and then return to you with honest humility and request your forgiveness. Thank you for sharing the secrets of your promises with me. And, God, thank you most of all for my salvation, which is your free gift to me, as one of your friends. Thank you, God.

New Testament verse for today: John 16:13

When the Holy Spirit, who is truth, comes, he shall guide you into all truth, for he will not be presenting his own ideas, but will be passing on to you what he has heard. He will tell you about the future.

One possible prayer for today:

God, thank you for sending your loving Holy Spirit to guide me into all truth. Thank you for working in my life through your loving Holy Spirit. Thank you for giving me the promise of an eternal future with you because I believe in you and your Son, Jesus. God, I do believe. Thank you for giving me the faith to believe.

My prayer for today—including any journaling thoughts I may want to add. Where am I today spiritually, emotionally, physically, financially, generally?

Today's Date: _____

Old Testament verse for today: Psalm 25:15 thru 18

My eyes are ever looking to the Lord for help, for he alone can rescue me. Come, Lord, and show me your mercy, for I am helpless, overwhelmed, in deep distress; my problems go from bad to worse. Oh, save me from them all! See my sorrows; feel my pain, forgive my sins.

One possible prayer for today:

God, I do look to you alone to help me through my problems. No one else can help me! No one else can give me the guidance that I need to get through this time in my life. Only you can rescue me! Lord, thank you for being there for me. Thank you for listening to my pleadings and my cries for help. Lord, I am overwhelmed and in deep distress. I am really hurting! And things seem to get worse instead of better. God, thank you for showing me your mercy at this time. Thank you for seeing my sorrows and for feeling my pain. Lord, thank you for coming quickly to show me your mercy. And, Lord, for any sin in my life, I confess it to you. Thank you for forgiving me. Thank you for being such a caring and loving God who is always there for me.

New Testament verse for today: II Corinthians 4:8 thru 10

We are pressed on every side by troubles, but not crushed or broken. We are perplexed because we don't know why things happen as they do, but we don't give up and quit. We are hunted down, but God never abandons us. We get knocked down, but we get up again and keep going. These bodies of ours are constantly facing death just as Jesus did; so it is clear to all that it is only the living Christ within who keeps us safe.

One possible prayer for today:

God, I feel just like this. I feel pressed on every side by my problems. I feel perplexed because I don't understand why things happen as they do. I feel hunted down by my problems. Lord, I may not be facing death, even though sometimes I feel like it might be easier to throw in the towel and die! So, Lord, I claim your promise that you will never abandon me. I claim your promise that the living Christ within me will not only keep me safe; but, will keep me from being crushed and broken; will help me to keep going and not quit. God, listen to my pleadings for your help. Please come quickly to my aid. Give me the wisdom and the guidance to make good decisions during this time of trial so that I don't create more and deeper problems. Thank you for hearing my prayers, Lord. Thank you for coming quickly to my aid.

My prayer for today—including any journaling thoughts I may want to add. Where am I today spiritually, emotionally, physically, financially, generally?

Today's Date: _____

Old Testament verse for today: Psalm 25:21

Assign me Godliness and Integrity as my bodyguards, for I expect you to protect me.

One possible prayer for today:

God, I expect so much from you. I ask so much from you. And you give me so much. And all you require from me is my love. What a one-sided relationship we have, O Lord. And yet, that is the relationship that you have designed for me so that I may spend eternity in your presence. Thank you for giving me such a one-sided relationship so that even I, in all my weakness, am able to keep my part of the bargain. I do love you, Lord. Thank you again and again for loving me.

New Testament verse for today: Hebrews 9:24 thru 26

For Christ has entered into heaven itself, to appear now before God as our Friend. It was not in the earthly place of worship that he did this, for that was merely a copy of the real temple in heaven. Nor has he offered himself again and again, as the high priest down here on earth offers animal blood in the Holy of Holies each year. If that had been necessary, then he would have had to die again and again, ever since the world began. But no! He came once for all, at the end of the age, to put away the power of sin forever by dying for us.

One possible prayer for today:

God, thank you for making Christ my friend! Thank you for sending Christ to die on the cross for my sins. Thank you for having a plan of salvation for me that is so simple that even I can avail myself of your plan. God, what a wonderful one-sided relationship you have designed for me. Thank you for loving me so much. Thank you for accepting my love.

My prayer for today—including any journaling thoughts I may want to add. Where am I today spiritually, emotionally, physically, financially, generally?

Today's Date: _____

Old testament verse for today: Psalm 26:1 thru 3

Dismiss all the charges against me, Lord, for I have tried to keep your laws and have trusted you without wavering. Cross examine me, O Lord, and see that this is so; test my motives and affections too. For I have taken your lovingkindness and your truth as my ideals.

One possible prayer for today:

God, you know my heart. There is nothing that I can do that can fool you. You know that I have tried to live as you would want me to live. You also know how often I fail. You have given me faith to trust you without wavering; and, I really try to do that. You know my motives and my affections. Lord, I do know that your lovingkindness and your truth are the ideals that I should have for my life. But, Lord, you know how often I fall short of these ideals. So, God, thank you for dismissing all the charges against me when I come to you with true humility and ask for your forgiveness. Thank you for wiping all these shortcomings from my record. Thank you for being such a loving and forgiving God to me.

New Testament verse for today: John 11:41b & 42a

"Father, thank you for hearing me. You always hear me, of course."

One possible prayer for today:

God, thank you for always hearing me, just as you always heard your Son, Jesus. Thank you for always listening to my prayers and pleadings. Thank you for never moving away from me, no matter what I do. So, God, just now, once again forgive me. Just now once again dismiss all the charges against me. Thank you, God, for dismissing all these charges against me.

My prayer for today—including any journaling thoughts I may want to add. Where am I today spiritually, emotionally, physically, financially, generally?

Today's Date: _____

Old Testament verse for today: Psalm 27:1 thru 3

The Lord is my light and my salvation: whom shall I fear? When evil men come to destroy me, they will stumble and fall! Yes, though a mighty army marches against me, my heart shall know no fear! I am confident that God will save me.

One possible prayed for today:

God, thank you for being my light and my salvation. Thank you for giving me the peace in my heart that passes all understanding. Thank you for protecting me from the evils in life that beset me on every corner. Thank you for giving me the confidence that I need to go about my every day life, knowing that you are always with me, guiding and protecting me. Thank you for being my personal God.

New Testament verse for today: Hebrews 3:6

But Christ, God's faithful Son, is in complete charge of God's house. And we Christians are God's house—he lives in us!—if we keep up our courage firm to the end, and our joy and our trust in the Lord.

One possible prayer for today:

God, thank you for being my light and my salvation. Thank you for putting your faithful Son, Jesus, in charge of everything, including my life, because he lives in me! What a wonderful premise. Thank you for letting Christ live in me. Thank you for giving me the strength and the courage to keep my faith firm to the end. Thank you for giving me the strength and the courage to keep my joy and trust in you and your Son, Jesus, firm and vibrant to the end. Thank you for your wonderful plan of salvation for me, Lord. Thank you for making that plan available to me. Thank you for always loving and caring for me. Thank you, God.

My prayer for today—including any journaling thoughts I may want to add. Where am I today spiritually, emotionally, physically, financially, generally?

Today's Date: _____

Old Testament verse for today: Psalm 27:11 Today's date;
Tell me what to do, O Lord, and make it plain because I am surrounded by waiting enemies.

One possible prayer for today:
Lord, this is a day when I feel beset on every side. This is a day when I need you to tell me exactly what to do—which way to turn—what decisions to make. Lord, I am coming to you to ask that you make it very plain which way I should turn. I can't seem to find a solution on my own. I need your help! Lord, please help me. Please be near to me. Please give me clear direction. Please let me listen to your direction and act as you would have me act. Thank you, Lord, for hearing me. Thank you for listening to me. Thank you for the help and the direction that you are going to give me. Thank you, Lord.

New Testament verse for today: Mark 10:27
Jesus looked at them intently, then said, "Without God, it is utterly impossible. But with God everything is possible."

One possible prayer for today:
God, thank you for being a God that makes everything possible! Thank you for being a God who can take the impossible and make it not only possible, but feasible. Thank you for taking my present problems and giving me a possible and feasible answer. Thank you for hearing me. Thank you for listening to me. Thank you for your help and the direction you are going to give me. Thank you for being the God of making all things possible! Thank you, God.

My prayer for today—including any journaling thoughts I may want to add. Where am I today spiritually, emotionally, physically, financially, generally?

Today's Date: _____

Old Testament verse for today: Psalm 27:13 & 14

I am expecting the Lord to rescue me again, so that once again I will see his goodness to me here in the land of the living. Don't be impatient! Wait for the Lord, and he will come and save you! Be brave, stouthearted and courageous. Yes, wait and he will help you.

One possible prayer for today:

God, thank you for that promise of the psalmist! I am expecting you to rescue me again from whatever problems I have again created by my actions. Thank you for giving me the patience I need to wait for you to save me. I must admit, Lord, that I get real impatient for you to respond to my needs and my prayers. So, help me not to be impatient. Help me to truly wait for you to act. Thank you for helping me to be brave, stouthearted and courageous. And, Lord, thank you for giving me the faith that I need to know that you will respond to my needs with your own plans and your own timing.

New Testament verse for today: Luke 12:21, 25 & 31

"Yes, every man is a fool who gets rich on earth but not in heaven. And besides, what's the use of worrying? What good does it do? Will it add a single day to your Life? Of course not! He will always give you all you need from day to day if you make the Kingdom of God your primary concern."

One possible prayer for today:

I know, Lord, that that promise sounds pretty good in principle. But, what about today when I don't have enough money to buy food for my family or to pay the rent? What about my car payments and the credit card payments? What do I do? Where should I turn? Maybe I have created this situation by not focusing on what you want of me. Maybe I have been too concerned about material things and not concerned enough about my spiritual life. Maybe I have been a fool pursuing earthly riches instead of trying to please you. Maybe I should have been asking for your help and guidance, and listening to you before I got into all of this problem instead of waiting until I had created the problem, and then come pleading. Lord, let me learn from my mistakes. But, right now, please give me the wisdom to make good decisions in this bad time for me and my family. Help me; but, let me learn to rely on you more all the time in every situation. Thank you, Lord, for putting up with me and for continuing to listen to me and to help me.

My prayer for today—including any journaling thoughts I may want to add. Where am I today spiritually, emotionally, physically, financially, generally?

Today's Date: _____

Old Testament verse for today: Psalm 28:6

Oh, praise the Lord, for he has listened to my pleadings! He is my strength, my shield from every danger. I trusted in him, and he helped me. Joy rises in my heart until I burst out in songs of praise to him.

One possible prayer for today:

God, let me always praise you for what you are doing and what you have done in my life. Thank you for always hearing my pleadings; and, thank you for responding to my pleadings by helping me. Thank you for being my strength, and my shield from every danger. Thank you for giving me the faith to trust you in all situations. Thank you for helping me. Thank you for restoring joy in my life so that I just cannot help praising your name and thanking you. Let me always sing your praises, Lord. Thank you, Lord.

New Testament verse for today: Acts 2:25 & 26

King David quoted Jesus as saying: "I know the Lord is always with me. He is helping me. God's mighty power supports me. No wonder my heart is filled with joy and my tongue shouts his praises! For I know all will be well with me in death—"

One possible prayer for today:

God, I know that you are always with me. I know that you are always helping me. I know that your mighty power is always there to support me. How can my heart not be filled with joy? How can my tongue not shout your praises? I know that you are always with me in life; and, I know that I have your promise that I will spend eternity with you if I will only accept your Son, Jesus, as my personal Savior. I do accept that gift, God. Thank you for making that gift available to me. Thank you for your help. Thank you for your mighty power. Thank you for your support in my every day struggles. Thank you, God.

My prayer for today—including any journaling thoughts I may want to add. Where am I today spiritually, emotionally, physically, financially, generally?

Today's Date: _____

Old Testament verse for today: Psalm 29:9

Oh, do not hide yourself when I am trying to find you. Do not angrily reject your servant. You have been my help in all my trials before; don't leave me now. Don't forsake me, O God of my salvation.

One possible prayer for today:

God, thank you for being there when I need you. Thank you for being there to help me in all my trials. Thank you for not rejecting me, even when I fail you. Thank you for never hiding yourself from me. Thank you for being the God of my salvation.

New Testament verse for today: I Thessalonians 5:24

May the God of peace himself make you entirely pure and devoted to God; and may your spirit and soul and body be kept strong and blameless until that day when our Lord Jesus Christ comes back again. God, who called you to become his child, will do all this for you, just as he promised.

One possible prayer for today:

God, thank you for being there when I need you. Thank you for giving me the strength and faith to be devoted to you. Thank you for never rejecting me. Thank you for forgiving me when I return to you so that my spirit and soul and body may appear blameless before you and Christ when Christ comes back again. Thank you for calling me to become your child. Thank you for your promises; and thank you for being a God who keeps and fulfills his promises. Thank you, God.

My prayer for today—including any journaling thoughts I may want to add. Where am I today spiritually, emotionally, physically, financially, generally?

Today's Date: _____

Old Testament verse for today: Psalm 30:1

I will praise you, Lord, for you have saved me from my enemies. You refuse to let them triumph over me.

One possible prayer for today:

Lord, thank you for always being there for me. There you for being someone to whom I may always turn for help. Thank you for always giving me the strength to get through the rough times. Thank you for saving me from my enemies and helping me to solve my problems. Thank you for giving me the triumphs that I have in my life. Thank you for being my loving and personal God.

New Testament verse for today: John 15:15

I no longer call you slaves, for a master doesn't confide in his slaves; now you are my friends, proved by the fact that I have told you everything the Father told me.

One possible prayer for today:

God, there is no question on how far you have gone to always be there for me! If I only believe, you have given me eternal life through your Son, Jesus. And, Jesus calls me His friend! How wonderful. This knowledge helps me to have the faith and confidence I need to tackle any problem and to hang in there when the going gets tough. It helps me to have the strength that I need to work through the hard times. Thank you, God, for all these wonderful promises that you have given to me. Thank you, again, for always being there for me.

My prayer for today—including any journaling thoughts I may want to add. Where am I today spiritually, emotionally, physically, financially, generally?

Today's Date: _____

Old Testament verse for today: Psalm 30:5

His anger last a moment; his favor lasts for life!

One possible prayer for today:

God, thank you for being merciful to me. Thank you for not staying angry at me. Thank you that your anger lasts only for a moment. And, God, thank you that your favor last for life. Thank you for being such a merciful God. Thank you.

New Testament verse for today: Romans 8:14

For all who are led by the Spirit of God are the sons of God.

One possible prayer for today:

God, I have asked you to take charge of my life. I have asked you to fill me with your Holy Spirit. I know that your promises are true; therefore, I can have confidence that your Holy Spirit is leading me. And, then I can have the confidence that I am one of your children! What a marvelous promise, Lord. How wonderful to operate with that confidence. Thank you, Lord, for leading me by your Spirit. Thank you for calling me one of your children.

My prayer for today—including any journaling thoughts I may want to add. Where am I today spiritually, emotionally, physically, financially, generally?

Today's Date: _____

Old Testament verse for today: Psalm 30:10 thru 12

Hear me, Lord; oh, have pity and help me. Then he turned my sorrow into joy! He took away my clothes of mourning and gave me gay and festive garments to rejoice in so that I might sing glad praises to the Lord instead of lying in silence in the grave.

One possible prayer for today:

Lord, on the days when I am hurting, let this plea of the Psalmist be my plea. And, Lord, if it is your will, let my result be the same as the result for the Psalmist! Hear my plea. Turn my sorrow into joy. Take away my mourning attitude and replace it with an attitude of joy. Let me sing praises to you always, Lord. Let my faith in you and in your plan for my life be so strong that I never cease praising you, Lord. Thank you for always being there for me, Lord. Thank you for your consistent love and care. Thank you, Lord.

New Testament verse for today: John 15:7 & 8

But if you stay in me and obey my commands, you may ask any request you like, and it will be granted! My true disciples produce bountiful harvest. This brings great glory to my father.

One possible prayer for today:

Lord, thank you for this promise. I know, Lord, that for this promise to be true for me, the key is whether or not I am a true disciple. If I am, then I know that I will only be asking for those things that are in line with your will for my life. I will be only asking for those things that, in fact, will bring glory to you. So, Lord, help me to live as one of your true disciples. Let me be so in touch with your will for my life that I do not ask for things that will not bring glory to you. Then, Lord, I know that my requests will be granted, and that I can produce bountiful harvests for you. Let me live in tune with your will for my life, Lord. Let me produce bountiful harvests and great glory for you.

My prayer for today—including any journaling thoughts I may want to add. Where am I today spiritually, emotionally, physically, financially, generally?

Today's Date: _____

Old Testament verse for today: Psalm 31:1 thru 5a

Lord, I trust in you alone. Don't let me enemies defeat me. Rescue me because you are the God who always does what is right. Answer quickly when I call to you; bend low and hear my whispered plea. Be for me a great Rock of safety from my foes. Yes, you are my Rock and my fortress; honor your name by leading me out of this peril. Pull me from the trap my enemies have set for me. For you are strong enough. Into your hand I commit my spirit.

One possible prayer for today:

God, that is a pretty awesome plea from your servant David; and, if I make that prayer to you, it pre-supposes that I am right and that my enemies are wrong. My enemies today are—(creditors, business transactions by competitors that are illegal, lying, sexual sins, drink or drug habits, stealing, dishonesty. Enemies can be things over which I have little control because others are involved, or things that are hurting my life over which I may be able to take control. Confess them here to God.) So, God, be my Rock. Be my Fortress. I cannot do it without you. Today, I am hurting and need you. Please help me, and Lord, I know that I am being selfish; but, if possible, please do it quickly!

New Testament verse for today: James 4:2b & 3

And yet the reason you don't have what you want is that you don't ask God for it. And even when you do ask you don't get it because your whole aim is wrong—you want only what will give you pleasure.

One possible prayer for today:

God, that really brings me to the place where the rubber meets the road! If I need correcting. If I am asking for the wrong things for the wrong reasons, please correct me. Help me to see the errors of my way and the errors in my thinking. But, God, as you correct me, please be gentle! Please remember that today I am pretty fragile. I need your guidance; I need your correction; and, I need a generous supply of wisdom and self control. But, I also need an overwhelming supply of your love. Please don't be too tough on me, Lord. Let me be listening for your guidance and extra sensitive to your leading. Thank you for correcting me gently!

My prayer for today—including any journaling thoughts I may want to add. Where am I today spiritually, emotionally, physically, financially, generally?

Today's Date: _____

Old Testament verse for today: Psalm 31:6

You have rescued me, O God who keeps his promises. I worship only you.

One possible prayer for today:

God, thank you for being a God who keeps his promises. Thank you for being a God who is worthy of my trust. Thank you for being a God who has the power to rescue me from every circumstances in which I put my trust in you. God, you know my heart. You know that I worship only you. Thank you for being a God who is so loving and kind that you accept my worship. Thank you, God.

New Testament verse for today: I Corinthians 3:11

And no one can ever lay any other real foundation than that one we already have—Jesus Christ.

One possible prayer for today:

God, thank you for being a God who keeps his promises. Thank you for being a God who is worthy of my trust. Thank you for being a God who laid the foundation for my salvation through your Son, Jesus. And, God, because you are a God worthy of my trust, I know that I can rely completely on your promise of salvation through Jesus. Thank you for being a God who has the power to rescue me from my sin and give me eternal life through your Son, Jesus. Thank you for this wonderful foundation you have laid for me. Thank you for making this marvelous plan of salvation available to me and making it so simple that I can understand it and accept it. Thank you, God.

My prayer for today—including any journaling thoughts I may want to add. Where am I today spiritually, emotionally, physically, financially, generally?

Today's Date: _____

Old Testament verse for today: Psalm 31:14 thru 17a

But I was trusting you, O Lord. I said, "You alone are my God; my times are in your hands. Rescue me from those who hunt me down relentlessly. Let your favor shine again upon your servant; save me just because you are so kind! Don't disgrace me, Lord, by not replying when I call to you for aid."

One possible prayer for today:

Lord, it is obvious that even David, whom you dearly loved, had enormous problems. His life didn't always go smoothly, or as he would have chosen for it to go. So, why should I think that my life should be any different? Why should I think that things should always go easy for me? Lord, I acknowledge that you alone are my God too. I acknowledge that my times are in your hands. I acknowledge that I am going to have some bad times. But, Lord, as David prayed, I pray that your favor will soon shine upon me once again. I thank you that you will help me through the morass that I feel that I am in at the present time. Let my faith remain strong, Lord. I need you more than ever right now. Comfort me and come to my aid, Lord. Thank you for hearing me and thank you for replying to me.

New Testament verse for today: Philippians 4:11b thru 13

—for I have learned how to get along happily whether I have much or little. I know how to live on almost nothing or with everything. I have learned the secret of contentment in every situation, whether it be with a full stomach or hunger, plenty or want; for I can do everything God asks me to with the help of Christ who gives me the strength and power.

One possible prayer for today:

God, above we saw that your servant David was in dire need. Here we see that your servant, the apostle Paul, also experienced great need. So, Lord, is there any reason why I shouldn't expect to face tough times in my life? Lord, give me the faith that David had to trust you in all situations. Give me the faith that Paul had that permits me to learn how to live in contentment no matter what I am experiencing. Give me the faith to trust you in all things and to know that your hand is guiding my life at all times. Thank you for giving me that faith right now when I need it. Thank you, Lord, for hearing my prayer and answering me.

My prayer for today—including any journaling thoughts I may want to add. Where am I today spiritually, emotionally, physically, financially, generally?

Today's Date: _____

Old Testament verse for today: Psalm 31:19

Oh, how great is your goodness to those who publicly declare that you will rescue them. For you have stored up great blessings for those who trust and reverence you.

One possible prayer for today:

God, let me always be strong enough in my faith to publicly declare your goodness and your love for me. Don't let me ever be ashamed of my belief and faith in you. And, then, God, I claim the Psalmist's promise that you have stored up great blessings for me if I trust and reverence you. God, I do trust you. I know that I sometimes fail to properly reverence you; so, Lord, continue to consider me a work in progress and, thank you for never giving up on me. Thank you for your patience, Lord.

New Testament verse for today: I Corinthians 10:29b thru 31

But why, you may ask, must I be guided and limited by what someone else thinks? If I can thank God for the food and enjoy it, why let someone spoil everything just because he thinks I am wrong? Well, I'll tell you why. It is because you must do everything for the glory of God, even your eating and drinking.

One possible prayer for today:

God, let me give you glory in everything I do. Let me use moderation in the things that may cause others to wonder about my commitment to you. Lord, my commitment doesn't vary, even if my actions sometimes don't show that commitment. Thank you for permitting me to enjoy good food and drink. Let me never be unthankful for what you permit me to have and to enjoy. Let me be considerate of the feelings of others, so that in my actions I show your love and concern to others. Thank you for helping me in this area, Lord.

My prayer for today—including any journaling thoughts I may want to add. Where am I today spiritually, emotionally, physically, financially, generally?

Today's Date: _____

Old Testament verse for today: Psalm 31:21

Blessed is the Lord, for he has shown me that his never failing love protects me like the walls of a fort!

One possible prayer for today:

Lord, what a wonderful thought that is! Thank you for giving me a love that is never failing. Thank you for protecting me like having the walls of a fort around me. Thank you for always being there for me, even when I fail you. Thank you, Lord. Thank you.

New Testament verse for today: Romans 8:1 thru 4

So there is now no condemnation awaiting those who belong to Christ Jesus. For the power of the life-giving Spirit—and the power is mine through Christ Jesus—has freed me from the vicious circle of sin and death. We aren't saved from sin's grasp by knowing the commandments of God, because we can't and don't keep them, but God put into effect a different plan to save us. He sent his own Son in a human body like ours—except that ours are sinful—and destroyed sin's control over us by giving himself as a sacrifice for our sins. So now we can obey God's laws if we follow after the Holy Spirit and no longer obey the old nature within us.

One possible prayer for today:

God, thank you for giving me Christ Jesus to forgive me of all my sins and to take them away never to be thought of again! What a great plan you provided for my salvation. Lord, I know that I can't meet all the requirements of your commandments. I know that I will continue to fall short of your ideal for my life. So, I thank you for giving me a different plan. Thank you for giving me a plan that I can follow—just believing and trusting in your Son, Jesus. God, I'm not sure that I always understand the part that your loving Holy Spirit plays in my life; but, I know that if I trust in Jesus as the sacrifice for my sins, that all of the rest will take care of itself. Thank you for making it so simple that even I can believe and trust.

My prayer for today—including any journaling thoughts I may want to add. Where am I today spiritually, emotionally, physically, financially, generally?

Today's Date: _____

Old Testament verse for today: Psalm 31:23 & 24

Oh, love the Lord, all you who are his people; for the Lord protects those who are loyal to him, but harshly punishes all who haughtily reject him. So cheer up! Take courage if you are depending on the Lord.

One possible prayer for today:

Lord, let me love you more. Don't ever let me become so proud that I even consider rejecting you in any manner. Lord, protect me at all times. Reward my loyalty with your everlasting protection. I am cheerful. I do take courage. Lord, I am depending on you and know that your protection is always there for me. Thank you, God, for your protection.

New Testament verse for today: Mark 5:36

But Jesus ignored their comments and said to Jairus, "Don't be afraid. Just trust me."

One possible prayer for today:

Lord, give me the faith to always trust you. You are my protection, Lord. I do depend on you at all times. I know that if my faith is strong enough I don't ever have to be afraid. All I need to do is trust. Give me the faith to always believe that strongly, Lord. Thank you for that gift of faith.

My prayer for today—including any journaling thoughts I may want to add. Where am I today spiritually, emotionally, physically, financially, generally?

Today's Date: _____

Old Testament verse for today: Psalm 32:1 & 2

What happiness for those whose guilt has been forgiven! What joys when sins are covered over! What relief for those who have confessed their sins and God has cleared their record.

One possible prayer for today:

God, what a wonderful God you are! Thank you for forgiving my guilt and giving me happiness. Thank you for covering over my sins and giving me joy. Thank you for clearing my record and giving me relief when I confess my sins to you and ask for your forgiveness. Thank you for being such a loving and forgiving. God.

New Testament verse for today: Galatians 2:20

I have been crucified with Christ: and I myself no longer live, but Christ lives in me. And the real life I now have within this body is a result of my trusting in the Son of God, who loved me and gave himself for me.

One possible prayer for today:

God, thank you for becoming man in the form of Jesus and dying on the cross for my sins. Lord, I know that I could never stand the pain of being crucified; but, you did that for me, so that my crucifixion is spiritual and not physical. I didn't have to bear all the pain. All I have to do is believe and trust in your plan for my salvation. Thank you for loving me so much that you gave yourself for me in the form of Jesus. Thank you, God.

My prayer for today—including any journaling thoughts I may want to add. Where am I today spiritually, emotionally, physically, financially, generally?

Today's Date: _____

Old Testament verse for today: Psalm 32:4 & 5

All day and all night your hand was heavy on me. My strength evaporated like water on a sunny day until I finally admitted all my sins to you and stopped trying to hide them. I said to myself, "I will confess them to the Lord." And you forgave me! All my guilt is gone.

One possible prayer for today:

God, you are so wonderful! Even when you lay a heavy hand of guilt on me, it is for my own good. Even when you withdraw some of your wonderful blessings from me, it is for my benefit to make me face up to my sins. And, Lord, you are so forgiving. When I finally admit my sins to you and stop trying to hide them, you are always ready to forgive and forget. When I confess them to you, you are always there for me. Thank you for forgiving me, Lord. Thank you for removing my guilt.

New Testament verse for today: Luke 7:50

And Jesus said to the woman, "Your faith has saved you; go in peace."

One possible prayer for today:

Lord, thank you for the consistency of your plan of salvation. Just as faith gave salvation to the woman in Jesus' time, so my faith will bring me eternal life in today's world. What a wonderful, consistent plan of salvation you have for all of us. Thank you for my salvation, Lord. Thank you for giving me the gift of faith so that I may avail myself of your plan of salvation. Thank you, Lord.

My prayer for today—including any journaling thoughts I may want to add. Where am I today spiritually, emotionally, physically, financially, generally?

Today's Date: _____

Old Testament verse for today: Psalm 32:6

Now I say that each believer should confess his sins to God when he is aware of them, while there is time to be forgiven. Judgment will not touch him if he does.

One possible prayer for today:

God, thank you for being there when I become aware of my sins and want to confess them to you. Thank you for making time for me to confess them. Thank you for forgiving me of my sins when I confess them. Thank you for removing me from the judgment of my sins when I confess them. Thank you, Lord, for your faithfulness of always forgiving me when I come back to you and confess my sins to you. Thank you, Lord.

New Testament verse for today: Hebrews 10:38 & 39

And those whose faith has made them good in God's sight must live by faith, trusting him in everything. Otherwise, if they shrink back, God will have no pleasure in them. But we have never turned our backs on God and sealed our fate. No, our faith in him assures our souls' salvation.

One possible prayer for today:

God, thank you for making me good in your sight because of my faith. Lord, I know that I would not and could not be good in your sight except for your forgiveness. Thank you for helping me to trust you in everything. Don't let me ever shrink back from trusting you, Lord. Let your pleasure always be in my life. Don't let me even think of turning my back on you, God. Thank you for the gift from you of my faith. Thank you for the assurance of my souls' salvation because of my faith. Thank you, God.

My prayer for today—including any journaling thoughts I may want to add. Where am I today spiritually, emotionally, physically, financially, generally?

Today's Date: _____

Old Testament verse for today: Psalm 32:7 & 8

You are my hiding place from every storm of life; you even keep me from getting into trouble! You surround me with songs of victory. I will instruct you (says the Lord) and guide you along the best pathway for your life; I will advise you and watch your progress.

One possible prayer for today:

God, thank you for being my hiding place from the storms of life. And, Lord, I need you a lot of the time. Lord, I know that you have kept me from getting into trouble many times; but, Lord, with my bull-headed ways, I still get into lots of trouble on my own! And, then after I have made the mistakes that cause me the trouble, I come running back to you to protect me. Thank you for instructing me, Lord. Let me heed your instructions all the time—not just when it looks like it fits into my plans. Let me accept your guidance along the best pathways for my life. Thank you for advising me and watching my progress. And, Lord, thank you for being patient with me and forgiving me when I don't take your advice. Thank you, Lord. Thank you for always being there as my hiding place, even after I have blundered out on my own without taking your advice.

New Testament verse for today: II Corinthians 5:9

So our aim is to please him always in everything we do, whether we are here in this body or away from this body and with him in heaven.

One possible prayer for today:

God, I have the feeling it will be easier for me to please you when I am with you in heaven than it is to please you while I am here on earth! Even though my aim and my goal is to please you in everything that I do, I know that I often fail to do that. I am pretty stubborn about getting my own way. Often, I think that I know the best way and forget to ask for your guidance. So, Lord, continue to help me. Continue to guide my pathways. And thank you for forgiving me when I fail you. Thank you, Lord.

My prayer for today—including any journaling thoughts I may want to add. Where am I today spiritually, emotionally, physically, financially, generally?

Today's Date: _____

Old Testament verse for today: Psalm 33:4 & 5

For all God's words are right, and everything he does is worthy of our trust. He loves whatever is just and good; the earth is filled with his tender love.

One possible prayer for today:

God, thank you for being worthy of my trust. Thank you for giving me words that are right. Thank you for giving me a boundless love that fills the earth. God, I know that I can never be just and good without your forgiveness, so thank you for always forgiving me when I come back to you and ask for forgiveness, no matter what I have done to fail you. Thank you for making me just and good in your sight; and, thank you for letting me enjoy the wonderful earth that you have filled with your tender love and made for my enjoyment. Thank you, Lord.

New Testament verse for today: Colossians 1:27b

And this is the secret: that Christ in your hearts is your only hope of glory.

One possible prayer for today:

God, thank you for these wonderful words that are right. Thank you for giving me Jesus, who is my only hope of glory. Thank you for always being worthy of my trust. Thank you for filling the earth with your tender love in the form of Jesus who died on the cross and rose again so that I might be washed clean from my sins. Thank you for providing that wonderful, loving plan for me. Thank you again, God, for making me just and good in your sight, not because of anything that I have done; but, because of your tender love for me. Thank you, God.

My prayer for today—including any journaling thoughts I may want to add. Where am I today spiritually, emotionally, physically, financially, generally?

Today's Date: _____

Old Testament verse for today: Psalm 33:18 thru 21

But the eyes of the Lord are watching over those who fear him, who rely upon his steady love. He will keep them from death even in times of famine! We depend upon the Lord alone to save us. Only he can help us; he protects us like a shield. No wonder we are happy in the Lord! For we are trusting him. We trust his holy name.

One possible prayer for today:

God, thank you for watching over me. You know my heart. You know that I fear you and I do rely upon your steady love. Thank you for that steady love. Thank you for keeping me safe at all times and in all circumstances. Lord, I do count on you and you alone to protect me and save me. Thank you for being my shield. Thank you for being a God worthy of my complete trust.

New Testament verse for today: Philippians 1:20

For I live in eager expectation and hope that I will never do anything that will cause me to be ashamed of myself but that I will always be ready to speak out boldly for Christ while I am going through all these trials here, just as I have in the past; and that I will always be an honor to Christ, whether I live or whether I must die.

One possible prayer for today:

God, please give me the strength to always witness about your love and the love and sacrifice of your Son, Jesus. Thank you for being with me at all times, whether I am going through times of ease or times of trial. Thank you for watching over me. Thank you for giving me the faith to depend upon you—and you alone—no matter what my trials. Thank you for being my shield in these times of trial. Thank you for helping me be an honor to Christ and to his love no matter what my circumstances. And, God, thank you for always being there to forgive me when I fail to live up to your expectations for me. Thank you for your everlasting love and forgiveness.

My prayer for today—including any journaling thoughts I may want to add. Where am I today spiritually, emotionally, physically, financially, generally?

Today's Date: _____

Old Testament verse for today: Psalm 33:22

Yes, Lord, let your constant love surround us, for our hopes are in your alone.

One possible prayer for today:

God, thank you for your constant love. Thank you for letting me feel your constant love surrounding me. When things go well, I need to remember to thank you more often. When things are going badly, when I am feeling pressures, when I don't know which way to turn, then my only hope is in you. You are always there for me, giving me the peace and confidence that can only come from you. Thank you for being my everlasting hope.

New Testament verse for today: Revelation 3:20

Look! I have been standing at the door and constantly knocking. If anyone hears me calling him and opens the door, I will come in and fellowship with him and he with me.

One possible prayer for today:

Lord, thank you for never giving up on me. Thank you for your constant love and thank you for your constant knocking on the door of my heart. Thank you for always being there anytime I open the door of my heart to admit you into my life. Thank you for always being ready to fellowship with me and permit me to fellowship with you. Thank you for your constant love. Thank you for letting me feel your constant love surrounding me at all times. Thank you, Lord.

My prayer for today—including any journaling thoughts I may want to add. Where am I today spiritually, emotionally, physically, financially, generally?

Today's Date: _____

Old Testament verse for today: Psalm 34:1 thru 3

I will praise the Lord no matter what happens. I will constantly speak of his glories and grace. I will boast of all his kindness to me. Let all who are discouraged take heart. Let us praise the Lord together, and exalt his name.

One possible prayer for today:

Lord, thank you for the faith that you have given me to praise you in all circumstances—no matter what is happening. Thank you for giving me the faith to always speak of your glories and grace. God, thank you for being so kind to me. Thank you for giving me an extra shot of faith and encouragement when I am discouraged. Let me always join in praising you for your love and your grace. Thank you, Lord.

New Testament verse for today: James 5:11b

Job is an example of a man who continued to trust the Lord in sorrow; from his experiences we can see how the Lord's plan finally ended in good, for he is full of tenderness and mercy.

One possible prayer for today:

God, I pray that you will not test me to the degree that you tested Job. I do pray that my faith would be as strong as Job's in the event that I have to undergo that kind of testing. I thank you for the promise that your plan for my life will end in good in your eyes. Lord, give me the faith and the strength to accept and praise you no matter what my circumstances, as I know that if I am trusting you, you are in charge of my circumstances and therefore what is happening in my life is your will for me at that time. Thank you for being a God full of tenderness and mercy.

My prayer for today—including any journaling thoughts I may want to add. Where am I today spiritually, emotionally, physically, financially, generally?

Today's Date: _____

Old Testament verse for today: Psalm 34:7 thru 9

For the Angel of the Lord guards and rescues all who reverence him. Oh, put God to the test and see how kind he is! See for yourself the way his mercies shower down on all who trust in him. If you belong to the Lord, reverence him; for everyone who does this has everything he needs.

One possible prayer for today:

God, please send your Angel to guard and rescue me. Let me give you the reverence and adoration that you deserve, Lord. God, I am putting my trust in you to help me solve my problems. You know that I have probably caused these problems by my own actions; yet, Lord, I plead for your mercies to shower down on me. I do trust in you. I do reverence you. Lord, give me what you want me to have. And, Lord, give me the faith to accept that what you give me is what you think is best for me at this time in my life. Thank you, God, for hearing my pleadings and responding to my prayers.

New Testament verse for today: I Peter 1:6 & 7

So, be truly glad! There is wonderful joy ahead, even though the going is rough for a while down here. These trials are only to test your faith, to see whether or not it is strong and pure. It is being tested as fire tests gold and purifies it—and your faith is far more precious to God than mere gold; so if your faith remains strong after being tried in the test tube of fiery trials, it will bring you much praise and glory and honor on the day of his return.

One possible prayer for today:

God, I admit. I am having real trouble being truly glad for my present problems! I know that you have a plan for my life. I know that you will restore the joy to my life. But, Lord, right now, I am hurting real bad! My faith is not wavering, Lord; but, I would really like you to help me get through this present mess real quick! I know that my faith is a gift from you. Let it be steadfast through these problems. I know that my faith is precious to you— more precious than gold. Let it come through this moment stronger than ever. Lord, I am counting on your help right now—and the ultimate reward of spending eternity with you. Thank you for helping me right now, Lord.

My prayer for today—including any journaling thoughts I may want to add. Where am I today spiritually, emotionally, physically, financially, generally?

Today's Date: _____

Old Testament verse for today: Psalm 34:18

The Lord is close to those whose hearts are breaking; he rescues those who are humbly sorry for their sins. The good man does not escape all troubles—he has them too. But the Lord helps him in each and every one.

One possible prayer for today:

God, thank you for always being there for me. Thank you for rescuing me when my heart is breaking and I turn to you—humbly coming before you and confessing my sins. Lord, I know that even when I have not turned away from you, I am going to confront problems. But, Lord, I claim the Psalmist's promise that you will help me in each and every one. Please help me just now, Lord. Please tell me which way to turn. Thank you for hearing me just now, Lord.

New Testament verse for today: II Thessalonians 3:5

May the Lord bring you into an ever deeper understanding of the love of God and of the patience that comes from Christ.

One possible prayer for today:

God, help me to trust you more when I am in trouble. Bring me into an ever deeper understanding of your love—which I know has no bounds. Please help me to have the additional patience I need when I am hurting and want my problems solved right now! Please draw me closer to Christ and take advantage of the patience that comes from knowing and believing in Christ. Thank you for making your love and Christ's love a resource that is always there for me and a resource on which I can count anytime I come to you. Thank you, God.

My prayer for today—including any journaling thoughts I may want to add. Where am I today spiritually, emotionally, physically, financially, generally?

Today's Date: _____

Old Testament verse for today: Psalm 36:5 & 6

Your steadfast love, O Lord, is as great as all the heavens. Your faithfulness reaches beyond the clouds. Your justice is as solid as God's mountains. Your decisions are as full of wisdom as the oceans are of water. You are concerned for men and animals alike.

One possible prayer for today:

God, thank you for being such a wonderful God. Thank you for being a steadfast God. Thank you for being such a faithful God whose faithfulness knows no end. Thank you for being such a wise God. Thank you for being a concerned God. Thank you for being concerned about the things that concern me. Oh Lord, you are so great and so deserving of all my praise. Thank you, God.

New Testament verse for today: Matthew 28:18

He told his disciples, "I have been given all authority in heaven and earth."

One possible prayer for today:

God, thank you for giving Jesus all authority in heaven and earth. Thank you that that authority includes your attributes of being steadfast, of having unlimited faithfulness, of being concerned for me at all times; and of being worthy of my honor and praise forever. Thank you for putting me under Christ's authority so that I may rest in the assurance that I have eternal life by believing in him. Thank you for your steadfast love and caring for me through Jesus. Thank you, God.

My prayer for today—including any journaling thoughts I may want to add. Where am I today spiritually, emotionally, physically, financially, generally?

Today's Date: _____

Old Testament verse for today: Psalm 36:7 & 8

How precious is your constant love, O God! All humanity takes refuge in the shadow of your wings. You feed them with blessings from your own table and let them drink from your rivers of delight.

One possible prayer for today:

God, thank you for your precious and constant love. Thank you for letting me take refuge in the shadow of your wings. Thank you for feeding me with blessings from your own table. Thank you for letting me drink from your rivers of delight. Lord, you know that I have some good days and some bad days; but, Lord, you are always there for me when I call on you. You are there with your constant love and blessings. Thank you, God, for always being there.

New Testament verse for today: Ephesians 4:32

Be kind to one another, tenderhearted, forgiving one another, just as God has forgiven you because you belong to Christ.

One possible prayer for today:

God, thank you for your constant love. How precious it is. Thank you for the blessings from your own table. And, God, what a wonderful blessing it is to have Christ as my Savior. What a wonderful blessing it is to be forgiven of my sins because of your gift of Christ. Lord, let me do a better job of being kind, tenderhearted, and forgiving of others. Help me to do a better job of following Christ's example, Lord. And, thank you for continuing to forgive me when I fail to follow that example. Thank you for being so good to me, Lord.

My prayer for today—including any journaling thoughts I may want to add. Where am I today spiritually, emotionally, physically, financially, generally?

Today's Date: _____

Old Testament verse for today: Psalm 36:9 & 10

For you are the Fountain of life; our light is from your Light. Pour out your unfailing love on those who know you! Never stop giving your salvation to those who long to do your will.

One possible prayer for today:

God, thank you for being my Fountain of life. Thank you for sharing your Light to my life. Thank you for pouring out your unfailing love to me because I know you and acknowledge you as the Lord of my life. Thank you for giving me your salvation. Thank you for making that plan of salvation so simple that even I can understand it. Lord, I do long to do your will. And, Lord, thank you for forgiving me when I fail you and return again and confess my failures to you. Thank you again for your unfailing love.

New Testament verse for today: I Peter 4:10

God has given each of you some special abilities; be sure to use them to help each other, passing on to others God's many kinds of blessings.

One possible prayer for today:

God, thank you for being my Fountain of Life. Thank you for sharing your Light to my life. Thank you for any special abilities that you have given to me. Thank you for giving me your salvation. Thank you for giving me the opportunity and the courage to tell others about your wonderful love and your wonderful plan of salvation. Thank you for making your plan of salvation so simple that I can understand it and I can tell others about it. Thank you for your unfailing love and for your blessings in my life with the abilities you have given me. Thank you, Lord.

My prayer for today—including any journaling thoughts I may want to add. Where am I today spiritually, emotionally, physically, financially, generally?

Today's Date: _____

Old Testament verse for today: Psalm 37:4 & 5

Be delighted with the Lord. Then he will give you all your hearts desires. Commit everything you do to the Lord. Trust him to help you do it and he will.

One possible prayer for today:

Lord, let me delighted with you—all the time. Not just when things go my way. I know that you will give me my hearts desires if I am delighted with you; because, if I am delighted with you at all times, then my will should be in tune with your will for my life at all times. Lord, that is a big challenge for me sometimes; because I like to go my own way and do things in my own way. So, help me, God. Let me always commit everything that I do to you. Let me trust you to lead me and to help me do what you lead me to do. And, Lord, then I do claim your promise that you will help me to do and to do it well. Give me the strength and the faith to follow your will for my life, Lord. And, God, thank you for treating me patiently when I fail to do that.

New Testament verse for today: Matthew 7:7 thru 11

Ask, and you will be given what you ask for. Seek, and you will find. Knock, and the door will be opened. For everyone who asks, receives. Anyone who seeks, finds. If only you will knock, the door will open. If a child asks his father for a loaf of bread, will he be given a stone instead? If he asks for fish, will he be given a poisonous snake? Of course not! And if you hardhearted, sinful men know how to give good gifts to your children, won't your Father in heaven even more certainly give good gifts to those who ask him for them?

One possible prayer for today:

God, what a great promise you have made to me through Jesus in these verses. Let me really believe that at all times, Lord. When the going gets tough; when things don't go the way I had planned, then sometimes I wonder if I can believe all this. Yet, I know that you always are leading me. I know that you have a plan for my life. I know that I will probably have some really rough times. So, Lord, let me cling to these promises when those rough times come. When I ask for something within your will for my life, please give me my request. When I knock, please answer. God, thank you for the good gifts that you have for me. Let me cling to that promise when I am really hurting. Thank you for that promise, Lord.

My prayer for today—including any journaling thoughts I may want to add. Where am I today spiritually, emotionally, physically, financially, generally?

Today's Date: _____

Old testament verse for today: Psalm 37:7a & 9b

Rest in the Lord; wait patiently for him to act. Those who trust the Lord shall be given every blessing.

One possible prayer for today:

God, forgive me for the times that I think that I know more than you do as to what is good for me in my life. Sometimes I don't wait patiently for you to act. Sometimes I rush out on my own because I don't think that you are moving as fast as I want and are not moving in the right direction! Sometimes I don't feel that I am being given every blessings that I want and that I deserve. So, Lord, forgive these human tendencies that are sometimes so strong in my life. Let me remember that you know what is best for me. You know what you want me to have. Let me accept what you give me with the faith and the confidence of really believing that what you have given me is, in fact, the blessing that you want me to have at that particular time. Lord, give me the extra shot of faith that I need just now to accept and believe as you want me to. Thank you, Lord, for helping me through this rough time.

New Testament verse for today: Philippians 4:4

Always be full of joy in the Lord; I say again, rejoice!

One possible prayer for today:

Lord, help me today to be full of joy in you and rejoice in you. I have been instructed again and again in your Word, the Bible, that I am to be happy and joyful in all things and at all times; but, today, I am struggling with that concept! I don't feel happy. I don't feel joyful. I don't feel like praising you for where I am. So, God, give me the strength and the faith that I need to get through this time. And, Lord, not only give me an extra shot of faith; but, give me extra forgiveness for being so caught up in my own world that I don't have the faith and the confidence in you that I need. Thank you for forgiving me these thoughts, Lord. But, you know my thoughts, so there is no need to try and hide them from you. Thank you for being there for me now, even if I am not worshipping you the way that I should. Thank you, Lord, for being there for me.

My prayer for today—including any journaling thoughts I may want to add. Where am I today spiritually, emotionally, physically, financially, generally?

Today's Date: _____

Old Testament verse for today: Psalm 37:11

But all who humble themselves before the Lord shall be given every blessing, and shall have wonderful peace.

One possible prayer for today:

Lord, I thank you for the peace that only you can give. I thank you that you love me and are patient with me. I thank you that I can humble myself before you with total confidence in your love and your kindness. Thank you, Lord, for the many, many, blessings you have given me; and, Lord, thank you for the greatest blessing of all—the wonderful peace you give me as I truly humble myself before you.

New Testament verse for today: Romans 5:8 & 9

But God showed his great love for us by sending Christ to die for us while we were still sinners. And since by his blood he did all this for us as sinners, how much more will he do for us now that he has declared us not guilty? Now he will save us from all of God's wrath to come.

One possible prayer for today:

God, what wonderful promises you have for us if we only believe in your Son, Jesus. Thank you for that great expression of your love in sending us the Christ. Thank you that you have wiped away my sins and declared me not guilty! Thank you for letting me come to you with all of my sin and forgiving me. Thank you for all you have done for me and all you are going to do for me. Thank you that by believing in Christ, I can be saved from all your wrath to come. Thank you for your great love, Lord. Thank you.

My prayer for today—including any journaling thoughts I may want to add. Where am I today spiritually, emotionally, physically, financially, generally?

Today's Date: _____

Old Testament verse for today: Psalm 37:23 & 24

The steps of good men are directed by the Lord. He delights in each step they take. If they fall it isn't fatal, for the Lord holds them with his hand.

One possible prayer for today:

God, thank you for directing my steps. Thank you for delighting in every step that I take. Thank you for being with me, even when I fall. Thank you for keeping those falls from being fatal. Thank you for being such a kind and loving God to me.

New Testament verse for today: Matthew 24:35

Heaven and earth will disappear, but my words remain forever.

One possible prayer for today:

Thank you, God, for the promise of your eternal nature and the eternal nature of your words and promises. Thank you that your promises include eternal life through belief in your Son, Jesus. Thank you for giving me the opportunity and the faith to believe in your words and your plan of salvation. Thank you for always being with me, Lord. Thank you.

My prayer for today—including any journaling thoughts I may want to add. Where am I today spiritually, emotionally, physically, financially, generally?

Today's Date: _____

Old Testament verse for today: Psalm 39:4 thru 7

Lord, help me to realize how brief my time on earth will be. Help me to know that I am here for but a moment more. My life is no longer than my hand! My whole lifetime is but a moment to you. Proud man! Frail as breath! A shadow! And all his busy rushing ends in nothing. He heaps up riches for someone else to spend. And so, Lord, my only hope is in you.

One possible prayer for today:

Lord, I realize that my life is but a moment in your timelessness. But, Lord, at the moment it is all that I know! It is my life. The only earthly life I have. So, Lord, help me to make the most of it for your service. Let some of my busy rushing be of value to you. Let your goals for my life become my goals for my life. Let me accumulate riches in heaven with you because I have loved you and adored you and worshipped you. Lord, let me always remember that my only hope is in you. And, Lord, when I do forget, thank you for always being there to forgive me.

New Testament verse for today: Galatians 3:11b

As the prophet Habakkuk says it, "The man who finds life will find it through trusting God."

One possible prayer for today:

God, you make things so simple! You make things so easy for me to understand if I will only listen to you. Thank you for making yourself available to me. Thank you for sending your loving Holy Spirit into my life to bring me to you. Thank you for letting me find the meaning of my life through trusting you. Thank you for my life, Lord. Thank you for giving me the joy of living that comes from knowing and trusting you. Thank you, God.

My prayer for today—including any journaling thoughts I may want to add. Where am I today spiritually, emotionally, physically, financially, generally?

Today's Date: _____

Old Testament verse for today: Psalm 40:1 thru 4

I waited patiently for God to help me; then he listened and heard my cry. He lifted me out of the pit of despair, out from the bog and the mire, and set my feet on a hard, firm path and steadied me as I walked along. He has given me a new song to sing, of praises to our God. Now many will hear of the glorious things he did for me, and stand in awe before the Lord, and put their trust in him. Many blessings are given to those who trust the Lord, and have no confidence in those who are proud, or who trust in idols.

One possible prayer for today:

God, you know that sometimes I have a hard time waiting patiently for you. You know that I want immediate answers to my prayers. I don't want to wait! But, God, I know that you are always there to listen to me. You will always hear my cry. In your own time, you will lift me out of the bog and the mire and set my feet on solid ground. You will always be there to steady me, even when I am in my lowest depths. Lord, let me sing your praises at all times. Let me testify to your love and your caring at all times—not just in the good times. I do trust you, and you only, Lord. Thank you for the promise of the return of your blessings. Give me the patience I need as I wait for you to answer my prayers.

New Testament verse for today: Hebrews 5:8 & 9

And even though Jesus was God's Son, he had to learn from experience what it was like to obey, when obeying meant suffering. It was after he had proved himself perfect in this experience that Jesus became the Giver of eternal salvation to those who obey him.

One possible prayer for today:

God, if your own Son had to suffer, there is no reason to think that I should not have to go through some bad times. And I know that my suffering is nothing compared to his! Lord, you also know that no matter how much I suffer, I will never become perfect. The only way I can be perfect in your eyes is because of what Christ did for me, and because you completely forgive me. So, because of Christ's suffering, I can have eternal salvation, if I only believe. God, I do believe. Help me to be patient in my time of suffering, knowing that it is your will for my life and knowing that you will give me the strength to get through this period, just as you gave Jesus strength to get through his suffering. Thank you, God.

My prayer for today—including any journaling thoughts I may want to add. Where am I today spiritually, emotionally, physically, financially, generally?

Today's Date: _____

Old Testament verse for today: Psalm 40:6

It isn't sacrifices and offerings which you really want from your people. Burnt animals bring no special joy to your heart. But you have accepted the offer of my lifelong service.

One possible prayer for today:

God, thank you for accepting the offer that I am capable of giving—that of my lifelong service to honor and praise you in all my circumstances. I will do my best to honor and praise you always. Thank you for being my own personal loving and caring God. And, God, when I fail you, thank you for always accepting me back, when I return in sincerity and humbleness. Thank you, God.

New Testament verse for today: Romans 10:12b & 13

They all have the same Lord who generously gives his riches to all those who ask him for them. Anyone who calls upon the name of the Lord will be saved.

One possible prayer for today:

Lord, I am asking for a generous supply of your riches. I am asking for a generous supply of faith so that I may always be able to honor and praise you—no matter what my circumstances. I am calling on your name for my salvation through your Son, Jesus. Thank you for providing such a simple means of salvation for me. Thank you for accepting my offer of lifelong service to you, and in return, giving me the eternal salvation that only you can give. Thank you, Lord.

My prayer for today—including any journaling thoughts I may want to add. Where am I today spiritually, emotionally, physically, financially, generally?

Today's Date: _____

Old Testament verse for today: Psalm 40:9 & 10

I have told everyone the Good News that you forgive men's sins. I have not been timid about it, as you well know, O Lord. I have not kept this Good News hidden in my heart, but have proclaimed your lovingkindness and truth to all the congregation.

One possible prayer for today:

God, thank you for forgiving my sins. That is absolutely wonderful Good News! Let me be faithful in telling others about your constant love and forgiveness. Thank you for letting me come to you and ask for forgiveness. Thank you for always hearing me. Thank you, Lord.

New Testament verse for today: Acts 1:8

But when the Holy Spirit has come upon you, you will receive power to testify about me with great effect, to the people in Jerusalem, throughout Judea, in Samaria, and to the ends of the earth, about my death and resurrection.

One possible prayer for today:

God, thank you for sending your loving Holy Spirit into my life to help me at all times and in all things. Thank you for helping me to testify about what your Son, Jesus, has done for me. Thank you for giving up Jesus to die on the cross and return to life so that my sins will not only be forgiven; but, they will be forgotten! What a wonderful promise that is, Lord. Thank you for that plan of salvation and thank you for your promise that I may have that salvation by simply believing in your Son, Jesus, as my personal Savior. I do believe, Lord. Thank you for giving me the faith to believe.

My prayer for today—including any journaling thoughts I may want to add. Where am I today spiritually, emotionally, physically, financially, generally?

Today's Date: _____

Old Testament verse for today: Psalm 40:11

Lord, don't hold back your tender mercies from me! My only hope is in your love and faithfulness.

One possible prayer for today:

Lord, thank you for being kind to me. Thank you for not holding back your tender mercies from me. Thank you for being worthy of my hope! I have no hope to solve my problems without your love, your faithfulness, and your tender mercies. Thank you for being such a benevolent God to me.

New Testament verse for today: Romans 12:12

Be glad for all God is planning for you. Be patient in trouble, and prayerful always.

One possible prayer for today:

God, sometimes that is very difficult for me to do. Sometimes I have a real hard time being glad for what is happening in my life! Many times I am not patient in trouble; and, God, I confess, sometimes I don't even want to pray and acknowledge your control of my life. I do confess my impatience. I confess my unhappiness with my circumstances. I confess my weakness to pray always. Lord, help me! Thank you for giving me the patience I need. Thank you for always being there when I do come to you to talk to you. Thank you for never turning a deaf ear. And, God, thank you for giving me the faith I need to really be glad for what you have planned for me. Thank you, God.

My prayer for today—including any journaling thoughts I may want to add. Where am I today spiritually, emotionally, physically, financially, generally?

Today's Date: _____

Old Testament verse for today: Psalm 40:16

But may the joy of the Lord be given to everyone who loves him and his salvation. May they constantly exclaim, "How great God is!"

One possible prayer for today:

God, how great you are! There is no question about that! Thank you for restoring to me the joy of my life. Lord, through problems in my life, I had lost my joy, and you have restored it to me. Thank you, God. God, I do love you and I revel in the joy of your salvation. Let me never forget how great you are!

New Testament verse for today: Galatians 5:6b & 11b

—for all we need is faith working through love. —salvation (comes) through faith in the cross of Christ alone.

One possible prayer for today:

Thank you for making salvation so simple, God. Thank you for making salvation possible if only I have faith in the cross of Christ. Nothing else is needed. How wonderful and how simple. Thank you for making it so simple that even I may understand it. And, God, thank you for giving me the gift of faith so that I may believe. Thank you for that gift of faith. Thank you, Lord.

My prayer for today—including any journaling thoughts I may want to add. Where am I today spiritually, emotionally, physically, financially, generally?

Today's Date: _____

Old Testament verse for today: Psalm 40:17

I am poor and needy, yet the Lord is thinking of me right now! O my God, you are my helper. You are my Savior; come quickly, and save me. Please don't delay!

One possible prayer for today:

God, you know that I always need you. And what a wonderful promise to know that you are always thinking of me—and that you are, in fact, thinking of me right now! Thank you, Lord, for thinking of me right now! God, thank you for always being my helper. Thank you for being my Savior. Thank you for always being there to save me. Thank you for always coming quickly to my aid. Thank you, God.

New Testament verse for today: Hebrews 11:22 & 23

Let us go right in, to God himself, with true hearts fully trusting him to receive us, because we have been sprinkled with Christ's blood to make us clean, and because our bodies have been washed with pure water. Now we can look forward to the salvation God has promised us. There is no room for doubt, and we can tell others that salvation is ours, for there is no question that he will do what he says.

One possible prayer for today:

God, thank you for thinking of me right now. Thank you for permitting me to come right in to you, fully trusting you to receive me. And, Lord, I know that you will receive me because of what your Son, Jesus, has done for me. Thank you for making such a wonderful plan of sprinkling me with Christ's blood so that I can be clean in your eyes. Thank you for the promise of my salvation. Thank you for giving me the confidence that there is no room for doubt about my salvation. because of what Christ has done for me. Thank you for your unquestionable promises. God, let me do my part of telling others what a wonderful and faithful God you are.

My prayer for today—including any journaling thoughts I may want to add. Where am I today spiritually, emotionally, physically, financially, generally?

Today's Date: _____

Old Testament verse for today: Psalm 42:1 & 2a

As the deer pants for water, so I long for you, O God. I thirst for God, the living God.

One possible prayer for today:

God, help me to echo the Psalmist's prayer in my life. Help me to long for an ever better relationship with you. Help me to always acknowledge that you are the one and only living God, a God who loves me and cares for me. Thank you for being such a loving and caring God.

New Testament verse for today: Luke 1:46b & 47

Oh, how I praise the Lord. How I rejoice in God my Savior!

One possible prayer for today:

God, I know that one way I may have an ever increasing relationship with you is to praise you always. Let my praise for you be ever in my heart and mind, and on my lips. Let me never forget to rejoice in the fact that you love me and care for me. Let me never forget to thank you for sending your Son, Jesus, to die on the cross for my sins and give me eternal salvation because of his sacrifice for me. Thank you, Lord. Thank you for being a God who is worthy of my praise and a God in whom I can continually rejoice. Thank you, God, for loving me and caring for me.

My prayer for today—including any journaling thoughts I may want to add. Where am I today spiritually, emotionally, physically, financially, generally?

Today's Date: _____

Old Testament verse for today: Psalm 42:5

Why then be downcast? Why be discouraged and sad? Hope in God! I shall yet praise him again. Yes, I shall again praise him for his help.

One possible prayer for today:

God, thank you for giving me the hope that I need, no matter how bad my circumstance may look at the moment. Thank you for helping me through the times when I feel downcast, discouraged and sad. Thank you for giving me the faith to be able to look ahead, counting on your many promises to help me, and know that you are always there with me. Let me praise you at all times, Lord. Let me know that I will be able to praise you for your help, as you once again guide me through the rocky times in my life. Thank you, God, for always being there for me.

New Testament verse for today: Romans 7:25

Who will free me from my slavery to this deadly lower nature? Thank God! It has been done by Jesus Christ our Lord. He has set me free.

One possible prayer for today:

God, thank you for setting me free from slavery to my base lower nature. Thank you for sending Christ to die on the cross so that all of my sins are wiped from the slate. Thank you for giving me that promise and that freedom. Yet, Lord, you know that I keep slipping back into my sinful ways. You know that I have to keep coming back to you and asking you once more to forgive me. And, God, thank you for your promise that you will always be there to forgive me. I know that many times when I am downcast, discouraged, and sad, it is because I have let my lower nature or my bad judgment cause me to make mistakes or make decisions that I know are not what you would have me do. So, Lord, help me through those times. I know that you have set me free. Now, I just have to have the consistency to take advantage of that freedom in a positive way that reflects my belief and trust in you. Thank you for helping me during these times of bad judgment, Lord. And thank you for forgiving me when I come to my senses and return to you.

My prayer for today—including any journaling thoughts I may want to add. Where am I today spiritually, emotionally, physically, financially, generally?

Today's Date: _____

Old Testament verse for today: Psalm 42:8

Yet day by day, the Lord also pours out his steadfast love upon me, and through the night I sing his songs and pray to God who gives me life.

One possible prayer for today:

Lord, thank you for loving me so much. Thank you for your steadfast love that never fails and never diminishes. Thank you for letting me love you in return. Thank you for accepting my love, even though it isn't always steadfast and sometimes I act like it has diminished. Thank you for letting me feel your love so that I may remember and reflect on that love whether I am busy during the day or lying and thinking during the night. Lord, even when I may get busy or self centered and forget about you, thank you for never forgetting about me.

New Testament verse for today: I Corinthians 13:7

If you love someone you will be loyal to him no matter what the cost. You will always believe in him, always expect the best of him, and always stand your ground in defending him.

One possible prayer for today:

Lord, I know that you love me. So, I know that you will always be loyal to me. I know that you will always believe in me and expect the best of me. And, God, I know that you will always defend me. I know that you have defended me to the greatest degree by giving your Son, Jesus, to die on the cross for my sins. Lord, let me somehow be capable of returning some of that love to you. Let me always believe in you. Let me always expect the best from you, and Lord, let me always stand my ground defending you. Thank you for your love, your belief, your expectation, and your defense for me, Lord. Help me to give my best to you.

My prayer for today—including any journaling thoughts I may want to add. Where am I today spiritually, emotionally, physically, financially, generally?

Today's Date: _____

Old Testament verse for today: Psalm 43:5

O my soul, why be so gloomy and discouraged? Trust in God! I shall again praise him for his wondrous help; he will make me smile again, for he is my God!

One possible prayer for today:

God, thank you for always being there for me. Thank you for being a God in whom I may justifiably trust! Thank you for being a God who deserves my praise. Thank you for always being there with your wondrous help. God, thank you for being my God, now and always.

New Testament verse for today: Hebrews 12:2 & 3

Keep your eyes on Jesus, our leader and instructor. He was willing to die a shameful death on the cross because of the joy he knew would be his afterwards; and now he sits in the place of honor by the throne of God. If you want to keep from being fainthearted and weary, think about his patience as sinful men did such terrible things to him.

One possible prayer for today:

God, thank you for giving me Jesus as an example. Thank you for reminding me that life is not always easy, just as it was not always easy for even your beloved Son. Just as you were always there for Jesus, thank you for always being there for me. Just as you had a plan for the life of Jesus, thank you for having a plan for my life. Lord, when I am faint-hearted and weary, when I am gloomy and discouraged, thank you for giving me Jesus as an example that if I will keep the faith; if I will keep my eyes on Jesus, you will reward me with not only eternal life with you and Jesus; but, you will make me smile again in my life here on earth. Thank you for being my wonderful, generous and caring God.

My prayer for today—including any journaling thoughts I may want to add. Where am I today spiritually, emotionally, physically, financially, generally?

Today's Date: _____

Old Testament verse for today: Psalm 46:1 & 2

God is our refuge and strength, a tested help in times of trouble. And so we need not fear even if the world blows up, and the mountains crumble into the sea.

One possible prayer for today:

God, in today's paper filled with articles of wars, hurricanes, mud slides, lives lost and people hungry and needy, sometimes a verse like this may sound a little "Pollyanna-ish." How can I not fear if those things are happening to me? How can I not fear if my mountain is crumbling into the sea? How can I not fear if my world is blowing up? Lord, I know that what you really want is for me to trust you no matter what is happening in my world. I know that what you really want is for me to have so much faith in you that I really believe that whatever happens in my life that it is the best thing for me because you are in charge and so it is your will for my life at that particular time. But, God, when my personal world is blowing up, and when my personal mountain is crumbling into the sea, I really hurt. That is when I especially need an extra shot of faith! That is when I especially need to feel your loving arms around me. So, help me, God. Help me to believe that much. Help me to believe that you are my refuge and my strength no matter what is happening to me. Give me that extra shot of faith that I need. Thank you, Lord, for hearing my prayer and for answering me when I need you the most. Thank you, God.

New Testament verse for today: II Corinthians 1:3 & 4

What a wonderful God we have—he is the Father of our Lord Jesus Christ, the source of every mercy, and the one who so wonderfully comforts and strengthens us in our hardships and trials.

One possible prayer for today:

God, thank you for this verse and this promise. Knowing that you and Jesus are always there for me is a help, even when I am really hurting and don't know where else to turn. Thank you for making Christ the source of my every mercy. Thank you for giving me Christ that I may turn to him for comfort and strength when I am really hurting. Thank you for always being there for me. Lord, in the name of your Son, Jesus Christ, be there for me right now. Give me the comfort and the strength that I need right now. Thank you for hearing my prayer right now, Lord. Thank you.

My prayer for today—including any journaling thoughts I may want to add. Where am I today spiritually, emotionally, physically, financially, generally?

Today's Date: _____

Old Testament verse for today: Psalm 48:1a
How great is the Lord! How much we should praise him.

One possible prayer for today:
God, thank you for being such a great God. Thank you for being the one and only true God. Thank you for being a God who is always worthy of my praise. Thank you for helping me to have the faith to always praise you more. Thank you, God.

New Testament verse for today: James 4:7
So give yourselves humbly to God. Resist the devil and he will flee from you.

One possible prayer for today:
God, I do give myself humbly to you. I do try to praise you with all my heart and with all my soul and with all my might. Thank you for giving me the strength to resist Satan and his attempts to turn me away from you. Thank you for causing Satan to flee from me. And, God, thank you for continuing to forgive me when I fail you, when my resistance to Satan is too low to cause him to flee from me. Thank you, God, for always being there to help me and to once again rescue me.

My prayer for today—including any journaling thoughts I may want to add. Where am I today spiritually, emotionally, physically, financially, generally?

Today's Date: _____

Old Testament verse for today: Psalm 50:4 thru 6

He has come to judge his people. To heaven and earth he shouts, "Gather together my own people who by their sacrifice upon my altar have promised to obey me." God will judge them with complete fairness, for all heaven declares that he is just.

One possible prayer for today:

God, thank you for being such a just God. Thank you for being so fair that you knew that I could not be perfect in your eyes no matter how many sacrifices I made on your altar, or how often I made them. Lord, I have promised that I will do my best to obey you; but, you know that I continually fall short of your perfect goals for me. So, God, in your marvelous love, understanding, and caring, you came up with another plan. One that I can meet. You gave me Jesus to die on the cross to wipe out all of my sin. What an incredible plan, God. Now you will judge me looking through the blood of your Son, Jesus. God, your fairness to me is almost unbelievable; but, I accept it because I believe in your Son. Thank you, God.

New Testament verse for today: I John 1:7

But if we are living in the light of God's presence, just as Christ does, then we have wonderful fellowship and joy with each other, and the blood of Jesus his Son cleanses us from every sin.

One possible prayer for today:

God, thank you for letting me live in the light of your presence. Thank you for the wonderful fellowship that I can have with you and Jesus. And, God, thank you for being the author of a plan for my salvation that lets me know that Christ's blood has cleansed me from every sin. Thank you for that wonderful plan which lets you judge me perfect in your eyes because of what Christ has done for me. Thank you, God.

My prayer for today—including any journaling thoughts I may want to add. Where am I today spiritually, emotionally, physically, financially, generally?

Today's Date: _____

Old Testament verse for today: Psalm 50:14 & 15

What I want from you is your true thanks; I want your promises fulfilled. I want you to trust me in your times of trouble, so that I can rescue you, and you can give me glory.

One possible prayer for today:

Lord, let me always be thankful to you in every situation; because, I know that that is what you want for my life at that particular time. In turn, let me fulfill all my vows to you. Forgive me for the times that I have not fulfilled the promises that I made to you. Let me trust you more all the time; not only in times of trouble, but in the good times too. And, Lord, I do trust you. And, Lord, I claim your promise to rescue me. Rescue me today from the perils that are attacking me. And, Lord, let me do my part. Let me glorify your name at all times. Thank you, Lord, for rescuing me.

New Testament verse for today: Acts 27:25

So take courage! For I believe God! It will be just as he said!

One possible prayer for today:

Thank you, Lord, for that reminder that it will always be just as you said. Thank you for always being there when I need you. Thank you for never giving up on me. Thank you for giving me the courage that I need in times of trouble. Thank you for giving me the faith to believe you at all times. Thank you for giving me a shot of courage when I need it the most. Thank you, God.

My prayer for today—including any journaling thoughts I may want to add. Where am I today spiritually, emotionally, physically, financially, generally?

Today's Date: _____

Old Testament verse for today: Psalm 50:23

But true praise is a worthy sacrifice; this really honors me. Those who walk my paths will receive salvation from the Lord.

One possible prayer for today:

God, let my life be lived in such a manner that all that I do praises you. Let me honor you with my thoughts and actions. And, Lord, thank you for your promise that if I do that, I will receive salvation from you. Thank you for making a path that I am able to follow. Thank you for your marvelous plan of salvation that is available to me.

New Testament verse for today: Acts 26:17 & 18

(God said to Paul) "And I will protect you from both your own people and the Gentiles. Yes, I am going to send you to the Gentiles to open their eyes to their true condition so that they may repent and live in the light of God instead of in Satan's darkness, so that they may receive forgiveness for their sins and God's inheritance along with all people everywhere whose sins are cleansed away, who are set apart by faith in me."

One possible prayer for today:

God, thank you for making your plan of salvation available to everyone. Thank you for making a plan available that rescues me from Satan's darkness. Thank you for forgiveness of my sins. Thank you for giving me the opportunity to believe in you, and then giving me the faith to avail myself of that opportunity. Thank you, God, for being so good to me.

My prayer for today—including any journaling thoughts I may want to add. Where am I today spiritually, emotionally, physically, financially, generally?

Today's Date: _____

Old Testament verse for today: Psalm 51:1 thru 3a

O loving and kind God, have mercy. Have pity upon me and take away the awful stain of my transgressions. Oh wash me, cleanse me from this guilt. Let me be pure again. For I admit my shameful deed.

One possible prayer for today:

God, thank you for being loving and kind to me. Thank you for showing me mercy. Thank you for taking pity on me when I sin against you. Thank you for washing me and cleansing me from the guilt of my sins. Thank you for making me pure again. Thank you for always accepting me back into your presence when I come before you and humbly admit my guilt and my shameful deeds. Thank you for being such a loving and forgiving God.

New Testament verse for today: Colossians 1:13 & 14

For he has rescued us out of the darkness and gloom of Satan's kingdom and brought us into the kingdom of his dear Son, who bought our freedom with his blood and forgave us all our sins.

One possible prayer for today:

God, what a wonderful God you are! Thank you for rescuing me from the darkness and gloom of Satan's kingdom. Thank you for bringing me into the kingdom of your dear Son, Jesus. Thank you for taking pity on me and showing me mercy. Thank you for making me pure again by giving me Jesus, who bought my freedom with his blood and forgave all my sins. What a wonderful promise, Lord. Thank you for giving me a plan where all my sins can be forgiven and erased from the slate of my life. Thank you, Lord.

My prayer for today—including any journaling thoughts I may want to add. Where am I today spiritually, emotionally, physically, financially, generally?

Today's Date: _____

Old Testament verse for today: Psalm 51:6 & 7

You deserve honesty from the heart; yes, utter sincerity and truthfulness. Oh, give me this wisdom. Sprinkle me with the cleansing blood and I shall be clean again. Wash me and I shall be whiter than snow.

One possible prayer for today:

God, there really isn't any use of my trying to be dishonest with you; because you know all of my innermost thoughts and desires. You made me and know my heart. So, God, not only give me the wisdom to be honest with you; but, give me the courage to deal with you truthfully and sincerely. Lord, I know that if I do this, you will, in fact, sprinkle me with the cleansing blood of your Son, Jesus. You will, in fact, wash me and make me whiter than snow as you forgive—and forget my sins. Thank you, Lord, for that promise. Thank you for your great plan of salvation. Thank you for giving me the wisdom to be honest in my prayers to you. Thank you, God.

New Testament verse for today: Acts 20:32

And now I entrust you to God and his care and to his wonderful words which are able to build your faith and give you all the inheritance of those who are set apart for himself.

One possible prayer for today:

How wonderful to be put into your trust, O Lord. How wonderful to know that I am in your care. Thank you for your words of encouragement that do build my faith. Thank you for making me your son so that I do have all the inheritance of one of your children. Thank you for setting me apart as one of your children. Thank you for loving me and continuing to forgive me. Thank you, Lord.

My prayer for today—including any journaling thoughts I may want to add. Where am I today spiritually, emotionally, physically, financially, generally?

Today's Date: _____

Old Testament verse for today: Psalm 51:9 thru 12

Don't keep looking at my sins—erase them from your sight. Create in me a new, clean heart, O God, filled with clean thoughts and right desires. Don't toss me aside, banished forever from your presence. Don't take your Holy Spirit from me. Restore to me again the joy of your salvation, and make me willing to obey you.

One possible prayer for today:

God, thank you for erasing my sins from your sight. Thank you for forgiving me over and over again—when I make the same mistakes over and over again. And, God, please help me. Help me to have a heart more in tune with your will for my life. Do, please, God, help me to have a heart filled with clean thoughts and right desires. Thank you for not ever completely tossing me aside and removing your Holy Spirit from me. Thank you for always being there to once again restore me to the joy of your salvation. Thank you, God. Thank you for helping me to be more willing to obey you.

New Testament verse for today: Acts 20:24

But life is worth nothing unless I use it for doing that work assigned to me by the Lord Jesus—the work of telling others the Good News about God's mighty kindness and love.

One possible prayer for today:

I know, God, that if I spend more time concentrating on what you want me to do, more time doing your work, more time thinking about your love and the great sacrifice Christ made for me, then I won't have as much time to think about things that are not pleasing to you. That will help me to have cleaner thoughts and desires more pleasing to you. So, help me, God. Help me to work on doing your work. Let my love for you become more apparent to those with whom I come in contact. Help create in me a cleaner heart by reminding me to do the work that Christ wants me to do. Thank you for helping me, God. And, God, thank you for forgiving me when I fail to live up to these goals.

My prayer for today—including any journaling thoughts I may want to add. Where am I today spiritually, emotionally, physically, financially, generally?

Today's Date: _____

Old Testament verse for today: Psalm 51:16 & 17

You don't want penance; if you did, how gladly I would do it! You aren't interested in offerings burned before you on the altar. It is a broken spirit you want—remorse and penitence. A broken and contrite heart, O God, you will not ignore.

One possible prayer for today:

God, you have told me in your scriptures that you made the world for me to enjoy; yet in that enjoyment, you always want me to put you first in my life and honor you first in all that I do. Lord, when I truly let you down; when I really sin against you, then I understand that you want me to acknowledge that sin from the bottom of my heart. You want me to acknowledge that you are, in fact, the Lord of my life. That is when you want my spirit to be broken before you. You want my true remorse and penitence. Lord, I have sinned against you. I have let you down. I acknowledge that sin and that failure. I am coming before you, Lord, with a spirit of remorse and penitence and a broken and contrite heart. And, Lord, I claim the Psalmist's promise that you will not ignore me in this time when I need your forgiveness. Thank you, God, for forgiving me.

New Testament verse for today: Luke 24:47

—that this message of salvation should be taken from Jerusalem to all the nations: There is forgiveness of sins for all who turn to me.

One possible prayer for today:

God, thank you for that promise. Thank you for giving me your Son, Jesus, that makes a plan for not only the forgiveness of my sins; but, for the promise of eternal life in your presence. Thank you, Lord, for forgiving me my sins and my failures. Thank you, God, for always being there for me.

My prayer for today—including any journaling thoughts I may want to add. Where am I today spiritually, emotionally, physically, financially, generally?

Today's Date: _____

Old Testament verse for today: Psalm 52:8 & 9

But I am like a sheltered olive tree protected by the Lord Himself. I trust in the mercy of God forever and ever. O Lord, I will praise you forever and ever for your punishment. And I will wait for your mercies—for everyone knows what a merciful God you are.

One possible prayer for today:

God, thank you for always protecting me. Thank you for punishing me properly for disobeying you. Thank you for being in charge of my life—even when my punishment is occurring. Thank you for being a God who I can always trust. Let me always have the faith to praise you, God, no matter what is happening in my life. And, God, thank you for giving me the faith to know that you will again restore your mercies to me. Thank you for being a loving and merciful God.

New Testament verse for today: Matthew 5:45b

For he gives his sunlight to both the evil and the good, and sends rain on the just and the unjust too.

One possible prayer for today:

God, I know that many times the bad things that occur in my life are things that I do not understand. I don't feel that I have disobeyed you or loved you less in any manner that should cause you to withdraw your blessings from me. And yet, bad things occur in my life. Things I don't understand. Things that I don't like. Things that hurt. I feel that I am being unfairly treated; and, sometimes that makes me feel that you are unfairly treating me. Lord, I know that I am supposed to be thankful in all things; so, help me, Lord. Give me the faith to honestly thank you at all times and in all things; because, I know that if it is occurring in my life, it is what you have planned for me. Help me, Lord. Give me the faith that I need. Thank you for forgiving my lack of faith and my lack of trusting you completely. Thank you, Lord.

My prayer for today—including any journaling thoughts I may want to add. Where am I today spiritually, emotionally, physically, financially, generally?

Today's Date: _____

Old Testament verse for today: Psalm 53:2

God looks down from heaven, searching among all mankind to see if there is a single one who does right and really seeks for God.

One possible prayer for today:

God, that is a little scary! To know that you are looking down from heaven to see if I am doing right and really seeking you. I think that I do most of the time. I think that I am trying to please you and live the way that you would want me to live. But, I know that I fail often. I know that I fall short of your goal. So, God, when that happens, I claim your promise of forgiveness. I claim your promise that you will remove my sins from me and remember them no more. Thank you for being faithful, Lord, even when I am not.

New Testament verse for today: Luke 6:31

Treat others as you want them to treat you.

One possible prayer for today:

Lord, that is something that I can really try to do. I know that I can't always please you. And, I know that I won't even always remember to treat others as I want them to treat me; but, at least, that is a goal that I can work on achieving. Help me in this one area today, Lord. Give me patience with my family, my co-workers, my neighbors, and anyone else with whom I come in contact. Let me be empathetic with others needs and problems. Thank you for helping me in this area, Lord.

My prayer for today—including any journaling thoughts I may want to add. Where am I today spiritually, emotionally, physically, financially, generally?

Today's Date: _____

Old Testament verse for today: Psalm 54:4
But God is my helper. He is a friend of mine!

One possible prayer for today:
What a wonderful thing it is, Lord, to know that you are my friend; and to know that you are always there to help me. Thank you for being such a faithful friend. Thank you for always being there to help me. Thank you, God.

New Testament verse for today: Romans 5:10
And since, when we were his enemies, we were brought back to God by the death of his Son, what blessings he must have for us now that we are his friends, and he is living within us!

One possible prayer for today:
God, thank you for turning me from one of your enemies into one of your friends. Thank you for sending your Son, Jesus, to bridge that gap between us and make me one of your friends. Thank you for the blessings you have given to me and the blessings you have in store for me as one of your friends. Thank you for living within me, directing my life, and continuing to forgive me when I stumble upon my life's path. Thank you for being such a wonderful friend.

My prayer for today—including any journaling thoughts I may want to add. Where am I today spiritually, emotionally, physically, financially, generally?

Today's Date: _____

Old Testament verse for today: Psalm 54:6

Gladly I bring my sacrifices to you; I will praise your name, O Lord, for it is good.

One possible prayer for today:

God, thank you for being so good to me. Thank you for your generosity to me so that I may in return give to you. Let me be a worthy steward of the gifts that you have given me. Let me be generous with my material gifts, as well as my time and my talent in returning to you a portion of what you have given me. Let me praise your marvelous name, Lord, in all that I do. Thank you for being such a worthy God; worthy of all my gifts and sacrifices.

New Testament verse for today: I Timothy 6:18 & 19

Tell them to use their money to do good. They should be rich in good works and should give happily to those in need, always being ready to share with others whatever God has given them. By doing this they will be storing up real treasure for themselves in heaven—it is the only safe investment for eternity! And they will be living a fruitful Christian life down here as well.

One possible prayer for today:

God, let me listen to your loving direction as I give of my time, talents, and money as you would have me give. Let me use my material blessings to do good to those in need. Let me be generous and rich in good works. Let me always be ready to share with others in need. Lord, help me to live a fruitful life here on earth, even as I store up treasures in heaven because you are so good to me that I could never give enough to deserve the wonders you have awaiting me. Thank you for being a God worthy of all my gifts.

My prayer for today—including any journaling thoughts I may want to add. Where am I today spiritually, emotionally, physically, financially, generally?

Today's Date: _____

Old Testament verse for today: Psalm 55:16 & 17

But I will call upon the Lord to save me—and he will. I will pray morning, noon, and night, pleading aloud with God; and, he will hear and answer.

One possible prayer for today:

God, thank you for giving me someplace to turn when I am in trouble. As the Psalmist said, if I call on you to save me, you will! Lord, let me have the faith to really believe that so that I also have the faith to always keep on praying—morning, noon, and night. Let me plead with you; and, Lord, please listen and answer my pleadings. I need your help now. I need your guidance now. Hear me and answer me, Lord. Thank you for hearing me and answering me.

New Testament verse for today: John 16:27

For the Father himself loves you dearly because you love me and believe that I came from the Father.

One possible prayer for today:

Father, thank you for loving me. Thank you for loving me both when things are going well and when things are not! I do love you and love your Son, Jesus; but, Lord, today I am hurting and having a real hard time thanking you and praising you. Thank you for this promise that you love me dearly. Thank you for never giving up on me, even when my faith wavers. Thank you, God.

My prayer for today—including any journaling thoughts I may want to add. Where am I today spiritually, emotionally, physically, financially, generally?

Today's Date: _____

Old Testament verse for today: Psalm 55:22

Give your burdens to the Lord. He will carry them. He will not permit the godly to slip or fall.

One possible prayer for today:

God, thank you for being there for me when I am feeling burdened. Thank you for letting me give you my burdens. Thank you for upholding me when I am in danger of slipping or falling. Thank you for the strength and guidance you give me when I need it the most. Thank you, Lord.

New Testament verse for today: Luke 8:48

"Daughter," he said to her, "your faith has healed you. Go in peace."

One possible prayer for today:

God, just as you healed this woman with your power, I know that you can remove all of my burdens and troubles from me when it is your will. So, God, I pray that you will take my burdens just now. I pray that you will carry them. I pray that you will not let me slip and fall under the load that I am presently feeling. I thank you that you are still there with all of your love, your power, and your ability to help me through these rough times. Give me the faith that this woman had. Give me the peace that you gave her. Give me the solution to my problems as you gave her a solution to hers. Thank you, Lord, for being as powerful today as you were then and as you have always been. Thank you for taking my burdens and giving me solutions. Thank you, Lord.

My prayer for today—including any journaling thoughts I may want to add. Where am I today spiritually, emotionally, physically, financially, generally?

Today's Date: _____

Old Testament verse for today: Psalm 56:3 & 4

But when I am afraid, I will put my confidence in you. Yes, I will trust the promises of God. And since I am trusting him, what can mere man do to me?

One possible prayer for today:

How wonderful you are, Lord, to be concerned about me. Thank you for caring about me. Thank you for giving me strength when I am afraid. Thank you for giving me the faith I need to really have confidence in you. God, I do trust your promises. I do have the confidence that as long as you are in charge of my life, I can know that whatever happens to me, it is your will, and I can accept it. Lord, let whatever you have in mind for me be as good and as comfortable for me as possible! Give me the strength to handle whatever occurs in a manner that would be pleasing to you.

New Testament verse for today: Matthew 21:21 & 22

Then Jesus told them, "Truly, if you have faith, and don't doubt, you can do things like this and much more. You can even say to this Mount of Olives, 'More over into the ocean,' and it will. You can get anything—anything you ask for in prayer—if you believe."

One possible prayer for today:

Lord, I don't understand that promise of Christ's. So far, in all of my prayers, I haven't moved any mountains! Maybe I don't have enough faith. Maybe I don't know how to pray. More likely, when I pray for the seemingly impossible, I am praying self-serving prayers that are not in line with your will for my life. So, Lord, help me to do a better job of coordinating my desires with your will. Let any mountains that I pray to move be only those mountains that you want moved! Lord, help me to live my life so that your will becomes my desire. Thank you, Lord, for helping me achieve that goal.

My prayer for today—including any journaling thoughts I may want to add. Where am I today spiritually, emotionally, physically, financially, generally?

Today's Date: _____

Old Testament verse for today: Psalm 56:9 thru 12

The very day I call for help, the tide of battle turns. My enemies flee! This one thing I know: God is for me! I am trusting God—oh, praise his promises! I am not afraid of anything mere man can do to me! Yes, praise his promises. I will surely do what I have promised, Lord, and thank you for your help.

One possible prayer for today:

Lord, I know that you are always there when I cry for help. So, help me today! Give me the wisdom, the courage, the strength, the persistence, and the faith to keep on trusting you in these difficult times. Lord, help my set of enemies—the problems I am facing—to flee! I do know that you are for me! I do know that I can trust you and count on your help. I do know that you are all powerful and that I should have no fear of my circumstances. Yes, Lord, I do praise your promises. I count on them. Lord, give me the strength to hold up my end of the contract—fulfilling my promises to you. Lord, I do thank you for your help. Thank you for your help. Thank you for being for me.

New Testament verse for today: I Thessalonians 5:9

For God has not chosen to pour out his anger upon us, but to save us through our Lord Jesus Christ.

One possible prayer for today:

God, thank you for that promise. No matter how bleak things look to me today, I know that you have chosen me to have eternal life through belief in your Son, Jesus. I know that no matter how much I hurt today, I can look forward to spending eternity with you. But, Lord, I need your help today. I thank you that you have not chosen to pour out your anger on me. So, Lord, turn on the blessings, I pray! Give me a solution to my problems, once more giving me firsthand knowledge that you are for me. Help me! Thank you, Lord, for hearing this plea and for answering my prayers.

My prayer for today—including any journaling thoughts I may want to add. Where am I today spiritually, emotionally, physically, financially, generally?

Today's Date: _____

Old Testament verse for today: Psalm 59:9 & 10a

O God my strength! I will sing your praises, for you are my place of safety. My God is changeless in his love for me and he will come and help me.

One possible prayer for today:

God, this is one of those days when I am having a hard time singing your praises! It is not a good day! In fact, I would have a hard time singing praises to anyone today. So, all I can do is claim the promise of the Psalmist that, in fact, you are my place of safety. That you are changeless in your love for me and that you will always be there for me, and that you will come and help me. Please come and help me, God. Please come to my rescue. Please give me the wisdom I need to get through this difficult time. Please give me an extra shot of faith to help me to truly trust you to help me. Thank you, Lord, for being patient with me when my faith in you gets weak. Thank you for being changeless in your love for me even though I may be unfaithful in my unwavering love for you. Thank you, God.

New Testament verse for today: John 14:15 & 16

If you love me, obey me; and I will ask the Father and he will give you another Comforter, and he will never leave you.

One possible prayer for today:

God, thank you for giving me Christ who makes such great promises to me at a time like this. I will really try to love and obey you and your Son, Christ. I will really try to believe, even in the rough times of my life. Thank you for sending your loving Holy Spirit to comfort me in my times of need. Thank you for the promise that your Holy Spirit will never leave me. And, God, thank you for giving me the shot of adrenaline and faith that I need—right now. Thank you, God.

My prayer for today—including any journaling thoughts I may want to add. Where am I today spiritually, emotionally, physically, financially, generally?

Today's Date: _____

Old Testament verse for today: Psalm 59:16

But as for me, I will sing each morning about your power and mercy. For you have been my high tower of refuge, a place of safety in the day of my distress.

One possible prayer for today:

Lord, how could I ever sing your praise enough? How could I ever worship you enough? You have done so much for me. You have protected me in times of trouble. You have been beside me in times of distress, keeping me safe. You are always there if and when I call on you. Yes, Lord, I know that things that I consider to be bad still happen to me. Yes, I still have troubles and problems; but, Lord, I know that I can always turn to you for comfort and for guidance. Knowing that you are there will give me courage and wisdom to face those problems better than if I tried to do it alone. Thank you for always being there for me, God.

New Testament verse for today: Matthew 28:20b

—and be sure of this—that I am with you always, even to the end of the world.

One possible prayer for today:

What a wonderful promise, Lord! Thank you for that promise. And I know that I can be sure that you are always there for me. I know that I can count on you to hear my prayers and to respond in a manner that is in line with your will for my life. Thank you, Lord, for always being there.

My prayer for today—including any journaling thoughts I may want to add. Where am I today spiritually, emotionally, physically, financially, generally?

Today's Date: _____

Old Testament verse for today: Psalm 59:17

O my strength, to you I will sing praises; for you are my high tower of safety, my God of mercy.

One possible prayer for today:

God, thank you for being my strength. Thank you for being my high tower of safety. Thank you for being my personal God of mercy. Lord, let me never forget to sing your praises. Don't let me get so busy, or so self satisfied, or so confident of my own self, that I forget that you are my God. You are my strength. You are my high tower of safety. And, God, thank you for being my God of mercy. One who cares for me at all times. Thank you, God.

New Testament verse for today: II Peter 3:18

But grow in spiritual strength and become better acquainted with our Lord and Savior Jesus Christ. To him be all glory and splendid honor, both now and forever more.

One possible prayer for today:

Lord, just as you are my strength, my tower of safety and my God of mercy, so let me do my part of worshipping you by becoming stronger spiritually because I become better acquainted with your Son, Jesus Christ. Lord, let me do my part of worshipping you by giving more glory and splendid honor in my life to Jesus. Let me keep my eye on the goals you have set for me. Thank you for giving me Christ as my personal Savior so that I may not only experience your love, your care, and your guidance in my life here on earth, but I may experience eternal life with you and Jesus in heaven. Thank you, Lord.

My prayer for today—including any journaling thoughts I may want to add. Where am I today spiritually, emotionally, physically, financially, generally?

Today's Date: _____

Old Testament verse for today: Psalm 60:6

God has promised to help us. He has vowed it by his holiness! No wonder I exult!

One possible prayer for today:

God, how wonderful. How could I ever ask for more than the knowledge that you have promised to help me. And you have vowed it by your holiness, which is something greater than I can even imagine! Yes, it is no wonder that I can exalt even in times of stress and potential problems. Thank you, God, for your promise to help even me.

New Testament verse for today: Matthew 11:28 thru 30

Come to me and I will give you rest—all of you who work so hard beneath a heavy yoke. Wear my yoke—for it fits perfectly—and let me teach you; for I am gentle and humble, and you shall find rest for your souls; for I give you only light burdens.

One possible prayer for today:

God, today I really need that promise that Christ gave. Today my yoke is not only heavy, it seems unbearable to me! Today I really feel that I cannot continue in my own strength. I have no place to turn but to you. Help me to trust Christ to carry my yoke. Give me the faith that I need to turn my problems over to Christ and believe that he will give me the strength to prevail. Please let me find rest for my soul, for it is weary and overwhelmed today. Let Christ give me only a light burden and remove the burdens of the world from my shoulders. Please, Lord!

My prayer for today—including any journaling thoughts I may want to add. Where am I today spiritually, emotionally, physically, financially, generally?

Today's Date: _____

Old Testament for today: Psalm 61:3 & 5

For you are my refuge, a high tower where my enemies can never reach me. For you have heard my vows, O god, to praise you every day, and you have given me the blessings you reserve for those who reverence your name.

One possible prayer for today:

God, thank you for being my refuge. Thank you for being a high tower that is beyond the reach of my enemies. Thank you for hearing my vows, Lord. Thank you for giving me the blessings that you reserve for those who reverence your name. Now, Lord, let me keep those vows. Let me praise you every day. Let me thank you every day for what you have done and are doing for me. Let me always reverence you, Lord.

New Testament verse for today: Acts 17:25b, 27, & 28

He himself (God) gives life and breath to everything, and satisfies every need there is. His purpose in all this is that they (all mankind) should seek after God, and perhaps feel their way toward him and find him—though he is not far from any of us. For in him we live and move and are! As one of your own poets says it, "We are the sons of God."

One possible prayer for today:

God, thank you for giving me life and breath. Thank you for satisfying all my needs. Thank you for never being very far from me. Thank you for calling me one of your sons! Lord, with all you have done for me, it makes it very easy for me to thank you and to reverence you every day. Thank you, God.

My prayer for today—including any journaling thoughts I may want to add. Where am I today spiritually, emotionally, physically, financially, generally?

Today's Date: _____

Old Testament verse for today: Psalm 62:1 & 2

I stand silently before the Lord, waiting for him to rescue me. For salvation comes from him alone. Yes, he alone is my Rock, my rescuer, defense and fortress. Why then should I be tense with fear when trouble comes?

One possible prayer for today:

God, thank you for always being there to rescue me. Thank you for being my Rock, my rescuer, my defense, and my fortress. Thank you for taking care of me when I stand silently before you, waiting for you to rescue me. Thank you for understanding my problems and giving me the strength that I need to confront and solve them. Thank you for removing my fear and tenseness in the midst of my troubles. Thank you for giving me the peace that can come only from you. Thank you, God.

New Testament verse for today: Philemon 1:3

May God our Father and the Lord Jesus Christ give you his blessings and peace.

One possible prayer for today:

God, thank you for the blessings that are mine as I trust in you. Thank you for the peace that only you can give. Thank you for giving me your Son, Jesus, through whom I may receive my salvation. Thank you, Lord.

My prayer for today—including any journaling thoughts I may want to add. Where am I today spiritually, emotionally, physically, financially, generally?

Today's Date: _____

Old Testament verse for today: Psalm 62:5 thru 7

But I stand silently before the Lord, waiting for him to rescue me. For salvation comes from him alone. Yes, he alone is my Rock, my rescuer, defense and fortress—why then should I be tense with fear when troubles come? My protection and success come from God alone. He is my refuge, a Rock where no enemy can reach me.

One possible prayer for today:

God, what a wonderful promise. Thank you for always being there to rescue me. Thank you for being the source and author of my salvation. Thank you for being my Rock, my rescuer, my defense, my fortress. Thank you for giving me the faith not to be tense when troubles come. Thank you for protecting me so that no enemy can reach me. Thank you, God.

New Testament verse for today: Romans 8:29

For from the very beginning God decided that those who came to him—and all along he knew who would—should become like his Son, so that his Son would be the First, with many brothers.

One possible prayer for today:

God, thank you for permitting me to come to you. Thank you for receiving me when I come to you. Thank you for always knowing that I would come to you. Thank for you making me like your Son. Thank you for being my Rock, and the author of my salvation.

My prayer for today—including any journaling thoughts I may want to add. Where am I today spiritually, emotionally, physically, financially, generally?

Today's Date: _____

Old Testament verse for today: Psalm 63:6 thru 8

I lie awake at night thinking of you—of how much you have helped me—and how I rejoice through the night beneath the protecting shadow of your wings. I follow close behind you, protected by your strong right arm.

One possible prayer for today:

God, I do rejoice at the thought of all that you have done for me. You have helped me so much. Thank you for helping me. Thank you for continuing to help me. Thank you for protecting me by your power and might—under the shadow of your powerful wings. Lord, let me always follow close behind you. Let me always listen to your leading in my life. Thank you for protecting me by your strong right arm. Thank you, Lord.

New Testament verse for today: Mark 16:15 & 16a

And he told them, "You are to go into all the world and preach the Good News to everyone, everywhere. Those who believe and are baptized will be saved."

One possible prayer for today:

God, when you have done so much for me. When you have protected me by the power of your right hand, how can I do less than tell everyone I know about the Good News that you have given your Son, Jesus, to die for my sins! Lord, I may not be articulate to always verbalize that Good News; but, let my life be lived so that it is a witness to that Good News. Let my life preach the love that you have shown for me. Thank you, God, for that Good News, and thank you for the personal salvation you have given to me. That, Lord, is Great News!

My prayer for today—including any journaling thoughts I may want to add. Where am I today spiritually, emotionally, physically, financially, generally?

Today's Date: _____

Old Testament verse for today: Psalm 65:3

Though sins fill our hearts, you forgive them all.

One possible prayer for today:

God, what a wonderful, loving, caring, and forgiving God you are. Thank you for being so wonderful to me. You know my heart. You know my thoughts. You know that I have a sinful nature. And, yet, Lord, you are always there to forgive all of my sins when I return to you and humbly confess my sins to you. Thank you for always being there to forgive all my sins, Lord.

New Testament verse for today: John 12:26

If these Greeks want to be my disciples, tell them to come and follow me, for my servants must be where I am. And if they follow me, the Father will honor them.

One possible prayer for today:

God, thank you for opening up your plan of salvation for everyone who will believe in your Son, Jesus. Thank you for opening up your plan of salvation for me. Help my faith to grow so that I do a better job of adhering to the principles that Christ laid down for his followers. Thank you for sending Christ to die on the cross so that my sins can be forgiven and forgotten. Thank you, God, for your wonderful Son, and for your wonderful plan of salvation which was freely given to me and is available to anyone who will believe.

My prayer for today—including any journaling thoughts I may want to add. Where am I today spiritually, emotionally, physically, financially, generally?

Today's Date: _____

Old Testament verse for today: Psalm 68:19

What a glorious Lord! He who daily bears our burdens also gives us our salvation.

One possible prayer for today:

God, thank you for being my personal glorious Lord! Thank you for daily bearing my burdens! Thank you for giving me my salvation! Thank you, God. Thank you.

New Testament verse for today: John 3:33 thru 36a

"Those who believe him discover that God is a fountain of truth. For this one—(Jesus) sent by God—speaks God's words, for God's Spirit is upon him without measure or limit. The Father loves this man because he is his Son, and God has given him everything there is. And all who trust him—God's Son—to save them have eternal life."

One possible prayer for today:

Lord, I do believe. I do want you to be a fountain of truth for me. Thank you for sending Jesus so that we can know him and trust him. Thank you for loving Jesus, and in turn, loving me. Thank you for giving me eternal life because of my belief. Help me to put away any unbelief, Lord. And, let me always thank you for all you have done for me and for loving me so much.

My prayer for today—including any journaling thoughts I may want to add. Where am I today spiritually, emotionally, physically, financially, generally?

Today's Date: _____

Old Testament verse for today: Psalm 60:13

But I keep right on praying to you, Lord. For now is the time—you are bending down to hear! You are ready with a plentiful supply of love and kindness. Now answer my prayer and rescue me as you promised.

One possible prayer for today:

I do keep right on praying, Lord. I do keep right on asking and pleading my case! Lord, you have promised that you are always bending down and listening. You have promised that you are always ready with a plentiful supply of love and kindness. Now, Lord, as the Psalmist prayed and wrote, answer my prayers and rescue me as you promised! Lord, I claim that promise—right now! Thank you for hearing me, Lord. Thank you for answering me.

New Testament verse for today: Matthew 18:19 & 20

"I also tell you this—if two of you agree down here on earth concerning anything you ask for, my Father in heaven will do it for you. For where two or three gather together because they are mine, I will be right there among them."

One possible prayer for today:

Lord, what a great promise Christ gave to us! If we ask and if we believe, it will be done! Lord, let me live my life with that confidence and that belief. Let me cultivate some other believing friends who can gather together with me, confident in the knowledge that you are there among us. And, Lord, let us ask and receive. And let us ask for those things that are in line with your will. Thank you, Lord, for giving us this promise through your Son, Jesus Christ.

My prayer for today—including any journaling thoughts I may want to add. Where am I today spiritually, emotionally, physically, financially, generally?

Today's Date: _____

Old Testament verse for today: Psalm 69:29 & 30

Rescue me, O God, from my poverty and pain. Then I will praise God with my singing! My thanks will be his praise.

One possible prayer for today:

God, I always need your help. Sometimes I feel that I need it more than other times—and this is one of those times! Please rescue me from my problems! Lord, I know that I must do the work, I must commit the decisions to action; but, I need your help in making the best decisions possible under these very trying circumstances. Lord, you know that I always try to praise you. You know that I always try my best to trust you and to turn to you for your guidance and help. So, God, I am turning to you again for your help. Please help me right now! Please give me the good sense I need to make the best possible decision— right now. Lord, I do thank you and praise you for your help. Thank you, Lord.

New Testament verse for today: Luke 17:6

If your faith were only the size of a mustard seed, Jesus answered, it would be large enough to uproot that mulberry tree over there and send it hurtling into the sea! Your command would bring immediate results.

One possible prayer for today:

God, I do need more faith. Please give me the shot of faith I need. I don't need to throw trees into the sea. I need to have a plan to solve my problems of the day. I wish that I could command them to be instantly solved. Maybe my faith isn't big enough, because I don't think that my problems are going to get solved that easily or quickly. But, God, I do trust you to give me the guidance I need. I trust you to be there for me to come to you and ask for help, and for you to answer. God, help me now. Help my faith in you to grow as I work through these problems in the best way I know how. Thank you for being there for me when I need you, Lord.

My prayer for today—including any journaling thoughts I may want to add. Where am I today spiritually, emotionally, physically, financially, generally?

Today's Date: _____

Old Testament verse for today: Psalm 69:32 & 33

The humble shall see their God at work for them. No wonder they will be so glad! All who seek for God shall live in joy. For Jehovah hears the cries of the needy ones, and does not look the other way.

One possible prayer for today:

God, I do humble myself before you; because, you know my heart. I can't fool you. And you know that if I am going to be honest, I don't have any place else to turn when I am in deep trouble. And, only you can make me glad again as I turn completely and helplessly to you. Let me seek you always, not just when I am in trouble. Let me live in joy. Lord, here my cries when I am needy. And, God, thank you for not turning the other way when I cry to you.

New Testament verse for today: Romans 8:24a & 25

We are saved by trusting. And trusting means looking forward to getting something we don't yet have—for a man (person) who already has something doesn't need to hope and trust that he will get it. But if we must keep trusting God for something that hasn't happened yet, it teaches us to wait patiently and confidently.

One possible prayer for today:

God, I really need that patience! The patience—and the faith—to keep trusting, and expectantly waiting—patiently and confidently—for you to help me in my times of trouble and to release me from the pain that I am presently experiencing. Lord, I do know that all things are possible through your power. You know the things that I want and you know the things that you want for me. Lord, I know that my goal is to want only those things that you want for me and not be impatient when I don't always get my way. Help me with my patience, Lord. Help me with my confidence so that I am expectantly awaiting only those things that fall within your will for my life. And, God, let me be confident in my salvation through my belief in your Son, Jesus Christ.

My prayer for today—including any journaling thoughts I may want to add. Where am I today spiritually, emotionally, physically, financially, generally?

Today's Date: _____

Old Testament verse for today: Psalm 70:1, 4 & 5

Rescue me, O God! Lord, hurry to my aid! Fill the followers of God with joy. Let those who love your salvation exclaim, "What a wonderful God he is!" But I am in deep trouble. Rush to my aid, for only you can help and save me. O Lord, don't delay.

One possible prayer for today:

God, thank you for always being there for me. Thank you for hurrying to my aid when I call on you .Thank you for your salvation that you have showered on me. Lord, I am calling on you. Thank you for hearing my pleas and rescuing me. Lord, thank you for rushing to my aid and not delaying. Thank you for being the one who can help and save me. Lord, let me always praise you and sing your praises of what a wonderful God you are to me. Thank you, Lord.

New Testament verse for today: I John 3:21 thru 23

But, dearly loved friends, if our consciences are clear, we can come to the Lord with perfect assurance and trust, and get whatever we ask for because we are obeying him and doing the things that please him. And this is what God says we must do: Believe on the name of his Son Jesus Christ, and love one another.

On possible prayer for today:

God, thank you for calling me your dearly loved friend. Lord, you know that my conscience could not be clear except that, in your love, you have forgiven me and removed the stain of my sin completely from my record! So, Lord, thank you for letting me come to you with perfect assurance and trust. Lord, let my pleadings for your help be in line with your will for my life. Let me live my life in a manner that is pleasing to you and in a manner that is in obedience to your plans for my life. Lord, I do believe in your Son, Jesus Christ, as my personal Savior. Let me show more love for others. So, Lord, I come to you again, pleading with you to hurry to my aid when I call. Thank you, Lord, for hearing me and rescuing me.

My prayer for today—including any journaling thoughts I may want to add. Where am I today spiritually, emotionally, physically, financially, generally?

Today's Date: _____

Old Testament verse for today: Psalm 71:1, 2, & 14

Lord, you are my refuge! Don't let me down! Save me from my enemies, for you are just! Rescue me! Bend down your ear and listen to my plea and save me. I will keep on expecting you to help me. I praise you more and more.

One possible prayer for today:

Lord, your Psalmist has prayed for rescue; and, I pray for rescue! Your Psalmist said to save him because You are just. I don't know that my life has been lived in such a manner that if You are just, You should save me; but, I am pleading with you anyway for your protection! I need your special help today because

And, Lord, I do expect you to help me! I cast myself on your mercy and your goodness; and, Lord, I will do my best to praise you more and more. Please give me the strength and the courage not only to face my problems today; but to do it in a manner that would be pleasing to you. Thank you for giving me the strength to make it through this day.

New Testament verse for today: John 17:2b & 3

He gives eternal life to each one You have given Him. And this is the way to eternal life— by knowing You, the only true God, and Jesus Christ, the one You sent to earth.

One possible prayer for today:

God, you love me so much. Thank you for loving me like you do; and, thank you for giving me the opportunity to experience eternal life. Thank you for making it possible; and, thank you for choosing me as one of your believers. Thank you for sending your Son to earth so that I could know Him. Thank you for being patient with me as I struggle with the daily cares of my world. Thank you for never letting go of me when I fail.

My prayer for today—including any journaling thoughts I may want to add. Where am I today spiritually, emotionally, physically, financially, generally?

Today's Date: _____

Old Testament verse for today: Psalm 71:3a

Be to me a great protecting Rock, where I am always welcome, safe from attacks.

One possible prayer for today:

God, you are my Rock. You are my Protector. And I know that I am always welcome when I come to you with a humble and a contrite heart, acknowledging your Lordship in my life. God, thank you for keeping me safe. Thank you for helping me through this day.

New Testament verse for today: John 6:39 & 40

And this is the will of God, that I should not lose even one of all those he has given me, but that I should raise them to eternal life as the Last Day. For it is my Father's will that everyone who sees his Son and believes on him should have eternal life—that I should raise him at the Last Day.

One possible prayer for today:

God, how wonderful to know that it is your will that Christ will not lose even one of those that has been given to him—and that includes me! All I have to do is believe. And, God, I do believe. I believe in your Son as my personal Savior; and, I do claim the promise that on the Last Day Christ will raise me to eternal life with him .What a great promise, Lord. Thank you for that promise and that confidence.

My prayer for today—including any journaling thoughts I may want to add. Where am I today spiritually, emotionally, physically, financially, generally?

Today's Date: _____

Old Testament verse for today: Psalm 71:6

Yes, you have been with me from birth and have helped me constantly—no wonder I am always praising you!

One possible prayer for today:

God, thank you for always being with me. Thank you for always helping me. Thank you for being constant in your love and your help. Lord, there are times when I feel that you aren't helping me. There are times when I feel that I am out there all alone. Yet, I know that you are there. You are always there. When I go through those times of doubt, Lord, please give me the shot of faith that I need. Let me, like the Psalmist, always praise you. Let me have the faith to know that you are always there—even in the bad times. Thank you, Lord, for always being there.

New Testament verse for today: Mark 13:31

"Heaven and earth shall pass disappear, but my words stand sure forever."

One possible prayer for today:

God, thank you for sending Christ to earth so that I can know that your plan of salvation is for real. Thank you for loving me that much! Thank you for the promise that no matter what happens, you are there for me. Thank you for giving me the faith that I need to always remember that promise. Thank you, God.

My prayer for today—including any journaling thoughts I may want to add. Where am I today spiritually, emotionally, physically, financially, generally?

Today's Date: _____

Old Testament verse for today: Psalm 71:7 & 8

My success—at which so many stand amazed—is because you are my mighty protector. All day long I'll praise and honor you, O God, for all you have done for me.

One possible prayer for today:

God, thank you for being my mighty protector. Thank you for all the success that you have permitted me to have. Lord, the reason that so many stand amazed at my success is because they know that I could not have done it on my own. They know that someone has to be helping me. Thank you, God, that you are the one who has helped me and continues to help me. Lord, let all that I do be an honor to your name and to the love and help that you have shown me. Let me praise you with my thoughts, words, and actions.

New Testament verse for today: Matthew 17:20b

"For if you had faith even as small as a tiny mustard seed you could say to this mountain, 'Move!' and it would go away. Nothing would be impossible."

One possible prayer for today:

God, when I realize your power, and realize that that power is all available to me, if I only have faith, that is not only awesome, but a little scary! I know that that power is available to me only when I am living in sync with your will for my life, Lord; but, I also know that if I have enough faith, there is nothing that I cannot accomplish with you in my corner. Thank you for being all powerful, Lord. Thank you for giving me the gift of faith. Thank you for letting me plug into your power to help me through the tough spots in my life, Lord. Please let me keep you in my thoughts all day long so that I may always have your enormous power available to me. Thank you, God.

My prayer for today—including any journaling thoughts I may want to add. Where am I today spiritually, emotionally, physically, financially, generally?

Today's Date: _____

Old Testament verse for today: Psalm 73:23 & 24

But even so, you love me! You are holding my right hand! You will keep on guiding me all my life with your wisdom and counsel; and afterwards receive me into the glories of heaven!

One possible prayer for today:

God, how wonderful you are! You love even me! You are always there to hold my right hand. You are always there to guide me. You are full of wisdom and counsel. God, thank you for loving me; for holding me and guiding me with your love; for giving me your wisdom and counsel; and, God, thank you, thank you, for giving me the knowledge that I can count on you receiving me into the glories of heaven! What a wonderful promise, Lord. Thank you. Thank you.

New Testament verse for today: Matthew 10:29 thru 31

Not one sparrow (What do they cost? Two for a penny?) can fall to the ground without your Father knowing it. And the very hairs of your head are all numbered. So don't worry! You are more valuable to him than many sparrows.

One possible prayer for today:

God, how can you love me so much? How can you be so concerned about me? Thank you for Christ's promise that you have even the hairs on my head numbered! Lord, if you have that kind of interest in me, why should I worry? You are in charge. You have a plan for my life today. Thank you for that plan. Thank you for giving me the faith and the confidence in that plan so that I do not have to worry. Thank you for making me feel comfortable with resting on your love and your concern. Thank you for making me feel valuable to you. Please, Lord, give me an extra shot of faith today, so that my faith in you and your plans for me truly do not waiver—no matter what kind of opportunities or challenges I face today. Thank you, Lord, for giving me that confidence.

My prayer for today—including any journaling thoughts I may want to add. Where am I today spiritually, emotionally, physically, financially, generally?

Today's Date: _____

Old Testament verse for today: Psalm 84:5

Happy are those who are strong in the Lord, who want above all else to follow your steps.

One possible prayer for today:

Lord, I do want to follow your steps; but, Lord, I keep stumbling! Please give me the strength to follow in your steps more closely; and, Lord, make me strong in you. Then, Lord, I claim the promise that I will be happy. Give me the happiness that you have promised, Lord, as I strive to follow you and honor you more consistently.

New Testament verse for today: John 6:29

Jesus told them, "This is the will of God, that you believe in the one he has sent."

One possible prayer for today:

God, I do believe in the one you sent, Jesus Christ. Thank you for sending Christ to die on the cross for my sins. Lord, let that belief in Christ grow each day, so that I am following your steps more closely. Thank you for your marvelous plan of salvation, God.

My prayer for today—including any journaling thoughts I may want to add. Where am I today spiritually, emotionally, physically, financially, generally?

Today's Date: _____

Old Testament verse for today: Psalm 84:10 thru 12

A single day spent in your Temple is better than a thousand anywhere else! I would rather be a doorman of the Temple of my God than live in palaces of wickedness. For Jehovah God is our light and our Protector. He gives us grace and glory. No good thing will he withhold from those who walk along his paths. O Lord of the armies of heaven, blessed are those who trust in you.

One possible prayer for today:

God, what a wonderful promise the Psalmist has given me in this thought. Being in your presence is so wonderful. Thank you for being my light and my protector. Thank you for giving me grace and glory. Lord, how wonderful it is to know that no good thing will you withhold from me if I walk along your paths. I claim that promise, Lord. I claim all the good things that you want me to have in my life. I do trust in you, Lord. Thank you for blessing me.

New Testament verse for today: Ephesians 2:8 & 9

Because of his kindness you have been saved through trusting Christ. And even trusting is not of yourselves; it too is a gift from God. Salvation is not a reward for the good we have done, so none of us can take any credit for it.

One possible prayer for today:

God, thank you for your grace and glory. Thank you for the wonderful gift of trusting Christ. Thank you for the gift of faith that permits me to have that trust. Thank you for giving me salvation through your Son, Jesus. Thank you for not making me earn that salvation, Lord, because you know that I could not have done that. Lord, I don't take any credit for my salvation. I just thank you for making it so easy and available to me. Thank you, God.

My prayer for today—including any journaling thoughts I may want to add. Where am I today spiritually, emotionally, physically, financially, generally?

Today's Date: _____

Old Testament verse for today: Psalm 86:1

Bend down and hear my prayer, O Lord, and answer me, for I am deep in trouble.

One possible prayer for today:

Lord, you know that many times there are circumstances that are seemingly beyond my control. You know that many times I do something that directly causes me major problems. Other times, it just seems that troubles come into my life over which I have no control. But, Lord, right now, whether it is something I have done or whether I am just the brunt of the problem, I have major problems with which I need your major help! Please hear my prayer, Lord. Please listen to my pleadings. Please give me the direction that I need. Thank you for hearing me, God. Thank you for listening to my problems and for giving me direction.

New Testament verse for today: I Peter 2:21 thru 24

This suffering is all part of the work God has given you. Christ, who suffered for you, is your example. Follow in his steps: He never sinned, never told a lie, never answered back when insulted; when he suffered, he did not threaten to get even; he left his case in the hands of God who always judges fairly. He personally carried the load of our sins in his own body when he died on the cross, so that we can be finished with sin and live a good life from now on. For his wounds have healed ours.

One possible prayer for today:

God, thank you for giving me Christ as an example. Thank you for the security I have in knowing that Christ has prepared the way for me to spend eternity with you. But, right now, Lord, I am really hurting because of my present situation. Right now, I have some hard decisions to make to get me out of the problems I have. Help me to have the strength to approach these problems in a manner that would be pleasing to you. Help me to retain my integrity and my dignity. Help me to be honest, to not lie or deceive, to not get insulting and threaten to get even. Let me leave my case in your hands and trust you to help me with the answers that are necessary to get through this period of my life. Thank you for hearing me, Lord. Thank you for helping me. Thank you for giving me the extra shot of faith that I need right now to trust you even more fully. Thank you for being there for me, Lord.

My prayer for today—including any journaling thoughts I may want to add. Where am I today spiritually, emotionally, physically, financially, generally?

Today's Date: _____

Old Testament verse for today: Psalm 86:3 thru 7

Be merciful, O Lord, for I am looking up to you in constant hope. Give me happiness, O Lord, for I worship only you. O Lord, you are so good and kind, so ready to forgive; so full of mercy for all who ask your aid. Listen closely to my prayer, O God. Hear my urgent cry. I will call to you whenever trouble strikes, and you will help me.

One possible prayer for today:

God, thank you for being merciful to me. I know that I fail you often. But, Lord, you are my only and constant hope. Thank you for the happiness that you give me. Thank you for being so good and kind to me. Thank you for forgiving me when I fail you. Thank you for being so full of mercy. Thank you for listening closely to my prayers, Lord. Thank you for always hearing my urgent cries. Lord, I do always turn to you when trouble strikes. Thank you for always being there to help me. Lord, I do worship only you. Thank you for being a God worthy of my worship.

New Testament verse for today: Hebrews 8:12

And I will be merciful to them in their wrongdoings, and I will remember their sins no more.

One possible prayer for today:

Lord, what a wonderful promise. Thank you for being merciful to me. Thank you for forgiving me of my failures. And, Lord, most of all, thank you for not only forgiving me, but for never remembering my sins again, once you have forgiven me. What a wonderful promise, Lord. Thank you, Lord, for that promise.

My prayer for today—including any journaling thoughts I may want to add. Where am I today spiritually, emotionally, physically, financially, generally?

Today's Date: _____

Old Testament verse for today: Psalm 86:11 thru 13a

Tell me where you want me to go and I will go there. May every fiber of my being unite in reverence to your name. With all my heart I will praise you. I will give glory to your name forever, for you love me so much! You are constantly so kind.

One possible prayer for today:

God, thank you for constantly being so kind to me. Thank you for guiding my life. Thank you for telling me where you want me to go. Lord, let me listen to your instructions. Let me follow your guidelines for my life. Let me always praise you with all my heart. Let me always give glory to your name. Thank you for loving me so much. Lord, let me reverence you more and more so that every fiber of my being reverences you. And, Lord, thank you for forgiving me when I fail to give you the reverence that you deserve. Thank you for always loving me, even when I fail you. Thank you, God.

New Testament verse for today: II Timothy 2:15

Work hard so God can say to you, "Well done." Be a good workman, one who does not need to be ashamed when God examines your work. Know what his Word says and means.

One possible prayer for today:

God, I know that I can only be a workman who does not need to be ashamed of my work in your eyes if you give me the strength and discipline that I need. I know that I do not have the strength and discipline on my own. I know that if I praise you with all my heart, that you will be close to me and help me at all times. I know that your Word tells me to reverence you more and more. Help me to learn to love you and trust you more in every situation in my life, Lord. Thank you, Lord, for helping me be a good workman who does not need to be ashamed in your eyes.

My prayer for today—including any journaling thoughts I may want to add. Where am I today spiritually, emotionally, physically, financially, generally?

Today's Date: _____

Old Testament verse for today: Psalm 91:2 & 9

This I declare, that he alone is my refuge, my place of safety; he is my God, and I am trusting him. For Jehovah is my refuge! I choose the God above all gods to shelter me.

One possible prayer for today:

God, how wonderful you are! Thank you for being my refuge and place of safety today. Thank you for being my God. Thank you for being trustworthy. Thank you for being the God above all other gods. Thank you for loving me and caring for me today. Thank you, God.

New Testament verse for today: Romans 5:17b & 21b

—all who take God's gift of forgiveness and acquittal are kings of life because of this one man, Jesus Christ. —now God's kindness rules—, giving us right standing with God and resulting in eternal life through Jesus Christ our Lord.

One possible prayer for today:

God, I accept your gift of forgiveness and acquittal through your plan of salvation made available through Jesus Christ. Thank you for that gift. Thank you for forgiving me and acquitting me. Thank you, God, that your kindness rules. Thank you that I can have right standing with you; and, God, thank you for giving me eternal life through Jesus Christ—my Lord.

My prayer for today—including any journaling thoughts I may want to add. Where am I today spiritually, emotionally, physically, financially, generally?

Today's Date: _____

Old Testament verse for today: Psalm 91:14

For the Lord says, "Because he loves me, I will rescue him; I will make him great because he trusts in my name. When he calls on me I will answer; I will be with him in trouble, and rescue him and honor him. I will satisfy him with a full life and give him my salvation.

One possible prayer for today:

Lord, I do love you. I do call on you continually for your help and your guidance. Thank you for your promise of rescue, for your promise of being with me in time of trouble, for your promise to rescue me, for your promise to satisfy me with a full life. Lord, I don't need to be made great. What I need is your love and your care. And, Lord, most of all thank you for your promise of salvation.

New Testament verse for today: II Timothy 1:9 & 10

It is he (God) who saved us and chose us for his holy work, not because we deserved it but because that was his plan long before the world began—to show his love and kindness to us through Christ. And now he has made all of this plain to us by the coming of our Savior Jesus Christ, who broke the power of death and showed us the way of everlasting life through trusting him.

One possible prayer for today:

Lord, thank you for not giving me what I deserve! Thank you for your continuous show of love and kindness to me. Thank you for sending your Son, Jesus, to break the power of death and to show me the way to everlasting life, if I will only trust him. Lord, thank you for giving me all these wonderful promises, and thank you for being a God who keeps his promises. Lord, I do believe in your Son, Jesus. Thank you for my salvation.

My prayer for today—including any journaling thoughts I may want to add. Where am I today spiritually, emotionally, physically, financially, generally?

Today's Date: _____

Old Testament verse for today: Psalm 92:1, 2, & 4

It is good to say, "Thank you" to the Lord, to sing praises to the God who is above all gods. Every morning, tell Him, "Thank you for your kindness," and every evening rejoice in all his faithfulness. You have done so much for me, O Lord. No wonder I am glad! I sing for joy.

One possible prayer for today:

God, "thank you" for being so good to me. "Thank you" for being above all other gods. "Thank you" for your kindness to me—yesterday, today and tomorrow. Lord, I do rejoice in your faithfulness. "Thank you" for doing so much for me. "Thank you" for being my God. Let me be faithful in worshipping you in all I do. "Thank you," God.

New Testament verse for today: John 8:12b

Jesus—"I am the light of the world. So if you follow me, you won't be stumbling through the darkness, for living light will floor your path.

One possible prayer for today:

God, thank you for sending your Son, Jesus, to guide me through the darkness of the days of my life. Thank you for having Christ flood my path with living light. Thank you for making Jesus the light of the world. Thank you for caring enough for me so that I don't have to stumble through life trying to rely on my own strength. Thank you for your love and Christ's light in my life. I claim your love and Christ's light for my strength today. Thank you, God.

My prayer for today—including any journaling thoughts I may want to add. Where am I today spiritually, emotionally, physically, financially, generally?

Today's Date: _____

Old Testament verse for today: Psalm 94:19

Lord, when doubts fill my mind, when my heart is in turmoil, quiet me and give me renewed hope and cheer.

One possible prayer for today:

God, thank you for being the God of peace. Thank you for being the God of renewed hope and cheer. Thank you for being there for me whenever I need you. Thank you for helping me through the periods of doubt and confusion. Be with me just now, Lord. Remove the dark cloud of confusion and unsettled feelings I have and replace them with the peace that only you can give. Thank you, Lord, for hearing this prayer.

New Testament verse for today: I John 1:5

This is the message God has given us to pass on to you: that God is Light and in him is no darkness at all.

One possible prayer for today:

Thank you for being the God of Light. Thank you for being a God who has no darkness in him. Thank you for removing the darkness from my life and replacing it with the light that only you can give. Thank you for being a God of mercy and forgiveness. Thank you for being my personal God.

My prayer for today—including any journaling thoughts I may want to add. Where am I today spiritually, emotionally, physically, financially, generally?

Today's Date: _____

Old Testament verse for today: Psalm 95:1 thru 3

Oh, come, let us sing to the Lord! Give a joyous shout in honor of the Rock of our salvation! Come before him with thankful hearts. Let us sing him psalms of praise. For the Lord is a great God, the great King of all gods.

One possible prayer for today:

Lord, let me always sing your praises. Let me always be joyous in my salvation which can come only through your marvelous plan. Let me always come before you with a thankful heart. Let me always be in awe of your wonderful power and majesty. Thank you, God, for being such a great God, and yet a God who loves me and cares about me. Thank you, God.

New Testament verse for today: I Peter 3:18

He (Christ) died once for the sins of all us guilty sinners, although he himself was innocent of any sin at any time, that he might bring us safely home to God.

One possible prayer for today:

God, thank you for being the Rock of my salvation and thank you for giving your Son, Jesus, as the sacrifice to make my salvation complete and secure. Thank you for being a God above all other gods. Thank you for being so loving to me that you had a plan for my salvation that covers all of my sins forever. Thank you for sending Jesus to bring me safely home to you. Thank you, God.

My prayer for today—including any journaling thoughts I may want to add. Where am I today spiritually, emotionally, physically, financially, generally?

Today's Date: _____

Old Testament verse for today: Psalm 96:4

For the Lord is great beyond description, and greatly to be praised. Worship only Him among the gods!

One possible prayer for today:

God, your wonder and your majesty are, indeed, beyond my ability to understand or describe! You are, indeed, greatly to be praised! So, God, today, I honor you. I praise you. I adore you. I thank you for being my God. I will worship only you and claim the blessing that you have promised to those who worship only you.

New Testament verse for today: Matthew 6:6 & 8

But when you pray, go away by yourself, all alone, and shut the door behind you and pray to your Father secretly, and your Father, who knows your secrets, will reward you. Remember, your Father knows exactly what you need even before you ask him!

One possible prayer for today:

God, that is almost scary to know that you know so much about me! You know my inner thoughts and desires! You know my needs, my dreams, my wishes, my secret thoughts! God, I thank you for being patient with me and rewarding me, as Christ promised, even though I don't deserve any rewards from you; because you know that my secret thoughts are not always what they should be. But, Lord, you always forgive me when I confess these thoughts to you. So, Lord, let me be in constant communication with you in my thoughts and my thanksgiving. God, I claim your rewards to me today. Thank you.

My prayer for today—including any journaling thoughts I may want to add. Where am I today spiritually, emotionally, physically, financially, generally?

Today's Date: _____

Old Testament verse for today: Psalm 100:1 thru 4

Shout with joy before the Lord, O earth! Obey him gladly; come before him, singing with joy. Try to realize what this means—the Lord is God! He made us—we are his people, the sheep of his pasture. Go thru his open gates with great thanksgiving; enter his courts with praise. Give thanks to him and bless his name.

One possible prayer for today:

God, thank you for being such a great God! Thank you for being the Lord over all! Thank you for letting me come thru your open gates with thanksgiving and letting me enter into your courts with praise. Lord, let me always come before you singing your praises. Let me come before you full of joy. Thank you for making me one of your people—one of your sheep—and one for whom you care deeply. Thank you for making me as I am. Let me always be thankful for all you have done for me. Let me always do my best to obey you and bless your name. Let me always realize that you are the Lord God of all! Thank you, Lord God.

New Testament verse for today: Hebrews 12:1b

Let us run with patience the particular race that God has set before us.

One possible prayer for today:

God, thank you again for being such a great God! Thank you for making me as I am. Thank you for giving me the ability to run the particular race that you have set before me. Let me run that race with patience. Let me run that race while singing your praises and always being thankful for all you have done for me. Let me run that race obeying you and blessing you as best I am able. Thank you for caring about me as I run the race that you have set before me. Thank you for always being there for me as I run the race you have set before me. Thank you, God, for the plan you have for my life.

My prayer for today—including any journaling thoughts I may want to add. Where am I today spiritually, emotionally, physically, financially, generally?

Today's Date: _____

Old Testament verse for today: Psalm 100:4b & 5

Give thanks to Him and bless his name. For the Lord is always good. He is always loving and kind, and his faithfulness goes on and on to each succeeding generation.

One possible prayer for today:

God, let me always remember to give thanks, no matter what my situation; because I know that it is your will! Thank you for always being good. Thank you for always being kind. Thank you for always being loving. Thank you for your everlasting faithfulness—for me and my family. Thank you for loving and forgiving me this day.

New Testament verse for today: Luke 18:7, 8a, & 13b

—don't you think that God will surely give justice to his people who plead with him day and night? Yes! He will answer them quickly! God, be merciful to me, a sinner.

One possible prayer for today:

God, sometimes knowing that you will give me justice is pretty scary! Maybe I don't want justice! Maybe I just want your love and your forgiveness. So, God, I do plead with you to answer me quickly. To always help me in my time of need, and God, thank you for being merciful to me, a sinner. Thank you, God.

My prayer for today—including any journaling thoughts I may want to add. Where am I today spiritually, emotionally, physically, financially, generally?

Today's Date: _____

Old Testament verse for today: Psalm 101:1 thru 4

I will sing about your loving-kindness and your justice, Lord. I will sing your praises! I will try to walk a blameless path, but how I need your help, especially in my own home, where I long to act as I should. Help me to refuse the low and vulgar things; help me to abhor all crooked deals of every kind, to have no part of them. I will reject all selfishness and stay away from every evil.

One possible prayer for today:

God, you know my heart. You know that I have every intention of keeping your praises constantly in my heart and on my lips. You know that I have every intention of trying to walk a blameless path, of refusing low and vulgar things, of abhorring deceit and dishonesty, of rejecting selfishness and evil. But, Lord, you also know how often I fail. You know how badly I need your help in every one of these areas. You know that even in my own home and with those close to me, I fail to live up to your goals for me. So, Lord, I do pray for your help. Give me the strength that I need to do better in all of these areas. And, Lord, when I fail you, thank you for always being there to forgive me when I return to you with a humble and a contrite heart. Thank you for your everlasting love, Lord.

New Testament verse for today: James 2:12

You will be judged on whether or not you are doing what Christ wants you to. So watch what you do and what you think; for there will be no mercy to those who have shown no mercy. But if you have been merciful, then God's mercy toward you will win out over his judgment against you.

One possible prayer for today:

God, thank you for being merciful to me. Give me the strength and the correct attitude toward others. Let me be merciful to those whose lives come in contact with mine. You know that I need your help in every area of my life. Lord, thank you for being such a merciful God that your mercy will win out over your judgment against me. Let your praises constantly be in my heart and mind and let me thank you always for being such a merciful God.

My prayer for today—including any journaling thoughts I may want to add. Where am I today spiritually, emotionally, physically, financially, generally?

Today's Date: _____

Old Testament verse for today: Psalm 103:1 thru 5

I bless the holy name of God with all my heart. Yes, I will bless the Lord and not forget the glorious things he does for me. He forgives all my sins. He heals me. He ransoms me from hell. He surrounds me with lovingkindness and tender mercies. He fills my life with good things! My youth is renewed like the eagle's!

One possible prayer for today:

God, let me always bless your holy name with all my heart. Lord, I know you do such wonderful things for me, and I thank you for that. I know that you forgive all my sins, and I thank you for that. I know that you have ransomed me from hell, and I thank you for that. I know that you have surrounded me with lovingkindness and tender mercies, and I thank you for that. But, Lord, today I am hurting and I need you to heal me—physically, mentally, and emotionally. I need my strength to be renewed like the eagle's. Lord, I thank you that you are hearing my prayer and that you will respond as it serves your needs, and I thank you for that. Lord, give me the strength to respond to your response to me and my prayers in a manner that would be pleasing to you. Thank you, Lord, for giving me that strength.

New Testament verse for today: I Corinthians 2:9b

—the Scriptures—say that no mere man has ever seen, heard or even imagined what wonderful things God has ready for those who love the Lord.

One possible prayer for today:

Lord, let me believe that promise more fully, for when I am hurting, I am caught up in the here and now, not in the everlasting! So, God, give me a stronger vision of the wonderful things that you have ready for me, for I do love you. I honor you with my prayers and my worship. Now, Lord, I need to have at least a little glimpse of the wonderful things you have in store for me, so that I can keep going today. Help me, Lord, and thank you for helping me.

My prayer for today—including any journaling thoughts I may want to add. Where am I today spiritually, emotionally, physically, financially, generally?

Today's Date: _____

Old Testament verse for today: Psalm 103:8 thru 12

He is merciful and tender toward those who don't deserve it; he is slow to get angry and full of kindness and love. He never bears a grudge, nor remains angry forever. He has not punished us as we deserve for our sins, for his mercy toward those who fear and honor him is as great as the height of the heavens above the earth. He has removed our sins as far away from us as the east is from the west.

One possible prayer for today:

Lord, what a wonderful set of promise the Psalmist has given us! You have been full of mercy and tenderness even when I don't deserve it. Thank you, God. Thank you for putting up with my human foibles. Thank you for not bearing a grudge against me when I continue to sin. Thank you for not remaining angry at me when I let you down. And, God, thank you so much for not punishing me as I deserve. And, thank you for removing my sins from me as far as the east is from the west. Thank you, God, for the scope of your mercy.

New Testament verse for today: Matthew 22:37 thru 39 & 40b

Jesus replied, "Love the Lord your God with all your heart, soul, and mind. This is the first and greatest commandment. The second more important is similar: Love your neighbor as much as you love yourself. Keep only these and you will find that you are obeying all the others."

One possible prayer for today:

Lord, when you love me so much, how can I do less than try to love you with all heart, soul, and mind? Let me love you more each day, Lord, as I rely on your guidance in my life. Let me be more concerned about others and not so caught up in my own problems, Lord. Thank you for loving me first so that I can love in turn.

My prayer for today—including any journaling thoughts I may want to add. Where am I today spiritually, emotionally, physically, financially, generally?

Today's Date: _____

Old Testament verse for today: Psalm 103:17 & 18

But the loving-kindness of the Lord is from everlasting to everlasting, to those who reverence Him; His salvation is to children's children of those who are faithful to His covenant and remember to obey Him.

One possible prayer for today:

God, thank you that your loving-kindness to me lasts forever. Thank you that all I have to do to claim that loving-kindness is to reverence you. Thank you for my salvation. Thank you for the promise of salvation to my children if I will be faithful and obey. Lord, You know that I do not always obey; but you have promised that when I return to you, you will always be there for me. Thank you, God, for your steadfast and everlasting love to me.

New Testament verse for today: James 3:13

If you are wise, live a life of steady goodness, so that only good deeds will pour forth. And if you don't brag about them, then you will be truly wise.

One possible prayer for today:

God, I know that in my life, good deeds do not always pour forth! And when I do happen to do something good, I can't wait to tell others what good things I have done! So, God, thank you for forgiving me when I fail to do good. Thank you for forgiving me when my ego gets in the way when I do happen to do something good. Thank you for helping me to do better on a consistent basis. Thank you for being everlasting in your goodness even though I am far from everlasting, or even consistent in mine.

My prayer for today—including any journaling thoughts I may want to add. Where am I today spiritually, emotionally, physically, financially, generally?

Today's Date: _____

Old Testament verse for today: Psalm 103:19 thru 22
The Lord has made the heavens his throne; from there he rules over everything there is. Bless the Lord, you mighty angels of his who carry out his orders, listening for each of his commands. Yes, bless the Lord, you armies of his angels who serve him constantly. Let everything everywhere bless the Lord. And how I bless him too!

One possible prayer for today:
God, how wonderful it is to have a God like you to worship who is so worthy of my praise and adoration. Thank you for ruling over everything from your throne in the heavens. Thank you for having armies of angels who listen to your every command, serving you constantly, and carrying out your orders. Lord, let me do my best to honor you with everything that I do. Let me do my best to also serve you constantly and carry out the plan you have for my life. And, Lord, thank you for always forgiving me when I fall short of meeting your plan for my life. Thank you for being such a wonderful, worthy and forgiving God.

New Testament verse for today: Ephesians 6:7 & 8a
Work hard and with gladness all the time, as though working for Christ, doing the will of God with all your hearts. Remember, the Lord will pay you for each good thing you do.

One possible prayer for today:
Lord, let my life be a blessing to you as I try to keep the model of Christ as my goal and inspiration. Let me work hard and with gladness in all that I do, doing my best to always do your will in everything. Like your mighty angels, let me listen to your commands for my life, carrying out your orders for me. And, Lord, I know that you will bless me as you see fit. I know that you have already give me the best payment that I could ever receive—eternal life with you because of what Christ has done for me. Thank you, Lord, for that wonderful payment.

My prayer for today—including any journaling thoughts I may want to add. Where am I today spiritually, emotionally, physically, financially, generally?

Today's Date: _____

Old Testament verse for today: Psalm 104:24 & 33 & 34

Lord, what a variety you have made! And in wisdom you have made them all! The earth is full of your riches. I will sing to the Lord as long as I live. I will praise God to my last breath! May he be pleased by all these thoughts about him, for he is my source of joy.

One possible prayer for today:

Lord, this is a great day! Thank you for this day! This is a day when I can look around and be absolutely amazed at your imagination. The beauty of the world. The sky. The trees and flowers. The birds and the little animals that are running around! God, how could you have been so creative? And how could you have made all of these things for me to enjoy? And, thank you for giving me the eyes, ears, and feeling to enjoy all the sights and sounds that you have made. Thank you for giving mankind the ability to use the things that you have made to give us the wonderful buildings and cars that we have at our disposal. Thank you, God, for being so wonderful to me!

New Testament verse for today: Matthew 6:19 thru 21

"Don't store up treasures here on earth where they can erode away or may be stolen. Store them in heaven where they will never lose their value, and are safe from thieves. If your profits are in heaven your heart will be there too."

One possible prayer for today:

God, I know that my ultimate reward will be in heaven based on my faith in you and the salvation you have provided for me through the death and resurrection of your Son, Jesus Christ. But, while I am here on earth, I am going to enjoy the wonderful blessings you have given to me. You made them for me to enjoy. You gave me the ability to enjoy them while I am here. I know that I have to keep in mind the ultimate goal of my life, which is to worship and adore you; so, today, I am worshipping you and adoring you for the great variety of the wonders you have made. Thank you, Lord, for your created wonders for me to enjoy.

My prayer for today—including any journaling thoughts I may want to add. Where am I today spiritually, emotionally, physically, financially, generally?

Today's Date: _____

Old Testament verse for today: Psalm 109:21

But as for me, O Lord, deal with me as your child, as one who bears your name! Because you are so kind, O Lord, deliver me.

One possible prayer for today:

Lord, today, I am feeling like a little child. I don't want to go out into the world and face today. The problems of today. The challenges of today. I just want to stay in bed and pull the covers over my head and have someone take care of me! So, God, I am counting on you to do that for me today. I know that I do have to go out and face my set of challenges for today. I can't stay in bed and pull the covers over my head. So, God, deal with me as your special child today. Guide my every step, every action, every word. Deliver me through this day. Give me the strength that I need. Thank you, God, for always being there when I need you. Let me feel close to you today.

New Testament verse for today: Romans 4:24b & 25

(We are assured)—that God will accept us—when we believe the promises of God who brought back Jesus our Lord from the dead. He died for our sins and rose again to make us right with God, filling us with God's goodness.

One possible prayer for today:

God, thank you for that promise to accept me. Lord, I do believe. Help me when my faith waivers. Give me an extra shot of faith! Lord, you loved me so much that you gave your Son, Jesus to die for my sins; but, then in your love, you had Christ rise again so that I could be right with you. Thank you, God. Thank you for filling me with your goodness today. Thank you for helping me to meet my challenges of today. Thank you again for accepting me just as I am. Thank you, God.

My prayer for today—including any journaling thoughts I may want to add. Where am I today spiritually, emotionally, physically, financially, generally?

Today's Date: _____

Old Testament verse for today: Psalm 109:26

Help me, O Lord my God! Save me because you are so loving and kind.

One possible prayer for today:

God, today I do need your help. Just as the Psalmist prayed for you to save, please save me! I am in deep trouble. I need your help to (name your need). God, I make lots of mistakes, and I probably brought this trouble on myself because of my actions ;but, I cannot see any way out of this problem. So, I plead with you to help me! Save me! Give me direction as to which way to turn and what decisions I should make. Oh God, thank you for hearing my prayer and thank you for giving me the direction I need.

New Testament verse for today: James 4:8a

And when you draw close to God, God will draw close to you.

One possible prayer for today:

Oh God, what a wonderful promise! Thank you for drawing close to me. Thank you for being there when I need you. God, I know that when I don't feel close to you, it is not because you have moved. It is because I have moved. My faith has been weak. My life has been out of kilter. My looking to you has waned or subsided. Let me take the steps of drawing close to you, knowing that you are always there. Thank you, God, for always being there. Help me not to draw away, so that in my times of trouble, I don't have to come back to you. I will already be feeling close to you and feeling the power that only you can provide.

My prayer for today—including any journaling thoughts I may want to add. Where am I today spiritually, emotionally, physically, financially, generally?

Today's Date: _____

Old Testament verse for today: Psalm 111:10

How can men be wise? The only way to begin is by reverence for God. For growth in wisdom comes from obeying his laws. Praise his name forever.

One possible prayer for today:

Lord, I need lots of wisdom because I often don't exhibit a lot of common sense when left to my own actions! I need the wisdom that you can offer. So, Lord, let me reverence you in my life, my thoughts, and my actions. Let me reverence you in all that I do. Let me work real hard at obeying your laws. And then, Lord, I claim the Psalmist's promise of growing wisdom. I need it, Lord. I claim it as a result of reverence for you and obeying your laws. And, God, let me praise your name for all my life. Let me do my little part to honor you with my life. Thank you, God, for forgiving me when I fail to live up to your ideals; and, thank you for giving me the wisdom to fail less often. Thank you, God.

New Testament verse for today: Romans 3:3b & 4

—just because they broke their promises to God, does that mean God will break his promises? Of course not! Though everyone else in the world is a liar, God is not. Do you remember what the book of Psalms says about this? That God's words will always prove true and right, no matter who questions them.

One possible prayer for today:

God, thank you for always being there for me, even when I am not there for you! Thank you for never breaking your promises to me, even when I break my promises to you. Thank you for always being there for me when I come to my senses and return to you. Thank you for always being full of forgiveness, even after I have failed you miserably and come crawling back to ask for forgiveness. Thank you that your words always prove true and right. Thank you, God.

My prayer for today—including any journaling thoughts I may want to add. Where am I today spiritually, emotionally, physically, financially, generally?

Today's Date: _____

Old Testament verse for today: Psalm 112:1

Praise the Lord! For all who fear God and trust in him are blessed beyond expression. Yes, happy is the man who delights in doing his commands.

One possible prayer for today:

God, let me always praise you and thank you with my thoughts and my actions. Let me love you and fear you at the same time; because, your love is unlimited and your power is awesome! Let me always trust you; and, then Lord, I claim the Psalmist's promises that I will be blessed beyond expression! Lord, let me delight in doing your commands; and, then I claim the Psalmist's promise of happiness. Lord, thank you for letting me praise and honor you. Thank you for accepting my simple actions of praise and honor to you. Thank you for loving me at all times. Thank you, Lord.

New Testament verse for today: Romans 2:7

He will give eternal life to those who patiently do the will of God, seeking for the unseen glory and honor and eternal life that he offers.

One possible prayer for today:

God, thank you for your promise of eternal life through belief in your Son, Jesus Christ. Thank you for making that plan of salvation available to me. Lord, you know that no matter how hard I try, I cannot always measure up to doing your will. You know that I often fail to meet your standards. And, yet, you love me and continue to offer me eternal life as long as I continue to believe in your Son, Jesus. What a sacrifice you made for me; and, how little you expect from me in return. Thank you for making it so easy for me to have eternal life. Thank you for the free gift you have offered me. Thank you for giving me the faith that I need to believe. Thank you, God.

My prayer for today—including any journaling thoughts I may want to add. Where am I today spiritually, emotionally, physically, financially, generally?

Today's Date: _____

Old Testament verse for today: Psalm 112:7

He (all who fear God) does not fear bad news, nor live in dread of what may happen. For he is settled in his mind that Jehovah will take care of him.

One possible prayer for today:

God, thank you for giving me the security of knowing that I do not have to fear bad news or live in dread of what may happen. Thank you for giving me the peace of knowing—of having it settled in my mind—that you will take care of me. Thank you for giving me the faith to believe that even when things may not go the way I want them to go. Let me have the faith to really believe that you are always in charge of the events of my life and give you thanks for whatever occurs in my life, because I know and accept that that is your will for me at that moment. Thank you for the strength and the faith to really believe that and to praise you at all times! Thank you, God.

New Testament verse for today: Hebrews 12:28

Since we have a kingdom nothing can destroy, let us please God by serving him with thankful hearts, and with holy fear and awe.

One possible prayer for today:

God, thank you for giving me the promise of an everlasting kingdom of being with you for eternity. Thank you for making that a kingdom that nothing can destroy. Let me live my life in such a manner that it is pleasing to you. Let me be thankful at all times, even though sometimes I have to look ahead at your future promises rather than feel sorry for myself because of my present circumstance. Let me serve you. Let me always have a thankful heart. And, Lord, I am in awe of your everlasting power, your continuing love, and your never ending forgiveness. Thank you for being such an awesome God.

My prayer for today—including any journaling thoughts I may want to add. Where am I today spiritually, emotionally, physically, financially, generally?

Today's Date: _____

Old Testament verse for today: Psalm 116:1, 2 & 5

I love the Lord because he hears my prayers and answers them. Because he bends down and listens. I will pray as long as I breathe! How kind he is! How good he is! So merciful, this God of ours.

One possible prayer for today:

God, I do love you. Thank you for forgiving me for not loving you more and showing it more often. Thank you for being merciful to me. Thank you for hearing my prayers and answering them. Thank you for giving me the wisdom to ask you for things that are in line with your will for my life. Thank you for being good, and kind, and merciful to me—today.

New Testament verse for today: John 5:24 & 34b

Jesus said, "I say emphatically that anyone who listens to my message and believes in God who sent me has eternal life, and will never be damned for his sins, but already has passed out of death into life. —believe in me and be saved."

One possible prayer for today:

Oh God, what a wonderful promise! How could I not love you when you sent your Son to give me such great promises of eternal life! Thank you for not damning me for my sins. Thank you that all I have to do the be saved is to believe in you and your Son Jesus. God, help me to overcome any hint of unbelief. Thank you for helping me, for loving me, and for forgiving me.

My prayer for today—including any journaling thoughts I may want to add. Where am I today spiritually, emotionally, physically, financially, generally?

Today's Date: _____

Old Testament verse for today: Psalm 117

Praise the Lord, all nations everywhere. Praise Him, all the peoples of the earth. For he loves us very dearly, And his truth endures. Praise the Lord.

One possible prayer for today:

God, I am having one of those days when I don't feel like praising anyone or anything—even you! So, today, I need your special help. I need to be reassured that you do love me dearly. I need to be reassured that your truth endures. I need to be reassured that your promises will all come true for me. God, help me today. Especially today. Give me the faith that I need for the challenges of today. Thank you, God, for loving me dearly and for letting me know—today—that you love me.

New Testament verse for today: John 4:22 & 23

For it's not where we worship that counts, but how we worship—is our worship spiritual and real? Do we have the Holy Spirit's help? For God is Spirit, and we must have his help to worship as we should. The Father wants this kind of worship from us.

One possible prayer for today:

God, help me! I do want to worship you. And I want my worship to be spiritual and real. And I know that I cannot do that without your loving Holy Spirit's help. God, please send your Holy Spirit to me right now to help me worship you right now the way that I should. You know that I am hurting. You know that I cannot worship you on my own the way that I should. I need your Holy Spirit's help. And you have promised that help for me—right now. Thank you, God, for that help and for putting up with me and for forgiving me when I feel the way that I do now. I know that that feeling only occurs because of my lack of faith. Thank you, Lord, for helping me right now.

My prayer for today—including any journaling thoughts I may want to add. Where am I today spiritually, emotionally, physically, financially, generally?

Today's Date: _____

Old Testament verse for today: Psalm 118:1 & 6 & 21

Oh, thank the Lord, for he's so good! His lovingkindness is forever. He is for me! How can I be afraid? What can mere man do to me? O Lord, thank you so much for answering my prayer and saving me.

One possible prayer for today:

God, you are so good; and, you are for me! What a wonderful promise. God, today, I am going to cling to that promise as I go about my day. I am going to try to remember you more often, thank you more often for all those things I normally take for granted, and thank you for answering my prayer and saving me. I do get caught up in my own agenda, Lord, and I can't figure out why everyone else doesn't want to march to my drummer! So, today, let me settle down, rely on you, trust you, and continually thank you for answering my prayer and saving me.

New Testament verse for today: Romans 4:4b & 5

—being saved is a gift: if a person could earn it by being good, then it wouldn't be free—but it is! It is given to those who do not work for it. For God declares sinners to be good in his sight if they have faith in Christ to save them from God's wrath.

One possible prayer for today:

God, how could anyone reject such a great gift? I know that I am not good. I know that sometimes I really mess up. I have all the ambitions, feelings, desires and excuses that anyone else has. But, God, you have given me the free gift of eternal life in your Son, Jesus. And all I have to do to take advantage of that gift is to believe! Wow! That is incredible! I could never achieve the goal of following all of your commandments and rules. But, you knew that, Lord. And you declared me—even sinful me—good in your sight if I believe. And, I do, Lord. Thank you for giving me the faith to believe. Thank you for declaring me good in your sight.

My prayer for today—including any journaling thoughts I may want to add. Where am I today spiritually, emotionally, physically, financially, generally?

Today's Date: _____

Old Testament verse for today: Psalm 118:24 & 25

This is the day that the Lord has made. We will rejoice and be glad in it. O Lord, please help us. Save us. Give us success.

One possible prayer for today:

Thank you, God, for making this day! God, don't let me judge the day by the weather! Let me rejoice because it is a day that you have made for me! Thank you, God, that I can rejoice and be glad in this day, because you are watching over me and love me. Thank you, God, for helping me this day. Thank you for saving me this day. Thank you, God, for giving me success this day in my endeavors. Thank you, God, that you will guide me, my thoughts, and my actions, so that they are acceptable to you. Thank you, God.

New Testament verse for today: Romans 5:1 & 2

So now, since we have been made right in God's sight by faith in His promises, we can have real peace with Him because of what Jesus Christ our Lord has done for us. For because of our faith, he has brought us into this place of highest privilege where we now stand, and we confidently and joyfully look forward to actually becoming all that God has had in mind for us to be.

One possible prayer for today:

Thank you, God, for making me right in your sight. Not because of anything that I have done to make me right, other than believing in you through faith in your Son, Jesus Christ. Thank you for giving me that wonderful peace that comes from that faith. Thank you for giving me the gift of faith. Thank you for helping me, sinner that I am, to become all that you had in mind for me. Thank you for forgiving me and never giving up on me. Thank you for who I am today. Thank you for helping me to become better in all ways today. Thank you, God.

My prayer for today—including any journaling thoughts I may want to add. Where am I today spiritually, emotionally, physically, financially, generally?

Today's Date: _____

Old Testament verse for today: Psalm 118:29

Oh, give thanks to the Lord, for He is good! For His lovingkindness is forever.

One possible prayer for today:

God, you are so good! Thank you for being so good to me. Thank you for helping me in every step of my life. My personal life. My business life. My relationships with my business associates and my family. My financial life. My social life. God, thank you for being concerned about every facet of my life. And, God, thank you that your lovingkindness does, in fact, last forever.

New Testament verse for today: Matthew 7:12

Jesus said, "Do unto others what you want them to do for you. This is the teaching of the laws of Moses in a nutshell."

One possible prayer for today:

God, how I sometimes struggle with this admonition. I don't treat others as I want to be treated in every situation. I am selfish and self-centered. I want my way. But, God, you always love me and want the best for me. I confess my selfishness and self-centeredness to you and thank you for forgiving me of those sins and traits. Thank you for continuing to work with me and on me and on my attitude and actions. Thank you for loving me, God. Help me to try harder to follow this admonition that has become known as "The Golden Rule." Let me try harder to make it a "Golden Rule" of my life.

My prayer for today—including any journaling thoughts I may want to add. Where am I today spiritually, emotionally, physically, financially, generally?

Today's Date: _____

Old Testament verse for today: Psalm 119:1 thru 3

Happy are all who perfectly follow the laws of God. Happy are all who search for God, and always do His will, rejecting compromise with evil, and walking only in His paths.

One possible prayer for today:

Lord, you know that I cannot do that! You know that I cannot perfectly follow your laws all the time and you know that I cannot always do your will! Who am I kidding? I sin all the time! I fall short of your goals for me consistently! And, I am not always happy. I am only human with all the ups and downs of any other person. But, Lord, I know that as long as I come back to you and ask for your forgiveness that you are always faithful to forgive me. Thank you for that. And, Lord, when I am not happy, it is usually because I am having my own little crisis of being concerned about me and my problems. No matter how large my problems may seem, Lord, I know that you care about me and can give me a peace that can only come from you. So help me to look to you and trust you more consistently and more fully. Then I know that my chances for continued happiness—or at least content-ment—are greater than if I try to go it alone.

New Testament verse for today: Romans 8:38 & 39

For I am convinced that nothing can ever separate us from His (God's) love. Death can't, and life can't. The angels won't, and all the powers of hell itself cannot keep God's love away. Our fears for today, our worries about tomorrow, or where we are—high above the sky, or in the deepest ocean—nothing will ever be able to separate us from the love of God demonstrated by our Lord Jesus Christ when He died for us.

One possible prayer for today:

God, that is the answer! I really don't need to worry or have my own personal identity crisis! For you are always there. Nothing—but my own rebellion—can ever separate me from your love. Thank you, God. Thank you for loving me; and forgiving me; and for always being there for me. Thank you. Thank you. Thank you.

My prayer for today—including any journaling thoughts I may want to add. Where am I today spiritually, emotionally, physically, financially, generally?

Today's Date: _____

Old Testament verse for today: Psalm 119:9

How can a young man stay pure? By reading your word and following its rules.

One possible prayer for today:

God, whether young or old, man or woman, it is tough to stay pure in today's world. There are so many things to tempt me. So, God, help me to stay as pure as possible. Help me to want to stay pure. Help me to keep my obligations, my promises, and my commitments. Help me to keep my commitments to you. Help me to study your word more so that I might have a solid guideline for my life. Thank you for giving me this guideline, and thank you for giving me the strength and the desire to follow that guideline more closely.

New Testament verse for today: Romans 11:29

For God's gifts and his call can never be withdrawn; he will never go back on his promises.

One possible prayer for today:

Wow! What a wonderful promise, Lord! Even though I may fail you, you have promised that your welcoming hand and your love is always extended to me! You have said that all I need to do is believe and trust, and to be fair and just and merciful. God, give me the desire, the strength, and the faith to do those things. Thank you for the gift of faith. Thank you for calling me to you. Thank you for never withdrawing those promises. Thank you, God, for accepting me. Thank you for helping me to follow your rules and to really try to stay pure.

My prayer for today—including any journaling thoughts I may want to add. Where am I today spiritually, emotionally, physically, financially, generally?

Today's Date: _____

Old Testament verse for today: Psalm 119:11

I have thought much about your words, and stored them in my heart so that they would hold me back from sin.

One possible prayer for today:

God, thank you for your words. Thank you for being an everlasting God so that your words are as applicable today as they were in the time of the Psalmist. Thank you for giving me the ability to store your words in my heart. Lord, when I am tempted, let me look to your words and to your advice to help me. Help me to have the strength to put sin and temptation behind me. Thank you for holding me back from sinning against you. And, God, thank you most of all for always forgiving me after I have sinned, but then return and honestly confess that sin to you. Thank you, God.

New Testament verse for today: I Corinthians 16:13

Keep your eyes open for spiritual danger; stand true to the Lord: act like men; be strong; and whatever you do, do it with kindness and love.

One possible prayer for today:

Lord, I know that I operate in an arena where sin abounds. I know that I am constantly beset with temptations. I also know that you have the power to keep me from the harm that sin brings into my life. I know that storing your words in my heart is one way of holding me back from sin. I know that you have given me the free will to make good decisions. So, God, help me to keep my eyes open for spiritual danger. Help me to shun situations where I would be tempted beyond my own ability to choose not to sin. Let me stand true to you, Lord. Let me be strong in my faith and in my commitment to you. And, Lord, let me live my life as an act of kindness and love for you, because you have been so kind, so loving, and so forgiving of me.

My prayer for today—including any journaling thoughts I may want to add. Where am I today spiritually, emotionally, physically, financially, generally?

Today's Date: _____

Old Testament verse for today: Psalm 119:29 thru 33

Keep me far from every wrong; help me, undeserving as I am, to obey your laws, for I have chosen to do right. I cling to your commands and follow them as closely as I can. Lord, don't let me make a mess of things. If you will only help me want your will, then I will follow your laws even more closely. Just tell me what to do and I will do it, Lord.

One possible prayer for today:

Lord, help me. The key to doing your will, as the Psalmist said, is choosing to do right and asking for your help to want to do your will. Lord, you have given me a free will. I can use it for either right or wrong. Help me to want to do right. Help me to choose to do right. Help me to listen to your leading and direction in my life. God, thank you for helping me. Thank you for caring about me and about what I do. Thank you for being my personal God.

New Testament verse for today: Hebrews 13:5b thru 6; and 8

For God has said, "I will never, never fail you nor forsake you." That is why we can say without any doubt or fear, "The Lord is my Helper and I am not afraid of anything that mere man can do to me." Jesus Christ is the same yesterday, today, and forever.

One possible prayer for today:

God, thank you for that promise! What a wonderful promise. Yes, there are times when I do feel forsaken, and there are other times when I feel you are watching over me very closely. Lord, give me the faith to believe it more often and more completely. Give me the faith to know that you are always my Helper. Thank you for forgiving me my fears and lack of faith. Thank you for never forsaking me. Lord, help me to never forsake you! Let me operate my life to be free from doubt and fear. Thank you for the faith and wisdom to make decisions so that it is easier to live without fear. Thank you again, Lord, for that great promise.

My prayer for today—including any journaling thoughts I may want to add. Where am I today spiritually, emotionally, physically, financially, generally?

Today's Date: _____

Old Testament verse for today: Psalm 119:43 & 49 & 58

May I never forget your words; for they are my only hope. Never forget your promises to me your servant, for they are my only hope. With all my heart I want your blessings. Be merciful just as you promised.

One possible prayer for today:

God, with all my heart I do want your blessings. I know that that may be selfish; but, Lord, I really want and need your blessings. Help me to remember your words. And as long as you have given me all the great promises you have given me in your Word, I am going to claim your blessings, expect your blessings, and thank you for your blessings! Thank you for being merciful, just as you promised. Be merciful to me today, Lord, as I stumble through the problems of today. Thank you for being my only hope.

New Testament verse for today: Matthew 6:27 & 34

Will all your worries add a single moment to your life? So don't be anxious about tomorrow. God will take care of your tomorrow too. Live one day at a time.

One possible prayer for today:

God, I don't know how Christ's admonition to live one day at a time fits into today's world where we need to plan each day, keep schedules, save for the future, buy insurance, and all the other things that are part of today's world. But, I do know that worrying isn't going to help! That isn't going to add any time to my life or add any pleasure to the time I have left. In many ways, I really don't have any choice but to put my life, my plans, my future, my all, into your hands, Lord. My life could end tomorrow and all the worrying that I have done about tomorrow would not have mattered. On the other hand, I do need to be responsible with the time and talent you have given me. So, Lord, help me to achieve the balance you want me to have in my life. Let me look to you more and rely on you more to live each day as if you were walking by my side, holding my hand. Because, you really are. Thank you, God, for giving me the balance I need in my life today. Then tomorrow, you and I together will face those problems! Thank you, God.

My prayer for today—including any journaling thoughts I may want to add. Where am I today spiritually, emotionally, physically, financially, generally?

Today's Date: _____

Old Testament verse for today: Psalm 119:114

You are my refuge and my shield, and your promises are my only source of hope.

One possible prayer for today:

Once again, Lord, I have gotten myself into a messy situation where I need your help. I don't know why I continue to make such thoughtless mistakes; but, I do! And, once again, I really need your help to give me direction to get out of this mess. You are my only source of hope! It may take a miracle to get me out of this one. But, I know that you are the source of all miracles. I know that I do not deserve your help. I also know that I must plead for it and I do. Thank you for hearing me, Lord. Thank you for being my refuge and my shield as I go through this trying time.

New Testament verse for today: Luke 11:13

And if sinful persons like yourselves give children what they need, don't you realize that your heavenly Father will do at least as much, and give the Holy Spirit to those who ask for Him?

One possible prayer for today:

God, I claim that promise that Christ stated. I know that you are the giver of every perfect gift, and I ask that you imbue me with your loving Holy Spirit. I know that maybe I am being manipulative in asking for that gift when I am also asking you to bail me out of a problem; but, Lord, I need your help. I need the help of your loving Holy Spirit. And, then I need to work harder at keeping in touch with you and relying on you for help and guidance on a day by day basis, rather than relying on my own lack of wisdom. Thank you for your help. Thank you for your loving Holy Spirit. Thank you for having your Son, Jesus, make intercession for me in my time of trouble.

My prayer for today—including any journaling thoughts I may want to add. Where am I today spiritually, emotionally, physically, financially, generally?

Today's Date: _____

Old Testament verse for today: Psalm 119:124 & 125

Lord, deal with me in lovingkindness, and teach me, your servant, to obey; for I am your servant; therefore give me common sense to apply your rules to everything I do.

One possible prayer for today:

God, sometimes I really do not use the common sense you have already given me! I continue to blow it! I am egotistical and self-centered! Lord, thank you for dealing with me in lovingkindness when I do blow it. Thank you for continuing to work with me, when anyone with less love than you, God, would have given up on me a long time ago. But, God, I am your servant. I do want to be receptive to your teaching. I do want to obey your rules. I do want to use common sense in applying your rules to my everyday life. Help me, God. Thank you for helping me to apply my common sense better, God. Thank you.

New Testament verse for today: Luke 11:9 & 10

And so it is with prayer—keep on asking and you will keep on getting; keep on looking and you will keep on finding; knock and the door will be opened. Everyone who asks receives; all who seek, find; and the door is opened to everyone who knocks.

One possible prayer for today:

God, that promise makes me feel better already. Thank you for that promise. Don't let me ever waiver in my asking, seeking, and knocking on your door. I know that sometimes my timetable does not coincide with yours; but, God, I know that you are listening. I know that you have a plan for my life. I know that you will help me. Lord, today I ask for another shot of faith to continue to ask, seek, and knock, even when the going is tough and sometimes my faith falters in believing that you do really listen and care. Thank you for listening and caring, Lord; and thank you for not giving up on me when my faith does waiver. Thank you again, Lord, for this promise.

My prayer for today—including any journaling thoughts I may want to add. Where am I today spiritually, emotionally, physically, financially, generally?

Today's Date: _____

Old Testament verse for today: Psalm 119:132

Come and have mercy on me as is your way with those who love you.

One possible prayer for today:

God, please come and have mercy on me today. I am hurting. I need your help. I need your guidance. I need to feel your loving arms around me. God, you know that I love you, so I am claiming this promise. Come, now, and have mercy on me!

New Testament verse for today: John 14:27

"I am leaving you a gift—peace of mind and heart! And the peace I give isn't fragile like the peace the world gives. So don't be troubled or afraid."

One possible prayer for today:

What a wonderful promise from Christ! Thank you for the gift of peace of mind and heart. Thank you for this minute coming to comfort me with that peace. Thank you for helping me to not be troubled or afraid. Thank you for giving me the faith that I need to get through this period. Thank you, God.

My prayer for today—including any journaling thoughts I may want to add. Where am I today spiritually, emotionally, physically, financially, generally?

Today's Date: _____

Old Testament verse for today: Psalm 119:169 & 170

O Lord, listen to my prayers; give me the common sense you promised. Hear my prayers; rescue me as you said you would.

One possible prayer for today:

Lord, you know that I need a lot of common sense! You know that I go off half cocked many times because I don't take a minute and ask for your guidance. You have promised to give me the common sense that I need. Let me take you up on your offer! You will listen to my prayers and help me, so let me remember to look to you for that help. And, Lord, when I make a blunder by acting without asking for your help, rescue me from that blunder. Thank you for being such a generous and forgiving God. Thank you.

New Testament verse for today: Colossians 2:6 & 7

And now just as you trusted Christ to save you, trust him, too, for each day's problems; live in vital union with him. Let your roots grow down into him and draw up nourishment from him. See that you go on growing in the Lord, and become strong and vigorous in the truth you were taught. Let your lives overflow with joy and thanksgiving for all he has done.

One possible prayer for today:

Thank you, God, for giving me salvation through your Son, Jesus. Thank you for permitting me to trust him to save me. Thank you for giving me the faith to trust him to help me with all my problems every day. Let my union with Christ grow stronger. Let me depend upon him and his guidance and draw strength and nourishment from that relationship. Let me keep on growing in that relationship. And, Lord, let my life always overflow with the joy and thanksgiving that can only come from trusting wholly in you and your Son, Jesus. Thank you for giving me that source of power, Lord, and let me continue to ask for your guidance and the common sense that you have promised.

My prayer for today—including any journaling thoughts I may want to add. Where am I today spiritually, emotionally, physically, financially, generally?

Today's Date: _____

Old Testament verse for today: Psalm 121:1 thru 8

Shall I look to the mountain gods for help? No! My help is from Jehovah who made the mountains! And the heavens too! He will never let me stumble, slip or fall. For he is always watching, never sleeping. Jehovah himself is caring for you! He is your defender. He protects you day and night. He keeps you from all evil, and preserves your life. He keeps his eyes upon you as you come and go, and always guards you.

One possible prayer for today:

What a wonderful God you are to me. To think that you are a God so powerful that you made all the earth, including the mountains, and the heavens too, and yet in all your power and might, you still care about me. Thank you for being a God who never sleeps. Thank you for watching my footsteps so that I need never worry about stumbling, slipping, or falling. Thank you for always watching over me, caring for me, defending me. Thank you for protecting me day and night. Thank you for keeping me from evil, for preserving my life, and for keeping your eye on me, always guarding me as I come and go. So, Lord, I know that with this promise, when troubles do assail me, then those times are your will for my life at that time. So, at those times, let me draw even closer to you, waiting for you to once again rescue me, praising you for your guidance, and asking for your help in learning whatever lessons you are trying to teach me. Lord, thank you for the faith to trust you at all times.

New Testament verse for today: Hebrews 4:12 & 13

For whatever God says to us is full of living power: it is sharper that the sharpest dagger, cutting swift and deep into our innermost thoughts and desires with all their parts, exposing us for what we really are. He knows about everyone, everywhere. Everything about us is bare and wide open to the all-seeing eyes of our living God; nothing can be hidden from him to whom we must explain all that we have done.

One possible prayer for today:

God, thank you for never sleeping. Thank you for always watching over me. Thank you for being such a powerful God. Thank you for knowing everything about me, and still loving me. Even though I can hide nothing from you, God, thank you for continuing to forgive me whenever I come to you and confess the sins that I have committed. Lord, I know that you want my love, my praise and you want my confession of all the sins I have committed. Thank you for knowing all my innermost thoughts and desires and still letting me come back to you for forgiveness. Thank you, God, for being such a loving and forgiving God.

My prayer for today—including any journaling thoughts I may want to add. Where am I today spiritually, emotionally, physically, financially, generally?

Today's Date: _____

Old Testament verse for today: Psalm 127:3

Children are a gift from God; they are his reward.

One possible prayer for today:

God, thank you for the gift of my children. Thank you for rewarding me with such a wonderful gift. God, I pray that I might treat this, your gift, with the love, the discipline, and the respect that such a great gift deserves. Please give me the guidance and the patience to be the kind of parent that you would have me to be. Thank you, God, for this reward.

New Testament verse for today: Ephesians 6:2 & 3

Honor your father and mother. This is the first of God's Ten Commandments that ends with a promise. And this is the promise: that if you honor your father and mother, yours will be a long life, full of blessing.

One possible prayer for today:

God, thank you for giving me a father and a mother whom I can truly honor. Thank you for giving me this blessing. Thank you for the promise that if I obey this command, I will have a long life, full of blessing. Lord, I claim this, your promise. And, Lord, help me to be the kind of parent that my children can honestly honor. Let me pass on your words to them so that they may come into salvation through your Son, Jesus. Thank you again, God, for being so good to me.

My prayer for today—including any journaling thoughts I may want to add. Where am I today spiritually, emotionally, physically, financially, generally?

Today's Date: _____

Old Testament verse for today: Psalm 128:1 & 2

Blessings on all who reverence and trust the Lord—and on all who obey Him! Their reward shall be prosperity and happiness.

One possible prayer for today:

God, some days that is a hard verse for me to accept. I have tried to reverence you and trust you; and, prosperity has still eluded me! What happened? Where have I erred? What more do I need to do? Lord, maybe the key is being willing to accept whatever you give me as being the prosperity that you have in mind for me at that time; and, be happy with what I have. Is that what I am supposed to do? Lord, please guide me in that area. Please forgive me for wanting more than I have and for expecting that I deserve more. What I really need is a change of heart to be happy with what I have. Please help me in this area of my life, Lord; and let me honor and praise you for all you have given me.

New Testament verse for today: John 20:31

—these are recorded so that you will believe that he (Christ) is the Messiah, the Son of God, and that believing in him, you will have life.

One possible prayer for today:

God, maybe that is my answer. If I believe that Christ is the Messiah and it is through my belief in Him that I have eternal life, maybe that puts things more into perspective. This life is all I know; but, if I can believe strongly enough in your promises, then the problems of this life may not seem so overwhelming. Then I can know that ultimately my troubles here will seem insignificant as I look toward an eternal reward with Christ in heaven. Yet, today, my problems do look overwhelming and there is no end in sight. So, God, I need you to forgive me for my lack of faith, and I need you to give me a shot of faith to get through this present situation. Please help me today, Lord. Let me feel your presence today so that I can keep my present problems in perspective. Thank you for helping me right now!

My prayer for today—including any journaling thoughts I may want to add. Where am I today spiritually, emotionally, physically, financially, generally?

Today's Date: _____

Old Testament verse for today: Psalm 130:3 thru 5

Lord, if you keep in mind our (my) sins then who can ever get an answer to his prayers? But you forgive! What an awesome thing that is! That is why I wait expectantly, trusting God to help, for he has promised.

One possible prayer for today:

God, I cannot even fathom that kind of love and forgiveness; but, do I ever claim it! Yes I do! I know that I sin regularly; but, Lord, you forgive. Thank you for forgiving me, Lord. Thank you for continuing to forgive me. I confess my sins to you and thank you for erasing them from my record! And, God, I do wait expectantly for answers to my prayers, trusting you to help me in all my times of need. My needs today are _____. Thank you for always being there for me.

New Testament verse for today: James 3:17 & 18

But the wisdom that comes from heaven is first of all pure and full of quiet gentleness. Then it is peace-loving and courteous. It allows discussion and is willing to yield to others; it is full of mercy and good deeds. It is wholehearted and straightforward and sincere. And those who are peacemakers will plant seeds of peace and reap a harvest of goodness.

One possible prayer for today:

God, maybe I would sin less, have less troubles, and get more answers to my prayers if I would put a higher priority in my life of following James admonitions in this verse. Lord, please give me wisdom. Please give me the wisdom to know when I should have a quiet spirit and when I should put up a fight. Please give me wisdom of knowing when I should be peace-loving and when I should take a stand, even if it means making someone unhappy. Help me to know when to yield and when not to yield. And, Lord, help me to always be straightforward and sincere. Thank you for forgiving me when I am duplicitous and less forthright. Help me today to know how I should act in every situation. Thank you, God, for your help.

My prayer for today—including any journaling thoughts I may want to add. Where am I today spiritually, emotionally, physically, financially, generally?

Today's Date: _____

Old Testament verse for today: Psalm 135:5 & 6

I know the greatness of the Lord—that He is greater far than any other god. He does whatever pleases Him throughout all of heaven and earth, and in the deepest seas.

One possible prayer for today:

God, how great Thou art! And, how I thank you and praise you for your greatness! And to think that you care for me and love me. How I thank you for that care and love. And, God, I thank you that you do whatever pleases you in all things and in all places of the earth. I thank you and praise you that you can use me to do your work here on earth. Please make my will more in line with your will for my life so that what I do pleases you more.

New Testament verse for today: Matthew 1:22 & 23

This will fulfill God's message through His prophets—Listen! The virgin shall conceive a child! She shall give birth to a Son, and He shall be called "Emmanuel" meaning "God is with us."

One possible prayer for today:

God, how I thank you for giving your Son as the perfect sacrifice for my sins. I cannot even conceive of that kind of a plan for the whole world. However, if it had been only me, you would have still done that just for me, because you love me so much. God, I thank you for your love. I thank you that you never give up on me. And, I thank you that today you are and will continue to be with me.

My prayer for today—including any journaling thoughts I may want to add. Where am I today spiritually, emotionally, physically, financially, generally?

Today's Date: _____

Old Testament verse for today: Psalm 136:1 thru 3

Oh, give thanks to the Lord, for he is good; his lovingkindness continues forever. Give thanks to the God of gods, for his lovingkindness continues forever. Give thanks to the Lord of lords, for his lovingkindness continues forever.

One possible prayer for today:

God, thank you for being eternal. Thank you for being consistent. Thank you for being the God of gods, and the Lord of lords. Thank you for being so good. And, Lord, thank you most of all for loving and caring about me.

New Testament verse for today: I John 4::9

God showed how much he loved us by sending his only Son into this wicked world to bring to us eternal life through his death. In this act we see what real love is: it is not our love for God, but his love for us when he sent his Son to satisfy God's anger against our sins.

One possible prayer for today:

God, thank you for your love. Thank you for showing that love to me by sending Jesus, your only Son, to die on the cross for my sins. Lord, your love is absolutely amazing. Thank you for showing me what real love is. Lord, thank you for forgiving me of my sins. Thank you for sending Jesus to satisfy your anger against my sin. Thank you, Lord.

My prayer for today—including any journaling thoughts I may want to add. Where am I today spiritually, emotionally, physically, financially, generally?

Today's Date: _____

Old Testament verse for today: Psalm 138:1

Lord, with all my heart I thank you. I will sing your praises before the armies of angels in heaven.

One possible prayer for today:

Lord, how wonderful you are. Even when I am really sagging from the stress and what seem to be insurmountable problems in my life, I know that you are there for me. Even when my problems are on the verge of overcoming me, let me remember to sing your praises. Thank you for giving me my own special angels to care for me when I am really hurting. Lord, no matter what my circumstances, let me sing your praises—not only before the angels; but before my friends and family.

New Testament verse for today: Luke 12:15

Beware! Don't always be wishing for what you don't have. For real life and real living are not related to how rich we are.

One possible prayer for today:

Lord, maybe that is much of my problem. Maybe I am spending too much of my time chasing worldly goods and riches. Maybe I am too caught up in material things that have no real lasting value. Lord, if that is what is causing me so much tension in my life, help me to reevaluate my goals and priorities. Help me to come to you with my goals and get your input on where my energies should be focused. Help me to live more as you would have me to live, Lord. And, Lord, if I am to make any major changes in my life style, I really need your help to make those adjustments. Help me, Lord; and let me be receptive to where you are leading me. Thank you, Lord, for being patient with me.

My prayer for today—including any journaling thoughts I may want to add. Where am I today spiritually, emotionally, physically, financially, generally?

Today's Date: _____

Old Testament verse for today: Psalm 138:2 & 3

I face your Temple as I worship, giving thanks to you for all your lovingkindness and your faithfulness, for your promises are backed by all the honor of your name. When I pray, you answer me, and encourage me by giving me the strength I need.

One possible prayer for today:

God, thank you for being such an honorable God. Thank you for your lovingkindness and your faithfulness. Thank you for all the many great promises you have made me. Thank you for hearing me and answering me when I pray. Thank you for encouraging me and giving me the strength that I need to face whatever challenges are before me. Thank you, God.

New Testament verse for today: Titus 2:11 thru 13

For the free gift of eternal salvation is now being offered to everyone, and along with this gift comes the realization that God wants us to turn from godless living and sinful pleasures and to live good, God-fearing lives day after day, looking forward to that wonderful time we've been expecting, when his glory shall be seen—the glory of our great God and Savior Jesus Christ.

One possible prayer for today:

God, thank you for your promise of the free gift of salvation that you offer to me. Thank you again for your lovingkindness and faithfulness. Help me, Lord, to turn from my sinful ways and so succeed more fully in living life day after day as you would have me to live. Thank you, Lord, for forgiving me when I fail to live up to your ideal for my life. Thank you for your promise that I may spend eternity with you and Jesus if I only believe. And, Lord, I do believe. Thank you, Lord, for that promise.

My prayer for today—including any journaling thoughts I may want to add. Where am I today spiritually, emotionally, physically, financially, generally?

Today's Date: _____

Old Testament verse for today: Psalm 138:7 & 8

Though I am surrounded by troubles, you will bring me safely through them. You will clench your fist against my angry enemies! Your power will save me. The Lord will work out his plans for my life—for your lovingkindness, Lord, continues forever. Don't abandon me—for you made me.

One possible prayer for today:

Lord, when I am in trouble, how wonderful it is to know that you are there to help me. How wonderful it is to know that you will bring me safely through these troubles. How wonderful to know that you will clench your fist against my angry enemies. Thank you, Lord. Thank you for using your power to save me. Thank you for working out your plans for my life. Thank you for your lovingkindness, Lord. Thank you for never abandoning me. Thank you, Lord.

New Testament verse for today: II Thessalonians 2:16 & 17

May our Lord Jesus Christ himself and God our Father, who has loved us and given us everlasting comfort and hope which we don't deserve, comfort your hearts with all comfort, and help you in every good thing you say and do.

One possible prayer for today:

God, thank you for giving me everlasting comfort and hope, even when I am surrounded by troubles. Even when I am facing my angry enemies, thank you for comforting my heart with all comfort. Thank you for working out your plans for my life, Lord, and thank you for helping me in every good thing that I say and do. Thank you, God, for loving me so much that you do all these things for me. Thank you, God.

My prayer for today—including any journaling thoughts I may want to add. Where am I today spiritually, emotionally, physically, financially, generally?

Today's Date: _____

Old Testament verse for today: Psalm 139:1 thru 7

O Lord, you have examined my heart and know everything about me. You know when I sit or stand. When far away you know my every thought. You chart the path ahead of me, and tell me where to stop and rest. Every moment, you know where I am. You know what I am going to say before I even say it. You both proceed and follow me, and place your hand of blessing on my head. This is too glorious, too wonderful to believe! I can never be lost to your spirit! I can never get away from God!

One possible prayer for today:

What a wonderful God you are! How wonderful it is to have you so concerned about me and have you care about me so much that you always know my heart and everything about me; to have you know when I sit or stand; to know my every thought; to chart my path and tell me where to stop and rest; to know what I am going to say; to proceed me and follow me; and, Lord, most of all, to place your hand of blessing on my head. Lord, your love for me is too glorious, too wonderful for me to even comprehend! Thank you for never letting me get away from you. Thank you for loving me always, Lord. Thank you.

New Testament verse for today: II Timothy 1:12b

For I know the one in whom I trust, and am sure that he is able to safely guard all that I have given him until the day of his return.

One possible prayer for today:

God, how could I not trust you completely? When you are so wonderful; when you know everything about me and still love me; when you have your hand of blessing on my head; Lord, who could I ever trust who would be more wonderful than you? I know that with your love and your concern that you can guard me every step of my life and you will be with me in eternity. Thank you, God.

My prayer for today—including any journaling thoughts I may want to add. Where am I today spiritually, emotionally, physically, financially, generally?

Today's Date: _____

Old Testament verse for today: Psalm 139:13 thru 16

You made all the delicate, inner parts of my body, and knit them together in my mother's womb. Thank you for making me so wonderfully complex! It is amazing to think about. Your workmanship is marvelous—and how well I know it. You were there while I was being formed in utter seclusion! You saw me before I was born and scheduled each day of my life before I began to breathe. Every day was recorded in your Book!

One possible prayer for today:

God, how wonderfully made I am. Thank you for making me such a unique and wonderful being. Thank you for knowing me and my life even before I was born. Thank you for scheduling every day of my life even before it began! Thank you for caring so much about me. Thank you for loving me and as a part of scheduling each day of my life, thank you for providing me with a marvelous plan of salvation. Thank you, Lord.

New Testament verse for today: Hebrews 6:18

He has given us both his promise and his oath, two things we can completely count on. For it is impossible for God to tell a lie. Now all those who flee to him to save them can take new courage when they hear such assurances from God; now they can know without a doubt that he will give them the salvation he has promised them.

One possible prayer for today:

God, thank you for all the wonderful promises you have given me. Thank you for being such a wonderful and steadfast God; a God who I can believe and take assurance from all his words. Thank you for being a God who cannot tell a lie. Thank you for planning my salvation as a part of scheduling each day of my life. Thank you, God.

My prayer for today—including any journaling thoughts I may want to add. Where am I today spiritually, emotionally, physically, financially, generally?

Today's Date: _____

Old Testament verse for today: Psalm 139:17 & 18

How precious it is, Lord, to realize that you are thinking about me constantly! I can't even count how many times a day your thoughts turn toward me. And when I waken in the morning, you are still thinking about me!

One possible prayer for today:

God, what a wonderful feeling to know that you are always thinking about me. Thank you for always thinking about me. Lord, no matter what I do, you are thinking about me and caring for me. You know, Lord, that I often think that I am too busy to think about you. And, most incredibly, when I am in trouble, or working through a problem—times when I need you most—at a time when I should be falling on my knees and asking for your help—I forget about thinking about you! And yet, Lord, when I remember that you are there for me, and then turn to you, you are, in fact, always there, waiting to help me. Waiting to give me strength. Waiting to advise me. Waiting to give me an extra shot of knowledge or faith to get me through my problem. Thank you, Lord, for always being there for me—morning, noon, nor night.

New Testament verse for today: Ephesians 2:18 & 19

Now all of us, whether Jews or Gentiles, may come to God the Father with the Holy Spirit's help because of what Christ has done for us. Now you are no longer strangers to God and foreigners to heaven, but you are members of God's very own family, citizens of God's country, and you belong to God's household with every other Christian.

One possible prayer for today:

God, no wonder you think about me constantly. You have made me a member of your household if I will only believe in your Son, Jesus. Thank you for giving me your loving Holy Spirit to help me come to you. Thank you for no longer considering me a stranger to you or a foreigner to heaven. Thank you for accepting me in everyway, God. Thank you.

My prayer for today—including any journaling thoughts I may want to add. Where am I today spiritually, emotionally, physically, financially, generally?

Today's Date: _____

Old Testament verse for today: Psalm 139:23 & 24

Search me, O God, and know my heart; test my thoughts. Point out anything you find in me that makes you sad, and lead me along the path of everlasting life.

One possible prayer for today:

God, thank you for being concerned about me and my life. I know that I cannot hide anything from you. I know that you are aware of my every innermost thought. You know every desire of my heart. God, thank you for pointing out the things in my thoughts and in my actions that make you sad. Thank you for being gentle with me when you do point these things out to me. And, Lord, thank you for providing a wonderful plan of salvation for me so that I may be confident of spending eternity with you. Thank you, Lord.

New Testament verse for today: Hebrews 7:24 & 25

But Jesus lives forever and continues to be a Priest so that no one else is needed. He is able to save completely all who come to God through him. Since he will live forever, he will always be there to remind God that he has paid for their sins with his blood.

One possible prayer for today:

God, thank you for Jesus. Thank you for sending Jesus to pay the price for my sins so that I may have everlasting life because of his sacrifice. Thank you for my confidence that I am saved completely because of what Jesus did for me. Thank you again, God, for your wonderful plan of salvation by sending Jesus to die for my sins. Thank you, God.

My prayer for today—including any journaling thoughts I may want to add. Where am I today spiritually, emotionally, physically, financially, generally?

Today's Date: _____

Old Testament verse for today: Psalm 141:1

Quick, Lord, answer me, for I have prayed. Listen when I cry to you for help.

One possible prayer for today:

Lord, I know that you hear me and I know that you listen to my pleadings and my prayers. Thank you for answering me when I call to you. Thank you for hearing my cries for help. And, Lord, if it be your will, please answer me quickly.

New Testament verse for today: Luke 18:27

He replied, "God can do what men can't."

One possible prayer for today:

God, I am counting that! I am counting on the fact that you can do things far beyond my ability to even envision them .That is why I am so comfortable praying to you and asking for your help. That is why I know that you can hear me and answer my prayers as it fits into your will for my life. Lord, thank you for being such a gracious God. Thank you again for hearing my pleadings and answering my prayers as you see fit. And, Lord, give me the faith and the patience to accept whatever answer you give me. Thank you, Lord, for giving me the confidence and faith I need to accept your will for my life.

My prayer for today—including any journaling thoughts I may want to add. Where am I today spiritually, emotionally, physically, financially, generally?

Today's Date: _____

Old Testament verse for today: Psalm 141:4

Take away my lust for evil things; don't let me want to be with sinners, doing what they do, sharing their dainties.

One possible prayer for today:

God, you know that I need your help in this area. You know that many times I enjoy things that I know you consider evil in your sight. So, Lord, this is an area where I need your help. I need you to help me to put these evil things out of my thoughts and out of my life. I need your help to take away my interest in these things. Give me the strength that I need to walk more closely the path that you would have me walk. And, Lord, when I fail you, thank you for continuing to forgive me.

New Testament verse for today: Hebrews 10:17

And then he (the Holy Spirit) adds, "I will never again remember their sins and lawless deeds."

One possible prayer for today:

Wow! What a wonderful promise! To think that if we confess our sins, they are not only forgiven, but they are never again remembered! What a wonderful God you are! How great in every way! Lord, to know that when I fail you, you not only forgive, but you forget, is beyond my comprehension. So, Lord, I just trust your Word to be true; and, I thank you again and again for being such a wonderful forgiving God to me.

My prayer for today—including any journaling thoughts I may want to add. Where am I today spiritually, emotionally, physically, financially, generally?

Today's Date: _____

Old Testament verse for today: Psalm 141:8a

I look to you for help, O Lord God. You are my refuge.

One possible prayer for today:

God, when the chips are down; when I don't have any place else to turn; I know that you are always there for me. You know that I am selfish, Lord. You know that many times I try to do it my way and don't include you; but, Lord, then I get into trouble and I come running back to you and plead for your help. And, Lord, you are always there. Thank you, Lord, for always being there. You are my only true refuge. Thank you, Lord.

New Testament verse for today: Hebrews 10:10, 12, 13 & 14

Under this new plan we have been forgiven and made clean by Christ's dying for us once and for all. —Christ gave himself to God for our sins as one sacrifice for all time, and then sat down in the place of highest honor at God's right hand, waiting for his enemies to be laid at his feet. For by this one offering he made forever perfect in the sight of God all those whom he is making holy.

One possible prayer for today:

God, thank you for not only being my refuge; but, thank you for making me perfect in your sight through my believe in your Son, Jesus. Thank you for forgiving me and making me clean in your sight because of Christ's sacrifice for my sins. Thank you for this marvelous plan that declares me perfect when there is no other way that I could ever be perfect in your eyes. Thank you for choosing to make me holy in your sight. Thank you, God.

My prayer for today—including any journaling thoughts I may want to add. Where am I today spiritually, emotionally, physically, financially, generally?

Today's Date: _____

Old Testament verse for today: Psalm 143:1 & 2

Hear my prayer, O Lord; answer my plea, because you are faithful to your promises. Don't bring me to trial! For compared to you, no one is perfect.

One possible prayer for today:

God, thank you for hearing my prayer. Thank you for answering my plea. Thank you for being faithful to your promises. And, Lord, thank you for not comparing me with you and your perfection. Thank you for loving me with all my warts and imperfections. Thank you for being such a loving and forgiving God to me.

New Testament verse for today: Galatians 5:22 & 23a

But when the Holy Spirit controls our lives he will produce this kind of fruit in us: love, joy, peace, patience, kindness, goodness, faithfulness, gentleness, and self-control.

One possible prayer for today:

God, thank you for hearing my prayer. Let me give the control of my life to the Holy Spirit. Let me be fruitful for you and your service by being loving, joyful, peaceable, patient, kind, good, faithful, gentle, and self-controlled. I know that I cannot achieve any consistency of any of these things without your help, Lord. So, help me. Thank you for loving me when I fail in producing these things in my life. Let me look to you for help more often, and let me listen to you and accept your help and your guidance more consistently. Thank you, God, for your help. Thank you for your loving Holy Spirit who will help me produce good fruit more often.

My prayer for today—including any journaling thoughts I may want to add. Where am I today spiritually, emotionally, physically, financially, generally?

Today's Date: _____

Old Testament verse for today: Psalm 143:8
Let me see your kindness to me in the morning, for I am trusting you. Show me where to walk, for my prayer is sincere.

One possible prayer for today:
Lord, thank you for being kind to me, not just in the morning, but all day long! Lord, I do trust you to help me and to guide me. Thank you for showing me where to walk. Thank you for answering my prayers when they are sincere. Thank you for listening to me, Lord.

New Testament verse for today: Hebrews 7:19b
But now we have a far better hope, for Christ makes us acceptable to God, and now we may draw near to him.

One possible prayer for today:
God, thank you for giving me Jesus so that I am acceptable to you. Thank you for giving me that hope. Thank you for letting me draw near to you so that I may feel your kindness all day long in my life. Thank you for drawing near to me and showing me where to walk. Thank you again, Lord, for letting me be acceptable to you and for receiving your unqualified love.

My prayer for today—including any journaling thoughts I may want to add. Where am I today spiritually, emotionally, physically, financially, generally?

Today's Date: _____

Old Testament verse for today: Psalm 143:10

Help me to do your will, for you are my God. Lead me in good paths, for your Spirit is good.

One possible prayer for today:

God, you know my heart. You know that I fail you often. So, I do need your help to do your will. Thank you for being my God. Thank you for leading me in good paths. Thank you for giving me the strength that I need to do your will more often and more consistently. Thank you, God, for being such a loving and forgiving God.

New Testament verse for today: Galatians 6:7 thru 10

Don't be misled; remember that you can't ignore God and get away with it: a man will always reap just the kind of crop he sows! If he sows to please his own wrong desires, he will be planting seeds of evil and he will surely reap a harvest of spiritual decay and death; but if he plants the good things of the Spirit, he will reap the everlasting life which the Spirit gives him. And let us not get tired of doing what is right, for after a while we will reap a harvest of blessing if we don't get discouraged and give up.

One possible prayer for today:

God, you do know my heart. You know when I am acting to please my own desires, and you know when I am acting as you would have me to act. Thank you for forgiving me when I am pleasing my own desires. Thank you for helping me to have the strength to plant the good things of the Spirit more often. Thank you for giving me everlasting life. Help me to not get tired of doing what is right. I need your help to always want to do what is right; because I often let my selfish desires come first. Thank you for your promise of a harvest of blessings if I don't get discouraged and give up. Thank you, God, for never giving up on me.

My prayer for today—including any journaling thoughts I may want to add. Where am I today spiritually, emotionally, physically, financially, generally?

Today's Date: _____

Old Testament verse for today: Psalm 145:1 thru 7

I will praise you, my God and King, and bless your name each day forever. Great is Jehovah! Greatly praise him! Let each generation tell its children what glorious things he does. I will meditate about your glory, splendor, majesty and miracles. Your awe-inspiring deeds shall be on every tongue: I will proclaim your greatness. Everyone will tell about how good you are, and sing about your righteousness.

One possible prayer for today:

God, I will praise you every day of my life. Even when I am hurting, I will praise you because only you can rescue me from my hurts. You are a great God! You deserve my praise. Let me tell everyone about what you have done for me. Don't let me ever be ashamed to tell others what a great God you are. I will not only think about your glory, splendor, majesty, and miracles; but, I will also think about all you have done for me. Let me always do my part of singing about your greatness, your goodness, and your righteousness. Thank you for being such a great God for me.

New Testament verse for today: Philippians 4:4

I strain to reach the end of the race and receive the prize for which God is calling us up to heaven because of what Christ Jesus did for us.

One possible prayer for today:

God, how could I not praise you always when you have done so much for me. Lord, no matter what my hurts may be here on earth today, I know that you have a prize awaiting me at the end of this earthly race—eternity with you and your Son, Jesus. Thank you for the promise of such a great prize for finishing the race here on earth. Thank you for sending your Son, Jesus, to die on the cross so that if I only believe, that prize can be mine. I do believe, Lord. Thank you for letting me know that that prize is waiting for me at the end of the face. And thank you for making it so easy for me to receive this prize. All I have to do is believe. Thank you, God.

My prayer for today—including any journaling thoughts I may want to add. Where am I today spiritually, emotionally, physically, financially, generally?

Today's Date: _____

Old Testament verse for today: Psalm 145:8 & 9

Jehovah is kind and merciful, slow to get angry, full of love. He is good to everyone, and his compassion is intertwined with everything he does.

One possible prayer for today:

God, I believe the Psalmist when he says all these good things about you. But if that is the case, then you must be very angry at me at this moment; or, else you have a plan for my life that is very different from what I had in mind! I am really hurting, God! I am not feeling very much of your love, compassion, and goodness today! What do I need to do? Where do I turn except to you? God, I know that you are in charge. I know that you are kind and merciful. I know that you are slow to get angry. God, if you are teaching me a lesson, let me learn quickly, as I am feeling a heavy burden right now. Let me feel your goodness and compassion again quickly, Lord. And, God, until my burden is lightened, I plead for the strength to bear up under it; and, I plead for the faith to continue to believe in your kindness and mercy. Help me, Lord. Help me soon! Thank you, Lord, for hearing my pleas.

New Testament verse for today: Romans 5:3, 4, & 5

We can rejoice, too, when we run into problems and trials for we know that they are good for us—they help us learn to be patient. And patience develops strength of character in us and helps us to trust God more each time we use it until finally our hope and faith are strong and steady. Then, when that happens, we are able to hold our heads high no matter what happens and know that all is well, for we know how dearly God loves us, and we feel this warm love everywhere within us because God has given us the Holy Spirit to fill our hearts with his love.

One possible prayer for today:

God, I really needed that promise. Hopefully my hope and faith are getting strong enough and steady enough for you to soon lighten my burdens. God, I do love you. I trust you. I admit that I could not get through this time without you. Let me hold my head high—only because I know you are there for me. I know how dearly you love me. Give me that warm feeling that can come only from your loving Holy Spirit at a time like this. Thank you for this promise, Lord.

My prayer for today—including any journaling thoughts I may want to add. Where am I today spiritually, emotionally, physically, financially, generally?

Today's Date: _____

Old Testament verse for today: Psalm 145:10 thru 13

All living things shall thank you, Lord, and your people will bless you. They will talk together about the glory of your kingdom and mention examples of your power. They will tell about your miracles and about the majesty and glory of your reign. For your kingdom never ends. You rule generation after generation.

One possible prayer for today:

God, it is so wonderful to have a God like you. So powerful. So glorious. So majestic. So full of miracles. Thank you for being an everlasting God. Thank you for being a God whose kingdom never ends. And, God, thank you most of all for being my personal God. For being a God who cares about me and the things that are important to me. Thank you for being my personal everlasting God. Thank you.

New Testament verse for today: Philippians 4:6 & 7

Don't worry about anything; instead, pray about everything; tell God your needs and don't forget to thank him for his answers. If you do this you will experience God's peace, which is far more wonderful than the human mind can understand. His peace will keep your thoughts and your hearts quiet and at rest as you trust in Christ.

One possible prayer for today:

God, thank you for being a God to whom I can bring my troubles. Thank you for being a God to whom I may pray about anything. Thank you for caring about my needs. Thank you for giving me the peace that only you can give. Thank you for giving me a peace that quiets my thoughts and my heart. Thank you for giving me Jesus, who died for my sins and rose again that I may have eternal life with you and with Jesus. Thank you, God, for being an everlasting God and for being a God who cares for me and who cares about my problems. Thank you, God, for caring for me.

My prayer for today—including any journaling thoughts I may want to add. Where am I today spiritually, emotionally, physically, financially, generally?

Today's Date: _____

Old Testament verse for today: Psalm 145:17 thru 21

The Lord is fair in everything he does, and full of kindness. He is close to all who call on him sincerely. He fulfills the desires of those who reverence and trust him; he hears their cries for help and rescues them. He protects all those who love him, but destroys the wicked. I will praise the Lord and call on all men everywhere to bless his holy name forever and forever.

One possible prayer for today:

Lord, thank you for being fair in everything you do. Thank you for being full of kindness to me. Thank you for being close to me when I sincerely call on you. Let me always do my part in reverencing you, and then, Lord, thank you for fulfilling all my desires as long as they are in line with your will for my life. I know that if I am truly reverencing you, then my desires will be in line with your will for me life. Thank you for hearing my cries and rescuing me when I call on you. Let me do my own part by blessing your holy name all of my life.

New Testament verse for today: I John 1:9

But if we confess our sins to him, he can be depended on to forgive us and to cleanse us from every wrong. And it is perfectly proper for God to do this for us because Christ died to wash away our sins.

One possible prayer for today:

God, thank you again for being close to me when I sincerely call on you. Thank you for giving me my desires when they are in line with your will for my life. Thank you for hearing me when I confess my sins to you. Thank you for being a dependable God who will hear me, and forgive me, and cleanse me from every wrong when I sincerely call on you. Thank you for giving me Christ who died for me and by dying, washed away my sins. Thank you for making such a proper plan and yet such a simple plan, so that even I can understand it and avail myself of this wonderful promise.

My prayer for today—including any journaling thoughts I may want to add. Where am I today spiritually, emotionally, physically, financially, generally?

Today's Date: _____

Old Testament verse for today: Psalm 147:11

But his joy is in those who reverence him, those who expect him to be loving and kind.

One possible prayer for today:

God, let me reverence you so that you have joy in me. Lord, I do expect you to be loving and kind. You have demonstrated that over and over again; and, Lord, I am just selfish enough to expect that your love and your kindness will continue. But, Lord, even if I have some tough times when I begin to question your kindness and how much you love me, help me with my faith. Continue to give me the faith to reverence you even in the tough times. Then I know that what you have in store for me is your will at that moment; and, that I will once again feel your love and your kindness. Thank you, Lord, for always being there for me—even in the tough times.

New Testament verse for today: Luke 21:33

And though all heaven and earth shall pass away, yet my words remain forever true.

One possible prayer for today:

God, thank you for that promise of your Son, Jesus. Thank you for reassuring me that your word is always true and that you are a God consistent in your love and your kindness for me. Thank you for being a God who has forgiven me and loves me all the time—even when I fail you. Thank you for always being there for me. Thank you, God.

My prayer for today—including any journaling thoughts I may want to add. Where am I today spiritually, emotionally, physically, financially, generally?

Today's Date: _____

Old Testament verse for today: Psalm 148:5

Let everything he has made give praise to him. For he issued his command, and they came into being; he established them forever and forever. His order will never be revoked.

One possible prayer for today:

God, let me do my part in praising you. Thank you for creating everything that there is. Thank you for having that kind of power. Thank you for the permanence of what you have created. Thank you that you are consistent. And, God, thank you in your consistent love and forgiveness of me. Thank you, God.

New Testament verse for today: I John 5:14 & 15

And we are sure of this, that he will listen to us whenever we ask him for anything in line with his will. And if we really know he is listening when we talk to him and make our requests, then we can be sure that he will answer us.

One possible prayer for today:

God, thank you again for your consistent love and forgiveness. Thank you for always being there for me when I call on you. Help me to learn to ask for those things that are in line with your will for my life and not just those selfish things that bring me pleasure. Let my requests be thoughtful and unselfish. Thank you for listening to me, and God, thank you for answering me. Thank you for giving me the faith to love you more even when your answer to me is "No"! Let my faith never waiver in knowing that you always love me and care for what is best for me.

My prayer for today—including any journaling thoughts I may want to add. Where am I today spiritually, emotionally, physically, financially, generally?

Today's Date: _____

Old Testament verse for today: Psalm 150:6
Let everything alive give praises to the Lord! You praise him!

One possible prayer for today:
God, thank you for my life. Thank you for letting me give you all my praise. Thank you for accepting my praises. Thank you for accepting me and loving me just the way I am. Thank you for giving me the ability to love and praise you. Thank you, Lord.

New Testament verse for today: Ephesians 5:19
Talk to each other much about the Lord, quoting psalms and hymns and singing sacred songs, making music in your hearts to the Lord.

One possible prayer for today:
God, help me to turn my thoughts more to you and what you want me to do with my life. Let me think about you and how wonderful you are to me. Let my heart sing out in praise of you. Thank you for giving me every breath that I take. Thank you for letting me praise you in my own humble way, and thank you for accepting the praise that I give you. Thank you for being such a loving and caring Lord. Thank you, Lord.

My prayer for today—including any journaling thoughts I may want to add. Where am I today spiritually, emotionally, physically, financially, generally?

Today's Date: _____

Old Testament verse for today: Proverbs 1:7

How does a man become wise? The first step is to trust and reverence the Lord!

One possible prayer for today:

God, I need lots of wisdom every day. I make lots of real bad decisions! I talk too much and say the wrong things, at the wrong times, to the wrong people. I confess those actions to you. Please help me to be wiser in my everyday actions—with my friends, my business associates, and especially, my family. Thank you for forgiving me my selfish and self-centered actions and decisions. Thank you for giving me extra wisdom for today. (or tomorrow, if this is an evening prayer)

New Testament verse for today: Matthew 4:4b

Christ said, "—the Scriptures tell us that bread won't feed men's souls: obedience to every word of God is what we need."

One possible prayer for today:

I know that I do not, and cannot obey every one of your words, God; but, I could try to do better than I am doing. And I could do better, with your help! And, I need your help! My soul needs a lift. This is not a good time in my life, God; and, I am hurting! Let me look to you for guidance more often and with more consistency than I have been doing. I confess my need to rely on you more. I know that if I sincerely confess that need and sincerely ask for your help, that even if I am having a bad day, you are there with me. I can count on that. My soul needs a boost today, Lord. Please give me that boost. Draw me closer to you, and let me learn to rely on you and your word more and more each day.

My prayer for today—including any journaling thoughts I may want to add. Where am I today spiritually, emotionally, physically, financially, generally?

Today's Date: _____

Old Testament verse for today: Proverbs 1:33

But all who listen to me shall live in peace and safety, unafraid. (Wisdom speaking)

One possible prayer for today:

Lord, I know that the first step to becoming wise is to trust in you. And you are the source of all wisdom. So let me listen to your wisdom. Let me live in peace and safety, unafraid, as I trust in you and the wisdom that comes from you and abiding by your will. Help me to listen to your wisdom, Lord.

New Testament verse for today: Romans 6:23

For the wages of sin is death, but the free gift of God is eternal life through Jesus Christ our Lord.

One possible prayer for today:

God, that makes it pretty simple! If all wisdom comes from you. If, in your wisdom, you have given me a free gift. If that free gift gives me eternal life. If not accepting that free gift gives me eternal death, that ought to be a pretty easy decision for me to make! Lord, I accept your free gift of eternal life through Jesus Christ, your Son and my Lord. Thank you for your wisdom. Thank you for your free gift of eternal life. Thank you for giving me the gift of faith so that I may accept your free gift. Thank you for being such a wise and wonderful Lord. Thank you. Thank you.

My prayer for today—including any journaling thoughts I may want to add. Where am I today spiritually, emotionally, physically, financially, generally?

Today's Date: _____

Old Testament verse for today: Proverbs 2:3 thru 5

Yes, if you want better insight and discernment, and are searching for them as you would for lost money or hidden treasure, then wisdom will be given you, and knowledge of God himself; you will soon learn the importance of reverence for the Lord and of trusting him.

One possible prayer for today:

Lord, let me really search for better insight and wisdom. Let me really want better insight and wisdom, as much or more than I want a lot of money or some other worldly pleasure. And, Lord, thank you for the promise that if I really search for better insight and wisdom, they will be given to me. Thank you for also permitting me to have knowledge of you. Lord, I do know the importance of reverence for you. I do know the importance of trusting you. Lord, when times are tough, give me the faith to reverence you and trust you even more. Thank you, God, for the insight and wisdom you have given me.

New Testament verse for today: I Timothy 6:6 thru 10

Do you want to be truly rich? You already are if you are happy and good. After all, we didn't bring any money with us when we came into the world, and we can't carry away a single penny when we die. So we should be well satisfied without money if we have enough food and clothing. But people who long to be rich soon begin to do all kinds of wrong things to get money, things that hurt them and make them evil-minded and finally send them to hell itself. For the love of money is the first step toward all kinds of sin. Some people have even turned away from God because of their love for it, and as a result have pierced themselves with many sorrows.

One possible prayer for today:

God, let me remember that I am really rich if I trust you and believe that what you have given me is what is best for me. Let me be happy with what you have given me and where you have placed me. Let me keep my material blessings in the proper focus as it relates to what you want for me. Lord, give me better insight and discernment in this area of my life. Let me keep focused on my reverence for you and trust in you in this area of my life. Give me the wisdom and knowledge that I need in this area, Lord. And, Lord, thank you for what you have given me to date.

My prayer for today—including any journaling thoughts I may want to add. Where am I today spiritually, emotionally, physically, financially, generally?

Today's Date: _____

Old Testament verse for today: Proverbs 2:6 thru 10

For the Lord grants wisdom! His every word is a treasure of knowledge and understanding. He grants good sense to the godly—his saints. He is their shield, protecting them and guarding their pathway. He shows how to distinguish right from wrong, how to find the right decision every time. For wisdom and truth will enter the very center of your being, filling your life with joy.

One possible prayer for today:

God, grant me the wisdom that I need to operate intelligently and effectively in the arena of life where you have placed me. Thank you for making your every word a treasure of knowledge and understanding. Let me listen to your words, Lord. Grant me the good sense that I need from you, Lord. Thank you for being my shield, protecting me and guarding my pathway. Lord, please always be by my side, helping me to distinguish right from wrong. Thank you for helping me to make the right decision every time. Thank you for letting wisdom and truth enter the very center of my being, and , Lord, thank you, thank you, for filling my life with joy.

New Testament verse for today: II Corinthians 12:8 & 9

Three different times I begged God to make me well again. Each time he said, "No, but I am with you; that is all you need. My power shows up best in weak people."

One possible prayer for today:

God, I know that sometimes I get frustrated when I don't get an immediate answer to my prayers. I know that sometimes the answer to my prayers is a "No" from you. I know that you can use me whether I am weak or strong. You can show your power through me as you see fit. And, Lord, when you do answer my prayers with a "No," that is the time when I especially need you to grant me an extra shot of wisdom. That is the time when I need an extra dose of common sense. That is the time when I especially need you as my shield, protecting me and guarding my pathway. That is the time when I more than ever need your help in making the right decision. So, God, be especially with me when you say "No" to my pleadings. Give me the faith at that time to trust you so much that my life continues to be filled with joy. Thank you, Lord, for being there for me when I most need you. Thank you for being all that I need.

My prayer for today—including any journaling thoughts I may want to add. Where am I today spiritually, emotionally, physically, financially, generally?

Today's Date: _____

Old Testament verse for today: Proverbs 3:3

Never forget to be truthful and kind. Hold these virtues tightly. Write them deep within your heart.

One possible prayer for today:

God, help me to always remember to be truthful and kind. Help me to hold these virtues tightly. Help me to commit them into my heart so strongly that they become a second nature to me. Thank you for helping me to live more as you would have me to live.

New Testament verse for today: Ephesians 5:2

Be full of love for others, following the example of Christ who loved you and gave himself to God as a sacrifice to take away your sins. And God was pleased, for Christ's love for you was like sweet perfume to him.

One possible prayer for today:

God, you know my heart. You know that I am selfish. You know that I am not always full of love for others. You know that I am more often apt to be full of love for myself. So, help me in this area of my life, God. Help me to do a better job of following the example that Christ set for me to follow. Thank you for being the author of love, and a God who loved me so much that he was willing to sacrifice his own Son to take away my sins. Thank you for the example of Christ's love. Thank you for his sacrifice. Lord, help me to conduct my life so that, at least once in a while, you can be pleased with me and my love for you and for others. Thank you, God, for continuing to forgive me when I fall short of your goal for me.

My prayer for today—including any journaling thoughts I may want to add. Where am I today spiritually, emotionally, physically, financially, generally?

Today's Date: _____

Old Testament verse for today: Proverbs 3:5 & 6

If you want favor with both God and man, and a reputation for good judgment and common sense, then trust the Lord completely; don't ever trust yourself. In everything you do, put God first, and he will direct you and crown your efforts with success.

One possible prayer for today:

God, what a wonderful promise! Let me trust you completely. Let me put you first in all that I do. And, God, I do claim the promise that you will direct me. You will crown my efforts with success. Thank you, God, for letting me trust you completely; and, thank you for giving me the success you want me to have. In turn, Lord, let me be delighted with the success you give me.

New Testament verse for today: Matthew 25:29

For the man who uses well what he is given shall be given more, and he shall have abundance. But from the man who is unfaithful, even what little responsibility he has shall be taken from him.

One possible prayer for today:

Lord, with each of your promises comes my responsibility. I know that. Thank you for what you have given me. Thank you for the life you have given me and the responsibility you have given me. Let me be faithful in even the smallest things that you have given me to do. Let me use well each talent, each minute, and each dollar you have entrusted to me. Please, Lord, help me to be faithful. I need your help to live up to your expectations of me. And, God, thank you for forgiving me when I don't live up to those expectations.

My prayer for today—including any journaling thoughts I may want to add. Where am I today spiritually, emotionally, physically, financially, generally?

Today's Date: _____

Old Testament verse for today: Proverbs 3:9 & 10

Honor the Lord by giving him the first part of all your income, and he will fill your barns with wheat and barley and overflow your wine vats with the finest wines.

One possible prayer for today:

Lord, I know that I could do better in my giving to you than I do; but, I also know that you want me to acknowledge the control you have over my entire life—including my finances; so, let me be consistent about giving you an offering of thanks and gratitude based on how wonderful you have been to me. And, then, Lord, maybe I am selfish; but I do claim the promise of the Proverbs writer, that you will open up the largesse of heaven and give me all the riches I could ever want! Thank you, Lord, for that promise. Let me be true to you and I know that you will be true to me.

New Testament verse for today: I Corinthians 3:19

For the wisdom of this world is foolishness to God. As it says in the book of Job, God uses man's own brilliance to trap him; he stumbles over his own "wisdom" and falls.

One possible prayer for today:

Well, God, I guess that that kind of says it all! I know that my wisdom is but foolishness to you. Yet, my wisdom is all I have unless I rely totally on you—and I know that is what you want me to do, and what I should do. So, God, let me look to you for all things. Let me not only give to you the first part of my income; but let me give to you the first part of all I am and have. Let me live my life in such a manner that—first and foremost—I honor you. Let me praise you in all that I do. Let me remember that you are the giver of every good and perfect gift, and remember to thank you for it. God, give me wisdom so that my wisdom is not quite so foolish!

My prayer for today—including any journaling thoughts I may want to add. Where am I today spiritually, emotionally, physically, financially, generally?

Today's Date: _____

Old Testament verse for today: Proverbs 3:13 thru 17
The man who knows right from wrong and has good judgment and common sense is happier than the man who is immensely rich! For such wisdom is far more valuable than precious jewels. Nothing else compares with it. Wisdom gives: A long good life; Riches; Honor; Pleasure; Peace.

One possible prayer for today:
God, that is an encouraging verse for me; because I probably will not ever be immensely rich! But, Lord, with your help, I can work hard on discerning between right and wrong and exercising good judgment and common sense. And I know that if I do live a life that exemplifies good judgment and common sense, I will feel good about myself; and that really is more important that having wealth and not feeling good about who I am and what I had to do to get that wealth. So, God, thank you for giving me the wealth that you have given me. Thank you for giving me the common sense and good judgment you have given me. Thank you for the peace and pleasure you have given me. And if any honor and riches come along, that will be a bonus! Thank you, God.

New Testament verse for today: Acts 16:30b & 31
Sirs, what must I do to be saved? They replied, Believe on the Lord Jesus and you will be saved, and your entire household.

One possible prayer for today:
God, thank you for providing a method for me to have eternal life through belief on your Son, Jesus. I'm human. I would like riches and honor, I would like to be known for my common sense and good judgment; but, God, these earthly pleasures fall short of the delight of knowing that you loved me so much that you sent Jesus to die on the cross so that my sins would be not only forgiven; but removed from even your memory! Thank you, God, for that wonderful promise. I do believe in your Son, Jesus; and I do claim your promise of eternal life.

My prayer for today—including any journaling thoughts I may want to add. Where am I today spiritually, emotionally, physically, financially, generally?

Today's Date: _____

Old Testament verse for today: Proverbs 3:21 thru 26

Have two goals: wisdom—that is, knowing and doing right—and common sense. Don't let them slip away, for they fill you with living energy, and are a feather in your cap. They keep you safe from defeat and disaster and from stumbling off the trail. With them on guard you can sleep without fear; you need not be afraid of disaster or the plots of wicked men, for the Lord is with you; he protects you.

One possible prayer for today:

God, thank you for helping me have more wisdom and common sense. Thank you for filling me with living energy. Thank you for keeping me from defeat, disaster, and stumbling off the trail. Thank you for letting me sleep without fear. Thank you for being with me and protecting me, Lord. Thank you for these promises.

New Testament verse for today: Romans 8:34

Who then will condemn us? Will Christ? No! For he is the one who died for us and came back to life again for us and is sitting at the place of highest honor next to God, pleading for us there in heaven.

One possible prayer for today:

God, how wonderful! How wonderful to know that when I fail; when I lack wisdom and common sense; when I am on the brink of disaster; I know that your loving Son, Jesus, is sitting next to you, pleading my case to you in heaven! What a wonderful plan and what a wonderful counselor pleading my case. Thank you for your love, Lord. Thank you for Christ's love. Thank you for Christ representing me to you when I fail. Thank you, Lord.

My prayer for today—including any journaling thoughts I may want to add. Where am I today spiritually, emotionally, physically, financially, generally?

Today's Date: _____

Old Testament verse for today: Proverbs 4:23

Above all else, guard your affections. For they influence everything else in your life.

One possible prayer for today:

God, give me the strength to properly guard my affections. You know my heart. You know that my human tendency is to think impure and unclean thoughts. You know that if I don't watch what I do, that I can fall into a thought process and a lifestyle that would not be pleasing to you. So, Lord, I ask for your help in this area. I ask you to give me the strength and the faith to look to you and then to listen to you as you guide me and help me in this area. Thank you, Lord, for listening to this prayer.

New Testament verse for today: Philippians 2:3 thru 6

Don't be selfish; don't live to make a good impression on others. Be humble, thinking of others as better than yourself. Don't just think about your own affairs, but be interested in others, too, and in what they are doing. Your attitude should be the kind that was shown us by Jesus Christ, who, though he was God, did not demand and cling to his rights as God.

One possible prayer for today:

God, please help me to guard my affections. Help me to be generous and unselfish. Help me to keep my ego in line so that I am not living to impress others, but, to impress you! Help me to show a genuine interest in others and in their lives and in their problems. Lord, I know that my attitude and actions will always fall way short of Christ's attitude; but help me to work on this area of my life so that what I do and say will be more pleasing to you and therefore bring more glory and honor to your name. Thank you for helping me in this area, Lord.

My prayer for today—including any journaling thoughts I may want to add. Where am I today spiritually, emotionally, physically, financially, generally?

Today's Date: _____

Old Testament verse for today: Proverbs 5:21

For God is closely watching you, and he weighs carefully everything you do.

One possible prayer for today:

God, thank you for watching me carefully. Thank you for weighing carefully everything that I do. And, God, thank you, most of all, for forgiving me completely when the scales on which you are weighing the things that I do, do not balance in your sight! Thank you for being a concerned God. Thank you for being a caring God. And thank you most of all for being a loving and forgiving God.

New Testament verse for today: Acts 9:31b

The believers learned how to walk in the fear of the Lord and in the comfort of the Holy Spirit.

One possible prayer for today:

God, I thank you that you have chosen me to be one of your believers. Although I love you, I also fear you. I fear your awesome power. I fear making conscious decisions that cause you to withdraw your freely given blessings from me. And, Lord, I know that all I have to do is to return to you and your love is so great that you will take me back and restore me into good grace with you again. Thank you for the comfort of your loving Holy Spirit. Thank you for making the Holy Spirit available to intercede for me. Thank you, God.

My prayer for today—including any journaling thoughts I may want to add. Where am I today spiritually, emotionally, physically, financially, generally?

Today's Date: _____

Old Testament verse for today: Proverbs 8:11 thru 13

For the value of wisdom is far above rubies; nothing can be compared to it. Wisdom and good judgment live together, for wisdom knows where to discover knowledge and understanding. If anyone respects and fears God, he will hate evil. For wisdom hates pride, arrogance, corruption and deceit of every kind.

One possible prayer for today:

God, please give me the wisdom that I need to get through this day. Give me the good judgment that I need right now. Let wisdom and good judgment live together in me and be exemplified in my life. You know that I love, respect, and fear you, God. Thank you for loving and caring for me. Thank you for giving me the wisdom, knowledge, and good judgment that I need today.

New Testament verse for today: II Corinthians 3:16 thru 18

But when anyone turns to the Lord from his sins, then the veil is taken away. The Lord is the Spirit who gives them life, and where he is there is freedom (from trying to be saved by keeping the laws of God). But we Christians have no veil over our faces; we can be mirrors that brightly reflect the glory of the Lord. And as the Spirit of the Lord works within us, we become more and more like him.

One possible prayer for today:

Lord, thank you for the wisdom you have given me. Thank you for choosing me and giving me the wisdom to accept your marvelous plan of salvation through the death and resurrection of your Son, Jesus. Thank you for giving me the knowledge about Jesus and your plan of salvation. Thank you for taking the veil away from my eyes and giving me the freedom to be saved by faith and not by keeping the law. Give me the wisdom and understanding to brightly reflect your glory. Help me to become more and more the person you would have me be. Thank you for wisdom. Thank you for knowledge. Thank you for my salvation.

My prayer for today—including any journaling thoughts I may want to add. Where am I today spiritually, emotionally, physically, financially, generally?

Today's Date: _____

Old Testament verse for today: Proverbs 9:10

For the reverence and fear of God are basic to all wisdom. Knowing God results in every other kind of understanding.

One possible prayer for today:

God, thank you for being a God that I can truly reverence without any question. Thank you for being a God who is so powerful that not only can I love you; but I can fear your power and might. Let me know you even better, God, so that I can grow in my understanding. Let me look to you for my guidance on a daily basis. Thank you, God, for being so wonderful in all ways.

New Testament verse for today: John 21:17b

Lord, you know my heart.

One possible prayer for today:

Lord, thank you for knowing me intimately. Thank you for knowing my every thought. Thank you for knowing my heart. Thank you for loving me even though you know my heart and know what a sinful person I am. Thank you for forgiving me when I sin. Lord, even though I reverence you and fear your mighty power, I love you for being so good to me and caring for me in every way and every circumstance. Thank you for loving me first, Lord.

My prayer for today—including any journaling thoughts I may want to add. Where am I today spiritually, emotionally, physically, financially, generally?

Today's Date: _____

Old Testament verse for today: Proverbs 11:28

Trust in your money and down you go! Trust in God and flourish as a tree!

One possible prayer for today:

God, how true! In times past, you have given me much in the way of material blessings, and I have fallen away from my dependence upon you. I have started to feel that I was pretty good in my own right and that I did not need to rely so completely on you for guidance in how to handle these many blessings in a way that is pleasing to you. Let me trust you more, God. Let me trust you more completely in all things. Let me flourish under your love and your guidance, Lord. Let me always look to you first for the direction in my life. And, God, thank you for forgiving me when I neglect to put you first.

New Testament verse for today: John 15:16

You didn't choose me! I chose you! I appointed you to go and produce lovely fruit always, so that no matter what you ask from the Father, using my name, he will give it to you.

One possible prayer for today:

God, thank you for choosing me through your Son, Jesus. Thank you for appointing me to go and produce lovely fruit always. Thank you for giving me the promise that if I do produce lovely fruit in your name that you will give me whatever I ask from you. But, God, I know that if I am in fact producing lovely fruit for you in your name that I will be asking for only those things that are in line with your will for my life. And, Lord, I know that if I do those things, you will let me flourish to the best of my ability. Thank you, Lord, for giving me such a great opportunity of serving you. Thank you for letting me flourish under your love and your guidance. Thank you, Lord.

My prayer for today—including any journaling thoughts I may want to add. Where am I today spiritually, emotionally, physically, financially, generally?

Today's Date: _____

Old Testament verse for today: Proverbs 14:12

Before every man there lies a wide and pleasant road that seems right but ends in death.

One possible prayer for today:

God, help me to distinguish those wide and pleasant roads that lie before me, but are roads that I should not take! I know that taking the easy way out sometimes looks so attractive; but, Lord, I also know that you will give me the strength and the courage to get through my hard times if I acknowledge your Lordship in my life and turn to you for guidance and direction. Help me to make wise choices in my life so that I lead a life that is pleasing to you. Help me to always look to you for guidance in my life; and Lord, please give me the guidance that I need—especially when I am struggling with problems and am tempted to take the easy way out. Thank you, Lord, for being the guide of my life.

New Testament verse for today: II Corinthians 4:17 & 18

These troubles and sufferings of ours are, after all, quite small and won't last very long. Yet this short time of distress will result in God's richest blessing upon us forever and ever! So we do not look at what we can see right now, troubles all around us, but we look forward to the joys in heaven which we have not yet seen. The troubles will soon be over, but the joys to come will last forever.

One possible prayer for today:

God, help me to look to you with unfailing faith to get me through these problems. I know that in your everlasting picture, my problems look finite! But in my life, they look gigantic right now! So I need another shot of your love and another shot of faith. I need to remember that you are in charge of my life. I need to remember that you love me and have a plan for my life. Thank you for giving me what I need right now. I know that you have prepared a home for me in heaven that will be absolutely wonderful. No problems and no trials. But, Lord, again I pray that you will help me—right now and right here on earth. Thank you for hearing my pleadings, oh Lord. Thank you for giving me the strength and the direction that I need right now.

My prayer for today—including any journaling thoughts I may want to add. Where am I today spiritually, emotionally, physically, financially, generally?

Today's Date: _____

Old Testament verse for today: Proverbs 14:26
Reverence for God gives a man deep strength; his children have a place of refuge and security.

One possible prayer for today:
God, thank you for the strength that you have given me as I reverence you. Thank you for the gift of faith you have given me. Thank you for giving my children the many blessings that you have given them. Thank you for giving my children a place of refuge and security. Thank you, God.

New Testament verse for today: Romans 8:30
And having chosen us, he called us to come to him; and when we came, he declared us "not guilty," filled us with Christ's goodness, gave us right standing with himself, and promised us his glory.

One possible prayer for today:
God, thank you for choosing me! Thank you for calling me to come to you. Thank you for accepting me when I came to you. Thank you for forgiving me of my sins and declaring me "not guilty." Thank you for filling me with Christ's goodness. Thank you for giving me right standing with you. Thank you for promising me your glory. Thank you for being such an awesome God. Thank you for giving me the deep strength you have given me. Thank you, God.

My prayer for today—including any journaling thoughts I may want to add. Where am I today spiritually, emotionally, physically, financially, generally?

Today's Date: _____

Old Testament verse for today: Proverbs 15:9

The Lord despises the deeds of the wicked, but loves those who try to be good.

One possible prayer for today:

Lord, thank you for loving me as long as I try to be good! Lord, you know that I often fail in that attempt! You know that my human frailties come into being more often than I would like; but, Lord, you know my heart. You know that I do genuinely try. And, Lord, thank you for continuing to forgive me when I fail.

New Testament verse for today: Hebrews 11:6

You can never please God without faith, without depending on him. Anyone who wants to come to God must believe that there is a God and that he rewards those that sincerely look for him.

One possible prayer for today:

God, thank you for the gift of faith that you have given to me. Thank you for giving me the faith to depend on you at all times—both in the good times and in the bad times. Thank you for rewarding me for sincerely looking for you, and for sincerely trying to be good. Thank you for letting me believe in you. Thank you for the wonderful plan you have for my life. Lord, let me always depend on you and thank you for whatever you have planned for my life.

My prayer for today—including any journaling thoughts I may want to add. Where am I today spiritually, emotionally, physically, financially, generally?

Today's Date: _____

Old Testament verse for today: Proverbs 15:33
Humility and reverence for the Lord will make you both wise and honored.

One possible prayer for today:
Lord, let me always remember that everything I am and everything I have is a gift from you. Every breath that I draw is a gift from you. My life always hangs in the balance of your love and your generosity. When I see the problems that could assail me and know that today I have been spared from those problems, I can only thank you for being so good to me today. Let me always be humble before your great power and might; and, let me always reverence your majesty as the Lord of everything. Give me the wisdom I need to live my life in a manner that is pleasing to you. Thank you, Lord, for putting up with me as I work through the challenges that I encounter, and in so doing, don't do it in humility and reverence for you. Thank you, God, for being a generous and loving God.

New Testament verse for today: John 16:23
At that time you won't need to ask me for anything, you can go directly to the Father and ask him, and he will give you what you ask for because you use my name. You haven't tried this before, (but begin now). Ask using my name, and you will receive, and your cup of joy will overflow.

One possible prayer for today:
Thank you, God, for making yourself so available to me because of what your Son, Jesus has done for me. Thank you for permitting me to come directly to you with my pleas, my petitions, and my praises. Thank you for giving me the things for which I ask as long as they are in line with your will for my life. And, God, thank you for not giving me the things for which I ask that are not in line with your will for my life. Because, I know that if I have asked and not received, it is because it is not good for me to have those things. Give me the wisdom and the confidence in you to accept your will in those matters. And, God, I know that if I am living in line with your will for my life, if I am reverencing you and showing you the proper humility, then, in fact, my cup of joy will overflow. Thank you, God.

My prayer for today—including any journaling thoughts I may want to add. Where am I today spiritually, emotionally, physically, financially, generally?

Today's Date: _____

Old Testament verse for today: Proverbs 16:1

We can make our plans, but the final outcome is in God's hands.

One possible prayer for today:

God, how wonderful it is for me to know that you are in charge of my life. Thank you for being the final authority as to what occurs in my life. Thank you for being concerned about me. Thank you for giving me the faith to willingly accept whatever outcome you have planned for me. Help me to praise you and thank you always.

New Testament verse for today: Colossians 3:17

And whatever you do or say, let it be as a representative of the Lord Jesus, and come with him into the presence of God the Father to give him your thanks.

One possible prayer for today:

God, let me always thank you in all things and at all times. Let my life be representative of the love you have shown me. Let me make my plans only after talking to you and listening to what you want me to do. Let me always be aware that the final outcome of my plans rest with you. So, Lord, let me come into your presence when I am making my plans, asking for your guidance and thanking you for your care, your concern, and your direction. Thank you, Lord.

My prayer for today—including any journaling thoughts I may want to add. Where am I today spiritually, emotionally, physically, financially, generally?

Today's Date: _____

Old Testament verse for today: Proverbs 16:3

Commit your work to the Lord, then it will succeed.

One possible prayer for today:

God, you know that sometimes that is hard for me to do. I like to take the bit in my teeth and run with it—do things my own way. But, Lord, help me. Give me the strength and the faith to commit all of my work to you. Be the center of my life and my work. And, Lord, I do claim the Psalmist's promise. If I honestly and humbly commit my work to you, then you will help me to succeed in what I do. I know that I can count on you, Lord. Help me to be more consistent so that you can count on me.

New Testament verse for today: Galatians 3:11b

God has said that the only way we can be right in his sight is by faith.

One possible prayer for today:

God, that is why I continue to pray for a greater amount of faith. I want to be right in your sight. I want to trust you in all things and have you guide my life in all things. Help me in my business life and in my personal life. Help me to always put my trust in you and not in my own false sense of wisdom or power. Thank you for giving me the faith that I need so that I can be right in your sight. Thank you, Lord, for the gift of faith.

My prayer for today—including any journaling thoughts I may want to add. Where am I today spiritually, emotionally, physically, financially, generally?

Today's Date: _____

Old Testament verse for today: Proverbs 16:9

We should make our plans—counting on God to direct us.

One possible prayer for today:

God, how wonderful it is to know that we can charge ahead, and that you will direct us if we are walking within your will. Lord, thank you for that promise. I do count on you to direct me, Lord; yet, I often charge ahead with my own agenda. Thank you for directing me, Lord. Thank you for letting me have the confidence I need to operate in my world. I know, Lord, that you are in charge of my life and all things. Don't let me get too busy or feeling so important that I forget that important fact, Lord; but, Lord, please just keep on directing me in your love and your forgiveness.

New Testament verse for today: Matthew 19:26b

"But with God, everything is possible."

One possible prayer for today:

Thank you, God, for making everything possible! Thank you for being so awesome that nothing is beyond your power! Thank you for being the Lord of my life! Thank you for directing me in all of my daily pursuits. Lord, let me always tap into your great power; and, use me as it fits your role for my life. But, Lord, if I may be selfish, please use me as a tool that continues to be in good health. Nevertheless, Lord, not my will; but, your will be done in my life.

My prayer for today—including any journaling thoughts I may want to add. Where am I today spiritually, emotionally, physically, financially, generally?

Today's Date: _____

Old Testament verse for today: Proverbs 16:20

God blesses those who obey him; happy the man who puts his trust in the Lord.

One possible prayer for today:

God, thank you for blessing me. I know that I do not always obey you. I know that I go my own way far too often without concern about what you want me to do; but, God, I do trust you. I do love you; and, even though my love is a human love—and therefore fallible—I know that your love is a divine love—and therefore infallible, and I thank you and praise you for that divine love. God, I know that I will be happy—no matter the circumstances—if I truly put my trust in you and learn to accept whatever you give me, because I will know that it is your will for me at that time. Give me that faith and confidence, Lord. Thank you for giving me that gift of faith.

New Testament verse for today: Act 10:37b

—there is a peace with God through Jesus, the Messiah, who is Lord of all creation.

One possible prayer for today:

Thank you for the peace that comes from a belief and a confidence in Jesus. Thank you for taking your Son from your right hand and sending him to die on the cross so that I might have eternal life. Thank you for making him my personal Messiah and Savior. God, to think that Christ was with you at the creation and then he came to earth to be my personal Savior is an overwhelming thought. Thank you for doing that for me, Lord. Thank you for loving me so much.

My prayer for today—including any journaling thoughts I may want to add. Where am I today spiritually, emotionally, physically, financially, generally?

Today's Date: _____

Old Testament verse for today: Proverbs 18:10

The Lord is a strong fortress. The godly run to him and are safe.

One possible prayer for today:

God, how wonderful it is to have you as my personal strong fortress. Thank you for always being there when I run to you. Thank you for keeping me safe. Lord, give me the wisdom to always run to you for protection and safety. Thank you for giving me the confidence that you are always there for me.

New Testament verse for today: Acts 10:42 & 43

And he (God) sent us to preach the Good News everywhere and to testify that Jesus is ordained of God to be the Judge of all—living and dead. And all the prophets have written about him, saying that everyone who believes in him will have their sins forgiven through his name.

One possible prayer for today:

God, what a wonderful strong fortress you are, who cannot only keep me safe; but, has provided a plan so that my sins may be forgiven if I only believe in your Son, Jesus. Thank you for keeping me safe. Thank you for ordaining Jesus to be my Judge. Thank you for giving me the faith to believe, so that I may have all my sins forgiven. Thank you, God, for being such a wonderful God who protects and forgives.

My prayer for today—including any journaling thoughts I may want to add. Where am I today spiritually, emotionally, physically, financially, generally?

Today's Date: _____

Old Testament verse for today: Proverbs 19:8

He who loves wisdom loves his own best interest and will be a success.

One possible prayer for today:

Lord, let me be more concerned about being wise than about collecting honors and worldly goods. Let me seek more of the wisdom that you can give to me so that I may be a better witness of your love and concern for me. Lord, I claim your promise that you will help me be the kind of success you want me to be. Let me rely more on your leading in my life and the wisdom that you have given me and that you will give me. Thank you, Lord, for being the author of all wisdom.

New Testament verse for today: Luke 6:27

Listen, all of you. Love your enemies. Do good to those who hate you. Pray for the happiness of those who curse you; implore God's blessing on those who hurt you.

One possible prayer for today:

God, not only do I need a generous supply of your wisdom to follow that advice, I also need an extra generous supply of love and patience! That's a real hard thing for me to do! When I have an enemy or someone that I know doesn't like me and treat me the way I think they should, I want all kinds of bad things to happen to them! I want to get even! Lord, help me to do a better job of loving my enemies; of doing good things to those who don't like me; of praying for good things to happen in the lives of those who treat me badly; and, Lord, help me to really pray for those who have hurt me. Please, God, give me the wisdom, the love, the faith, and the patience to work a lot harder to do those things. And, Lord, when I let you down, thank you for not treating me the way I treat others when they have let me down.

My prayer for today—including any journaling thoughts I may want to add. Where am I today spiritually, emotionally, physically, financially, generally?

Today's Date: _____

Old Testament verse for today: Proverbs 19:23
Reverence for God gives life, happiness, and protection from harm.

One possible prayer for today:
Lord, I do reverence you. I do worship you. And, God, I do know that all life comes from you. Sometimes I am not happy. And sometimes I don't feel that protection from harm. What have I done wrong, Lord? Where have I failed? I know that you cannot fail, so what has happened? Lord, give me the faith to go on believing. Give me the comfort that I need at this moment to feel your protection. Give me happiness again. Thank you, Lord, for hearing me.

New Testament verse for today: John 1:1 thru 5
Before anything else existed, there was Christ, with God. He has always been alive and is himself God. He created everything there is—nothing exists that he didn't make. Eternal life is in him, and this life gives light to all mankind. His life is the light that shines through the darkness—and the darkness can never extinguish it.

One possible prayer for today:
Lord, let me keep this thought in my mind as I encounter the bad times. Christ has always been there and therefore will always be there for me. He created me as he created all things. He made me in his image. Thank you for the eternal life that I have through Christ. Thank you for always giving that light and thank you that the darkness—and my dark times—can never extinguish the light that Christ gives. Thank you, God.

My prayer for today—including any journaling thoughts I may want to add. Where am I today spiritually, emotionally, physically, financially, generally?

Today's Date: _____

Old Testament verse for today: Proverbs 20:24

Since the Lord is directing our steps, why try to understand everything that happens along the way?

One possible prayer for today:

Lord, please give me the faith to accept that challenge! I am always trying to figure out why this or that happened. I am always looking for a reason that a certain event has occurred, when what I really need to do is accept that you are in charge of my life and that my obligation to you is to accept what has happened and honor you with my reaction to whatever happens. Lord, many times I need more faith to accomplish that. So, today, give me the faith that I need to honor you today with whatever is happening in my life. Thank you, Lord, for being in charge. Thank you for giving me the faith that I need—even if just for today.

New Testament verse for today: I Corinthians 10:13

But remember this—the wrong desires that come into your life aren't anything new and different. Many others have faced exactly the same problems before you. And no temptation is irresistible. You can trust God to keep the temptation from becoming so strong that you can't stand up against it, for he has promised this and will do what he says. He will show you how to escape temptation's power so that you can bear up patiently against it.

One possible prayer for today:

God, please give me the help that I need today to do just that—to bear up patiently against the temptation that has come into my life. I can't do it alone, Lord. I need your help! I need to feel your presence in my life—right now! I need to hear you speak to me in some manner that makes me feel your love and your caring. And, Lord, please be gentle with me as you give me the power that I need. Please don't be angry with me for getting myself into this situation. I am looking to you for your help, Lord. I claim Paul's promise in this verse that you will do this for me. Thank you, Lord. Thank you for hearing me and helping me.

My prayer for today—including any journaling thoughts I may want to add. Where am I today spiritually, emotionally, physically, financially, generally?

Today's Date: _____

Old Testament verse for today: Proverbs 22:4

True humility and respect for the Lord lead a man to riches, honor and a long life.

One possible prayer for today:

God, let me have the proper humility and respect for you. Let me always acknowledge your awesome power and reverence your greatness. Let me always thank you for being so kind to me. And, Lord, I claim the Psalmist's promise of riches, honor, and a long life. Thank you, God.

New Testament verse for today: John 8:36

So if the Son sets you free, you will indeed be free.

One possible prayer for today:

God, thank you for setting me free through the death and resurrection of your Son, Jesus. Thank you for that marvelous plan of salvation made so simple that even I can accept it. Lord, I know that no matter what happens to me on this earth, that I can count on spending eternity in your presence. And, God, when I am really in trouble, that assurance is even better than the promise of riches, honor, and long life. Lord, I do thank you for the many blessings you have given me and are giving me in this earthly life; but, even more, Lord, I thank you for your Son, Jesus, setting me free from the bondage of sin. Thank you, Lord.

My prayer for today—including any journaling thoughts I may want to add. Where am I today spiritually, emotionally, physically, financially, generally?

Today's Date: _____

Old Testament verse for today: Proverbs 22:17 through 19

Listen to this advice; follow it closely, for it will do you good, and you can pass it on to others; Trust in the Lord.

One possible prayer for today:

God, what wonderful advice! Thank you for being such a loving and gracious God that I can trust in you always and completely. Thank you for always being there for me when I need you. Thank you for always having my best interest at heart, even if it sometimes does not seem like it. Thank you, God.

New Testament verse for today: John 6:68b & 69

You (Jesus) alone have the words that give eternal life, and we believe them and know you are the holy Son of God.

One possible prayer for today:

God, thank you for giving me your one and only Son that I may have eternal life through my belief in Him. Thank you for giving Jesus—and Jesus alone—the words that give eternal life. Thank you that I believe and that I may count on your promise of eternal life. Sometimes this life doesn't seem too good, Lord, so thank you for giving me the hope of a better life with you in eternity. Thank you again, Lord, for the gift of your only Son.

My prayer for today—including any journaling thoughts I may want to add. Where am I today spiritually, emotionally, physically, financially, generally?

Today's Date: _____

Old Testament verse for today: Proverbs 30:5

Ever word of God proves true. He defends all who come to him for protection. Do not add to his words, lest he rebuke you, and you be found a liar.

One possible prayer for today:

God, thank you for being the God of truth. Thank you for being a God whose words prove true. Thank you for being a God who always does what he says he is going to do. Thank you for the protection that you have given—and are giving—me. And, God, don't let me be one who embellishes your words. Let me be true to your words and the meaning of them. What you have said needs no embellishment, Lord. Thank you for being the kind of God you are.

New Testament verse for today: Matthew 4:10

"Get out of here, Satan," Jesus told him. "The scriptures say, 'Worship only the Lord God. Obey only him.' "

One possible prayer for today:

God, because your words prove true, please give me the strength and the faith to try to always follow your teachings. I know that I cannot always follow them. I know that I will fail. I know that my humanity—my selfishness—my weakness—my ego—will get in the way with regularity; but, Lord, let me always return to you, knowing that when I return to you, you will take me back into your fellowship. So, Lord, let me always worship only you. Let me obey you and you only. When I feel tempted, let me have the strength to say, like Jesus, "Get out of my life, Satan!"

My prayer for today—including any journaling thoughts I may want to add. Where am I today spiritually, emotionally, physically, financially, generally?

Today's Date: _____

Old Testament verse for today: Ecclesiastes 2:24 & 25a

So I decided that there was nothing better for a man to do than to enjoy his food and drink, and his job. Then I realized that even this pleasure is from the hand of God. For who can eat or enjoy apart from him? For God gives those who please him wisdom, knowledge, and joy.

One possible prayer for today:

God, thank you for making my life as pleasant as it is. Thank you for permitting me to enjoy good food and drink. Thank you for giving me a job that I can enjoy. And, Lord, on those day that I do not enjoy my job, give me the patience and the wisdom to do it well anyway. Thank you for reminding me that all I have is a gift from you and that I cannot really enjoy what I have apart from you—without giving you the thanks for all I have. Thank you, God, for giving me the wisdom, knowledge and joy that you have given me.

New Testament verse for today: Luke 36:37

Try to show as much compassion as your Father does. Never criticize or condemn—or it will all come back on you. Go easy on others; then they will do the same for you.

One possible prayer for today:

God, let me use the wisdom you have given me to be kind to others. Let me continually show compassion to others. Don't let me criticize, or condemn or judge others; because I know that I do lots of things for which I could be criticized or judged more harshly. God, thank you for being such a loving and forgiving God for me. Thank you, Lord.

My prayer for today—including any journaling thoughts I may want to add. Where am I today spiritually, emotionally, physically, financially, generally?

Today's Date: _____

Old Testament verse for today: Ecclesiastes 3:11

Everything is appropriate in its own time. But though God has planted eternity in the hearts of men, even so, man cannot see the whole scope of God's work from beginning to end.

One possible prayer for today:

God, thank you for being the God who rules over all things. Thank you for making things appropriate in their own time. Thank you for planting eternity in my heart. And, Lord, thank you for not burdening me with complete foreknowledge of all your work. Thank you for letting me live my life one day at a time. And, God, thank you for being with me every single day of my life.

New Testament verse for today: Matthew 6:31 thru 33

So don't worry at all about having enough food and clothing. Why be like the heathen? For they take pride in all these things and are deeply concerned about them. But your heavenly Father already knows perfectly well that you need them, and he will give them to you if you give him first place in your life and live as he wants you to.

One possible prayer for today:

Lord, this promise of Christ's has always bothered me. I know that you have always taken care of me. I know that I have never gone without an adequate amount of food or enough clothing; but, Lord, what about all the people who believe in you that do not have enough food and clothing? I know that you can see the whole scope of your work from beginning to end and that I cannot see beyond this moment. And I know that you always have a plan for everyone's life. So, God, please give me the faith to trust you in all things and for all things. Give me a concern for others that will help your cause. Thank you for always taking care of me and those who are dear to me. God, give comfort to those who do not have enough of their basic needs. Help me to understand what part you want me to play in the scope of your work.

My prayer for today—including any journaling thoughts I may want to add. Where am I today spiritually, emotionally, physically, financially, generally?

Today's Date: _____

Old Testament verse for today: Ecclesiastes 3:12 & 13
So I conclude that, first, there is nothing better for a man than to be happy and to enjoy himself as long as he can; and second that he should eat and drink and enjoy the fruits of his labors, for these are gifts from God.

One possible prayer for today:
God, thank you for giving me enjoyment in life. Let me learn to be thankful in all things— even during those days when I am facing obstacles. Let me look at those obstacles as lessons that you want me to learn. And, Lord, for the good times—when I truly do enjoy the times and the fruits of my labor, I thank you. Thank you for giving me enough to eat and drink; and, thank you for all your many gifts to me. Thank you, God, that on most days, I can really enjoy the life that you have permitted me to live. Thank you, God.

New Testament verse for today: Luke 6:45
A good man produces good deeds from a good heart. And an evil man produces evil deeds from his hidden wickedness. Whatever is in the heart overflows into speech.

One possible prayer for today:
God, let my heart be pure and right with you. Let the many gifts that you have given me produce in me a good heart, good deeds, and speech that is acceptable to you. Let my heart be so in tune with your will for my life, that when things do not go as I would like them to go, my speech still overflows with praise to you. Give me the strength that I need to keep my heart right with you, Lord. And, Lord, thank you for your patience and your forgiveness when I fail you in this area of my life.

My prayer for today—including any journaling thoughts I may want to add. Where am I today spiritually, emotionally, physically, financially, generally?

Today's Date: _____

Old Testament verse for today: Ecclesiastes 3:14

And I know this, that whatever God does is final—nothing can be added or taken from it; God's purpose in this is that man should fear the all-powerful God.

One possible prayer for today:

God, thank you for being all-powerful. Thank you for not only being such a powerful God I should fear you; but, for being an all-loving God that never gives up on loving even me— no matter what I do. Thank you for being the final authority in my life; but, thank you for being a loving final authority if I will only turn to you and trust you to help me. Thank you, God, for helping me.

New Testament verse for today: Luke 12:8

And I assure you of this: I, the Messiah, will publicly honor you in the presence of God's angels if you publicly acknowledge me here on earth as your Friend.

One possible prayer for today:

God, thank you for giving your Son, Jesus, to be my Friend here on earth and to publicly honor me before your angels, if I will only believe in him and acknowledge him in my life. What a wonderful gift, Lord. Thank you for that gift. To be acknowledged to you—an all-powerful God—is an awesome honor. Thank you for giving me that plan made so simple to follow. All I have to do is believe. Thank you, God. I do believe.

My prayer for today—including any journaling thoughts I may want to add. Where am I today spiritually, emotionally, physically, financially, generally?

Today's Date: _____

Old Testament verse for today: Ecclesiastes 3:22

So I saw that there is nothing better for men than that they should be happy in their work, for that is what they are here for, and no one can bring them back to life to enjoy what will be in the future, so let them enjoy it now.

One possible prayer for today:

God, thank you for giving me a life that has many pleasant moments and events in it. Thank you for permitting me to enjoy what I do each day. Lord, I know that all of life cannot always be pleasant. I know that there will always be snags in the daily current of live and business; but, it is wonderful to know that we can have abundant life through belief in your Son, Jesus. Thank you for making a world that can have many wonderful days in it. Thank you, God.

New Testament verse for today: Romans 8:31 & 32

What can we ever say to such wonderful things as these? If God is on our side, who can ever be against us? Since he did not spare even his own Son for us but gave him up for us all, won't he also surely give us everything else?

One possible prayer for today:

Thank you, God, for all the wonderful things that you have given me. Thank you for all the wonderful promises I have on which I can rely. Thank you for always being on my side. Thank you for giving me the knowledge that no one or no thing can really stand against me. Thank you for giving me your Son, Jesus, through whom I may receive eternal life. Thank you for all you have done for me and given me. Thank you, God.

My prayer for today—including any journaling thoughts I may want to add. Where am I today spiritually, emotionally, physically, financially, generally?

Today's Date: _____

Old Testament verse for today: Ecclesiastes 4:9 & 10

Two can accomplish more than twice as much as one, for the results can be much better. If one falls, the other pulls him up: but if a man falls when is alone, he's in trouble.

One possible prayer for today:

God, thank you for giving me friends who will help me when I am in trouble. Thank you for giving me friends who will pull me up when I fall. Lord, let me work at surrounding myself with people who will be there for me when I need them. And, Lord, in turn let me be there for others when they are in trouble or when they fall. Let me be ready with the help that they need in their time of trouble. Give me a kind and helpful heart, Lord. Help me to be more concerned about others.

New Testament verse for today: James 5:19 & 20

Dear brothers, if anyone has slipped away from God and no longer trusts the Lord, and someone helps him understand the Truth again, that person who brings him back to God will have saved a wandering soul from death, bringing about the forgiveness of his many sins.

One possible prayer for today:

God, thank you for giving me friends who will pull me up when I fall. Thank you for giving me caring friends who will work at bringing me back to you if I ever slip away. Lord, we know that you will always welcome any of us back with open arms when we come back to you and humbly ask for your forgiveness of our sins. Thank you for always being there to forgive me when I come back to you. And, Lord, thank you for giving me friends who care enough to help me come back to you whenever I start to slip away from your love and your care. Thank you, Lord.

My prayer for today—including any journaling thoughts I may want to add. Where am I today spiritually, emotionally, physically, financially, generally?

Today's Date: _____

Old Testament verse for today: Ecclesiastes 4:18

Tackle every task that comes along, and if you fear God you can expect his blessing.

One possible prayer for today:

God, today I need your help. Today I need the fulfillment of the promise in this verse. Today, I have a real task in front of me that I am not sure I know how to solve. So, God, I need your help. I need your blessing. I need your guidance. Thank you, God, for being there for me today when I need you the most. Thank you for helping me tackle my task today. And, God, I know that if I get so wrapped up in what I am doing that I forget about you, I know that you will never forget about me. Thank you, God, for being so faithful to me.

New Testament verse for today: Philippians 4:19

And it is he who will supply all your needs from his riches in glory, because of what Christ Jesus has done for us.

One possible prayer for today:

What a wonderful promise, Lord. I claim that promise today. For me. Today. I claim that promise that you will supply all my needs today from your riches in glory. Thank you, Lord, for letting me call on your great power. Thank you for giving me the guidance that I need today. And, God, most of all, thank you for giving me Christ as my personal Savior. Thank you, God.

My prayer for today—including any journaling thoughts I may want to add. Where am I today spiritually, emotionally, physically, financially, generally?

Today's Date: _____

Old Testament verse for today: Ecclesiastes 5:19

Well, one thing, at least, is good: it is for a man to eat well, drink a good glass of wine, accept his position in life, and enjoy his work whatever his job may be, for however long the Lord may let him live.

One possible prayer for today:

Lord, it is obvious that you want me to be able to live life "to the max!" Thank you for that encouragement. Lord, thank you for giving me all the good things that you have given me. Thank you for giving me the challenges that make my life more interesting. Thank you for letting me have food and drink, and to be able to enjoy them. Thank you for my ability to work and achieve. Lord, thank you for life itself; and, thank you for giving me the gift of eternal life, so that when this life ends, I may experience an even greater eternal life in your presence.

New Testament verse for today: John 1:17 & 18

For Moses gave us only the Law with its rigid demands and merciless justice, while Jesus Christ brought us loving forgiveness as well. No one has ever actually seen God, but, of course, his only Son has, for he is the companion of the Father and has told us all about him.

One possible prayer for today:

God, thank you for giving me your only Son, who knows you and has told me about you. Thank you for giving me a new set of rules that make it possible for me to live life to "to the max" and still live without guilt as long as I live within your will for my life. Thank you for the loving forgiveness that your Son, Jesus, brought to me. Thank you, God, for being so wonderful to me.

My prayer for today—including any journaling thoughts I may want to add. Where am I today spiritually, emotionally, physically, financially, generally?

Today's Date: _____

Old Testament verse for today: Ecclesiastes 5:20

And, of course, it is very good if a man has received wealth from the Lord, and the good health to enjoy it. To enjoy your work and to accept your lot in life—that is indeed a gift from God. The person who does that will not have to look back with sorrow on his past, for God gives him joy.

One possible prayer for today:

Lord, thank you for what you have given me. Sure, I am selfish. I would always like more; but, Lord, you have given me what you want me to have, and I thank you for it. Please give me the faith to always accept my lot in life. Please give me that gift. And, Lord, I know that the only way that I can ever truly accept all that occurs in my life—good or bad—and accept it with equanimity, is to truly trust you and put you in charge of my life. Give me the faith to do a better job of that, Lord. Thank you for giving me the faith that I need.

New Testament verse for today: John 1:12 & 13

But to all who received him, he gave the right to become children of God. All they needed to do was to trust him to save them. All those who believe this are reborn!—not a physical rebirth resulting from the human passion or plan—but from the will of God.

One possible prayer for today:

Lord, thank you for that promise. Thank you for giving me the right to become one of your children! What a privilege! And to think that all I need to do is to trust you. And, if I do that you have promised to save me. I will be reborn into your eternal Kingdom. Thank you, God, for making this plan available to me. Thank you for giving me the faith to accept this and to believe it. Thank you for letting me put my trust in you and have the knowledge that I won't have to look back on my life with sorrow; but will know that I will have joy. Thank you, God.

My prayer for today—including any journaling thoughts I may want to add. Where am I today spiritually, emotionally, physically, financially, generally?

Today's Date: _____

Old Testament verse for today: Ecclesiastes 7:14

Enjoy prosperity whenever you can, and even when hard times strike, realize that God gives one as well as the other—so that everyone will realize that nothing is certain in this life.

One possible prayer for today:

Lord, let me always keep that in mind. Let me be willing to honestly thank you for the good times as well as the bad times; because I know that if I am living within your will, then both the good times and the bad times are your plans for me at that moment. Let me be properly humble and thankful during the good times; and, Lord, give me the faith to be properly thankful and optimistic during the bad times. Let me be thankful to you at all times, Lord.

New Testament verse for today: John 14:13 & 14

You can ask him (the Father) for anything, using my name, and I will do it, for this will bring praise to the Father because of what I, the Son, will do for you. Yes, ask anything, using my name, and I will do it!

One possible prayer for today:

Lord, I know that I can ask anything from you, using your Son's name, and you will do it. But, Lord, I know that for me to get my request, I have to be asking for things that are in line with your will for my life. Thank you for showing me the things that you want me to request from you, Lord. Thank you for showing me how you want me to live my life. Thank you for working in my life in such a manner that I will be asking for things that are in line with your will for my life. Thank you for helping me to ask for the things you want me to have in both the good times and the bad, Lord. Thank you for directing my life, Lord.

My prayer for today—including any journaling thoughts I may want to add. Where am I today spiritually, emotionally, physically, financially, generally?

Today's Date: _____

Old Testament verse for today: Ecclesiastes 11:1 & 2

Give generously, for your gifts will return to you later. Divide your gifts among many, for in the days ahead you yourself may need much help.

One possible prayer for today:

Lord, thank you for giving me the time, talent and funds to be able to give. Even if I have little, I can give something to others. Let me be wise in my gifts. Let me look to you for guidance in properly giving of my time, my talents, and my funds. Lord, let me be generous, as you have been generous with me. Thank you, Lord, for your generosity.

New Testament verse for today: John 12:28

Father, bring glory and honor to your name.

One possible prayer for today:

Lord, let me bring glory and honor to your name because of my actions. Let me bring glory and honor to your name because of the way I use my time, talents, and funds for your service. Lord, thank you for using me as it serves your purposes. And, Lord, if it is your will, thank you for using me in a way where I may remain healthy in all aspects of my life. Thank you for being so good to me, Lord. Thank you for letting me do my part to bring glory and honor to your name.

My prayer for today—including any journaling thoughts I may want to add. Where am I today spiritually, emotionally, physically, financially, generally?

Today's Date: _____

Old Testament verse for today: Ecclesiastes 11:4

If you wait for perfect conditions, you will never get anything done.

One possible prayer for today:

God, thank you for giving me the faith to push ahead even when I cannot clearly see how I am going to get where I am planning on going! Only by faith in you can I continue to feel confident in pursuing a difficult path that has a lot of stumbling blocks along the way. God, I know that seldom do you give me a perfect condition; but, I also know that you are always with me to guide me through the rough spots. Thank you, God, for always being with me whether the condition are perfect or not.

New Testament verse for today: Matthew 34:42

So be prepared, for you don't know what day your Lord is coming.

One possible prayer for today:

God, I know that the only time my life is going to be perfect all the time is when I am in your presence in eternity. So, help me to always be prepared for the event that takes me from this life to eternity with you. Lord, I don't know when that will occur, so let me live in such close harmony with you that I am always ready. Then I can eagerly anticipate that perfect condition that you will provide for me. Thank you, God, for the security of that promise. In the meantime, let me live my life doing the things that you want me to do, working in the conditions that you are providing for me now.

My prayer for today—including any journaling thoughts I may want to add. Where am I today spiritually, emotionally, physically, financially, generally?

Today's Date: _____

Old Testament verse for today: Ecclesiastes 12:13

Here is my final conclusion: fear God and obey his commandments, for this is the entire duty of man.

One possible prayer for today:

God, I do love you and yet I fear your mighty power. I try to obey your commandments; but, I know that I often fail. I cannot live up to those ideals that you outlined for me. So, Lord, I will continue to love you and know that you have a plan for my life that makes my salvation possible, even though I continue to fall short of your goals for me. Thank you for being so generous, Lord.

New Testament verse for today: Colossians 2:13 thru 15

You were dead in sins, and your sinful desires were not yet cut away. Then he gave you a share in the very life of Christ, for he forgave all your sins, and blotted out the charges proved against you, the list of his commandments which you had not obeyed. He took this list of sins and destroyed it by nailing it to Christ's cross. In this way God took away Satan's power to accuse you of sin, and God openly displayed to the whole world Christ's triumph at the cross where sins were taken away.

One possible prayer for today:

God, what a wonderful plan you made for my salvation! You knew that I couldn't keep your commandments. You knew that I would continually fail. So, you gave me Christ! Thank you for forgiving me all my sins! Thank you for blotting out all the charges proved against me! Thank you for forgiving me all the commandments which I had disobeyed. Thank you for nailing all of my sins and the charges against me on Christ's cross! Thank you for taking away Satan's power to accuse me of all my sins. Thank you for openly displaying to the whole world Christ's triumph on the cross. Thank you, God, for your love and your wonderful plan of salvation for me because of your love for me.

My prayer for today—including any journaling thoughts I may want to add. Where am I today spiritually, emotionally, physically, financially, generally?

Today's Date: _____

Old Testament verse for today: Isaiah 1:18

Come, let's talk this over! Says the Lord: no matter how deep the stain of your sins, I can take it out and make you as clean as freshly fallen snow. Even if you are stained as red as crimson, I can make you white as wool! If you will only let me help you, if you will only obey, then I will make you rich!

One possible prayer for today:

What a wonderful God you are! Thank you for that promise. Thank you for your promise to me that no matter what my sin—no matter what!—you will remove it from me and make me as clean as freshly fallen snow. Thank you, God, for doing that for me. Even if I have done the worst things imaginable, if I come to you and truly and humbly confess, you will make me as white as wool. Lord, help me. Help me to obey you. And, Lord, I claim your promise, that if I will do those things, you will make me rich. Thank you for being such a wonderful God. Thank you. Thank you.

New Testament verse for today: John 11:25 thru 26a

Jesus told her, (Martha) "I am the one who raises the dead and gives them life again. Anyone who believes in me, even though he dies like anyone else, shall live again. He is given eternal life for believing in me and shall never perish. Do you believe this?"

One possible prayer for today:

Lord, I do believe this! I believe that your son, Jesus, is the one who gives eternal life. Thank you for giving me Jesus so that I may have eternal life. Thank you for giving me the faith to believe. Thank you for your wonderful plan of salvation that is mine if I will only truly believe. Lord, I do believe. Lord, I claim your promises that you will cleanse me from all my sins and give me eternal life through your Son, Jesus. Thank you, Lord. Thank you.

My prayer for today—including any journaling thoughts I may want to add. Where am I today spiritually, emotionally, physically, financially, generally?

Today's Date: _____

Old Testament verse for today: Isaiah 5:16

But the Lord of Hosts is exalted above all, for he alone is holy, just and good.

One possible prayer for today:

God, thank you for being a Lord who is exalted above all. Thank you for being a Lord who is holy, just and good. Thank you for being my personal Lord. Thank you for caring for me in all things and at all times. Lord, I love you and adore you. Let me do my part of honoring you with my life and my actions so that I do my best to give you the adoration and exaltation that you desire in my life. Thank you, Lord, for being such a wonderful, patient, loving God.

New Testament verse for today: Luke 11:36

If you are filled with light within, with no dark corners, then your face will be radiant too, as though a floodlight is beamed upon you.

One possible prayer for today:

Let me light shine from within because of my love and faith in you, Lord. Let me get rid of all the dark corners of my life. Let the floodlight of your love and your compassion shine through me today because I am doing my best to live as you want me to live, Lord. Thank you for giving me the joy in my life that permits me to be a radiant witness for you. Thank you, Lord.

My prayer for today—including any journaling thoughts I may want to add. Where am I today spiritually, emotionally, physically, financially, generally?

Today's Date: _____

Old Testament verse for today: Isaiah 6:3b

Holy, holy, holy is the Lord of Hosts; the whole earth is filled with his glory.

One possible prayer for today:

God, thank you for being holy. Thank you for loving me, even though you are holy and I am sinful. Thank you for cleansing me of my sin through the blood of your Son, Jesus. Thank you for giving me this wonderful world to enjoy. Thank you for filling that wonderful world with your glory. As I look at your wonderful world, let me always remember to thank you and worship you in all that I do. Thank you for being the Lord of everything.

New Testament verse for today: Romans 3:27 & 28

Then what can we boast about doing, to earn our salvation? Nothing at all. Why? Because our acquittal is not based on our good deeds; it is based on what Christ has done and our faith in him. So it is that we are saved by faith in Christ and not by the good things we do.

One possible prayer for today:

God, thank you for filling the earth with your glory. Thank you that, as a part of filling the earth with your glory, you choose to send your Son, Jesus, to earth to pay the price for my sins. Thank you for making that plan so that I do not have to earn my salvation; because, if I had to earn it, I know that I would fail. Thank you for acquitting me of my sins without my having to do any good deeds; because, I know that I could not do enough good deeds to wipe out my sins. Thank you for Christ. Thank you for giving me the faith to believe in Christ so that my salvation comes from that alone. Thank you, God, for that wonderful plan as a part of your glory on earth.

My prayer for today—including any journaling thoughts I may want to add. Where am I today spiritually, emotionally, physically, financially, generally?

Today's Date: _____

Old Testament verse for today: Isaiah 8:13 & 14a

Don't fear anything except the Lord of the armies of heaven! If you fear him, you need fear nothing else. He will be your safety.

One possible prayer for today:

Lord, what a powerful God you are—Lord of the armies of heaven! What a wonderful name, so worthy of my praise! And, God, I do fear you. I reverence you. I adore you. I thank you for being my personal God. And, God, with you on my side, I thank you and praise you that I have no need to fear anything else. Thank you, God, for being my safety. Thank you, God, for your mighty power that is at work for me—personally. Thank you, God.

New Testament verse for today: Matthew 24:46 & 47

Blessings on you if I return and find you faithfully doing your work. I will put such faithful ones in charge of everything that I own!

One possible prayer for today:

Lord, what a wonderful thought! Here you are, the Lord of the armies of heaven, and your Son, Jesus, has promised that if I am faithful in doing the work that you have given me to do, that I will be in charge of everything you own! Lord, I am not worthy of that kind of largesse and power. I am not worthy to be in charge of anything that you own. On my own merit, I am not even worthy to be called one of your children. But, Lord, you have made me worthy by your magnificent love. And, only because of your love and the free gift of your salvation can I be worthy in your eyes. Thank you, God, for making me worthy in your eyes because of the free gift of forgiveness that you have given me.

My prayer for today—including any journaling thoughts I may want to add. Where am I today spiritually, emotionally, physically, financially, generally?

Today's Date: _____

Old Testament verse for today: Isaiah 9:2

The people who walk in darkness shall see a great Light—a Light that will shine on all those who live in the land of the shadow of death.

One possible prayer for today:

God, thank you for sending the Light of the World. Thank you for sending a Light that shines on all of us who live under the bondage of sin and the cares of this world. Thank you for knowing that we needed this Light to permit us to have a perfect fellowship with you. Thank you, God.

New Testament verse for today: John 17:9 & 10

My plea is not for the world but for those you have given me because they belong to you. And all of them, since they are mine, belong to you; and you have given them back to me with everything else of yours, and so they are my glory!

One possible prayer for today:

God, thank you for sending the Light to me. Thank you for sending your Son, Jesus, to be the Light of the World. Thank you for permitting me to become one of Jesus' followers. Thank you for the promise that I belong to you and to your Son, Jesus. Thank you for counting me among those who Christ considers his glory. Thank you for loving me so much.

My prayer for today—including any journaling thoughts I may want to add. Where am I today spiritually, emotionally, physically, financially, generally?

Today's Date: _____

Old Testament verse for today: Isaiah 9:6

For unto us a Child is born; unto us a Son is given; and the government shall be upon his shoulder. These will be his royal titles: "Wonderful," "Counselor," "The Mighty God," "The Everlasting Father," "The Prince of Peace." His ever-expanding, peaceful government will never end. He will rule with perfect fairness and justice from the throne of his father David. He will bring true justice and peace to all the nations of the world. This is going to happen because the Lord of heaven's armies has dedicated himself to it!

One possible prayer for today:

God, thank you for planning such a great and wonderful plan of salvation through your Son, Jesus Christ, and then following through on that plan when it fit your timing. Thank you for giving us this wonderful Son who is our Mighty God and Everlasting Father. Thank you that Jesus rules with you in perfect fairness and justice. And, Lord, thank you that you and Jesus rule with compassion and caring so that you continue to forgive my sins when I fail to live up to my end of the bargain. Thank you, God, for sending Jesus to be such a loving Savior.

New Testament verse for today: Hebrews 9:13 thru 15

And if under the old system the blood of bulls and goats and the ashes of young cows could cleanse men's bodies from sin, just think how much more surely the blood of Christ will transform our lives and hearts. His sacrifice frees us from the worry of having to obey the old rules, and makes us want to serve the living God. For by the help of the eternal Holy Spirit, Christ willingly gave himself to God to die for our sins—he being perfect, without a single sin or fault. Christ came with this new agreement so that all who are invited may come and have forever all the wonders God has promised them. For Christ died to rescue them from the penalty of the sins that they had committed while still under that old system.

One possible prayer for today:

God, thank you for giving your Son, Jesus, as a sacrifice for the sins of the world. Thank you for giving me this new system of salvation. Thank you for letting Christ give himself to you to shed his blood for me so that the stains of my sins are forever removed from my record. Thank you for this new plan of salvation that permits me to inherit all the wonders that you have promised me. Thank you, God, for being so wonderful to me.

My prayer for today—including any journaling thoughts I may want to add. Where am I today spiritually, emotionally, physically, financially, generally?

Today's Date: _____

Old Testament verse for today: Isaiah 12:2 & 3

See, God has come to save me! I will trust and not be afraid, for the Lord is my strength and song; he is my salvation. Oh, the joy of drinking deeply from the Fountain of Salvation.

One possible prayer for today:

Thank you, God, for always being there to save me. Thank you that I can trust in you and not be afraid of what I am facing in my life. Thank you for being my strength; and, thank you for giving me a song in my heart. Thank you for being my salvation. God, thank you for giving me the faith to drink deeply from the Fountain of Salvation. Thank you for making that plan of salvation available to me. Thank you, God.

New Testament verse for today: John 6:47

"How earnestly I tell you this—anyone who believes in me already has eternal life!"

One possible prayer for today:

Thank you, God, for providing such a wonderful plan for me to know that I have eternal life through my belief in your Son, Jesus. Thank you for permitting me to drink from that marvelous Fountain of Salvation that you have provided. Thank you for the gift of faith. Thank you, God, for being so good to me.

My prayer for today—including any journaling thoughts I may want to add. Where am I today spiritually, emotionally, physically, financially, generally?

Today's Date: _____

Old Testament verse for today: Isaiah 25:1

Lord, I will honor and praise your name, for you are my God; You do such wonderful things! You planned them long ago, and now you have accomplished them, just as you said!

One possible prayer for today:

God, it is so wonderful to have a God like you on my side. You are a God that is not only all powerful; but, Lord, you are timeless! I thank you and honor you and praise you, O God, for being my personal God; for doing such wonderful things for me; for being a timeless God that carries out your plans throughout the ages! Thank you for accomplishing the things that you have done for me, God. Thank you, God.

New Testament verse for today: Luke 19:38

"God has given us a King!" they exulted. "Long live the King! Let all heaven rejoice! Glory to God in the highest heavens!"

One possible prayer for today:

God, thank you for giving us your Son, Jesus. I know that he was not a king in the manner that was expected; but, I also know that he was a King far beyond what was expected. He was a King that could give me eternal life if I only believe in Him. And, God, I do believe. Thank you for giving me the faith to believe. Thank you for making this plan in the beginning of time and for carrying it out so that I may believe and have eternal life. You always accomplish your purposes, Lord. Thank you for permitting me to be a part of that eternal plan. Thank you, God.

My prayer for today—including any journaling thoughts I may want to add. Where am I today spiritually, emotionally, physically, financially, generally?

Today's Date: _____

Old Testament verse for today: Isaiah 26:3 & 4

He will keep in perfect peace all those who trust in him, whose thoughts turn often to the Lord! Trust in the Lord God always, for in the Lord Jehovah is your everlasting strength.

One possible prayer for today:

God, thank you for keeping me in perfect peace. Thank you for being the kind of God in whom I can confidently put my trust. Thank you for being the kind of God where it is easy for me to think of you often and praise you as I go through my day. Lord, let me trust you always and let me trust you more completely. Thank you, God, for being my everlasting strength. Lord, be my special strength today.

New Testament verse for today: Luke 7:23b

Blessed is the one who does not lose his faith in me.

One possible prayer for today:

Lord, thank you for the gift of faith that you have given to me. Please, Lord, don't let that faith in you ever waiver. You are so wonderful. When I acknowledge that you can keep me in perfect peace, and that you can be my everlasting strength, how could my faith ever falter? Lord, thank you for giving me your blessing and that of your Son, Jesus, if I don't ever lose my faith. Thank you, Lord, for being so good to me.

My prayer for today—including any journaling thoughts I may want to add. Where am I today spiritually, emotionally, physically, financially, generally?

Today's Date: _____

Old Testament verse for today: Isaiah 26:7 & 8

But for good men the path is not uphill and rough! God does not give them a rough and treacherous path, but smoothes the road before them. O Lord, we love to do your will! Our hearts desire is to glorify your name.

One possible prayer for today:

God, let me genuinely love to do your will. Give me a heart that is in tune with your will for my life. Let my hearts desire always be to glorify your name. Then, Lord, please smooth the road of my life for me. Help me through the rough spots that are presently confronting me. Help me overcome the treacherous path that I have been experiencing and that still is in front of me. Give me the faith and the wisdom to get through this period and continue to glorify your name even as I am encountering these obstacles. Thank you for the promise that you will once again give me a smooth road on which to live my life.

New Testament verse for today: Hebrews 10:17

And then he adds, "I will never again remember their sins and lawless deeds."

One possible prayer for today:

God, what a wonderful promise! Even when I have let you down, when I return to you, you wipe the slate clean! You have promised that once you have done that, you will never again remember what I have done for which you have forgiven me. What a promise! What a loving and generous God you are. Thank you, God, for being so loving and wonderful to me.

My prayer for today—including any journaling thoughts I may want to add. Where am I today spiritually, emotionally, physically, financially, generally?

Today's Date: _____

Old Testament verse for today: Isaiah 26:12

Lord, grant us peace; for all we have and are has come from you.

One possible prayer for today:

Lord, let me always acknowledge that all I am; all I can become; all I have; and, all that I will ever have has come from you. You have permitted me to be a steward of my life and my material things while here on earth; but, life is fleeting, and I need to always remember that you are the author of all things—including my life. Lord, do grant me a peace that only you can give. Grant me the peace that comes from accepting you as the Lord of my life and acknowledging your Lordship in all areas of my life. Thank you for being such a great and loving God. Thank you again, God, for the peace that only you can give.

New Testament verse for today: Mark 4:40

And he (Jesus) asked them, "Why were you so fearful? Don't you even yet have confidence in me?"

One possible prayer for today:

Lord, please give me the faith to have confidence at all times and in all things in you and your Son, Jesus Christ. Don't let me be fearful. Only by truly believing and by having that faith can I also have the peace that only you can give. Let me have the confidence I need to understand and accept that you are in control of my life; and, that that is always good, even though I may be going through some hard times. Lord, thank you for giving me the faith that I need to have the confidence that can result in that perfect peace. Thank you, Lord.

My prayer for today—including any journaling thoughts I may want to add. Where am I today spiritually, emotionally, physically, financially, generally?

Today's Date: _____

Old Testament verse for today: Isaiah 30:18

Yet the Lord still waits for you to come to him, so he can show you his love; he will conquer you to bless you, just as he said. For the Lord is faithful to his promises. Blessed are those who wait for him to help them.

One possible prayer for today:

Thank you, Lord, for waiting for me to come to you. Thank you for showing me your love. Thank you for conquering me just so that you can bless me. Thank you for being faithful to all your promises. Thank you for blessing me when I wait for you to help me. Thank you for your help, Lord.

New Testament verse for today: Luke 10:25 thru 27

One day an expert on Moses' laws came to test Jesus' orthodoxy by asking him this question: "Teacher, what does a man need to do to live forever in heaven?" Jesus replied, "What does Moses' law say about it?" "It says," he replied, "that you must love the Lord your God with all your heart, and with all your soul, and with all your strength, and with all your mind. And you must love your neighbor just as much as you love yourself." "Right!" Jesus told him. "Do this and you shall live!"

One possible prayer for today:

God, you know that I do not have the continued singlemindedness and strength to love you with everything that I have or everything that I am. Yet, I do love you. I try to love you more. I just get sidetracked fairly often. That is why it is so wonderful that you continue to wait for me to come back to you even when I have strayed away. Lord, please keep conquering me to bless me. Please don't ever give up on me! I will keep on trying to love you more; but, Lord, when I fail, then I will claim your promise that you will always be faithful to your promises to wait for me and to continue to forgive me and then promptly forget my sins. Thank you, Lord.

My prayer for today—including any journaling thoughts I may want to add. Where am I today spiritually, emotionally, physically, financially, generally?

Today's Date: _____

Old Testament verse for today: Isaiah 30:21

And if you leave God's paths and go astray, you will hear a Voice behind you say, "No, this is the way; walk here."

One possible prayer for today:

God, how wonderful you are to promise to guide me gently. How I claim this verse for my life. I know that I sin. I know that I leave your paths and go astray; but, Lord, let me always listen for your voice telling, "No, this is the way; walk here." Guide me gently, Lord. Speak to me in a way that I can unmistakenly understand. Thank you for your gentle guidance, Lord.

New Testament verse for today: Colossians 1:22 & 23a

He has done this through the death on the cross of his own human body, and now as a result Christ has brought you into the very presence of God ,and you are standing there before him with nothing left against you—nothing left that he could even chide you for; the only condition is that you fully believe the Truth, standing in it steadfast and firm, strong in the Lord, convinced of the Good News that Jesus died for you ,and never shifting from trusting him to save you. This is the wonderful news that came to each of you and is now spreading all over the world.

One possible prayer for today:

God, thank you for guiding me gently. Thank you for telling me which path to take. Thank you for giving your own life through the human body of your Son, Jesus, that even when I do leave your paths and go astray, I can still stand before you with nothing left that you can even chide me for, because of what Christ has done for me. All I have to do is believe, Lord. And, Lord, I do believe. I am convinced of the Good News that Christ died for my sins and that they are removed from your sight. Lord, I will never shift in my trust in this belief. Thank you for this wonderful news. Thank you for this wonderful gift.

My prayer for today—including any journaling thoughts I may want to add. Where am I today spiritually, emotionally, physically, financially, generally?

Today's Date: _____

Old Testament verse for today: Isaiah 33:2

But to us, O Lord, be merciful, for we have waited for you. Be our strength each day and our salvation in the time of trouble.

One possible prayer for today:

Lord, thank you for continuing to be merciful to me. Thank you for giving me the wisdom and the patience to wait for you. Thank you for being my strength each day. Thank you for being my salvation in time of trouble. Thank you for always giving me hope when my troubles seem too big to handle. Thank you for being my personal God.

New Testament verse for today: John 10:28

I give them eternal life and they shall never perish. No one shall snatch them away from me.

One possible prayer for today:

God, what a wonderful promise. Thank you for providing me a plan for eternal life. Thank you for making that plan so simple and yet so solid that no one can ever snatch me away from you. Thank you for giving me the promise that if I believe, I will never perish. Thank you, Lord, for your amazing love.

My prayer for today—including any journaling thoughts I may want to add. Where am I today spiritually, emotionally, physically, financially, generally?

Today's Date: _____

Old Testament verse for today: Isaiah 33:21 & 22

The glorious Lord will be to us a wide river of protection, and no enemy can cross. For the Lord is our Judge, our Lawgiver, and our King; he will care for us and save us.

One possible prayer for today:

God, thank you for that wonderful promise. Thank you for being a wide river of protection for me. Thank you for keeping my enemies away. Thank you for being my Judge, my Lawgiver, and my King. Thank you for caring for me and saving me. Thank you for being such a wonderful, patient, loving God. Thank you for never giving up on me, God.

New Testament verse for today: Luke 6:38

For if you give, you will get! Your gift will return to you in full and overflowing measure, pressed down, shaken together to make room for more, and running over. Whatever measure you use to give—large or small—will be used to measure what is given back to you.

One possible prayer for today:

Lord, when you have promised to be my protector and my Savior, why should I be selfish in my giving of myself and my talents to others who need help. Help me, Lord, to be generous in all my ways and with all the things that you have given to me to use as I see fit. Thank you for forgiving my selfish ways, Lord. Thank you for helping me to give more of my time, my energy, and my material blessings to others in your name, Lord. And, then, Lord, maybe this is another example of my selfishness; but, I claim your promise that you will return even more; but, I know that promise is only if I keep on giving even more! Thank you, Lord, for showing the way to give. You gave your only Son, Jesus, to die for my sins. Anything that I could do would look pretty easy compared to your gift to me. Thank you, Lord.

My prayer for today—including any journaling thoughts I may want to add. Where am I today spiritually, emotionally, physically, financially, generally?

Today's Date: _____

Old Testament verse for today: Isaiah 27:16 & 17

Lord of hosts, God of Israel enthroned above the cherubim, you alone are God of all the kingdoms of the earth. You alone made heaven and earth. Listen as I plead; see me as I pray.

One possible prayer for today:

God, what a wonderful God you are. Thank you for being the Lord of Hosts and for being the God that is enthroned above the cherubim. Thank you for being the God of all the kingdoms of the earth. Thank you for being the God that made the heaven and the earth for me to enjoy. And God, right now, thank you for listening to me as I plead; thank you for seeing me as I pray. Thank you for caring about me—just now. Thank you for being such an awesome God, and yet loving and caring for me.

New Testament verse for today: Romans 12:10 & 11

Love each other with brotherly love and affection and take delight in honoring each other. Never be lazy in your work but serve the Lord enthusiastically.

One possible prayer for today:

God, when you are so awesome and still have time to love and care for me, shouldn't I be able to take a little time to show brotherly love and concern for those with whom I associate? When you have honored me by calling me one of yours, shouldn't I be able to take some delight in others? Lord, give me the strength and consistence not to be lazy in my work—as long as I am doing something that is in line with your will for my life. Lord, you have been so good to me and have done so much for me, help me to do more for you. I need your help, Lord; but, let me try harder to serve you more consistently and enthusiastically.

My prayer for today—including any journaling thoughts I may want to add. Where am I today spiritually, emotionally, physically, financially, generally?

Today's Date: _____

Old Testament verse for today: Isaiah 40:8

The grass withers, the flowers fade, but the Word of our God shall stand forever.

One possible prayer for today:

God, it is apparent that as life moves ahead, that man is very mortal. Not only does the grass wither and the flowers fade; but, I know that I am not going to live forever either! So, Lord, I put my faith in you and in your word. Thank you for being an immortal God. Thank you for giving me your word which will stand forever. Thank you, God.

New Testament verse for today: I Corinthians 13:12 & 13

Now all that I know is hazy and blurred, but then I will see everything clearly, just as clearly as God sees into my heart right now. There are three things that remain—faith, hope, and love—and the greatest of these is love.

One possible prayer for today:

God, I don't understand immortality. I don't understand how you could have always been and always will be. In my mortal mind, I really can't comprehend these things. So, the things that I know are hazy and blurry. Your ways are so far above my ways that I really cannot comprehend them. But, you see clearly all things; and, I know that when I see you face to face, then I will see everything clearly. In the meantime, Lord, give me the things that are important to serve you while I am here on earth. Give me the faith that I need to follow you more consistently. Thank you for the hope that you have given me—the hope of salvation as well as the everyday hope of things here on earth. And, Lord, thank you for giving me the love that I need to go through each day. Love for you, for my family, and for my neighbors, associates, and acquaintances. Thank you, God.

My prayer for today—including any journaling thoughts I may want to add. Where am I today spiritually, emotionally, physically, financially, generally?

Today's Date: _____

Old Testament verse for today: Isaiah 40:25 & 26

"With whom will you compare me? Who is my equal?" Asks the Holy One. Look up into the heavens! Who created all those stars? As a shepherd leads his sheep, calling each by its pet name, and counts them to see that none are lost or strayed, so God does with the stars and planets!

One possible prayer for today:

God, thank you for being such a great and awesome God. There is no one who can compare with you; and, yet, Lord, you care for me! You care for the things that are cares for me. On one hand you call the stars by their pet names, and on the other hand you listen to my prayers when I call on you for help. What an awesome God you are! Thank you for being my personal God. Thank you for being not only the shepherd of the stars, but my own personal shepherd. Thank you, God.

New Testament verse for today: Ephesians 3:20

Now glory be to God who by his might power at work within us is able to do more than we would ever dare to ask or even dream of—infinitely beyond our highest prayers, desires, thoughts, or hopes.

One possible prayer for today:

God, how great it is to have you as my personal God! How great it is to be able to call on all that mighty power which can be put to work within me. Lord, let me always give you the glory. Let me ask only for those things that are in line with your will for me life. And, Lord, when I do dream, let those dreams, those desires, those prayers, those thoughts, and those hopes be dreams, desires, thoughts, hopes, and prayers that will be pleasing to you. Lord, I know that I can call on that great power and get anything that is in line with your will. Lord, make me want the things that you want, so that when you look down from the heavens, you will have a pet name for me as one who loves you, just as you have pet names for the stars. Thank you, God, as you continue to work in my life.

My prayer for today—including any journaling thoughts I may want to add. Where am I today spiritually, emotionally, physically, financially, generally?

Today's Date: _____

Old Testament verse for today: Isaiah 40:27 thru 30

Don't you yet understand? Don't you know by now that the everlasting God, the creator of the farthest parts of the earth, never grows faint or weary? No one can fathom the depths of his understanding. He gives power to the tired and worn out, and strength to the weak. Even the youths shall be exhausted, and the young men will all give up. But they that wait upon the Lord shall renew their strength. They shall mount up with wings like eagles; they shall run and not be weary; they shall walk and not faint.

One possible prayer for today:

God, help me to not only understand; but, to believe and live like I really believe! You are so powerful! You are so awesome! You created everything! And, God, thank you for never growing faint or weary. Lord, I know that I can never fathom the depths of your understanding, so let me just take you and your promises by faith. Thank you for giving me power when I am tired and worn out. Thank you for giving me strength when I am weak. Thank you for renewing my strength if I will only wait on you. And, Lord, I claim your promise that once again I will mount up with wings like eagles; that I will run and not be weary; and that I shall walk and not be faint. Thank you for those great promises, Lord.

New Testament verse for today: Mark 9:23b

"Anything is possible if you have faith."

One possible prayer for today:

Lord, please give me that faith! I know that all of the promises you made are all mine to claim. All I need is faith. So, give me that extra shot of faith whenever I need it the most. Give me that extra shot of faith when I am tired and weary so that I can truly believe. Then I know that I will have the ability to face any problem that is confronting me and work through it in a manner that is your will. Let me always have the faith to know that sometimes my plans are not your plans. Sometimes my timing is not your timing. Then, Lord, I need the strength, the patience, and the faith to wait on you. Then, in your timing, you will once again let me mount up with wings like eagles. Thank you, Lord, for helping me through the bad times until I can soar again.

My prayer for today—including any journaling thoughts I may want to add. Where am I today spiritually, emotionally, physically, financially, generally?

Today's Date: _____

Old Testament verse for today: Isaiah 41:10

Fear not, for I am with you. Do not be dismayed. I am your God. I will strengthen you; I will uphold you with my victorious right hand.

One possible prayer for today:

God, what a wonderful promise! Lord, I know that if I have enough faith, enough confidence, that I really do not ever need to fear. I never need to feel dismayed. All I really need to remember is that you are my God. You are always there. You will give me the strength that I need, if I will only call on you for help and rely on that help. And, Lord, I do claim your promise that you will uphold me with your victorious right hand. No one can stand against you, Lord. Thank you for being my friend, and thank you for being in my corner, strengthening me and upholding me with your victorious right hand.

New Testament verse for today: I Corinthians 10:26

For the earth and every good thing in it belongs to the Lord and is your to enjoy.

One possible prayer for today:

God, when I know that you are on my side; when I know that you are upholding me with your victorious right hand; when I know that everything—the earth and every good thing in it—belongs to you; and I know that it is mine to enjoy; how could I not be overflowing with thankfulness to you? You are such a great God to give me this beautiful world to enjoy. Lord, even on the days when I am really feeling down and feeling like the weight of the world is on my shoulders, all I have to do is look around and know that you are such a great God. That you have indeed made a wonderful world with many beautiful things that are free for me to enjoy. Let me have the ability to look on the bright side when I am feeling sad and lonely. Let me look around and know that you are a wonderful God who made a world of things that I may enjoy at any time.

My prayer for today—including any journaling thoughts I may want to add. Where am I today spiritually, emotionally, physically, financially, generally?

Today's Date: _____

Old Testament verse for today: Isaiah 43:1 thru 3a

But now the Lord who created you says, Don't be afraid, for I have ransomed you; I have called you by name; you are mine. When you go through deep waters and great trouble, I will be with you. When you go through rivers of difficulty, you will not drown! When you walk through the fire of opposition, you will not be burned up—the flames will not consume you. For I am the Lord your God, your Savior, the Holy One of Israel.

One possible prayer for today:

God, thank you for these wonderful promises. Thank you for being my Savior. Thank you for ransoming me. Thank you for calling me by my name and making me yours. Thank you for being with me when I go through deep waters and great trouble. Thank you for keeping me from drowning when I face rivers of difficulty. Thank you for keeping me safe in the fire of opposition. Thank you for being my God and my Savior in all the circumstances of my life. Thank you, God.

New Testament verse for today: John 3:18 thru 21

There is no eternal doom awaiting those who trust him to save them. But those who don't trust him have already been tried and condemned for not believing in the only Son of God. Their sentence is based on this fact: that the Light from heaven came into the world, but they loved the darkness more than the Light, for their deeds were evil. They hated the heavenly Light because they wanted to sin in the darkness. They stayed away from that Light for fear their sins would be exposed and they would be punished. But those doing right come gladly to the Light to let everyone see that they are doing what God wants them to.

One possible prayer for today:

God, thank you for the promise that there is no eternal doom awaiting me if I trust in you. Thank you for ransoming me. Thank you for giving me the faith to believe in your only Son. Thank you for sending your Light from heaven. Thank you for helping me to do right in your eyes, so that you will always be with me when I go through deep waters and great trouble. Thank you for giving me the faith to believe so that whether I am facing rivers of difficulty or fires of opposition, I will neither drown or be consumed. Thank you again and again for being my Savior.

My prayer for today—including any journaling thoughts I may want to add. Where am I today spiritually, emotionally, physically, financially, generally?

Today's Date: _____

Old Testament verse for today: Isaiah 43:13

From eternity to eternity I am God. No one can oppose what I do.

One possible prayer for today:

God, you are so awesome! You can do what you want to do and no one can oppose it. Thank you for using that awesome power in love and kindness. Thank you for using that awesome power to love and take care of me. Thank you for being the one and only eternal God. Thank you for responding to my love for you. Thank you, God.

New Testament verse for today: Hebrews 4:16

So let us come boldly to the very throne of God and stay there to receive his mercy and to find grace to help us in our times of need.

One possible prayer for today:

What a wonderful God you are to give me the confidence to come boldly to your very throne. And, then to stay there to receive your mercy and help. Thank you for helping me in my times of need. Thank you for listening to me when I call to you. Thank you for the mercy that I can receive when I come boldly—and yet humbly—before your very throne. Thank you for being such a powerful, merciful God.

My prayer for today—including any journaling thoughts I may want to add. Where am I today spiritually, emotionally, physically, financially, generally?

Today's Date: _____

Old Testament verse for today: Isaiah 43:25

I, yes, I alone am he who blots away your sins for my own sake and will never think of them again.

One possible prayer for today:

God, that promise overwhelms me! To consider that kind of forgiveness is almost more than I can comprehend! You, who is almighty and powerful will blot away my sins for your own sake; and, then, unbelievable but true, you will never think of them again! God, thank you for blotting out my sins. Thank you for never throwing them back in my face again. Thank you for forgiving me again and again. Thank you for being a God who, when I say "I'm sorry, God, I did that again," you say, "Did what again?", because you have promised to never think of them again. Thank you. Thank you. Thank you.

New Testament verse for today: Romans 1:16 & 17

For I am not ashamed of this Good News about Christ. It is God's powerful method of bringing all who believe it to heaven. This message was preached first to the Jews alone, but now everyone is invited to come to God in this same way. This Good News tells us that God makes us ready for heaven—makes us right in God's sight—when we put our faith and trust in Christ to save us. This is accomplished from start to finish by faith. As the scripture says it, "The man who finds life will find it through trusting God."

One possible prayer for today:

God, thank you for bringing me this Good News about Christ. Thank you for promising me that if I believe it you will bring me to heaven. Thank you for making that Good News to everyone—including me. Thank you for making me ready for heaven—making me right in your sight. I do trust Christ to save me, Lord. Thank you for making that wonderful plan available even to me.

My prayer for today—including any journaling thoughts I may want to add. Where am I today spiritually, emotionally, physically, financially, generally?

Today's Date: _____

Old Testament verse for today: Isaiah 45:7 & 8

I form the light and make the dark. I send good times and bad. I, Jehovah, am he who does these things. Open up, O heavens. Let the skies pour out their righteousness. Let salvation and righteousness sprout up together from the earth. I, Jehovah, created them.

One possible prayer for today:

God, what a wonderful and powerful God you are! How could I not worship you? How could I not stand in awe of you? Thank you for being a God who is so powerful that you have formed the light and the dark. Thank you for being a God who is in charge of the good times and the bad times in my life. Thank you for making the good times far outweigh the bad times! Thank you for opening up the heavens to pour your righteousness out on me. Thank you for making a plan of salvation that encompasses me, if I only believe. God, I do believe. Thank you for your righteousness and your salvation.

New Testament verse for today: I John 5:9 & 10

We believe men who witness in our courts, and so surely we can believe whatever God declares. And God declares that Jesus is his Son. All who believe this know in their hearts that it is true. If anyone doesn't believe this, he is actually calling God a liar, because he doesn't believe what God has said about his Son.

One possible prayer for today:

God, I do believe you. You are so awesome. You are so magnificent. You made the light and the dark. And, God, you declared that Jesus was your Son. This was your promise so that I could have a perfect relationship with you that would not have been possible any other way. Because of your Son, Jesus, I can have that relationship. I sin. I confess my sin to you. You forgive me because of the blood your Son, Jesus, shed on the cross. You forgive me. You wipe the slate of my sinful life clean. Then in my humanness, I sin again. And then when I come humbly back to you and ask for forgiveness again, you forgive me again, and again, and again! What an awesome, powerful, and yet loving and caring God you are. Thank you, God, for loving and caring for me.

My prayer for today—including any journaling thoughts I may want to add. Where am I today spiritually, emotionally, physically, financially, generally?

Today's Date: _____

Old Testament verse for today: Isaiah 45:22 & 23

Let all the world look to me for salvation! For I am God; there is no other. I have sworn by myself and I will never go back on my word, for it is true—that every knee in all the world shall bow to me, and every tongue shall swear allegiance to my name.

One possible prayer for today:

Lord, your power and your might are awesome! There is no other place to turn for salvation. You alone are God. I accept that there is no other. Lord, I do bow humbly before you, honoring your Holy Name. I thank you for choosing me to be one of your people. Thank you, Lord.

New Testament verse for today: Luke 1:37

"For every promise from God shall surely come true."

One possible prayer for today:

Lord, thank you for being so faithful. Thank you for being the God who makes every promise come true. Thank you for being the author of my salvation. Thank you for letting that salvation come to even me. Thank you, Lord.

My prayer for today—including any journaling thoughts I may want to add. Where am I today spiritually, emotionally, physically, financially, generally?

Today's Date: _____

Old Testament verse for today: Isaiah 46:4

I will be your God through all your lifetime, yes, even when your hair is white with age. I made you and I will care for you. I will carry you along and be your Savior.

One possible prayer for today:

What a wonderful promise, Lord. Thank you for your promise to be my personal God throughout my entire life! Thank you for making me. Thank you for your promise to care for me. Thank you for your promise to carry me along. Thank you for your promise to be with me, even when I get old and may be unlovable. Thank you for your promise to be my Savior. Thank you, God, for being consistent and everlasting.

New Testament verse for today: Acts 2:21

But anyone who asks for mercy from the Lord shall have it and be saved.

One possible prayer for today:

God, thank you for your promise of salvation. Thank you for always being there when I need your mercy. Thank you for always hearing me. Thank you for making such a wonderful plan of salvation for me. Thank you for giving me the faith to accept your plan of salvation for me. Thank you for caring enough about me to do all these wonderful things. Thank you, Lord.

My prayer for today—including any journaling thoughts I may want to add. Where am I today spiritually, emotionally, physically, financially, generally?

Today's Date: _____

Old Testament verse for today: Isaiah 46:9b & 10

For I am God—I only—and there is no other like me who can tell you what is going to happen. All I say will come to pass, for I do whatever I wish.

One possible prayer for today:

God, thank you for being so awesome. Thank you for being so consistent. Thank you for always being there for me and doing what you said you were going to do. Thank you for being a God like no other god. Thank you for knowing the future and for knowing that I am going to be with you in heaven for eternity. Even though you can do whatever you wish, thank you for wishing to guide me and to give me a plan for eternal life that is easy for me to follow. All I have to do is believe. Thank you, Lord.

New Testament verse for today: II Corinthians 6:16b

For you are God's temple, the home of the living God, and God has said of you, "I will live in them and walk among them, and I will be their God and they shall be my people."

One possible prayer for today:

God, thank you for living in me and walking with me. Thank you for being my God and for making me one of your people. Lord, many times my thoughts and my actions make me ashamed to realize that I am one of your temples; that you live in my heart. But, God, there is no other God like you that continues to forgive and forget when I come back to you and humbly confess that I have left your path. Thank you for continuing to forgive me, God. Thank you for never giving up on me. Thank you for being such a wonderful God to me.

My prayer for today—including any journaling thoughts I may want to add. Where am I today spiritually, emotionally, physically, financially, generally?

Today's Date: _____

Old Testament verse for today: Isaiah 49:13 thru 16a

Sing for joy, O heavens; shout, O earth. Break forth with song, O mountains, for the Lord has comforted his people, and will have compassion upon them in their sorrow. Yet they say, "My Lord deserted us; he has forgotten us." Never! Can a mother forget her little child and not have love for her own son? Yet even if that should be, I will not forget you. See, I have tattooed your name upon my palm.

One possible prayer for today:

God, thank you for being an ever-loving and everlasting God. Thank you for being a God of comfort. Thank you for being a God of compassion. Thank you for being a God that does not—and in fact—cannot forget me! Thank you for making me your child, for loving me as your child, and for tattooing my name upon the palm of your hand. Thank you again, God, for your wonderful comfort and compassion to me.

New Testament verse for today: Ephesians 1:5

His unchanging plan has always been to adopt us into his own family by sending Jesus Christ to die to us. And he did this because he wanted to!

One possible prayer for today:

God, thank you again for being an ever-loving and everlasting God. Thank you for making a plan to adopt me into your family. Thank you for sending Jesus Christ to die on the cross for my sins so that I may appear blameless before you. Thank you for wanting me to be a part of your family so much that you sent Jesus to die on the cross to redeem me from my life of sin. Thank you for adopting me as your child. Thank you for loving me as your child.

My prayer for today—including any journaling thoughts I may want to add. Where am I today spiritually, emotionally, physically, financially, generally?

Today's Date: _____

Old Testament verse for today: Isaiah 53:4 thru 6

Yet it was our grief he bore, our sorrows that weighed him down. And we thought his troubles were a punishment from God, for his own sins! But he was wounded and bruised for our sins. He was chastised that we might have peace; he was lashed—and we were healed! We are the ones who strayed away like sheep! We, who left God's path to follow our own .yet God laid on him the guilt and sins of every one of us!

One possible prayer for today:

God, how could you have been so loving to each of us that you sacrificed your only Son so that I could have eternal life? I can't even understand that kind of love! You sent your Son, Jesus, to bear my grief, my sorrows, my troubles, and my punishment, my wounds and my bruises! He took my punishment so that I could have peace. Thank you, God, for that peace. Thank you for healing me and saving me from eternal damnation because of my sins. Thank you for sending Christ to take away my guilt and stain of sin. Thank you, God, for your marvelous plan of salvation.

New Testament verse for today: Acts 13:38 & 39

Brothers! Listen! In this man Jesus, there is forgiveness for your sins! Everyone who trusts in him is freed from all guilt and declared righteous—something the Jewish law could never do.

One possible prayer for today:

God, how wonderful your plan is for each of us—and for me personally; consistent throughout the scriptures from the Old Testament through the New Testament. How wonderful that I can have the assurance that I have forgiveness for my sins. How wonderful to know that I can be freed from all guilt. How wonderful to be declared righteous in your eyes. Thank you, Lord, for that freeing and redeeming love expressed through your Son, Jesus. Thank you, God.

My prayer for today—including any journaling thoughts I may want to add. Where am I today spiritually, emotionally, physically, financially, generally?

Today's Date: _____

Old Testament verse for today: Isaiah 53:11 & 12

And when he sees all that is accomplished by the anguish of his soul, he shall be satisfied; and because of what he has experienced, my righteous Servant shall make many to be counted righteous before God, for he shall bear all their sins. Therefore I will give him the honors of one who is mighty and great, because he has poured out his soul unto death. He was counted as a sinner, and he bore the sins of many, and he plead with God for sinners.

One possible prayer for today:

God, thank you for that marvelous plan of salvation you devised so many years ago. Thank you for permitting me to become aware of that marvelous plan. Thank you for accepting me and counting me righteous—not because of anything that I have done to be righteous—but only because I believe. Thank you for providing a substitute who bore all my sins and who plead to you for me and for the salvation of my soul. Thank you, God, for being such a great and loving God that you would provide such a plan for me.

New Testament verse for today: Galatians 2:16

And yet we Jewish Christians know very well that we cannot become right with God by obeying our Jewish laws, but only by faith in Jesus Christ to take away our sins. And so we, too, have trusted Jesus Christ, that we might be accepted by God because of faith—and not because we have obeyed the Jewish laws. For no one will ever be saved by obeying them.

One possible prayer for today:

God, thank you for providing Christ as the way to salvation. Thank you for sending your Son, Jesus, to pour out his soul unto death. Thank you for providing Jesus to bear my sins and to plead with you for the salvation of my soul. Thank you for caring enough about me to know that I could never be saved by obeying a set of laws. Thank you for giving me the faith to believe that by accepting Christ as my personal Savior, I could have my sins forgiven and be made righteous in your eyes. And God, I know that that is the only way I could ever be righteous in your eyes. God, thank you for that plan. Thank you for your love that made that plan work for me.

My prayer for today—including any journaling thoughts I may want to add. Where am I today spiritually, emotionally, physically, financially, generally?

Today's Date: _____

Old Testament verse for today: Isaiah 55:6

Seek the Lord while you can find him .Call upon him now while he is near.

One possible prayer for today:

Lord, I do seek you. Thank you for being near to me. Thank you for making yourself available so that I may find you. Thank you for waiting for me to seek you and not giving up on me. I do call upon you, Lord. Please listen and answer my pleadings.

New Testament verse for today: Romans 10:8 thru 11

For salvation that comes from trusting Christ—which is what we preach—is already within easy reach of each of us; in fact, it is as near as our own hearts and mouths. For if you tell others with your own mouth that Jesus Christ is your Lord, and believe in your own heart that God has raised him from the dead, you will be saved. For it is by believing in his heart that a man becomes right with God; and with his mouth he tells others of his faith, confirming his salvation. For the scriptures tell us that no one who believes in Christ will ever be disappointed.

One possible prayer for today:

God, how easy you made it to seek you and to find you. To make finding you possible, you sent your own Son to earth in the form of a man, to walk on this earth and show the way to you. What a wonderful plan, God. Thank you. Lord, I believe. I believe in my own heart that Jesus Christ is my Lord, and that you raised him from the dead. Thank you for putting up with my unbelief until I too could be saved by my simple act of belief. Thank you, God. I claim the promise that Christ will never disappoint me, if I truly trust in him, honor him, and do my best to follow his teachings.

My prayer for today—including any journaling thoughts I may want to add. Where am I today spiritually, emotionally, physically, financially, generally?

Today's Date: _____

Old Testament verse for today: Isaiah 55:7

Let men cast off their wicked deeds; let them banish from their minds the very thought of doing wrong! Let them turn to the Lord that he may have mercy upon them, and to our God, for he will abundantly pardon!

One possible prayer for today:

God, you are so incredible! Knowing that you will continue to abundantly pardon me is an awesome thought! Lord, you know that I do try to cast off my wicked deeds. You know that I do try to banish from my mind the very thought of doing wrong. But, Lord, you know my every thought. You know my heart. You know that I often fail you in these feeble, human attempts of mine. But, Lord, I know that when I turn to you, you will always have mercy on me; and, you will continue to abundantly pardon me. Thank you, Lord, for your wonderful, unrelenting love.

New Testament verse for today: Revelations 2:7

Let this message sink into the ears of anyone who listens to what the Spirit is saying to the churches: To everyone who is victorious, I will give fruit from the Tree of Life in the Paradise of God.

One possible prayer for today:

Lord, let this message sink into my ears so that I will be victorious as I live for you and worship you to the best of my ability. Let me listen to your loving Holy Spirit as he offers to direct my life. Lord, I want to be with you to be given fruit from the Tree of Life in your Paradise. Thank you for your promise that your love will be broad enough and forgiving enough, that if I continue to turn to you, these rewards will be mine. Thank you, God, for your wonderful, unrelenting love.

My prayer for today—including any journaling thoughts I may want to add. Where am I today spiritually, emotionally, physically, financially, generally?

Today's Date: _____

Old Testament verse for today: Isaiah 55:10 & 11

As the rain and snow come down from heaven and stay upon the ground to water the earth, and cause the grain to grow and to produce seed for the farmer and bread for the hungry, so also is my Word. I send it out and it always produces fruit. It shall accomplish all I want it to and prosper everywhere I send it.

One possible prayer for today:

God, thank you for being so powerful. Thank you for being in charge of all things, whether it is the weather, the crops, or the prospering of your Word. Thank you for sending your Word to me so that I may experience your salvation. Thank you for letting your Word prosper in me. Thank you, Lord.

New Testament verse for today: II Corinthians 6:1 & 2

As God's partners we beg you not to toss aside this marvelous message of God's great kindness. For God says, "Your cry came to me at a favorable time, when the doors of welcome were wide open. I helped you on a day when salvation was being offered." Right now God is ready to welcome you. Today he is ready to serve you.

One possible prayer for today:

God, thank you for sending your Word to me. Thank you for making my heart open so that I did not toss aside your marvelous message of kindness and salvation. Thank you for throwing the doors of welcome wide open for me. Thank you for helping me. Thank you for your salvation that you made available to me. Thank you for being there to welcome me and to serve me. Thank you for wanting your salvation to prosper in me.

My prayer for today—including any journaling thoughts I may want to add. Where am I today spiritually, emotionally, physically, financially, generally?

Today's Date: _____

Old Testament verse for today: Isaiah 58:6 thru 9

No, the kind of fast I want is that you stop oppressing those who work for you and treat then fairly and give them what they earn. I want you to share your food with the hungry and bring right into your homes those who are helpless, poor and destitute. Clothe those who are cold and don't hide from relatives who need your help. If you do these things, God will shed his own glorious light upon you. He will heal you; your godliness w ill lead you forward, and goodness will be a shield before you, and the glory of the Lord will protect you from behind. Then when you call, the Lord will answer. "Yes, I am here," he will quickly reply. All you need to do is to stop oppressing the weak, and to stop making false accusations and spreading vicious rumors!

One possible prayer for today:

God, you are obviously a God much concerned about fairness in all my dealings. You are concerned about my sharing all the great things that you have given me and done for me. Help me to be more fair; more honest; more giving. And, then, God, I do claim the promises mentioned. Please shed your glorious light upon me. Heal me. Lead me always with your godliness. Shield me with your goodness. Protect me from behind with your glory. Answer me when I call. Lord, I know that you will do your part. Please help me to do mine!

New Testament verse for today: John 8:51

With all the earnestness I have I tell you this—no one who obeys me shall ever die!

One possible prayer for today:

God, what a great promise your Son, Christ has given me. I know that I have the obligation to believe and to obey. But what wonderful rewards, Lord! Thank you for the promise of eternal life. Help me to not only believe and obey, but to put my belief into action as Isaiah challenged me to do.

My prayer for today—including any journaling thoughts I may want to add. Where am I today spiritually, emotionally, physically, financially, generally?

Today's Date: _____

Old Testament verse for today: Isaiah 58:10 & 11

Feed the hungry! Help those in trouble! Then your light will shine out from the darkness, and the darkness around you shall be as bright as day. And the Lord will guide you continually, and satisfy you with all good things, and keep you healthy too; and you will be like a well-watered garden, like an ever-blooming spring.

One possible prayer for today:

God, I know that when I am in trouble, I really like it when people reach out to help me. I like it when they aren't judgmental and quick to blame my troubles on my own bad judgment. So, Lord, let me treat others in trouble as I would like to be treated. Let me feed the hungry and help the troubled. Let my light shine out to those in trouble; but, let that light shine only as a reflection of your love. Don't let me get caught up in trying to get the credit for myself. And, Lord, I do claim your promise that if I do my part, you will guide me continually. You will satisfy me with all good things. You will keep me healthy. And, I will be like a well-watered garden and an ever-blooming spring. Thank you for that promise, Lord.

New Testament verse for today: John 14:1 thru 3a

Let not your heart be troubled. You are trusting God, now trust in me. There are many homes up there where my Father lives, and I am going to prepare them for your coming. When everything is ready, then I will come and get you, so that you can always be with me where I am.

One possible prayer for today:

God, I know that you look at the big picture. Many times I can't see longer than through the day, if that long! I know that I have a home with you for eternity if I believe in you through your Son, Jesus. And I do! I am trusting Christ to take me into your presence for eternity. But, God, I do have to get through my daily life here before I can enjoy that eternity with you. So, help me now, please! Give me the strength to help others even when I don't feel like it. Give me the faith to trust you more, even when I am hurting. Thank you for always being there for me, Lord. Thank you.

My prayer for today—including any journaling thoughts I may want to add. Where am I today spiritually, emotionally, physically, financially, generally?

Today's Date: _____

Old Testament verse for today: Isaiah 59:1 & 2

Listen now! The Lord isn't too weak to save you. And he isn't getting deaf! He can hear you when you call! But the trouble is that your sins have cut you off from God. Because of sin, he has turned his face away from you and will not listen any more.

One possible prayer for today:

God, I know that I am a sinner. I know that I am weak and you are strong. I know that you can save me any time you choose to do so. I know you are not getting deaf. I know that you are always there for me when I return to you and confess my sins to you. Lord, I know that it is my sin that has cut me off from you, not anything that you have done. Please forgive me for letting you down. Please forgive me for turning away from you. Thank you for not continuing to turn away from me when I return to you. Thank you, Lord.

New Testament verse for today: Galatians 3:21b & 22

If we could be saved by his laws, then God would not have had to give us a different way to get out of the grip of sin—for the Scriptures insist we are all its prisoners. The only way out is through faith in Jesus Christ; the way of escape is open to all who believe him.

One possible prayer for today:

God, thank you for recognizing that I could not get out of the grip of sin and become pleasing to you by obeying your laws. Thank you for providing another way for my salvation. Thank you for providing an easier way for me and one that works for me. Thank you for offering your Son, Jesus, as a sacrifice for my sins. Thank you for making it so that all I have to do is believe in Jesus as my Savior. Thank you for giving me the faith to make that decision. Thank you for freeing me from the grip of sin through that belief. Thank you for providing that way of escape for me. I do believe, Lord. Thank you, Lord.

My prayer for today—including any journaling thoughts I may want to add. Where am I today spiritually, emotionally, physically, financially, generally?

Today's Date: _____

Old Testament verse for today: Isaiah 61:10 & 11

Let me tell you how happy God has made me! For he has clothed me with garments of salvation and draped me about with the robe of righteousness. I am like a bridegroom in his wedding suit or a bride with her jewels. The Lord will show the nations of the world his justice; all will praise him. His righteousness shall be like a budding tree, or like a garden in early spring, full of young plants springing up everywhere.

One possible prayer for today:

God, thank you for the joy you have given me. Thank you for being so good to me in every way. Lord, thank you most of all for my salvation that you have provided for me through the gift of your Son, Jesus. Thank you for making me righteous in your eyes because of that gift. Thank you for being a just and yet loving God. Thank you for all the blessings you have given.

New Testament verse for today: II Corinthians 1:2

May God our Father and the Lord Jesus Christ mightily bless each one of you, and give you peace.

One possible prayer for today:

God, thank you for your many blessings. Thank you for the peace you have given me. Thank you for the joy you have given me. Thank you for my salvation through your Son, Jesus, which is a reason that I can experience the peace and joy you have given me. Thank you for being such a generous and loving God.

My prayer for today—including any journaling thoughts I may want to add. Where am I today spiritually, emotionally, physically, financially, generally?

Today's Date: _____

Old Testament verse for today: Isaiah 64:4

For since the world began no one has seen or heard of such a God as ours, who works for those who wait for him.

One possible prayer for today:

God, thank you for being a God like no other god! Thank you for being so great that I have never seen or heard of another God like you. Thank you for working for me, if I wait for you. Thank you for putting up with me and loving me just as I am. Thank you, God.

New Testament verse for today: Romans 3:25 & 26

For God sent Jesus Christ to take the punishment for our sins and to end all God's anger against us. He used Christ's blood and our faith as the means of saving us from his wrath. In this way he was being entirely fair, even though he did not punish those who sinned in former times. For he was looking forward to the time when Christ would come and take away those sins. And now in these days also he can receive sinners in this same way, because Jesus took away their sins.

One possible prayer for today:

God, again thank you for being like no other god. Thank you for being a God who cares about me. Thank you for being a God who has a plan for forgiving my sins. Thank you for sending Jesus Christ to take my punishment and to remove any anger you have toward me. Thank you for Christ's blood. Thank you for giving me the faith to believe so that I may be forgiven. Thank you for this marvelous plan of forgiveness. Thank you for taking away my sins. Thank you, God.

My prayer for today—including any journaling thoughts I may want to add. Where am I today spiritually, emotionally, physically, financially, generally?

Today's Date: _____

Old Testament verse for today: Isaiah 64:8 & 9

And yet, O Lord, you are our Father. We are the clay and you are the Potter. We are all formed by your hand. Oh, be not so angry with us, Lord, nor forever remember our sins. Oh, look and see that we are all your people.

One possible prayer for today:

God, thank you for being my heavenly Father. Thank you for being such a loving Potter. Thank you for forming me and giving me life. And, God, thank you for not remaining angry with me when I fail you. Thank you for not remembering my sins. Thank you for always remembering that I am one of your people. Thank you, God.

New Testament verse for today: I Corinthians 8:2 & 3

If anyone thinks he knows all the answers, he is just showing his ignorance. But the person who truly loves God is the one who is open to God's knowledge.

One possible prayer for today:

God, sometimes I think that I am pretty smart. When that happens, it doesn't seem long until I make some mistake that brings me back down to size. So, God, let me always be open to your instruction and your knowledge. Your way is so much better than my way. Thank you for being concerned about me. Thank you for never giving up on me. Thank you for continuing to show me your knowledge. Lord, let me always be receptive to that knowledge.

My prayer for today—including any journaling thoughts I may want to add. Where am I today spiritually, emotionally, physically, financially, generally?

Today's Date: _____

Old Testament verse for today: Isaiah 66:2

My hand has made both earth and skies, and they are mine. Yet I will look with pity on the man who has a humble and a contrite heart, who trembles at my word.

One possible prayer for today:

God, you are so wonderful. You are so powerful. You are so imaginative. When I look around me and see all the wonderful things that you have created, I am amazed that even in your magnificence, that you could have had the imagination to create all these things. Whether we are looking at the most beautiful and fragile of the flowers, the majestic peaks of the mountains, or something as peculiar as a giraffe, Lord, you made them all! Amazing. And then to think that with all that power and imagination, you will still look on me in pity and in love if I will only truly worship you. Thank you, Lord, for using your amazing power to still love and care for me. Lord, let me be humble before you. Let me have contrite heart as it relates to you. Let me on one hand, tremble at your word, and on the other hand, rejoice in your love for me. Thank you, Lord, for who you are.

New Testament verse for today: Romans 14:8

Living or dying we follow the Lord. Either way we are his. Christ died and rose again for this very purpose, so that he can be our Lord both while we live and when we die.

One possible prayer for today:

God, thank you for being my Lord no matter what happens to me—living or dying. With the amazing power that you have, how could I question your ability to take care of me during life or during death? Thank you for Christ's death and his resurrection; because it is by those acts and that plan that I have your assurance that you are with me in life and in death. Thank you, God, for including me in that plan.

My prayer for today—including any journaling thoughts I may want to add. Where am I today spiritually, emotionally, physically, financially, generally?

Today's Date: _____

Old Testament verse for today: Isaiah 66:13

I will comfort you there as a little one is comforted by its mother.

One possible prayer for today:

God, thank you for the comfort that I can have by knowing that you love me and care for me in all my activities. Thank you for being such a loving God who cares for me and continues to rescue me from the mistakes I make in my human sinful nature. Thank you for loving me and caring for me. Thank you, God.

New Testament verse for today: Titus 2:14

He died under God's judgment against our sins, so that he could rescue us from constantly falling into sin and make us his very own people, with cleansed hearts and a real enthusiasm for doing kind things for others.

One possible prayer for today:

God, thank you for comforting me. Thank you for giving me the comfort of knowing that I may have salvation by believing in your Son, Jesus. Thank you for giving up your Son, Jesus, to take away all my sins if I will only confess them and believe in Christ's redeeming power. Thank you for making me one of your very own people. Thank you for giving me a cleansed heart. Thank you for the comfort that comes from knowing your Son. Jesus. Thank you, God.

My prayer for today—including any journaling thoughts I may want to add. Where am I today spiritually, emotionally, physically, financially, generally?

Today's Date: _____

Old Testament verse for today: Jeremiah 1:5

I knew you before you were formed within your mother's womb; before you were born I sanctified you and appointed you my spokesman to the world.

One possible prayer for today:

God, your wonders never cease. To think that you have known each of us, including me, before I was born is an awesome thought. To know that you had a plan for my life before I was born shows your love and concern for me. Lord, I know that if I love you, I need to honor you always and be willing to speak of my faith in you. Let all my life—my actions and my speech—speak of your love for me and my love for you. Thank you, Lord, for making me so special in your eyes.

New Testament verse for today: Colossians 3:16

Remember what Christ taught and let his words enrich your lives and make you wise; teach them to each other and sing them out in psalms and hymns and spiritual songs, singing to the Lord, with thankful hearts.

One possible prayer for today:

God, thank you for enriching my life with your many promises. Thank you for the wisdom that you have given me. Let me do my part in responding to your love for me by teaching others of your love and goodness. Let me remember to praise you always, singing your praises. And, Lord, let me always be thankful for all you have done for me and given me. Let my heart sing with thanksgiving to you. Thank you, Lord, for being so good to me.

My prayer for today—including any journaling thoughts I may want to add. Where am I today spiritually, emotionally, physically, financially, generally?

Today's Date: _____

Old Testament verse for today: Jeremiah 7:23

Obey me and I will be your God and you shall be my people; only do as I say and all shall be well!

One possible prayer for today:

Help me to obey you, Lord. Give me the strength and the self discipline I need to obey you better than I could do on my own. Lord, I claim your promise that all shall be well with me. I need your help in all that I do. Thank you, Lord, for answering my prayer and giving me the strength to obey you.

New Testament verse for today: Romans 6:15

Does this mean that now we can go ahead and sin and not worry about it? (For our salvation does not depend on keeping the law, but on receiving God's grace!) Of course not!

One possible prayer for today:

Lord, thank you for giving me the faith to believe in you. I know that I don't always obey you. I know that I continue to sin, whether I want to or not! I know that I could not keep all the precepts of your law. So, Lord, thank you for saving me by your grace. Thank you for that grace. Thank you for not holding my disobedience against me. Thank you for forgiving me when I confess my disobedience to you. Thank you, Lord.

My prayer for today—including any journaling thoughts I may want to add. Where am I today spiritually, emotionally, physically, financially, generally?

Today's Date: _____

Old Testament verse for today: Jeremiah 9:23 & 24

The Lord says: Let not the wise man bask in his wisdom, nor the mighty man in his might, nor the rich man in his riches. Let them boast in this alone. That they truly know me, and understand that I am the Lord of justice and of righteousness whose love is steadfast; and that I love to be this way.

One possible prayer for today:

Lord, let me truly know you. How can I do that better? Hopefully by praying to you; communicating with you; reading and studying your word; waiting and listening for you to speak to me in the various ways that you use to reach your people today. Don't let me get caught up in who I am, whether I am in good times or bad; riches or poverty; health or sickness. Let me always acknowledge that you are the Lord of justice and righteousness. Thank you for your promise that your love for me is steadfast. And, Lord, thank you for loving to be that way, and for always being that way.

New Testament verse for today: Galatians 2:19

—for it was through reading the Scriptures that I came to realize that I could never find God's favor by trying—and failing—to obey the laws. I came to realize that acceptance with God comes by believing in Christ.

One possible prayer for today:

Lord, I know that I am unable to earn your love by my good works. I know that your love is freely given to all who believe in you and believe in your Son, Jesus Christ. I know that you accept and love me just as I am; but, that your hope is that I will, in fact, get to know you better and therefore honor you more. But, Lord, I also know that in the final test of my love, what really counts is my acceptance of eternal life through the gift of your Son. I believe, Lord. Thank you for giving me such a simple plan that even I can follow it.

My prayer for today—including any journaling thoughts I may want to add. Where am I today spiritually, emotionally, physically, financially, generally?

Today's Date: _____

Old Testament for today: Jeremiah 10:6

Lord, there is no other god like you. For you are great and your name is full of power. Who would not fear you, O King of nations? (And that title belongs to you alone!) Among all the wise men of the earth and in all the kingdoms of the world there isn't anyone like you.

One possible prayer for today:

God, Jeremiah wrote that prayer hundreds of years ago, and yet it is as true today as it was when Jeremiah lived and prayed. Thank you for being a consistent God, both for Jeremiah way back then and for me today. Thank you for being so great! Thank you for being so full of power that even your name is full of power! Thank you for being above all other gods that people have ever worshipped! And, Lord, with all that power, thank you for loving me and being concerned about me and the things that concern me today. Thank you, Lord.

New Testament verse for today: Philippians 1:6

And I am sure that God who began the good work within you will keep right on helping you grow in his grace until his task within you is finally finished on that day when Jesus Christ returns.

One possible prayer for today:

God, because of your greatness; because of your consistency; and because of your power, I can take heart that you will never give up on me as long as I honor and worship you. I know that you called me and that you are working within my life as much as I will let you. I know that I have a free will and that I often thwart the work that you are trying to do in me; but, Lord, please don't give up on me. Let me grow in your grace. Keep on building the good work within me that you want me to do. And thank you for the promise that Christ will return to take me home with him.

My prayer for today—including any journaling thoughts I may want to add. Where am I today spiritually, emotionally, physically, financially, generally?

Today's Date: _____

Old Testament verse for today: Jeremiah 10:10

But the Lord is the only true God, the living God, the everlasting King. The whole earth shall tremble at his anger; the world shall hide before his displeasure.

One possible prayer for today:

Lord, your power can be real scary! You are so powerful! You are the only true and everlasting God. Thank you for loving me so that I do not have to hide in fear from your displeasure. Thank you for being a gracious God. Thank you for accepting my prayers for forgiveness. Lord, if you remembered my sins, I would have to constantly hide. But, you don't. You forgive. What a wonderful God you are. Thank you for being so mighty, and yet being so loving.

New Testament verse for today: Mark 11:4 thru 6

Jesus told them, "Go back to John and tell him about the miracles you've seen me do—the blind people I've healed, and the lame people now walking without help, and the cured lepers, and the deaf who hear, and the dead raised to life; and tell him about my preaching the Good News to the poor. Then give him this message, 'Blessed are those who don't doubt me.' "

One possible prayer for today:

God, thank you for letting Christ have your power here on earth so that he could do the marvelous miracles that he did. Thank you for that living testimony to your great and everlasting power. And, thank you that this testimony was centered in Christ's love, so that I can know that you are a God of love. Therefore, I do not have to fear your awesome power; but, can worship you in love and in adoration. Thank you, God, for the living testimony Christ gave me to your everlasting power—and love. Thank you, God.

My prayer for today—including any journaling thoughts I may want to add. Where am I today spiritually, emotionally, physically, financially, generally?

Today's Date: _____

Old Testament verse for today: Jeremiah 10:23

Lord, I know it is not within the power of man to map his life and plan his course—so you correct me, Lord; but please be gentle. Don't do it in your anger, for I would die.

One possible prayer for today:

In the world's scheme of things, Lord, I know that I am really insignificant. Yet, I know that you love me. That does not make me insignificant. That makes me important in your sight. I know that I can make decisions and then something over which I have no control will totally change the result that I had intended, so, ultimately, my fate is in your hands. I know that I make lots of mistakes, God, and I know that I do need continuous correcting; but, Lord, please correct me gently. Please be gentle with the correction of my errors. Thank you, Lord, for your gentle correction.

New Testament verse for today: John 12:46 & 57

"I have come as a light to shine in this dark world, so that all who put their trust in me will no longer wander in the darkness. If anyone hears me and doesn't obey me, I am not his judge—for I have come to save the world and not to judge it."

One possible prayer for today:

God, what a wonderful promise your Son, Jesus, has given me. He has not come to judge me, but to save me. How wonderful that is! Thank you for giving me the light that Jesus brings to my life. Thank you for giving me the faith to trust Jesus and to do my best to obey his teachings. And, Lord, thank you for the promise that Christ did not come to judge me, but to save me.

My prayer for today—including any journaling thoughts I may want to add. Where am I today spiritually, emotionally, physically, financially, generally?

Today's Date: _____

Old Testament verse for today: Jeremiah 17:5

The Lord says: Cursed is the man who puts his trust in mortal man and turns his heart away from God.

One possible prayer for today:

God, don't let me ever turn my heart away from you. Let me always be aware that everything I have is a gift from you and that my obligation is to be a good steward of what you have given me. Don't let me put my trust in men for my security or my salvation. Lord, don't even let me trust myself except as you give me the power and the guidance to handle each day as it arrives. Thank you, Lord, for giving me the faith to always put my trust in you.

New Testament verse for today: Philippians 4:8b

Fix your thoughts on what is true and good and right. Think about things that are pure and lovely, and dwell on the fine, good things in others. Think about all you can praise God for and be glad about.

One possible prayer for today:

God, sometimes I have a real hard time always thinking about the good things in others. I can be pretty nasty in my thoughts about others pretty easily! So, God, help me to think about all the good things in others. Help me to think about all the things that are true and good and right in my life. Help me to think about all the things that are pure and lovely. Help me to think about the fine, good things in others today. And, Lord, especially for today, let me really concentrate on all the reasons I can praise you. Let me concentrate on all the reasons I have to be glad. Thank you, Lord, for giving me so many things for which I can praise you and for which I can be glad. Thank you for being so good to me. Let me be a good steward today of all the gifts you have given me.

My prayer for today—including any journaling thoughts I may want to add. Where am I today spiritually, emotionally, physically, financially, generally?

Today's Date: _____

Old Testament verse for today: Jeremiah 17:7

But blessed is the man who trusts in the Lord and has made the Lord his hope and confidence.

One possible prayer for today:

Lord, when things are going well, I sometimes get comfortable in my own strength and in my own decision-making ability; but, when things get tough, I know that my only real hope and confidence must be in you! I don't really have any control over many parts of my life and my circumstances; yet, you are always in charge of all things. Lord, you are my only hope and confidence. Thank you for blessing me for my faith in you.

New Testament verse for today: Mark 10:14b & 15

"Let the children come to me, for the Kingdom of God belongs to such as they. Don't send them away! I tell you as seriously as I know how that anyone who refuses to come to God as a little child will never be allowed into his Kingdom."

One possible prayer for today:

God, my trust and confidence in you must be the same trust and confidence that a little child has in a loving person who is giving loving care. Sometimes that is hard for me to do. Sometimes I want to take charge of things over which I have no control. But, I know that I must continue to have the faith of a little child for a loving parent, for you are my Heavenly Father. Thank you for being my Heavenly Father. Thank you for loving me so much. Thank you, God.

My prayer for today—including any journaling thoughts I may want to add. Where am I today spiritually, emotionally, physically, financially, generally?

Today's Date: _____

Old Testament verse for today: Jeremiah 17:14

Lord, you alone can heal me, you alone can save, and my praises are for you alone.

One possible prayer for today:

How wonderful it is, Lord, to have a God like you who can heal and can save. And, Lord, as Jeremiah said, you are the only one who can do those things. Lord, I do praise you, and you alone! Thank you for being a healing, caring and saving God. Lord, as the Psalmist said, I have never heard of another God like you! I do praise you, and honor you, and thank you, God.

New Testament verse for today: I Corinthians 8:6

But we know that there is only one God, the Father, who created all things and made us to be his own, and one Lord, Jesus Christ, who made everything and gives us life.

One possible prayer for today:

Thank you, God, for your awesome power; for your creative imagination and skills; for being the one and only true God. Thank you for giving us your Son, Jesus Christ, who made everything and gives us life; and gives us everlasting life. Thank you for your power; for your majesty; and yet with all that power, thank you for giving us your love; and, for making that love in the form of a man, Jesus. Thank you, God.

My prayer for today—including any journaling thoughts I may want to add. Where am I today spiritually, emotionally, physically, financially, generally?

Today's Date: _____

Old Testament verse for today: Jeremiah 17:17

Lord, don't desert me now! You alone are my hope.

One possible prayer for today:

Lord, how true that is! You alone are my hope! Thank you for being consistent. I know that I do not have to worry about you deserting me. I know that you will always be there for me. I know I can trust you and count on you at all times. Thank you, Lord, for being my hope at all times.

New Testament verse for today: II Corinthians 5:20b & 21

—receive the love he offers you—be reconciled to God. For God took the sinless Christ and poured into him our sins. Then, in exchange, he poured God's goodness into us.

One possible prayer for today:

God, I accept your love. You are my only hope. Thank you for offering me your love. Thank you for letting me be reconciled to you. Thank you for taking my sins away and remembering them no more. Thank you for giving me that marvelous plan of salvation through the death and resurrection of your sinless Son, Jesus. Thank you for permitting me to have some of your goodness in me. Thank you for being so good to me, God. Thank you for being not only my only hope, but a wonderful and marvelous hope. Thank you, God.

My prayer for today—including any journaling thoughts I may want to add. Where am I today spiritually, emotionally, physically, financially, generally?

Today's Date: _____

Old Testament verse for today: Jeremiah 20:13

Therefore I will sing out in thanks to the Lord! Praise him! For he has delivered me, poor and needy, from my oppressors.

One possible prayer for today:

God, thank you for always being there for me. Let me sing your praises at all times. Thank you for hearing my prayers. Thank you for giving me the patience and the faith that I need at this time in my life. Thank you, Lord.

New Testament verse for today: Revelations 7:16 & 17

They will never be hungry again, nor thirsty, and they will be fully protected from the scorching noontime heat. For the Lamb standing in front of the throne will feed them and be their Shepherd and lead them to the springs of the Water of Life. And God will wipe their tears away.

One possible prayer for today:

God, what a wonderful expectation! Thank you for the promise that if I remain faithful in my belief in you, that you will remain faithful in your ultimate care for me. Thank you for sending Christ to be my Shepherd. Thank you for promising to ultimately wipe all of my tears away. Thank you for helping me today, as I do my best to live for you and trust you to help me in my troubles and problems today. Thank you for giving me these promises, Lord.

My prayer for today—including any journaling thoughts I may want to add. Where am I today spiritually, emotionally, physically, financially, generally?

Today's Date: _____

Old Testament verse for today: Jeremiah 29:11 thru 13

For I know the plans I have for you, says the Lord. They are plans for good and not for evil, to give you a future and a hope. In those days when you pray, I will listen. You will find me when you seek me, if you look for me in earnest.

One possible prayer for today:

God, thank you for having a plan for my life. Thank you for making that plan a plan for good and not for evil. Thank you for making that plan a plan that gives me a future and a hope. Thank you for promising to hear me when I pray to you. Thank you for promising to listen to my prayers. Thank you for promising that if I seek you in earnest that you will be there for me and that you will let me find you. Thank you for being such a wonderful and caring God.

New Testament verse for today: Philippians 1:9 thru 11

My prayer for you is that you will overflow more and more with love for others, and at the same time keep on growing in spiritual knowledge and insight, for I want you always to see clearly the difference between right and wrong and to be inwardly clean, no one being able to criticize you from now until the Lord returns. May you always be doing those good, kind things which show you are a child of God, for this will bring praise and glory to the Lord.

One possible prayer for today:

God, thank you for having a plan for my life. Thank you that as a part of that plan you will give me the heart and concern for others. Thank you for helping me to grow in spiritual knowledge and insight. Thank you for helping me to distinguish between right and wrong. Thank you for helping me to remain inwardly clean. Thank you for helping me really try to do those good and kind things which will bring praise and glory to you. Lord, you know that doing those things is not my nature. So, Lord, I really need lots of help. I claim your promise that when I pray, you will listen. Thank you for helping me in this area, Lord. And thank you for forgiving me when I fail you in this area. Thank you again for having such a wonderful plan for my life.

My prayer for today—including any journaling thoughts I may want to add. Where am I today spiritually, emotionally, physically, financially, generally?

Today's Date: _____

Old Testament verse for today: Jeremiah 33:2 & 3

The Lord, the Maker of heaven and earth—Jehovah is his name—says this: Ask me and I will tell you some remarkable secrets about what is going to happen here.

One possible prayer for today:

God, thank you for sharing your secrets with me. Thank you for giving me your book, the Bible, which tells me what I need to know to have eternal life with you. Thank you for not keeping secret your marvelous plan of salvation through your Son, Jesus. Thank you for sharing that plan with the world, so that we have the opportunity to avail ourselves of your perfect plan for our lives. Thank you for giving me the faith so that I may receive salvation through your Son, Jesus. Thank you for sharing this remarkable plan with me.

New Testament verse for today: Ephesians 1:13 & 14

And because of what Christ did, all you others too, who heard the Good News about how to be saved, and trusted Christ, were marked as belonging to Christ by the Holy Spirit, who long ago had been promised to all of us Christians. His presence within us is God's guarantee that he really will give us all that he promised: and the Spirit's seal upon us means that God has already purchased us and that he guarantees to bring us to himself. This is just one more reason for us to praise our glorious God.

One possible prayer for today:

God, thank you for sharing your marvelous plan of salvation with me. Thank you for marking me as belonging to Christ by the Holy Spirit. Thank you for giving me that promise and for keeping that promise. Thank you for giving me this guarantee that you will always keep your promises to me. Thank you for putting your loving Holy Spirit's seal on me guaranteeing me that you have purchased me and will bring me to you. Let me always praise you, my glorious God. Thank you, God.

My prayer for today—including any journaling thoughts I may want to add. Where am I today spiritually, emotionally, physically, financially, generally?

Today's Date: _____

Old Testament verse for today: Lamentations 3:21, 22a, 23 thru 26

Yet there is one ray of hope: his compassion never ends. Great is his faithfulness; his lovingkindness begins afresh each day. My soul claims the Lord as my inheritance; therefore I will hope in him. The Lord is wonderfully good to those who wait for him, to those who seek him. It is good both to hope and wait quietly for the salvation of the Lord.

One possible prayer for today:

What wonderful promises, O Lord! No matter how bad things may look, there is always that ray of hope! Thank you, Lord, for your never ending compassion. Thank you for your great faithfulness. Thank you for your fresh lovingkindness each and every day. I do claim you, Lord, as my inheritance. I do hope in you and wait for you to help me. And, God, I do claim this promise that you will be wonderfully good to me if I seek you and wait for you to help me. Thank you, Lord, for that hope and for that promise.

New Testament verse for today: Romans 12:3b

Be honest in your estimate of yourselves, measuring your value by how much faith God has given you.

One possible prayer for today:

Lord, I thank you for the faith you have given me. I thank you for that measure of faith that is particularly mine. Let me be honest in my estimate of myself. I know that you love me. I know that you have given me the faith to get through all kinds of problems, if I will just exercise that faith. So, God, I do wait for you to help me. I ask for whatever faith I need for today. Thank you, God, for hearing and answering this prayer.

My prayer for today—including any journaling thoughts I may want to add. Where am I today spiritually, emotionally, physically, financially, generally?

Today's Date: _____

Old Testament verse for today: Lamentations 3:31 thru 33

For the Lord will not abandon him forever. Although God gives him grief, yet he will show compassion too, according to the greatness of his lovingkindness. For he does not enjoy afflicting men and causing sorrow.

One possible prayer for today:

God, thank you for being a God who is so full of lovingkindness to me. Thank you for promising me that even in my grief I know that you will not abandon me forever. Thank you for your compassion to me. Thank you for helping me at all times. Lord, I claim the promise that you do not enjoy my afflictions and my sorrows. I claim the promise that you will show me your compassion. Please let that compassion come quickly, Lord. Please shower me with your great lovingkindness again. Thank you, God, for remembering me in my distress.

New Testament verse for today: I Peter 1:21

Because of this, your trust can be in God who raised Christ from the dead and gave him great glory. Now your faith and hope can rest in him alone.

One possible prayer for today:

Thank you for being such a great and loving God. Thank you for being a God who is worthy of my complete trust. Thank you for being the Rock upon whom I can rest my faith and hope. Thank you for being a God who raised Christ from the dead so that I could have eternal life with you and your Son Jesus, if I will only believe. God, I do believe. Even though I am going through a period of distress, Lord, I look to you to show me your great compassion. My faith and trust do rest in you alone. Thank you for being a God who never lets me down. Thank you, Lord.

My prayer for today—including any journaling thoughts I may want to add. Where am I today spiritually, emotionally, physically, financially, generally?

Today's Date: _____

Old Testament verse for today: Lamentations 3:55 thru 57

But I called upon your name, O Lord, from deep within the well, and you heard me! You listened to my pleading; you heard my weeping! Yes, you came at my despairing cry and told me not to fear.

One possible prayer for today:

God, thank you for hearing me no matter how far I may have fallen away from you. Lord, even if I am in the depth of despair, when I humbly cry to you, you hear me. You listen to my pleading. You react with lovingkindness to my weeping. Thank you for being there for me so that even in the depth of my despair, I can turn to you, and if my faith in you is strong enough, you have the strength to remove my fear from me. Give me the faith that I need in this time of pleading and weeping, Lord. Remove my fear from me. Thank you, Lord, for being a God who can remove my fear. Thank you for always being there to listen to me, no matter what my circumstances.

New Testament verse for today: Romans 8:33

Who dares accuse us whom God has chosen for his own? Will God? He is the one who has forgiven us and given us right standing with himself.

One possible prayer for today:

God, what a wonderful promise! No matter how bad things may look in my life, I need to realize that you are always there to listen to me; to hear my pleading and my weeping. And no matter how bad things may look to me right now, I know that you have chosen me for your own. You don't accuse me or forsake me. You are there promising me forgiveness and right standing with you. Thank you for those promises, Lord. Thank you for giving me these promises on which I can rely to give me hope and encouragement. Thank you for being such a loving and forgiving God to me.

My prayer for today—including any journaling thoughts I may want to add. Where am I today spiritually, emotionally, physically, financially, generally?

Today's Date: _____

Old Testament verse for today: Lamentations 3:58

O Lord, you are my lawyer! Plead my case! For you have redeemed my life.

One possible prayer for today:

God, how exciting to consider! How wonderful to know that you are on my side! Thank you for being on my side. Thank you for pleading my case. And, God, thank you most of all for redeeming my life and providing me a plan of salvation through the gift of your Son, Jesus Christ.

New Testament verse for today: Romans 8:11

And if the Spirit of God, who raised up Jesus from the dead, lives in you, he will make your dying bodies live after you die, by means of the same Holy Spirit living within you.

One possible prayer for today:

Thank you for this wonderful promise, Lord. If you had the power to raise Jesus from the dead; and, if that Spirit is available to me today; and, if you are pleading my case as my lawyer, I know that you will take care of me for eternity! What a wonderful God you are! How loving you are! What great hope you give me for an eternity with you! Thank you, God, for giving me that hope and for giving me the faith to claim that hope. Thank you, God.

My prayer for today—including any journaling thoughts I may want to add. Where am I today spiritually, emotionally, physically, financially, generally?

Today's Date: _____

Old Testament verse for today: Ezekiel 33:12

For the good works of a righteous man will not save him if he turns to sin; and the sins of an evil man will not destroy him if he repents and turns from his sins.

One possible prayer for today:

God, you are so loving and kind, and so full of forgiveness. Thank you for continuing to forgive me if I continue to repent. I know that I cannot earn your love and your salvation by any good works that I do. I know that I must turn my life over to you and do my best to let you be in charge. If I do that, Lord, you will keep your promise to me and give me salvation through your Son, Jesus. Thank you, Lord, for that promise.

New Testament verse for today: Mark 3:35

"Anyone who does God's will is my brother, and my sister, and my mother."

One possible prayer for today:

Lord, what a privilege to be in your family! Christ has said that if I do your will, I am in the family of God. Help me to be more consistent in doing your will, Lord. Give me the strength and the faith to follow your guidance more closely. And, God, thank you for letting me be in your family.

My prayer for today—including any journaling thoughts I may want to add. Where am I today spiritually, emotionally, physically, financially, generally?

Today's Date: _____

Old Testament verse for today: Ezekiel 34:31

You are my flock, the sheep of my pasture. You are my men and I am your God, so says the Lord.

One possible prayer for today:

God, thank you for taking care of me as a shepherd takes care of his sheep. Thank you for including me as one of your flock. Thank you for being my God. Thank you for this promise.

New Testament verse for today: Matthew 12:50

Then he (Jesus) added, "Anyone who obeys my Father in heaven is my brother, sister, and mother!"

One possible prayer for today:

God, how exciting to know that if I believe, if I obey you, that Christ considers me part of the family! What a wonderful thought. What a wonderful family to join! God, thank you for giving me that opportunity. Thank you for giving me the faith to believe and obey. And, God, thank you for forgiving me when I fail. Thank you, Lord.

My prayer for today—including any journaling thoughts I may want to add. Where am I today spiritually, emotionally, physically, financially, generally?

Today's Date: _____

Old Testament verse for today: Ezekiel 36:26 & 27

And I will give you a new heart—I will give you new and right desires—and put a new spirit within you. I will take out your stony hearts of sin and give you new hearts of love. And I will put my Spirit within you so that you will obey my laws and do whatever I command.

One possible prayer for today:

God, thank you for giving me a new heart—one with new and right desires; because, you know that left to my own devices and actions, I don't always have the right desires! Thank you for giving me the opportunity to have a new spirit. Thank you for removing my stony heart of sin. Thank you for sending your loving Holy Spirit into my life so that I will want to obey your laws and do whatever you command. Thank you for loving me enough to put up with me, to be patient with me, and to give me all these wonderful blessings and promises. Thank you, Lord.

New Testament verse for today: II Corinthians 5:17

When someone becomes a Christian he becomes a brand new person inside. He is not the same anymore. A new life has begun!

One possible prayer for today:

Thank you for making me a brand new person inside, God. Thank you for giving me new life through the gift of your Son, Jesus. Thank you for making salvation possible for even a sinner like me. Lord, you paid such a price for my salvation; and, yet you make it so easy and simple for me. Thank you, Lord. Thank you.

My prayer for today—including any journaling thoughts I may want to add. Where am I today spiritually, emotionally, physically, financially, generally?

Today's Date: _____

Old Testament verse for today: Daniel 2:19b thru 22

Then Daniel praised the God of heaven, saying, "Blessed be the name of God forever and ever, for he alone has all wisdom and all power. World events are under his control. He removes kings and sets others on their thrones. He gives wise men their wisdom, and scholars their intelligence. He reveals profound mysteries beyond man's understanding. He knows all hidden things, for he is light, and darkness is no obstacle to him."

One possible prayer for today:

God, thank you for being all knowing and all powerful. Thank you for being a God who has no obstacles that you cannot overcome. Let me always bless your name in all that I do and all that I think. Thank you for having all wisdom and power. Lord, thank you for sharing with me that portion of your wisdom and power that I need to get through today. Lord, thank you for being concerned about me and the things that concern me, even though all world events are under your control. Thank you for your love and care for me.

New Testament verse for today: I Corinthians 1:24b & 25

Christ himself is the center of God's wise plan for their salvation. This so called "foolish" plan of God is far wiser than the wisest plan of the wisest man, for God in his weakness—Christ dying on the cross—is far stronger than any man.

One possible prayer for today:

God, thank you for your wisdom and your power. Thank you that in all of your wisdom, you provided a plan for my salvation that is so simple that even I can understand it and avail myself of it. Thank you for permitting yourself to become weak through the death of Jesus, so that I might become strong and perfect in your sight because I am forgiven of all my sins. Thank you for being such a wise, wonderful, and powerful God; and, yet so caring and generous to me. Thank you, God.

My prayer for today—including any journaling thoughts I may want to add. Where am I today spiritually, emotionally, physically, financially, generally?

Today's Date: _____

Old Testament verse for today: Daniel 9:4b

"O Lord," I (Daniel) prayed, "you are a great and awesome God; you always fulfill your promises of mercy to those who love you and who keep your laws."

One possible prayer for today:

Lord, I agree with Daniel. You are a great and awesome God. Thank you for your greatness. Thank you for being so awesome. And, God, thank you for always fulfilling your promises of mercy to those who love you and who keep your laws. You know, Lord, that I love you. You also know that I do not always keep your laws. Yet you also know that I try. And, God, one of your promises is that you will never quit forgiving me when I come back to you and humbly ask for your forgiveness. Thank you for your awesome promises, God.

New Testament verse for today: II Corinthians 5:1

For we know that when this tent we live in now is taken down—when we die and leave these bodies—we will have wonderful new bodies in heaven, homes that will be ours forevermore, made for us by God himself, and not by human hands.

One possible prayer for today:

What a wonderful promise, God. How great to know that this is one more of your promises—that when I die I will be with you for eternity if I only believe in your Son, Jesus Christ. God, sometimes this body does let me down. Sometimes it is difficult to continue. Yet, knowing what is in store for me—an eternity with you with a new heavenly body—that gives me strength and encouragement. God, thank you for preparing a body made for me by your own hands. Thank you, God.

My prayer for today—including any journaling thoughts I may want to add. Where am I today spiritually, emotionally, physically, financially, generally?

Today's Date: _____

Old Testament verse for today: Daniel 9:9

But the Lord our God is merciful, and pardons even those who have rebelled against him.

One possible prayer for today:

God, thank you for being merciful to me, a sinner. One who has rebelled against you just by being me! Just by being full of myself, instead of full of you. No matter how deep and vile my sins, Lord, you continue to forgive when I come back to you with honesty and humility. Thank you for continuing to pardon me and forgive my sins and my rebellion. Thank you for always listening to me and hearing me. Thank you, God.

New Testament verse for today: Ephesians 6:18

Pray all the time. Ask God for anything in line with the Holy Spirit's wishes. Plead with him, reminding him of your needs, and keep praying earnestly for all Christians everywhere.

One possible prayer for today:

God, thank you for letting me come back to you again and again with my prayers and my needs. Thank you for always being there for me. Thank you for letting me plead with you. Lord, today you know that I am hurting a lot—so I am pleading! I want something very badly that is not going my way. Maybe I am selfish. Maybe I am wanting something that is not in line with your loving Holy Spirit's wishes for my life. So, Lord, let me lean on you for your answer. Let me accept that answer when it comes as being what the Holy Spirit wants for my life right now. Help me to see things from your perspective. Give me the good judgment to work through this problem in a manner that would be pleasing to you and bring glory to your name. Help me to have the good judgment not to try to solve this on my own and in my own way. Help me, Lord. I really need your help today!

My prayer for today—including any journaling thoughts I may want to add. Where am I today spiritually, emotionally, physically, financially, generally?

Today's Date: _____

Old Testament verse for today: Hosea 6:3

Oh, that we might know the Lord! Let us press on to know him, and he will respond to us as surely as the coming of dawn or the rain of early spring.

One possible prayer for today:

Lord, help me to know you better. How do I do that? By studying your scriptures? By taking more time and communicating with you? I do want to press on to know you, God. I desire a closer relationship with you. I do want you to be a friend of mine. And, God, I do count on your responding to me. I do trust that you are as consistent in caring for me and responding to my needs and my pleas as the coming of dawn or the rain of early spring. Thank you, God, for your consistency.

New Testament verse for today: Matthew 18:3 & 4

"Unless you turn to God from your sins and become as little children, you will never get into the Kingdom of Heaven. Therefore anyone who humbles himself as this little child, is the greatest in the Kingdom of Heaven."

One possible prayer for today:

God, though I try, I continue to sin. Thank you for forgiving me each time I sin. Lord, I am not sure that I really understand Christ's admonition of becoming like a little child. I am older than a little child. I live a life more in tune with how old I am. But, Lord, I think Christ was telling me to have a faith in you like a little child has in a loving parent. A little child's life is totally dependent on someone taking care of him or her. I think that Christ was telling me to trust you in all things and in all circumstances just as a little child trusts whoever is taking care of him or her. God, I want to do that. Help me to do that. When my faith wanes, give me another shot of faith! And, God, thank you for never giving up on me as long as I try!

My prayer for today—including any journaling thoughts I may want to add. Where am I today spiritually, emotionally, physically, financially, generally?

Today's Date: _____

Old Testament verse for today: Hosea 6:6

I don't want your sacrifices—I want your love; I don't want your offerings—I want you to know me.

One possible prayer for today:

Lord, I do want to know you better than I do. I want to give you the offering of my life lived for you. Help me to know you better, Lord. Give me the self discipline to spend more time reading your Word, talking to you and communicating with you; and, then listening for you to speak to me. Thank you, Lord, for being patient with me as I work toward knowing you better.

New Testament verse for today: Mark 12:28 thru 31

One of the teachers of religion who was standing there listening to the discussion realized that Jesus had answered well. So he asked, "Of all the commandments, which is the most important?" Jesus replied, "The one that says, 'Hear, O Israel! The Lord our God is the one and only God. And you must love him with all your heart and soul and mind and strength.' "The second is: 'You must love others as much as yourself.' No other commandments are greater than these."

One possible prayer for today:

God, that is probably how I learn to know you better. I just need to love you more. I need to love you with all my heart, my soul, my mind ,and my strength. And, I know that I really have to work on loving others more. Lord, you know me. You know my selfish attitudes. You know that I usually put myself first. Lord, help me to love you more. Help me to be less selfish. Let me be more concerned about others and not so caught up in my own problems. Thank you, Lord, for letting me know how I can know you better.

My prayer for today—including any journaling thoughts I may want to add. Where am I today spiritually, emotionally, physically, financially, generally?

Today's Date: _____

Old Testament verse for today: Hosea 10:12

Plant the good seeds of righteousness and you will reap a crop of my love; plow the hard ground of your hearts, for now is the time to seek the Lord, that he may come and shower salvation upon you.

One possible prayer for today:

Lord, I need your love. I really do. So, it may be selfish; but, I really want to plant the good seeds of righteousness and plow the hard ground of my heart. I do seek you, Lord. I turn my life over to you and ask you to help me in my everyday life. Thank you for my salvation, Lord. Thank you for showering me with your love and your salvation.

New Testament verse for today: Matthew 7:20

Yes, the way to identify a tree or a person is by the kind of fruit produced.

One possible prayer for today:

Lord, let my fruit be pleasing to you. Let me be identified as one of your followers by the fruit of my life. You have done so much for me. You have promised me eternal life through your marvelous plan of salvation. You have given up your only Son for my salvation. Let me do my small part by believing and then acting on that belief to produce fruit pleasing to you. Thank you for being patient with me, Lord, as I live my life.

My prayer for today—including any journaling thoughts I may want to add. Where am I today spiritually, emotionally, physically, financially, generally?

Today's Date: _____

Old Testament verse for today: Hosea 12:6

Oh, come back to God. Live by the principles of love and justice, and always be expecting much from him, your God.

One possible prayer for today:

God, don't let me leave you so that I have to come back to you! Let me try harder to live by your principals of love and justice. Help me to do that. Let me turn to you for guidance and strength. And, God, I do expect much from you. Thank you for meeting my expectations.

New Testament verse for today: Mark 11:22 thru 25

In reply Jesus said to the disciples, "If you only have faith in God—this is the absolute truth—you can say to this Mount of Olives, 'Rise up and fall into the Mediterranean,' and your command will be obeyed. All that's required is that you really believe and have no doubt! Listen to me! You can pray for anything, and if you believe, you have it; it's yours! But when you are praying, first forgive anyone you are holding a grudge against, so that your Father in heaven will forgive you your sins too."

One possible prayer for today:

Lord, I do expect much from you all the time. I do pray for the things that are important to me. I do have the gift of faith that you have given to me. Lord, don't let me misuse that faith. Don't let me misuse the wonderful power of prayer that is available to me. Don't let me be asking the impossible only to get my own way or to simply have more of my own pleasure and ease. I know that all power is yours. I ask for guidance in calling on that power in a manner that is in line with your will. Let my faith grow. Let my prayers result in powerful things being accomplished; but, let those powerful things be for your honor and glory and not for my own selfish desires.

My prayer for today—including any journaling thoughts I may want to add. Where am I today spiritually, emotionally, physically, financially, generally?

Today's Date: _____

Old Testament verse for today: Joel 2:13b

Return to the Lord your God, for he is gracious and merciful. He is not easily angered; he is full of kindness, and anxious not to punish you.

One possible prayer for today:

Lord, let me always return to you. Don't let me stray so far that the return is much of a trip! I thank you and praise you that you are so gracious and merciful. I thank you and praise you that you are not easily angered. I thank you and praise you that you are so full of kindness. And, Lord, I thank you and praise you that you are not anxious to punish me. I know that I often let you down; but, Lord, you never let me down. Thank you.

New Testament verse for today: Matthew 10:32

If anyone publicly acknowledges me as his friend, I will openly acknowledge him as my friend before my father in heaven.

One possible prayer for today:

God, what a wonderful promise from your Son, Jesus! How could anyone have a better friend? Help me to have the strength to always acknowledge Jesus by the way I live; by the way I talk; by the way I go about my daily activity; by the way I interact with my friends and acquaintances. How exciting to know that if I do my part, Christ will acknowledge me as his friend to you, God. Thank you for that promise.

My prayer for today—including any journaling thoughts I may want to add. Where am I today spiritually, emotionally, physically, financially, generally?

Today's Date: _____

Old Testament verse for today: Joel 2:32a

Everyone who calls upon the name of the Lord will be saved.

One possible prayer for today:

Thank you for making salvation available to everyone—even me! Thank you for giving me a plan for salvation on which I can count and rely. Thank you for being such a loving and gracious Lord. Thank you. Thank you.

New Testament verse for today: Ephesians 2:10

It is God himself who has made us what we are and given us new lives from Christ Jesus; and long ages ago he planned that we should spend these lives helping others.

One possible prayer for today:

God, thank you for making such a wonderful plan for my new life through your Son, Jesus Christ. Thank you for forgiving me of all my sins—no matter how sordid they may be. Let me follow your plan of helping others come to know you and know how much you love them .Let my life and my actions be a witness to your wonderful love. Help me strengthen my faith in you. Help me to look to you for my help so that I may be of more help to others in their walk of faith. Thank you for your help, Lord.

My prayer for today—including any journaling thoughts I may want to add. Where am I today spiritually, emotionally, physically, financially, generally?

Today's Date: _____

Old Testament verse for today: Amos 5:14a

Be good, flee from evil—and live! Then the Lord God of Hosts will truly be your Helper.

One possible prayer for today:

Lord, help me to flee from evil. Help me to be good in your eyes. Lord, please be my helper. Please let me live with all of the great benefits you planned for me. Be my helper always, Lord. Thank you for being my helper and thank you for always being there for me.

New Testament verse for today: John 10:9 & 10b

Yes, I am the Gate. Those who come in by way of the Gate will be saved and will go in and out and find green pastures. My purpose is to give life in all its fullness.

One possible prayer for today:

God, thank you for giving me your Son, Jesus, as the Gate for my life. Thank you for choosing me to be one who can come and go by way of this Gate. Thank you for extending that saving grace to me. Thank you for leading my life into green pastures. Thank you for your goal for me that my life should be lived in all of its fullness. Let me always turn to you for my leading, Lord, and lead me into the continued fullness of my life. Thank you for that leading and for that fullness, Lord.

My prayer for today—including any journaling thoughts I may want to add. Where am I today spiritually, emotionally, physically, financially, generally?

Today's Date: _____

Old Testament verse for today: Jonah 2:7

When I had lost all hope, I turned my thoughts once more to the Lord. And my earnest prayer went to you in your holy Temple.

One possible prayer for today:

God, when things are hopeless for me, I know that you are always there for me. I know that I, like Jonah, can turn my thoughts to you. I know that I can offer up my earnest prayer to you in your holy Temple; and Lord, I know that you will hear me and that you will answer my prayer as it fits your plans for my life. Thank you, Lord, for always being in your holy Temple waiting for me to call on you. Thank you for always hearing me, Lord. Thank you for giving me the faith and the patience to accept your plans in my life.

New Testament verse for today: Romans 12:1

And so, dear brothers, I plead with you to give your bodies to God. Let them be a living sacrifice, holy—the kind he can accept. When you think of what he has done for you, is that too much to ask?

One possible prayer for today:

God, I need your help to be able to live in such a manner that my life—my body—is an acceptable sacrifice to you. I know that I fail you often. I know that I get my own agenda in front of your agenda for my life. I know that you love me without reservation. Let me do more to love you and honor you with my life. Let me have the strength and the faith that I need to truly be an acceptable living sacrifice to you. Thank you, God, for being patient with me as I continue to work on properly honoring you with my life. Thank you for never giving up on me.

My prayer for today—including any journaling thoughts I may want to add. Where am I today spiritually, emotionally, physically, financially, generally?

Today's Date: _____

Old Testament verse for today: Jonah 2:9

I will never worship anyone but you! For how can I thank you enough for all you have done? I will surely fulfill my promises. For my deliverance comes from the Lord alone.

One possible prayer for today:

God, I know that my life is in your hands and that my deliverance comes from you alone. I know that I can never adequately thank you for all you have done for me. But, Lord, help me to be faithful to you in worshipping only you and you alone. Help me to be faithful in fulfilling my promises to you. Help me to live my life as a testimony to your love for me, even though I fail and continue to let you down by my actions. Thank you, God, for never letting me down.

New Testament verse for today: Philippians 2:13

For God is at work within you, helping you want to obey him, and then helping you do what he wants.

One possible prayer for today:

God, thank you for that promise of your help. I really need your help within me to obey you. I have all these things that can tempt me that are probably things that you would not want me to do; and, on my own, I know that I do not always have the strength to resist. Even though I want to obey you, I don't always do it. So, Lord, help me to not only want to obey you; but, help me to do what you want me to do. Thank you, Lord, for your help. And, Lord, thank you for continuing to forgive me when I fail in my goal of obeying you and doing the things that you want me to do.

My prayer for today—including any journaling thoughts I may want to add. Where am I today spiritually, emotionally, physically, financially, generally?

Today's Date: _____

Old Testament verse for today: Micah 6:8

No, he (God) has told you what he wants, and this is all it is: to be fair and just and merciful, and to walk humbly with your God.

One possible prayer for today:

God, that is great! That actually seems like something that I could do! And, God, thank you for telling me what you expect from me and thank you for making it so simple. I humble myself before you, God; and yet, on the other hand, I walk proudly knowing that you are my God and that you love me just as I am. Thank you, God, for being such a great and merciful God.

New Testament verse for today: Romans 11:22

Notice how God is both kind and severe. He is very hard on those who disobey, but very good to you if you continue to love and trust him.

One possible prayer for today:

God, thank you for forgiving me when I do disobey. Thank you for being so good to me when I continue to love and trust you. You know that I don't always do what I should do; and, many times don't even do what I want to do; but, Lord, when I do disobey, please scold me gently. Please don't be too hard on me. And thank you for always keeping the door open for me to come back to you. Thank you that your kindness never ends when I do come back to love and trust you.

My prayer for today—including any journaling thoughts I may want to add. Where am I today spiritually, emotionally, physically, financially, generally?

Today's Date: _____

Old Testament verse for today: Micah 7:7

As for me, I look to the Lord for his help; I wait for God to save me; he will hear me.

One possible prayer for today:

Lord, I always look to you for my help. Thank you for always being there for me. Lord, I wait for you to help me, to deliver me, to save me. I thank you for always hearing me. Lord, I acknowledge that I cannot do it alone. I need your help to get me through my every-day challenges. Thank you, Lord, for being such a wonderful God.

New Testament verse for today: Acts 15:8

God, who knows men's hearts, confirmed the fact that he accepts Gentiles by giving them the Holy Spirit, just as he gave him to us.

One possible prayer for today:

God, thank you for making your plan of salvation available to everyone—regardless of race, creed, color, culture, or whatever. Thank you for permitting me, a sinner, to come into a saving knowledge of you through your Son, Jesus, the Christ. Thank you for sending your loving Holy Spirit into my life so that I may have even greater communion with you. God, you are so wonderful to me, a forgiven sinner. Thank you, Lord.

My prayer for today—including any journaling thoughts I may want to add. Where am I today spiritually, emotionally, physically, financially, generally?

Today's Date: _____

Old Testament verse for today: Micah 7:9b

God will bring me out of my darkness into the light and I will see his goodness.

One possible prayer for today:

God, thank you for giving me the faith to know that no matter how dismal things may look today, that you will once again bring me out of my pain and into the joy that only you can give. Thank you for letting me know that once again I will see and feel your goodness. Thank you for always being there for me, no matter how bad things look today. Lord, bring me back into your light and your goodness quickly, for today I am hurting and need extra strength and extra loving care from you. Thank you, God, for giving me what I need today.

New Testament verse for today: II Corinthians 7:1

Having such great promises as these, dear friends, let us turn away from everything wrong, whether of body or spirit, and purify ourselves, living in the wholesome fear of God, giving ourselves to him alone.

One possible prayer for today:

God, you are such a great and wonderful God. Thank you for always being there for me to bring me out of the darkness and into your light and letting me once again experience your goodness. So, Lord, with such a great promise, let me do my best to turn away from everything wrong; to live as pure a life as I can possibly live; to live in a wholesome fear of you because of your great power. But, God, let me also live in the comfort of knowing what a loving and faithful God you are, even though you have all this great power. Thank you for not only being all powerful, but being all loving and forgiving. Lord, give me the strength to really work at living as you would have me live. And, Lord, thank you for forgiving me when I fail.

My prayer for today—including any journaling thoughts I may want to add. Where am I today spiritually, emotionally, physically, financially, generally?

Today's Date: _____

Old Testament verse for today: Micah 7:18 & 19

Where is another God like you, who pardons the sins of the survivors among his people? You cannot stay angry with your people, for you love to be merciful. Once again you will have compassion on us. You will tread our sins beneath your feet; you will throw them into the depths of the ocean.

One possible prayer for today:

God, what a wonderful promise! To think that you will actually throw my sins—and your remembrance of them into the depths of the ocean. God, thank you for that promise. Thank you for pardoning me. Thank you for not staying angry with me. Thank you for loving to be merciful to me, sinful though I am. Thank you, again and again, Lord, for that great promise.

New Testament verse for today: John 3:16 & 17

For God loved the world so much that he gave his only Son so that anyone who believes in him shall not perish but have eternal life. God did not send his Son into the world to condemn it, but to save it.

One possible prayer for today:

Wow! God, how wonderful! Thank you for being such a loving God! Thank you for giving your Son to me—to even me—so that if I only believe in him—and I do!—that you have guaranteed me eternal life! Wow! What an act of love and what a promise! God, I thank you for that love. I thank you that you did not send your Son to condemn me, but to save me. Thank you, Lord, for being such a loving God.

My prayer for today—including any journaling thoughts I may want to add. Where am I today spiritually, emotionally, physically, financially, generally?

Today's Date: _____

Old Testament verse for today: Nahum 1:7

The Lord is good. When trouble comes, he is the place to go! And he knows everyone who trusts in him!

One possible prayer for today:

God, thank you for knowing me, as I do trust in you! Thank you for being a good God! Thank you for always being there when trouble comes into my life! Thank you for especially being there for me today.

New Testament verse for today: John 6:37

But some will come to me—those the Father has given me—and I will never, never reject them.

One possible prayer for today:

God, thank you for giving me to Jesus. Thank you for letting me come to him; and, God, thank you for Christ's promise that he will never, never reject me. Thank you for all the love that you have shown to me through your Son, Jesus.

My prayer for today—including any journaling thoughts I may want to add. Where am I today spiritually, emotionally, physically, financially, generally?

Today's Date: _____

Old Testament verse for today: Habakkuk 2:4

Note this: Wicked men trust themselves alone, and fail; but the righteous man trusts in me, and lives!

One possible prayer for today:

God, let me trust in you always for all things. Don't let me trust in my own wiles and devices; or my own supposed ability and talent! I know that if I do that, I will ultimately fail. Let me trust in you alone, Lord. And let me live with honor and success as you guide my life.

New Testament verse for today: Ephesians 6:10 & 11

—I want to remind you that your strength must come from the Lord's mighty power within you. Put on all of God's armor so that you will be able to stand safe against all strategies and tricks of Satan

One possible prayer for today:

Thank you for giving me the strength that I need to get through this day, Lord. Thank you for giving me all the armor I need to withstand the temptations that are going to confront me today. Thank you for keeping me safe from all the strategies and tricks that the world will offer me today, Lord; things that would not be pleasing to you. Thank you for always helping me, Lord. Thank you for your mighty power that I can have within me, Lord, if I will only claim it.

My prayer for today—including any journaling thoughts I may want to add. Where am I today spiritually, emotionally, physically, financially, generally?

Today's Date: _____

Old Testament verse for today: Habakkuk 2:14

The time will come when all the earth is filled, as the waters fill the sea, with an awareness of the glory of the Lord.

One possible prayer for today:

Lord, let my time be now when I am always aware of your glory. Don't let me every consider that all I have and all that is in the earth could possibly come from anyone or anything other than you. Thank you for your power and your glory. Thank you for filling the earth with your glory. And, Lord, thank you for letting me enjoy that glory.

New Testament verse for today: Luke 6:35

Love your enemies! Do good to them! Lend to them! And don't be concerned about the fact that they won't repay. Then your reward from heaven will be very great, and you will truly be acting as sons of God: for he is kind to the unthankful and to those who are very wicked.

One possible prayer for today:

Lord, those are really tough challenges for me to obey! I have a real hard time loving my enemies. I don't want to do good to them! I want to get even with them! And I certainly don't want to give them money that I am never going to get back! But, Lord, then I need to remember that the earth is yours. You are a God that has filled the earth with your glory. You are kind to the wicked and the unthankful. Lord, if I am going to do my part of living as you would have me to live, I need your help in matters like these. I need your instruction as to how to handle challenges like these in my everyday life. Lord, help me to understand exactly the role you would have me to play in this area. Thank you for instructing me, Lord.

My prayer for today—including any journaling thoughts I may want to add. Where am I today spiritually, emotionally, physically, financially, generally?

Today's Date: _____

Old Testament verse for today: Habakkuk 2:20

But the Lord is in his holy Temple; let all the earth be silent before him.

One possible prayer for today:

Lord, your might and power are so awesome that if I really think about it, I would be always in reverence to you. You are mighty. You are holy. You are an awesome God; but, you are also a loving and a merciful God. So, in addition to those times when I need to be silent before you and listen to your direction for my life, I know that there are times when I can sing and dance and praise you with ever fiber in my body—whether it be in silence or with a joyful noise.

New Testament verse for today: Romans 11:33

Oh, what a wonderful God we have! How great are his wisdom and knowledge and riches! How impossible it is for us to understand his decisions and his methods!

One possible prayer for today:

God, thank you for being so wonderful, so full of wisdom and knowledge and riches. Thank you for loving me and letting me love you in return. Thank you for giving me some small part of your wisdom so that I can operate successfully in my every day world. Thank you for giving me the faith to accept the decisions you have made that effect my life in a manner that I don't understand. Help me to always acknowledge your Lordship in my life. Give me the faith to never doubt you and your decisions and your methods.

My prayer for today—including any journaling thoughts I may want to add. Where am I today spiritually, emotionally, physically, financially, generally?

Today's Date: _____

Old Testament verse for today: Habakkuk 3:2

O Lord, now I have heard your report, and I worship you in awe for the fearful things that you are going to do. In this time of our deep need, begin again to help us, as you did in years gone by. Show us your power to save us. In your wrath, remember mercy.

One possible prayer for today:

God, you are all powerful. I do worship you in awe for all your power and might. You know my need, Lord. You know that I need your help. Thank you for always being there to listen to my pleadings and to help me. Thank you for showing your great power to help me. Lord, no matter what my sin, thank you for forgiving me and for turning your wrath away from me and showing me mercy. Thank you, Lord, for your great mercy.

New Testament verse for today: Galatians 4:6 & 7

And because we are his sons God has sent the Spirit of his Son into our hearts, so now we can rightly speak of God as our dear Father. Now we are no longer slaves, but God's own sons. And since we are his sons, everything he has belongs to us, for that is the way God planned.

One possible prayer for today:

God, thank you for calling me one of your sons. Thank you for turning your wrath away from me. Thank you for loving me and guiding me as one of your sons. Thank you for letting me come to you as one of your sons and knowing that you will use your great power to help me. Thank you for making your world a place where I can exist and enjoy. Thank you for giving me access to everything that you have; because, in your love, you made me one of your children. Thank you, God.

My prayer for today—including any journaling thoughts I may want to add. Where am I today spiritually, emotionally, physically, financially, generally?

Today's Date: _____

Old Testament verse for today: Habakkuk 3:3

I see God moving across the deserts from Mount Sinai. His brilliant splendor fills the earth and sky; his glory fills the heavens, and the earth is full of his praise! What a wonderful God he is!

One possible prayer for today:

God, thank you for being an everlasting God who is full of brilliant splendor; who fills the earth and the sky with his splendor; whose glory fills the heavens. Lord, thank you for being such a wonderful God. Thank you for being just as wonderful and full of splendor as you were in the days of Habakkuk. Lord, let me do my small part of praising you so that I help the earth be full of praise for you. Thank you, Lord, for your splendor and glory.

New Testament verse for today: John 14:6

Jesus told him, "I am the Way—yes, and the Truth and the Life. No one can get to the Father except by means of me."

One possible prayer for today:

God, I know that for me to experience the true joy that you have planned for me, I have to come to you through your Son, Jesus. Lord, your world is full of incredible splendor and glory; but, the way to experience all that you have planned for me is to accept Christ as my Savior. Let me come into your presence and fully experience all your power, glory, and splendor by acknowledging that you are my personal God, and that I can gain admittance to being called one of your children only through Christ. Thank you, Lord, for letting that plan be so simple that even I can find the Way. Thank you, God.

My prayer for today—including any journaling thoughts I may want to add. Where am I today spiritually, emotionally, physically, financially, generally?

Today's Date: _____

Old Testament verse for today: Habakkuk 3:18 & 19a

Yet I will rejoice in the Lord: I will be happy in the God of my salvation. The Lord God is my strength.

One possible prayer for today:

God, thank you for being the God of my strength. Thank you for being the God of my salvation. Thank you for being a God who is worthy at all times of all the honor and glory that I can give to you. Thank you for making me one of your children so that I can rejoice in you. Thank you for the happiness that comes from being one of your children. Thank you, God, for my salvation.

New Testament verse for today: Philippians 3:29

But our homeland is in heaven, where our Savior the Lord Jesus Christ is; and we are looking forward to his return from there.

One possible prayer for today:

God, thank you for being my strength today. Thank you for my salvation through your Son, Jesus. Thank you for all the good things that you do for me here on earth so that I can rejoice in you and be happy and certain of my salvation. Thank you for promising me a homeland in heaven with you and your Son, Jesus. Thank you for the certainty of my salvation through the shed blood of Jesus so that I can look forward eagerly to his return from heaven. Thank you for your wonderful love and for your wonderful plan of salvation for me. Thank you, God.

My prayer for today—including any journaling thoughts I may want to add. Where am I today spiritually, emotionally, physically, financially, generally?

Today's Date: _____

Old Testament verse for today: Zephaniah 3:17 & 18a

For the Lord your God has arrived to live among you. He is a mighty Savior. He will give you victory. He will rejoice over you in great gladness; he will love you and not accuse you. Is that a joyous choir I hear? No, it is the Lord himself exulting over you in happy song.

One possible prayer for today:

God, thank you for coming to live among men in the form of your Son, Jesus. Thank you for sending us a mighty Savior. Thank you for giving us the victory of eternal life through the death and resurrection of your Son, Jesus. Thank you for rejoicing in gladness over each and every one who accepts Jesus as their Savior. Thank you for loving me and not accusing me. Thank you for always being there to forgive me when I humbly return to you and ask for your forgiveness, no matter how deep the stain of my sin. Lord, thank you for exulting over me in happy song! What a wondrous and glorious God you are. Thank you, God.

New Testament verse for today: John 13:20

Truly, anyone welcoming my messenger is welcoming me. And to welcome me is to welcome the Father who sent me.

One possible prayer for today:

God, thank you for sending your Son, Jesus, to live among men so that I might have eternal life. Thank you for permitting me to welcome Jesus into my heart as my Savior. Thank you for that beautiful concept that welcoming Jesus is to welcome you, God. Thank you for making a plan of salvation that is so simple that even I may understand it and avail myself of it. And, God, I do believe. Thank you for accepting my simple belief. Thank you, God, for your salvation message through your Son, Jesus.

My prayer for today—including any journaling thoughts I may want to add. Where am I today spiritually, emotionally, physically, financially, generally?

Today's Date: _____

Old Testament verse for today: Zechariah 1:5b

—remember—God's Word endures!

One possible prayer for today:

God, that's not only a great promise; but, a pretty scary one! Your word does endure. And, if I commit my life to you and follow your instructions, I can claim all of your great promises. What a great feeling that is to know that your Word endures and that your promises are constant. On the other hand, if I choose not to follow your instructions and rebel against you, your Word, and the punishment contained in that Word also endures! And that is pretty scary. Thank you, God, that your Word endures; and thank you, God, that you continue to forgive me even when I fail you, and that promise of forgiveness also endures. Thank you! Thank you! Thank you!

New Testament verse for today: Romans 9:15 & 16

God said to Moses, "If I want to be kind to someone, I will. And I will take pity on anyone I want to." And so God's blessings are not given just because someone decides to have them or works hard to get them. They are given because God takes pity on those he wants to.

One possible prayer for today:

God, that is also pretty scary as well as being pretty exciting! Please choose me as one on whom you take pity. I know that I cannot earn your favor. I know that your favor comes from faith in you and belief on your Son, Jesus Christ, as my Savior. Lord, help my belief to be more constant as each day passes, and help my faith to grow with each day and each experience. Not only in the good times; but, also when trials and challenges confront me. Help me to never waiver in looking to you for my help and guidance. And, God, thank you for deciding to take pity on me. No matter what my circumstances, let me always remember to thank you.

My prayer for today—including any journaling thoughts I may want to add. Where am I today spiritually, emotionally, physically, financially, generally?

Today's Date: _____

Old Testament verse for today: Zechariah 4:6b

Not by might, nor by power, but by my Spirit, says the Lord of Hosts—you will succeed because of my Spirit, though you are few and weak.

One possible prayer for today:

God, I know that you are an everlasting God. Just as you took care of your people in Old Testament days by the power of your Spirit, I know that you can take care of me today with that same power. Thank you for giving me your Holy Spirit to help me and to protect me from the challenges I face. Even though I have no ability to solve my problems on my own, your wonderful, loving Holy Spirit is there to help me. Thank you, Lord, for helping me in my weakness.

New Testament verse for today: I Peter 3:15

Quietly trust yourself to Christ your Lord, and if anybody asks why you believe as you do, be ready to tell him, and do it in a gentle and respectful way.

One possible prayer for today:

God, please give me the strength and the courage to always let others know how good you are to me. Thank you for strengthening my belief so that I am firm in my faith and trust in you in all circumstances. Let my life be a witness to your great and everlasting love. Thank you for helping me to grow in my faith and trust in you, Lord.

My prayer for today—including any journaling thoughts I may want to add. Where am I today spiritually, emotionally, physically, financially, generally?

Today's Date: _____

Old Testament verse for today: Zechariah 8:16

"Here is your part: Tell the truth. Be fair. Live at peace with everyone. Don't plot harm to others; don't swear that something is true when it isn't! How I hate that sort of thing!" says the Lord.

One possible prayer for today:

Lord, you really lay out what you want me to do and how you want me to live. Thank you for being so precise. On the other hand, I know that I have a hard time even following those simple rules on a consistent basis. I am much too human sometimes! I am greedy. I am self-centered. I don't always act like I want to live at peace with everyone. I probably stretch the truth. So, Lord, even with these simple set of rules, I know that I fail you. So, thank you for forgiving me, Lord, when I fail. Thank you for your patience.

New Testament verse for today: Luke 18:17

"For the Kingdom of God belongs to men who have hearts as trusting as these little children's. And anyone who doesn't have that kind of faith will never get within the Kingdom's gates."

One possible prayer for today:

Lord, let my faith in you be as pure and trustworthy as a child who has a loving father. Let me acknowledge you as the Lord of my Life in all that I do. God, there are a lot of things that I don't understand about you and your actions; but, Lord, I don't need to understand all of those things. Probably if I could understand everything about you, you wouldn't be God. So, without questioning, I accept my faith in you and in your Son, Jesus, as being the only way to eternal life. And, God, thank you for that plan of eternal life. Thank you for making it so simple that even I can understand it. Thank you for choosing me to be one of your family of believers. Thank you, God.

My prayer for today—including any journaling thoughts I may want to add. Where am I today spiritually, emotionally, physically, financially, generally?

Today's Date: _____

Old Testament verse for today: Zechariah 12:8

The Lord will defend the people of Jerusalem; the weakest among them will be as mighty as King David! And the royal line will be as God, like the Angel of the Lord who goes before them!

One possible prayer for today:

God, what an awesome and powerful God you are! Thank you for being such an awesome and powerful God. Lord, just as you were awesome and powerful in Zechariah's time, I know that you have that same power and might to help me today. I know that no matter how weak I may be, you can help me to be as strong as I need to be to accomplish whatever task you have for me to accomplish. Thank you for being a God who is not only awesome and powerful; but, a God who is loving and caring for me. Thank you for being my own personal awesome, powerful, loving and caring God.

New Testament verse for today: I Peter 1:18 & 19

God paid a ransom to save you from the impossible road to heaven which your fathers tried to take, and the ransom he paid was not mere gold or silver, as you very well know. But he paid for you with the precious lifeblood of Christ, the sinless, spotless Lamb of God.

One possible prayer for today:

God, you are so awesome and so powerful that you could have done anything you wanted to do to bring salvation to me. Yet, you loved me so much that you came up with a plan that involved giving your sinless, spotless, Son to die on the cross for my sins. Your power never wanes or fades, and neither does your love. Even in my weakness, you provided a plan for my salvation that even I could understand and accept. Thank you for your awesome power and might. Thank you for your love and care. And, God, thank you for the wonderful gift of your Son through whom I may experience eternal life. Thank you for caring enough about me to give me the faith to believe in your Son. God, I do believe. Thank you for choosing me to believe and helping me to believe.

My prayer for today—including any journaling thoughts I may want to add. Where am I today spiritually, emotionally, physically, financially, generally?

Today's Date: _____

Old Testament verse for today: Malachi 3:10

Bring all the tithes into the storehouse so that there will be food enough in my Temple; if you do, I will open up the windows of heaven for you and pour out a blessing so great you won't have room enough to take it in! Try it! Let me prove it to you!

One possible prayer for today:

God, I know that my belief in you should have some kind of a reaction on my part. Your servant Malachi has challenged us to give to your work; to bring offerings to your house of worship; to tithe! Lord, let me be faithful in doing my part in giving back to you. I know that all I am and all I have has come from you. I am only a steward of the many blessings you give to me. Let me always remember that fact, and let me do my part in giving back to you. And, Lord, then I selfishly claim your promise that you will open up the windows in heaven and give me blessings so great that I won't be able to comprehend them all. I do claim that promise, Lord; and, thank you for giving me that promise.

New Testament verse for today: I Corinthians 4:20

The Kingdom of God is not just talking; it is living by God's power.

One possible prayer for today:

God, that is certainly your challenge to me—to put my "money where my mouth is"! Talk is cheap! But, living for you on a daily basis in the world in which I operate can be a challenge. And, I cannot do that without your help. I cannot do that without your power. So, God, give me that power. Thank you for giving me that power today, Lord.

My prayer for today—including any journaling thoughts I may want to add. Where am I today spiritually, emotionally, physically, financially, generally?

Special Reflections
I Want to Remember

Today's date   Reflect on Page #   What Was Special

_____   _____   _____

_____   _____   _____

_____   _____   _____

_____   _____   _____

_____   _____   _____

_____   _____   _____

_____   _____   _____

_____   _____   _____

_____   _____   _____

_____   _____   _____

_____   _____   _____

_____   _____   _____

_____   _____   _____

_____   _____   _____

_____   _____   _____

Today's date   Reflect on Page #   What Was Special

—————————   —————————   ———————————————

—————————   —————————   ———————————————

—————————   —————————   ———————————————

—————————   —————————   ———————————————

—————————   —————————   ———————————————

—————————   —————————   ———————————————

—————————   —————————   ———————————————

—————————   —————————   ———————————————

—————————   —————————   ———————————————

—————————   —————————   ———————————————

—————————   —————————   ———————————————

—————————   —————————   ———————————————

—————————   —————————   ———————————————

—————————   —————————   ———————————————

—————————   —————————   ———————————————

—————————   —————————   ———————————————

—————————   —————————   ———————————————

—————————   —————————   ———————————————

—————————   —————————   ———————————————

Today's date	Reflect on Page #	What Was Special
_____	_____	_____
_____	_____	_____
_____	_____	_____
_____	_____	_____
_____	_____	_____
_____	_____	_____
_____	_____	_____
_____	_____	_____
_____	_____	_____
_____	_____	_____
_____	_____	_____
_____	_____	_____
_____	_____	_____
_____	_____	_____
_____	_____	_____
_____	_____	_____
_____	_____	_____
_____	_____	_____
_____	_____	_____

Today's date   Reflect on Page #   What Was Special

_____   _____   _____

_____   _____   _____

_____   _____   _____

_____   _____   _____

_____   _____   _____

_____   _____   _____

_____   _____   _____

_____   _____   _____

_____   _____   _____

_____   _____   _____

_____   _____   _____

_____   _____   _____

_____   _____   _____

_____   _____   _____

_____   _____   _____

_____   _____   _____

_____   _____   _____

_____   _____   _____

_____   _____   _____

_____   _____   _____

Today's date	Reflect on Page #	What Was Special
_____	_____	_____
_____	_____	_____
_____	_____	_____
_____	_____	_____
_____	_____	_____
_____	_____	_____
_____	_____	_____
_____	_____	_____
_____	_____	_____
_____	_____	_____
_____	_____	_____
_____	_____	_____
_____	_____	_____
_____	_____	_____
_____	_____	_____
_____	_____	_____
_____	_____	_____
_____	_____	_____
_____	_____	_____
_____	_____	_____

Today's date	Reflect on Page #	What Was Special
_____	_____	_____
_____	_____	_____
_____	_____	_____
_____	_____	_____
_____	_____	_____
_____	_____	_____
_____	_____	_____
_____	_____	_____
_____	_____	_____
_____	_____	_____
_____	_____	_____
_____	_____	_____
_____	_____	_____
_____	_____	_____
_____	_____	_____
_____	_____	_____
_____	_____	_____
_____	_____	_____
_____	_____	_____

Today's date   Reflect on Page #   What Was Special

_____   _____   _____

_____   _____   _____

_____   _____   _____

_____   _____   _____

_____   _____   _____

_____   _____   _____

_____   _____   _____

_____   _____   _____

_____   _____   _____

_____   _____   _____

_____   _____   _____

_____   _____   _____

_____   _____   _____

_____   _____   _____

_____   _____   _____

_____   _____   _____

_____   _____   _____

_____   _____   _____

_____   _____   _____

_____   _____   _____

Today's date   Reflect on Page #   What Was Special

_____   _____   _____

_____   _____   _____

_____   _____   _____

_____   _____   _____

_____   _____   _____

_____   _____   _____

_____   _____   _____

_____   _____   _____

_____   _____   _____

_____   _____   _____

_____   _____   _____

_____   _____   _____

_____   _____   _____

_____   _____   _____

_____   _____   _____

_____   _____   _____

_____   _____   _____

_____   _____   _____

_____   _____   _____

_____   _____   _____

Today's date	Reflect on Page #	What Was Special
_____	_____	_____
_____	_____	_____
_____	_____	_____
_____	_____	_____
_____	_____	_____
_____	_____	_____
_____	_____	_____
_____	_____	_____
_____	_____	_____
_____	_____	_____
_____	_____	_____
_____	_____	_____
_____	_____	_____
_____	_____	_____
_____	_____	_____
_____	_____	_____
_____	_____	_____
_____	_____	_____
_____	_____	_____
_____	_____	_____

Today's date   Reflect on Page #   What Was Special

_____   _____   _____

_____   _____   _____

_____   _____   _____

_____   _____   _____

_____   _____   _____

_____   _____   _____

_____   _____   _____

_____   _____   _____

_____   _____   _____

_____   _____   _____

_____   _____   _____

_____   _____   _____

_____   _____   _____

_____   _____   _____

_____   _____   _____

_____   _____   _____

_____   _____   _____

_____   _____   _____

_____   _____   _____

_____   _____   _____

Today's date	Reflect on Page #	What Was Special
_____	_____	_____
_____	_____	_____
_____	_____	_____
_____	_____	_____
_____	_____	_____
_____	_____	_____
_____	_____	_____
_____	_____	_____
_____	_____	_____
_____	_____	_____
_____	_____	_____
_____	_____	_____
_____	_____	_____
_____	_____	_____
_____	_____	_____
_____	_____	_____
_____	_____	_____
_____	_____	_____
_____	_____	_____

Today's date	Reflect on Page #	What Was Special
————————	————————	————————————
————————	————————	————————————
————————	————————	————————————
————————	————————	————————————
————————	————————	————————————
————————	————————	————————————
————————	————————	————————————
————————	————————	————————————
————————	————————	————————————
————————	————————	————————————
————————	————————	————————————
————————	————————	————————————
————————	————————	————————————
————————	————————	————————————
————————	————————	————————————
————————	————————	————————————
————————	————————	————————————
————————	————————	————————————
————————	————————	————————————
————————	————————	————————————

Today's date	Reflect on Page #	What Was Special
_____	_____	_____
_____	_____	_____
_____	_____	_____
_____	_____	_____
_____	_____	_____
_____	_____	_____
_____	_____	_____
_____	_____	_____
_____	_____	_____
_____	_____	_____
_____	_____	_____
_____	_____	_____
_____	_____	_____
_____	_____	_____
_____	_____	_____
_____	_____	_____
_____	_____	_____
_____	_____	_____
_____	_____	_____
_____	_____	_____

Today's date   Reflect on Page #   What Was Special

_____   _____   _____

_____   _____   _____

_____   _____   _____

_____   _____   _____

_____   _____   _____

_____   _____   _____

_____   _____   _____

_____   _____   _____

_____   _____   _____

_____   _____   _____

_____   _____   _____

_____   _____   _____

_____   _____   _____

_____   _____   _____

_____   _____   _____

_____   _____   _____

_____   _____   _____

_____   _____   _____

_____   _____   _____

_____   _____   _____

Today's date   Reflect on Page #   What Was Special

_____   _____   _____

_____   _____   _____

_____   _____   _____

_____   _____   _____

_____   _____   _____

_____   _____   _____

_____   _____   _____

_____   _____   _____

_____   _____   _____

_____   _____   _____

_____   _____   _____

_____   _____   _____

_____   _____   _____

_____   _____   _____

_____   _____   _____

_____   _____   _____

_____   _____   _____

_____   _____   _____

_____   _____   _____

Today's date   Reflect on Page #   What Was Special

_____   _____   _____

_____   _____   _____

_____   _____   _____

_____   _____   _____

_____   _____   _____

_____   _____   _____

_____   _____   _____

_____   _____   _____

_____   _____   _____

_____   _____   _____

_____   _____   _____

_____   _____   _____

_____   _____   _____

_____   _____   _____

_____   _____   _____

_____   _____   _____

_____   _____   _____

_____   _____   _____

_____   _____   _____

About the Author

Dave Noland has spent his entire business career in the St. Paul/Minneapolis area of Minnesota. He was reared on a farm in southwestern Minnesota and accepted Christ as his personal Savior at the age of ten. Although never in any kind of full-time Christian service, Dave has had a very active personal devotional life, which has resulted in the chosen verses and prayers offered in this book. These have been instrumental in providing Dave a solid foundation of trust in God as his friend during the good and the bad times in his life. Hopefully, you will find them helpful in your personal devotional life.

Printed in the United States
18972LVS00001B/1-30